Jennifer R. Strawbridge
**The Pauline Effect**

# Studies of the Bible
and Its Reception

---

Edited by
Dale C. Allison, Jr., Christine Helmer,
Thomas Römer, Choon-Leong Seow,
Barry Dov Walfish, Eric Ziolkowski

# Volume 5

Jennifer R. Strawbridge
# The Pauline Effect

The Use of the Pauline Epistles
by Early Christian Writers

DE GRUYTER

Winner of the 2014 SBL–De Gruyter Prize for Biblical Studies and Reception History

ISBN 978-3-11-057815-7
e-ISBN (PDF) 978-3-11-044654-8
e-ISBN (EPUB) 978-3-11-044546-6
ISSN 2195-450X

**Library of Congress Cataloging-in-Publication Data**
A CIP catalog record for this book has been applied for at the Library of Congress.

**Bibliographic information published by the Deutsche Nationalbibliothek**
The Deutsche Nationalbibliothek lists this publication in the Deutsche Nationalbibliografie;
detailed bibliographic data are available on the Internet at http://dnb.dnb.de.

© 2015 Walter de Gruyter GmbH, Berlin/Boston
This volume is text- and page-identical with the hardback published in 2015.
Typesetting: Konrad Triltsch, Print und digitale Medien GmbH, Ochsenfurt
Logo: Martin Zech
Printing and binding: CPI books GmbH, Leck

♾ Printed on acid-free paper
Printed in Germany

www.degruyter.com

# Preface

It is a delight to offer thanks to those who have made this study possible. This work began life as a doctoral thesis at the University of Oxford, where I benefitted greatly from the support and communities of Keble College and the Faculty of Theology and Religion. For the outstanding instruction and support of my supervisors, Professor Christopher Rowland and Professor Teresa Morgan, I am especially grateful. Their encouragement, scholarship, persistence, challenging conversation, and careful reading of innumerable drafts shaped this project immensely. I only hope that in my own vocation I can imitate a small part of their pedagogical care, grace, and whole-hearted investment. Professor Alexandra Brown first introduced me to the study of the New Testament and Professor Christopher Beeley to the study of Patristics, and to both of them I am forever indebted and grateful. Moreover, they have served as mentors and conversation partners on this journey, offering significant encouragement. I have also benefitted from the suggestions of those who read and commented on substantial parts or even the whole of this study at different stages: Professor Alexandra Brown, Professor Edwin Craun, Marlys Craun, Professor David Lincicum, Dr Ian Boxall, Kylie Crabbe, Dr Sarah Apetrei, Dr Mary Marshall, Dr Benjamin Edsall, the SBL-DeGruyter Prize committee, and an anonymous reviewer. I am also grateful to Megan Kearney for her vital assistance with the index. My examiners, Professor Mark Edwards and Professor Judith Kovacs, provided helpful questions and challenging criticisms for further reflection and offered much encouragement not only in the examination but also in conversations that have followed. No doubt all those named will find something with which to disagree and I am sure I have fallen short of their suggestions in many places, but I hope they realise how much this project owes to them.

This study was also enabled by generous financial support from a number of organizations. The support of St Mary's Episcopal Church in Arlington, Virginia set me on my feet in Oxford, along with awards from Keble College, the Faculty of Theology and Religion, and the Bampton Trust. Colleagues at Keble offered invaluable support, including sabbatical leave in Trinity Term 2013 for which I am unspeakably grateful, especially to the Governing Body, the Advowsons Committee, the Revd Robert Grimley, the Revd Darren McFarland, as well as the many students who gave of their time and gifts and enabled the Chapel community at the College to flourish. Grants from Sons and Friends of the Clergy and the English Clergy Association allowed me to spend much of my sabbatical leave ensconced in the Widener Library at Harvard, and the warm hospitality, kindness, conversation, and endearing friendship of the Brothers of the Society of St John the Evangelist offered the space for me to complete a draft in Cambridge, Mass.

Earlier portions of chapter 2 first appeared in *Studia Patristica* (vol. XLIII; Leuven: Peeters Press, 2013) and a portion of chapter 5 was among material I contributed to a jointly authored paper with Benjamin Edsall in the *Journal for the Study of the New Testament*, 2015, vol 37 (3). I am grateful for the opportunity to reprint some of that material here. I am also thankful to DeGruyter and the Society of Biblical Literature for creating a prize for Biblical Studies and Reception History and for their work to increase the visibility of reception history within the wider academic community. Thank you to the SBL-DeGruyter Prize committee for their encouragement and for awarding a prize that would lead to this publication and to Albrecht Döhnert and Alissa Jones Nelson at De Gruyter for accepting this work. I am particularly grateful to Sophie Wagenhofer, Angelika Hermann, and the editorial team at De Gruyter for their expert guidance throughout the process of publication.

A number of friends and colleagues have been willing to share their time and ideas with me, helping to clarify much of my thinking. Without their support, my life and this study would be much the worse. Dr Bronwyn Johnston walked the length of the dissertation with me, including numerous study excursions, and especially helping in the final weeks of revision and editing with a red pen and boundless humour and tea. Dr Sarah Apetrei, Dr Mary Marshall, and Kylie Crabbe all made suggestions and critiques that improved this work and served as a sounding board and conversation partners throughout. I am grateful for their thought-provoking conversation, careful reading, and cherished friendship. Numerous friends, teachers, and colleagues also offered support through the platforms of the Oxford New Testament, Reception History, and Patristics Seminars, including but not limited to Professor John Muddiman, Professor Markus Bockmuehl, Dr Nick King, Dr Christopher Hays, Nicholas Moore, Benjamin Edsall, Jonathan Downing, Simon Cuff, and Peter Anthony. Alongside these friends and colleagues, the prayers, friendship, and encouragement of Peter and Bea Groves, Jonathan and Amanda Phillips, a clergy colleague group, Melissa and David Cox, the Keble College Chapel community, Richard Metzger, Eric and Cara Strawbridge, and Craig and Sue Strawbridge engenders a debt of gratitude that will not be forgotten. Ultimately, this is for my grandmother Ruth, who in her 100th year was clear that we always needed a minister and a doctor in the family. For her confidence, encouragement, love, and humour, I am most grateful.

Jennifer R. Strawbridge
Oxford
St Matthew, 2015

# Contents

**Chapter One: Introduction —— 1**
1.1 Reception History and Christian Formation —— 1
1.2 Surveys within New Testament Studies —— 4
1.3 Surveys in Ancient Historical Studies —— 7
1.4 A Database of Pauline References —— 10
1.5 From Quantity to Quality: The Four Pericopes —— 12
1.6 Defining References and Setting Boundaries —— 18
1.7 Conclusion —— 22

**Chapter Two: 1 Corinthians 2.6–16: Wisdom leads a soul to God —— 24**
2.1 Early Christian Writers and 1 Corinthians 2 —— 24
2.2 Rhetorical Manoeuvres & Apologetic Discourse —— 28
2.3 Exegesis of difficult texts —— 38
2.4 Wisdom and formation —— 43
2.5 Conclusions —— 52

**Chapter Three: Ephesians 6.10–17: spiritual armour...to wage a spiritual war —— 57**
3.1 Early Christian Writers and Ephesians 6 —— 57
3.2 Spiritual Forces of Wickedness (Eph 6.12) —— 62
3.3 Fiery Darts of the Evil One (Eph 6.16) —— 69
3.4 Wrestling: For our struggle is not against flesh and blood (Eph 6.12) —— 74
3.5 Take up the whole armour of God (Eph 6.11 and 6.13) —— 77
3.5.1 What is the armour of God? —— 78
    Baptism —— 78
    Prayer, Faith, and Wisdom —— 80
3.5.2 Taking up the armour of God —— 82
    Excursus: Some Challenges —— 88
3.6 Conclusions —— 93

**Chapter Four: 1 Corinthians 15.50–58: Resolve me of all ambiguities —— 97**
4.1 Early Christian Writers and 1 Corinthians 15 —— 97
4.2 The Valentinians and their Influence —— 102
4.3 Irenaeus of Lyons —— 108
4.4 Tertullian —— 114
4.5 Origen —— 119

4.6 Conclusions: Resurrection, Hermeneutics, and Formation —— 124

**Chapter Five: Colossians 1.15–20: There was a time when he was not —— 135**
5.1 Early Christian Writers and Colossians 1 —— 135
5.2 Christological Titles and their Implications —— 138
5.2.1 εἰκὼν τοῦ θεοῦ τοῦ ἀοράτου: "Image of the invisible God" —— 140
5.2.2 πρωτότοκος πάσης κτίσεως: "First-born of all creation" —— 149
    Excursus on *Prayer of Joseph* —— 153
5.2.3 θρόνοι εἴτε κυριότητες: "Thrones and Dominions" —— 155
5.2.4 ἡ κεφαλὴ τοῦ σώματος, τῆς ἐκκλησίας: "The head of the body, the Church" —— 160
5.3 Close Connections with John 1 and Philippians 2 —— 162
5.4 Concluding Remarks: Why Colossians 1.15–20? —— 167
5.4.1 Colossians 1.15–20 and the Arian Controversy —— 169

**Chapter Six: Conclusion —— 174**

**Appendix: Introduction —— 182**
A.1 Databases —— 182
A.1.1 Reference (R) —— 183
A.1.2 Possible Reference (PR) —— 184
A.1.3 Reference Not Found (RNF) —— 184

**Appendix A: 1 Corinthians 2.6–16 —— 186**

**Appendix B: Ephesians 6.10–17 —— 209**

**Appendix C: 1 Corinthians 15.50–58 —— 226**

**Appendix D: Colossians 1.15–20 —— 238**

**Bibliography —— 260**
B.1 Primary Sources —— 260
B.2 Reference Works —— 269
B.3 Secondary Sources —— 270

**Index of Ancient Sources —— 289**

**Index of Subjects —— 303**

# Chapter One: Introduction

> *All Scripture is divinely inspired and useful for teaching, for reproving, and for instruction in righteousness.*[1]

## 1.1 Reception History and Christian Formation

The concluding words of the second letter of Peter include a reflection on "our beloved brother Paul" who "wrote to you according to the wisdom given to him, speaking of this as he does in all his letters (2 Pet 3.15)." Considered one of the last canonical texts written, the Petrine epistle's final words underscore an early understanding of Paul as one who is wise and the authoritative status of his letters. But what is the influence of the Pauline epistles more broadly in early Christianity? How are the wisdom of Paul and the authority of his letters claimed by the earliest Christian writers?

In this study, I explore the use of Paul and his letters by early Christian writers of the first three centuries and examine how their interpretation of Paul's words contributes to our understanding of Christian formation.[2] This project is a study of the effects of selected Pauline excerpts on early Christians as dis-

---

[1] 2 Tim 3.16, quoted by Origen, *Hom.Judic*, 5.1 (*FC* 119). New Testament citations are taken from the 27th edition of *Novum Testamentum Graecae* and translations are from the NRSV. Unless otherwise indicated, the translations of Latin and Greek patristic texts are my own with significant phrases included with the English. The source for the Greek or Latin texts is listed in the footnotes and where the translation has been adapted from another, that source is also given. It is worth noting that the histories of transmission of early Christian texts vary and this study primarily uses the critical editions and translations from *GCS*, *SC*, *CCL* and, when these are not available, Loeb and Migne. Origen's texts are in both Greek and Latin, since some of his works are only extant through preservation in the later Latin writings of Rufinus.

[2] Early Christian papyrological references to Pauline writings attest to a collection of letters addressed to seven churches: see Harry Gamble, *Books and Readers in the Early Church: A History of Early Christian Texts* (New Haven, Conn: Yale University Press, 1995), 60–63. Therefore, when this study refers to Pauline epistles in the time before the Nicene Council (325 C.E.), it includes both of the Thessalonian and Corinthian correspondences, Galatians, Philippians, Philemon, Romans, Colossians, and Ephesians (Colossians and Philemon were often grouped together as letters addressed to the same community). This project also considers Hebrews (claimed to be Pauline by *1 Clement*) and the pastoral epistles of Timothy and Titus (claimed to be Pauline by Irenaeus, Tertullian, and some Valentinian writings; see Elaine Pagels, *The Gnostic Paul: Gnostic Exegesis of the Pauline Letters* [Philadelphia: Trinity Press International, 1992], 4–5).

cerned through the lens of early Christian writing or, more precisely, the pens of early Christian writers. By adapting a methodology from ancient historical studies and creating a survey of all possible references to the Pauline writings in early Christian Latin and Greek texts, this study identifies and focuses upon four of the most frequently cited Pauline passages in ante-Nicene writings: 1 Cor 2.6–16, Eph 6.10–17, 1 Cor 15.50–58, and Col 1.15–20.[3] Certainly lists have been produced before this project that tell us which *books* of the New Testament were most utilised within a specific time period. But unlike the chapters that follow, these lists do not include the detail of specific *verses* nor have they moved beyond the level of asking questions about why such frequently occurring texts might be important to study.

How does the widespread and frequent use of the four Pauline passages identified by this project shape early Christian writings, their doctrine and discourse? And how, secondarily, might these texts illuminate early Christian formation? Does a community of interpretation emerge from early Christian uses of the most frequently cited Pauline texts? What themes are apparent as each pericope is articulated, adopted, expanded, and combined with other scriptural texts and theological concepts by early Christians as they seek to understand and to live by words of Scripture?[4] That the most frequently cited texts are found in the context of some of the central pre-Nicene theological debates—Irenaeus' understanding of salvation and recapitulation, Origen's understanding of scriptural interpretation, Clement's understanding of teaching, Tertullian's understanding of resurrection—cannot be an accident. The Pauline texts most frequently used by early Christian writers are not random. They are closely connected with the developing doctrines and debates of ante-Nicene Christianity.

Early Christian use of these four Pauline pericopes is also closely connected with aspects of Christian formation. "Formation" can be a rather contentious term, often conflated with Christian pedagogy or catechesis which are more difficult to determine in this early time period. Understood within an early Christian context, writings function formatively in a direct way as they purport to teach the basics of the faith and to define doctrine in the face of opposition.[5] Formation,

---

[3] Limiting the time period of this study to Christian writings before 325 C.E. is not to suggest that the Council of Nicaea brings the period of early Christianity to a close. Rather, recognising the surge of Christian texts after this period, the Council of Nicaea serves as a necessary, though artificial, end point in this time of momentous change for Christianity in the Roman Empire.
[4] Angela Russell Christman, *'What Did Ezekiel See?': Christian Exegesis of Ezekiel's Vision of the Chariot from Irenaeus to Gregory the Great* (BiAC 4; Leiden: Brill, 2005), 3.
[5] See Quintilian, *The Orator's Education* (ed. D.A. Russell; Cambridge, Mass: Harvard University Press, 2001); G. Kennedy, *The Art of Rhetoric in the Roman World, 300 B.C.–A.D. 300* (Princeton,

however, may also be indirect, with an intention to frighten off those who might attempt to influence early Christians in a different or even harmful way. Our use of formation as a category, therefore, depends on understanding the purpose of writing. It is also intimately connected to the art of persuasion, which "is the central element to all ancient conceptions of rhetoric" and discourse.[6] Understood in a rhetorical context, the concept of formation includes defence and explanation (apologetic), teaching and paraenesis (didactic), and exhortation especially directed at those who are not insiders or new initiates (protreptic).[7] Thus, formation is expanded analogously with rhetoric to include all texts. All writings have a formative aspect to them since all texts are written to persuade. They are, therefore, an essential part of the process of developing Christians in the faith. The communicative aim of a text is to form.[8] This understanding of formation underscores the serious attention ancient writers paid to what was written and said and, in the context of this study, *prima facie* the seriousness with which early Christian writers cite and use the writings of Paul in their own works.

The way Pauline passages are used in sources such as the writings of early Christians, therefore, can offer insights into understanding the formation of Christian communities and identities. This is especially true in light of an understanding of formation within a Graeco-Roman context as that which takes place beyond an explicitly educational setting and conveys the sense of a broader cultural and rhetorical understanding of persuasion and its part in setting the boun-

---

NJ: Princeton University Press, 1972); Frances M. Young, "The Rhetorical Schools and their Influence on Patristic Exegesis," in *The Making of Orthodoxy: Essays in Honour of Henry Chadwick* (ed. Rowan Williams; Cambridge: Cambridge University Press, 1989), 182–199; 186–187.
**6** Dennis L. Stamps, "The Use of the Old Testament in the New Testament as a Rhetorical Device: A Methodological Proposal" in *Hearing the Old Testament in the New Testament* (ed. Stanley Porter; Grand Rapids, Mich: Eerdmans, 2006), 9–37; 26.
**7** Sterling divides the three modes of discourse into diatribe, paraenetic, and protreptic rather than apologetic, protreptic, and didactic as described by Grant and Rankin. See Gregory E. Sterling, "Hellenistic Philosophy and the New Testament," in *A Handbook to the Exegesis of the New Testament* (ed. Stanley Porter; NTTS 25; Leiden: Brill, 1997), 313–358; 322–325; David Rankin, *From Clement to Origen: The Social and Historical Context of the Church Fathers* (Farnham: Ashgate, 2007), 6; Kennedy, *Art of Rhetoric*; Mark J. Edwards et al., "Introduction: Apologetics in the Roman World," in *Apologetics in the Roman Empire: Pagans, Jews, and Christians* (ed. Mark J. Edwards, Martin Goodman, and Simon Price; Oxford: Oxford University Press, 1999), 1–14; 1; Robert M. Grant, *The Greek Apologists of the Second Century* (Philadelphia: Westminster, 1988), 9.
**8** See Frances M. Young, *Biblical Exegesis and the Formation of Christian Culture* (Cambridge: Cambridge University Press, 1997) who writes that "the object of every discourse was persuasion" (100).

daries of practice and belief.⁹ What follows is not a comprehensive study of the nature of Christian formation, but rather, an exploration of how early Christians' use of a specific text in their writings contributes to the formation of their doctrines and discourse.

Based on a comprehensive survey of Pauline references in ante-Nicene literary sources, I offer a detailed account of 1 Cor 2.6–16, Eph 6.10–17, 1 Cor 15.50–58, and Col 1.15–20 as these texts are adapted to suit different communities at a time when the status of Christianity was undergoing great change in the Roman Empire. From this analysis and with a better grasp of early Christian use of these four texts, one of the most significant findings of this project emerges: a definition of Christian formation as progress from one level of wisdom to another. This insight, alongside the methodology on which the project is founded, contributes to valuable reflections on the ways that these four frequently-cited passages were used to form and persuade early Christians and, in the process, to shape Christianity as a system of belief and practice.

## 1.2 Surveys within New Testament Studies

In recent years, scholarship on early Christianity has seen a surge of interest in the reception history of the New Testament and the interpretation of Scripture by early Christian writers.[10] As Candida Moss writes in her study of early Christian martyrdom, reception histories of the New Testament can be divided into two distinct approaches: biblical interpretation within the work of one particular au-

---

**9** Cribiore, in her comprehensive study of school exercises, makes a similar distinction concerning school papyri when she writes that concepts of school and education are determined "on the basis of the activity carried on, rather than in terms of the identity of the person teaching, the student-teacher relationship, or the premises where teaching takes place" (Raffaella Cribiore, *Writing, Teachers, and Students in Graeco-Roman Egypt* [Atlanta, Ga: Scholars Press, 1996], 6).
**10** See Maurice F. Wiles, *The Divine Apostle: The Interpretation of St. Paul's Epistles in the Early Church* (Cambridge: Cambridge University Press, 1967); Pagels, *Gnostic Paul*; Young, *Biblical Exegesis*; Annewies van den Hoek, "Techniques of Quotation in Clement of Alexandria: A View of Ancient Literary Working Methods," *VC* 50, no. 3 (1996): 223–243; Francesca Cocchini, *Il Paolo di Origene: Contributo alla storia della recezione delle epistole paoline nel III secolo* (Verba Seniorum 11; Rome: Edizioni Studium, 1992); Ernst Dassmann, *Der Stachel im Fleisch: Paulus in der frühchristlichen Literatur bis Irenäus* (Münster: Aschendorff, 1979); Andreas Lindemann, *Paulus im ältesten Christentum: d. Bild d. Apostels u. d. Rezeption d. paulin. Theologie in d. frühchristl. Literatur bis Marcion*, (BHT 58; Tübingen: Mohr, 1979); Candida Moss, *The Other Christs: Imitating Jesus in Ancient Christian Ideologies of Martyrdom* (New York/Oxford: Oxford University Press, 2010); Ben C. Blackwell, "Paul and Irenaeus," in *Paul and the Second Century* (eds. Michael F. Bird and Joseph R. Dodson; London/New York: T&T Clark, 2011), 190–206; 190.

thor, and the reception of a particular New Testament text as traced through the writings of early Christians.¹¹ The first approach is confined to the evidence of extant texts of an early Christian writer, thereby making this approach problematic for the study of most authors who wrote before the fourth century.¹² The second approach, Moss surmises, is too often hampered by the narrow criteria by which scholars identify scriptural references. In other words, reception history is limited both "temporally, in that the majority of studies focus on later patristic authors, and generically, in that the material examined is confined to citation and commentary."¹³ While I have narrowed the emphasis of this study to the letters attributed to Paul,¹⁴ at the same time I have maintained a broad focus across a wide range of authors and genres within pre-Nicene Christianity. By concentrating on the most frequently used Pauline passages in early Christian literary sources, I offer an approach for managing early Pauline reception in a coherent and justifiable way. In the process, I also provide a middle way between Moss's two criticisms of early biblical reception, since this project is limited neither to one author nor to one scriptural text.

Despite the surge in scholarship on the reception of Pauline texts in early Christian writings, the approach of examining the use of Pauline texts across all extant writings in a given time period has not been investigated extensively.

---

**11** Moss, *Other Christs*, 2–3. See also the recent works of Riemer Roukema and Benjamin White on the reception of 1 Cor 15: Riemer Roukema, "Origen's Interpretation of 1 Corinthians 15," in *Gelitten, Gestorben, Auferstanden: Passions- und Ostertraditionen im antiken Christentum* (eds. Tobias Nicklas, Andreas Merkt, and Joseph Verheyden; WUNT 2; Tübingen: Mohr [Siebeck], 2010), 329–342; Riemer Roukema, "Paulus' verhandeling over de opstanding. 1 Korintiërs 15," *Int* 21, no. 2 (2013): 33–35; Benjamin L. White, *Remembering Paul: Ancient and Modern Contests over the Image of the Apostle* (Oxford: Oxford University Press, 2014), 158–165.
**12** Origen, writing in the 3rd century, is an exception to this difficulty since a large number of his commentaries, homilies, apologies, and treatises are extant.
**13** Moss, *Other Christs*, 3.
**14** The reasons for focusing on letters attributed to Paul in this study are three-fold. The first is practical, as an investigation of all New Testament texts in this time period would be impossible to handle within the confines of a single monograph. Space limitations, therefore, necessitate a narrower focus. The second is the agreement amongst many scholars that Paul's letters circulated together very early (see Gamble, *Books and Readers*, 58–65, 140–143, and 271n71 for bibliographic references). These texts were known to early Christian writers and as this study will demonstrate, used by them within a wide range of debates. The third is the authoritative nature of Paul the apostle for early Christian writers. Just as scholars of ancient history focus on the writings of Homer and find that references to Homer are not simply about the content of the text cited but the authority given to the author by using a Homeric text, so this study focuses on the writings of Paul as one whose authority gives weight to early Christians' words. This third point will be further discussed in this introduction and in the chapter on 1 Cor 2.6–16.

Judith Kovacs emphasises the need for a comprehensive study of early Christian reception of Pauline texts, writing that, "the fragmentary evidence of interpretation of the [...] Pauline letters remains largely unexplored."[15] For example, within her focused study of Origen's use of excerpts from 1 Corinthians, Kovacs is astounded that "there is not one study [...] of the seventy-three pages of fragments from Origen's homilies on 1 Corinthians."[16] Accordingly, in the following chapters I concentrate on how early Christians were using parts of the Pauline epistles across a wide range of texts—including some which remain untranslated and are rarely cited in secondary sources—and in the process seek to fill this gap in scholarship.

In addition to Kovacs, scholars such as Larry Hurtado, Stephen Llewelyn, and Peter Gorday provide further support for the importance of a comprehensive survey of biblical references as a foundation for engaging early Christian reception of Scripture and as a starting point for examining how early Christians were using these texts. Hurtado argues that early Christian papyri and literary texts "reflect attitudes, preferences, and usages of many Christians more broadly in the second and third centuries."[17] Recognising the potential importance of the texts occurring with the greatest frequency, Hurtado offers a list of the extant copies of each canonical book of the New Testament within early Christian papyri.[18] Llewelyn, as a part of the series *New Documents Illustrating Early Christianity*, presents a more extensive survey which includes the number of references to each biblical book in extant papyrus, parchment, and patristic sources, but without explanation.[19] With these brief surveys in mind, Hurtado concludes that, "assuming that the comparative numbers of extant copies of texts reflect the comparative numbers of copies circulating in the ancient setting of these copies, we can infer the relative popularity of texts in these Christian circles."[20] Referring to his own limited survey, he offers the challenge along with his hope that "this de-

---

**15** Judith Kovacs, "Servant of Christ and Steward of the Mysteries of God," in *In Dominico Eloquio, In Lordly Eloquence: Essays on Patristic Exegesis in honour of Robert Louis Wilken* (eds. Paul M. Blowers, et al.; Grand Rapids, Mich: Eerdmans, 2002), 147–171; 149–150.
**16** Kovacs, "Servant of Christ," 149–150.
**17** Larry W. Hurtado, *The Earliest Christian Artifacts: Manuscripts and Christian Origins* (Grand Rapids, Mich: Eerdmans, 2006), 27.
**18** Hurtado, *Earliest Christian Artifacts*, 210–229 (Appendix 1).
**19** Stephen R. Llewelyn, *New Documents Illustrating Early Christianity: A Review of the Greek Inscriptions and Papyri Published in 1982–1983*, (vol. 7; North Ryde, NSW: Ancient History Documentary Research Centre of Macquarie University, 1994), 257–261.
**20** Larry W. Hurtado, "Early Christian Manuscripts as Artifacts," in *Jewish and Christian Scripture as Artifact and Canon* (eds. Craig A. Evans and H. Daniel Zacharias; London/New York: T&T Clark, 2009), 66–81; 68.

liberately limited and somewhat preliminary analysis of the texts that are attested in Christian manuscripts of the second and third centuries will at least have demonstrated that it is worthwhile to give attention to these matters."[21] Hurtado comments in particular that this sort of survey is "insufficiently noted in current discussion and debates about Christianity" in antiquity.[22] He is clear that if more attention were given to surveys of attested texts and comparative references, scholars would "likely have some direct indication of what texts were read and their comparative popularity."[23]

## 1.3 Surveys in Ancient Historical Studies

While the importance of surveys of biblical texts is noted within reception historical and biblical studies, how such a survey may be compiled and its results analysed has not been addressed. Thus, I drew on a method worked out by scholars of ancient history, at least two of whom created comprehensive surveys in order to understand the nature and indebtedness to literary authorities in Graeco-Roman pedagogy. This method, as established by scholars of ancient history Raffaella Cribiore and especially Teresa Morgan, is a wide ranging survey of references to authors such as Homer, Menander, and Isocrates in Graeco-Roman school-text papyri. Such a study finds that a large number of extracts from the works of Homer present an "important test-case for our understanding of what literature was taught" and thus formed the emerging core of Graeco-Roman literate education.[24] Certainly the assumption that all of Homer was used equally is not unfounded, especially if one bases such conclusions on the accounts of education offered by Quintilian.[25] However, a survey of Homeric references in papyrological

---

**21** Hurtado, *Earliest Christian Artifacts*, 40.
**22** Hurtado, *Earliest Christian Artifacts*, 40. See also Pagels, *Gnostic Paul*, 7–8 where she describes a survey of the use of the Pauline epistles within second century Valentinian texts in order to determine the hermeneutical methods used by Valentinian exegetes. She offers the caveat that "much of the work of gathering and comparing such sources […] remains to be completed in future studies" (8).
**23** Hurtado, *Earliest Christian Artifacts*, 40. Although Hurtado does not refer to the studies of Morgan or Cribiore, his words echo theirs in this conclusion.
**24** Teresa Morgan, *Literate Education in the Hellenistic and Roman Worlds* (Cambridge: Cambridge University Press, 1998), 105. According to Morgan, within the confines of Graeco-Roman literate education, it is possible to determine the emerging core of "what most people learned, what they learned first, and in the case of reading, what they went on practising the longest" (Morgan, *Literate Education*, 38).
**25** Quintilian, *Orat*, 1.8.1–12 and 10.1.46. See also Morgan, *Literate Education*, 105.

and literary texts reveals a different story and begins to paint a new picture of the importance and use of Homer's writings within the ancient world.[26] Such a survey therefore enables the discovery of the most frequently cited Homeric texts in school-text papyri and consequently, based on this quantitative data, opens the door for a qualitative analysis of the ways these texts were being used.[27] Morgan's method does not simply quantify citation but analyses the distribution of passages in school-text papyri, offering direct evidence of the use of these texts in teaching since each reference is from the hand of a student or teacher.

As a foundation for this study, I adapt this method of surveying extant texts in Graeco-Roman literate education and apply it to early Christian writings. Morgan's method, however, must be adapted and not adopted in full because the focus of this study is not on papyrological texts—a study which would be hampered and limited by the paucity of extant sources—but on early Christian literary texts.[28] By adapting the method in this way, this project draws on Morgan's own observation that the results of the survey on the use of Homer in school exercises are *mirrored* by the results of a survey on the use of Homer in literary texts from the same time period. Thus, the first books of Homer's *Iliad*, frequently

---

[26] See Morgan, *Literate Education*, 94–119.

[27] Narrowing the results of the survey further, Morgan determines that Books 1 and 2 from Homer's *Iliad* are the most frequently cited Homeric excerpts in Graeco-Roman school exercises (Morgan, *Literate Education*, 106–107). Therefore, these two books would have played a significant role in Graeco-Roman literate education and constitute the emerging core of what early Graeco-Roman people may have learned.

[28] While more than a thousand Homeric papyri have been discovered (Raffaella Cribiore, *Gymnastics of the Mind: Greek Education in Hellenistic and Roman Egypt* [Princeton, NJ: Princeton University Press, 2001], 194) only two-hundred papyri containing Pauline texts are extant and only three of these are identified as possible school exercises (*P.Oxy.* 2.209, *P.Lond.Lit.* 207, and *P.Mich.* 926). Thus, while papyri provide evidence for early Christian formation and education using Pauline texts, they cannot provide a concrete answer to the research questions of this study, especially if the focus is limited only to Pauline school-text papyri. For more on the connection between early Christian papyri and education, see: AnneMarie Luijendijk, *Greetings in the Lord: Early Christians and the Oxyrhynchus Papyri* (HTS 60; Cambridge, Mass: Harvard University Press, 2008), 57–58 and 67–70; Kim Haines-Eitzen, *Guardian of Letters: Literacy, Power and the Transmitters of Early Christian Literature* (Oxford: Oxford University Press, 2000), 78 and 91; Theodore C. Skeat, "Early Christian Book-Production: Papyri and Manuscripts," in *The West from the Fathers to the Reformation* (ed. G.W.H. Lampe; *The Cambridge History of the Bible* 2; Cambridge: Cambridge University Press, 1969), 54–79; 73; Martin Hengel, *Studies in the Gospel of Mark* (trans. John Bowden; Eugene, Ore: Wipf & Stock, 2003), 79; Malcolm Choat, "Echo and Quotation of the New Testament Papyrus Letters to the end of the 4th Century," in *New Testament Manuscripts: Their Texts and their World* (eds. Thomas Kraus and Tobias Nicklas; Leiden/Boston: Brill, 2006), 267–292; 283.

cited and distributed throughout school-text papyri, are also frequently cited and distributed throughout literary texts from the same period. Certainly, this study of the use of Paul's writings recognises that the connection between literary sources and pedagogy is more tenuous than school-text papyri and pedagogy. In this way therefore, the conclusions which can be drawn differ from those of Morgan since the subject matter is not school-texts but sophisticated literary constructs.

Nevertheless, the methodological insights established by Morgan and the clear connection between educational and literary texts offer a way to deal with Pauline references in early Christian texts that is consistent and manageable. Based on the conclusion that the number of textual references in ancient school exercises coincides with the literary reception of the same texts, something about how early Christian writing was shaped by the most frequently cited Pauline texts can be explored. What does the frequent citation of certain Pauline passages and the ways in which they were used say about what was important to early Christians? Moreover, what might these uses contribute to an understanding of Christianity as a system of practice and belief? The method as set forth by Morgan is adapted with the assumption that the frequency of citation will aid understanding of how and why Pauline texts were a particularly important resource for early Christians.

In his study of Origen's use of Paul's letter to the Romans, Peter Gorday argues that highly cited Pauline texts help to illuminate the hermeneutical approach of early Christians to Scripture. "What matters," he writes, "aside from their sheer frequency (which is not to be ignored), is how one *weighs* these citations and allusions: in what context do they appear, across how many works are they scattered, [and] how central do they seem to be to an argument [...] we still need an adequate hermeneutic of the use of texts" in order to grasp what early Christians understood of Scripture in general and the Pauline epistles in particular.[29] This study follows both of Gorday's suggestions, determining not only the sheer frequency of Pauline texts in early Christian writings, but taking this further by examining the context, distribution, and content of their use. Therefore, as the approach offered by scholars of ancient history enabled them to draw qualitative conclusions about the use of Graeco-Roman texts in an educational context, so this adapted approach enables qualitative conclusions about the use of Pauline texts by early Christians. Only by establishing the context in

---

[29] Peter Gorday, "Paulus Origenianus: The Economic Interpretation of Paul in Origen and Gregory of Nyssa," in *Paul and the Legacies of Paul* (ed. William S. Babcock; Dallas: Southern Methodist University Press, 1990), 141–163; 351n2; italics original.

which these references occur in early Christian texts and how they are used, do the quantitative results of the survey become qualitative. Furthermore, this method also enables both the identification and an analysis of four frequently cited passages of Paul which, to my knowledge, have not been identified before nor has a study focused in-depth on the use of these four passages in early Christian writings.

## 1.4 A Database of Pauline References[30]

The database on which this study is based contains 27,051 references to the Pauline epistles in pre-Nicene sources.[31] The excerpts that make up this comprehensive survey include texts in varying modes of philosophical and intellectual discourse, including apologetic, protreptic, and didactic texts.[32] Within the initial survey, excerpts from literary sources make up ninety-eight percent of the references,[33] with only 207 possible Pauline references in papyri from this time period[34] and 115 possible epigraphic references.[35]

---

30 This database will be available online as a searchable digital resource from September 2016.
31 This does not mean that excerpts from Paul appear in 27,051 different texts, but that each separate reference could be regarded as a separate decision to use the Pauline passage. See Morgan, *Literate Education*, 54.
32 See Rankin, *Clement to Origen*, 6–8. See also Sterling, "Hellenistic Philosophy," 322–325.
33 The primary sources for literary references include *Biblia Patristica, Sources chrétiennes, Patrologia Latina, Patrologia Graeca, Clavia Patrum Graecorum,* and *Instrumenta Patristica,* as well as electronic databases such as *Thesaurus Linguae Graecae, Patrologia Latina Database, Biblindex* (an updated version of *Biblia Patristica*), and *Cetedoc Library of Christian Latin Texts*.
34 While the focus of this study is restricted to literary texts, papyrological texts as a whole and especially documentary texts, while largely ignored in biblical studies, do serve as a point of comparison and an additional witness to the use of a text by early Christians. In particular, Pauline references found in school exercises and letters enable further study of the links between early Christian teaching and Scripture, as well as questions about networks for early Christian education, especially through the occurrence of scribal markers called *nomina sacra*. See Luijendijk, *Greetings in the Lord*, 57–58, 67–69, 122–123; Macquarie University Ancient History Documentary Research Centre, "Papyri from the Rise of Early Christianity in Egypt: Conspectus of Texts," Conspectus XIX.A, 13.
35 This study also initially considered epigraphic references, although they are not literary or documentary texts but inscriptions such as engravings on house lintels, columns, tombs and sarcophagi. While the use of archaeological evidence in the form of epigraphy and epitaphs adds yet another dimension, engaging a context in which early Christians were using Scripture, the lack of clarity and precision with regards to dating and identification means that they do not feature in this project.

While references from the works of Origen of Alexandria constitute approximately one-half of all pre-Nicene Pauline references, the works of Eusebius of Caesarea, Tertullian, Clement of Alexandria, and Irenaeus of Lyons also feature prominently. Nevertheless, the database is not limited to their writings and includes more than 230 works by more than 75 ante-Nicene authors. Figure I illustrates the distribution of these Pauline references within literary sources.[36]

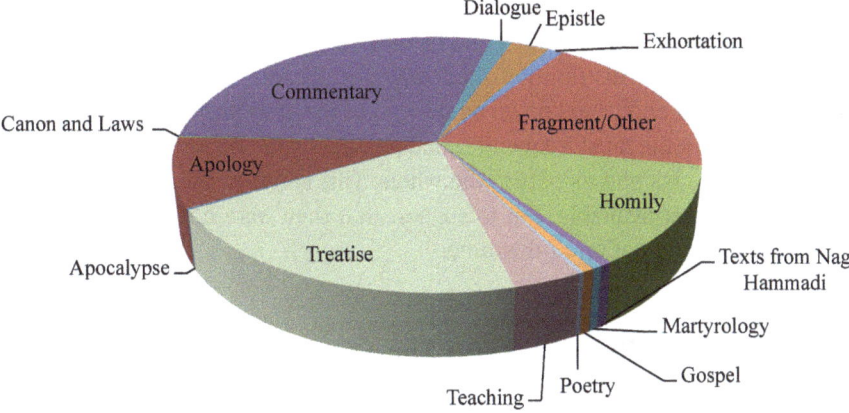

**Figure 1:** Pauline References by Genre (categories per *Sources chrétiennes*)

That Pauline references may be found across such a wide range of authors and within such a wide variety of texts suggests that the most highly cited passages were at the forefront of the minds of early Christian writers for a variety of purposes. My treatment of a range and variety of scriptural references, authors, and texts, therefore, strengthens any qualitative conclusions drawn from this quantitative data.[37]

The creation of this database of references to Pauline texts in early Christian sources revealed that certain clusters of passages were cited at a much higher rate than others.[38] The identity of these pericopes is significant in itself, prompt-

---

**36** The texts are divided according to the categories identified by *Sources chrétiennes*.
**37** van den Hoek, "Techniques of Quotation," 230–234.
**38** In terms of numbers, the most frequently cited pericopes are as follows with the approximate number of citations in parenthesis: 1 Cor 2.6–16 (691); Col 1.15–20 (673); Phil 2.6–8 (568); Eph 6.10–17 (466); 1 Cor 15.50–58 (404); 1 Cor 1.20–24 (382); Rom 8.14–17 (227); Eph 2.11–15 (159); and Rom 8.30–39 (142). Note that because Phil 2 and Col 1 are so frequently found together in early Christian writings and are used similarly in Christological arguments, the

ing questions about why these texts occur in such great quantity and how early Christians were using them. Also noteworthy is the discovery that almost every verse of the letters attributed to Paul by early Christians is represented in the database, confirming scholarly suggestions that Paul's letters were circulating together from a very early time.[39] If the survey had revealed a large number of references to a small number of Pauline texts, the conclusion for this project might be very different, suggesting instead that early Christians were working from selected collections of Pauline texts and pericopes. That almost every part of the Pauline letters is represented, even though some at a much higher rate and with a much wider distribution than others, indicates that all of Paul's texts were being used and were known by the end of the ante-Nicene period. Morever, it intimates that the most frequently cited passages were known beyond a collection of select texts and as part of the whole. This is not to claim that select collections were not available, but to suggest that they were not the only Pauline documents in circulation at this time.

## 1.5 From Quantity to Quality: The Four Pericopes

Based on a collation of references to texts attributed to Paul in ante-Nicene Christian writings, this study establishes which parts of the Pauline epistles were most used by early Christians—1 Cor 2.6–16, Eph 6.10–17, 1 Cor 15.50–58, and Col 1.15–20—and then determines how the use of these passages affects and shapes early Christian writings and how, secondarily, they might illuminate an understanding of Christian formation. Having determined the methodology and the desirability of examining the early reception of Pauline writings in general, I offer a glimpse at some of the conclusions that emerge from this project.

While the four passages that serve as a focal point for each chapter were selected because of the frequency with which they are cited, the treatment of each passage addresses the context in which these passages appear; how they are used and scattered across and throughout early Christian writings; what role they play in early Christian debate; and the variety of hermeneutical approaches with which they are utilised. Given that specific images, phrases, and key words

---

focus of this study was restricted to Col 1 but includes many notes and references to Phil 2 in the fifth chapter.

**39** Verses not present include 40 verses of Romans; 21 verses of 1 Corinthians; 32 verses of 2 Corinthians; 13 verses of Galatians; 3 verses of Ephesians; 14 verses of Philippians; 4 verses of Colossians; 12 verses of 1 Thessalonians; 7 verses of 2 Thessalonians; 14 verses of 1 Timothy; 18 verses of 2 Timothy; 9 verses of Titus; 5 verses of Philemon.

began to emerge across genres and across time, each chapter has been divided into sections and follows a particular image or theme chronologically by author in order to discern the diversity and, in some places, the consistency of early Christian use.[40] In this way, a phrase such as "image of the invisible God" from Col 1.15 could be followed through different authors, looking at the ways the phrase is used across time, genre, and location. Moreover, the process of focusing on concepts and images picked up by authors from the four Pauline texts also highlights key issues woven into an author's writing as the words of Paul are taken up, adapted, modified, and reworked within a significant number of early Christian texts. Irenaeus' theological understanding of recapitulation, Tertullian's focus on the substance of Christ, Origen's interpretation of Scripture, and Clement's focus on formation all come into play when these Pauline texts are used and adapted within their writings. Because theology and the exposition of Scripture are so essentially connected in this time period, part of this study also contributes to reflection on broader theological topics such as Christology, cosmology, eschatology, and anthropology. The Pauline text that links each early Christian writer within a chapter serves "as an exegetical linchpin holding together a complex web of passages"[41] and images. These images and phrases, therefore, are interpreted with sensitivity both to the specifics of use by a particular author and the larger contours and context of Scripture in early Christian debate.[42] As excerpts from each Pauline passage are received and appropriated

---

[40] The exception to this division is chapter 4 on 1 Cor 15, which is divided chronologically by author.
[41] Christman, *What Did Ezekiel See*, 98.
[42] Many authoritative and reliable studies exist on biblical interpretation in early Christianity. These include Andreas Lindemann, *Paulus im ältesten Christentum: Das Bild d. Apostels u. d. Rezeption d. paulinischen Theologie in d. frühchristl. Theologie bis Marcion* (BHT 58; Tübingen: Mohr, 1979); Charles Kannengiesser, *Handbook of Patristic Exegesis: The Bible in Ancient Christianity*, (FOC 1–2; Leiden: Brill, 2003); Bertrand de Margerie, *Introduction à l'histoire de l'exégèse* (vol. 1–4; Initiations; Paris: Cerf, 1980–1990); Henning Graf Reventlow, *History of Biblical Interpretation* (trans. Leo G. Perdue; 4 vols. of SBSt; Leiden/Boston: Brill, 2010); Manlio Simonetti, *Biblical Interpretation in the Early Church: An Historical Introduction to Patristic Exegesis* (trans. John A. Hughes; Edinburgh: T&T Clark, 1994); Karlfried Froehlich, *Biblical Interpretation in the Early Church* (Sources of Early Christian Thought; Philadelphia: Fortress Press, 1984); Robert M. Grant, *A Short History of the Interpretation of the Bible* (London: SCM Press, 1984); Donald K. McKim, *Historical Handbook of Major Biblical Interpreters* (Downers Grove, Ill: InterVarsity Press, 1998); Alan J. Hauser and Duane F. Watson, eds., *A History of Biblical Interpretation. Vol. 1: The Ancient Period* (Grand Rapids, Mich/Cambridge: Eerdmans, 2003); Young, *Biblical Exegesis*; *Ancient Christian Commentary on Scripture* series (29 vols; Downers Grove, Ill: InterVarsity Press); *The Church's Bible* series (4 vols.; Grand Rapids, Mich: Eerdmans, 2003–); *Novum Testamentum Patristicum*; and *Ein patristischer Kommentar zum Neuen Testa-*

within early Christian writings, their use can only be fully understood in the context of "the perceived overarching plan, plot, or argument of a literary work."[43]

The themes that become the focus of individual chapters are not simply repeated between one author and the next, and the intention is not to discover or follow the evolution of a particular use or passage chronologically. Rather, in order to engage as fully as possible with the use of excerpts from each Pauline pericope, each chapter concentrates on a small selection from early Christian writings that use excerpts from the respective passage. This selection emphasises themes, words, and images used by multiple authors for diverse purposes as they explicate theological concepts, defend the Christian faith, and engage with opponents, students, and theological concepts and constructs within their works.[44] Therefore, each chapter provides an in-depth examination of the texts that best expose the ways a passage was used by a multitude of early Christian writers and as such, major examples of the different types of interpretation of each Pauline pericope become this study's focus.[45]

With a focus on significant aspects of early Christian use of the four Pauline pericopes, each chapter assumes a similar structure as I set forth the multiplicity of authors examined in order to establish how these Pauline passages may have shaped early Christian writings and doctrinal development. Beginning with an account of the context of each pericope within the epistle as a whole, a brief survey of modern scholarship follows, situating the pericope both in its scriptural context and within current scholarly debate. This is particularly important since three of the four passages—a portion of 1 Cor 2, Col 1, and Eph 6—are

---

*ment* (2 vols; Göttingen: Vandenhoeck & Ruprecht, 2007–). For a more detailed overview and review of works up to 2006 on patristic biblical interpretation, see: Johannes Van Oort, "Biblical Interpretation in the Patristic Era, a 'Handbook of Patristic Exegesis' and Some Other Recent Books and Related Projects," *VC* 60, no. 1 (2006): 80–103.

**43** Young, *Biblical Exegesis*, 7.

**44** The only texts excluded from the study are those which could not be found, either because the text itself could not be found or because upon consultation, a reference could not be determined. Nevertheless, these texts are included in the appendices since they are listed in indices such as *Biblia Patristica*. Earlier fragments from writers like Clement of Rome and many anonymous Valentinian texts do not give enough context or content to draw out an extensive exegesis in the body of the chapter and therefore are primarily cited in the notes and appendix. Other examples and related references from early Christian texts can be found in the footnotes, which evidence the breadth of material considered.

**45** In this way, each chapter could become a monograph in itself (following the model of Christman's monograph on the patristic use of a portion of Ezek 1), but it would be one that asks a different research question.

## 1.5 From Quantity to Quality: The Four Pericopes

the subject of debates within modern scholarship concerning their authenticity as a Pauline text.

As Ian Boxall explains in his reception history of Patmos, this section on modern scholarship "seeks to describe the imaginative space offered to interpreters by the ambiguities and multivalency of the text, which might have been obscured by scholarly focus on a narrow set of questions and interests."[46] References to modern scholarship acknowledge the scholarly debates and ambiguities surrounding the text considered in each chapter. The brief overview of modern scholarship is both "retrospective (reflecting knowledge of readings already uncovered)" and "prospective (setting out possible ambiguities yet to be explored)."[47] The context within Scripture and within modern scholarship for the passage discussed in each chapter allows for comparison and even critique of modern interpretation by some of the earliest reception of these texts. This result is best described by Young, who concludes that even though early Christian "exegetical methods have often been dismissed because of their so-called disregard of history," from the use of biblical texts by early Christians, "we might learn much."[48]

The four chapters which follow this introduction focus on one of the four highly cited Pauline pericopes and begin with a chapter on 1 Cor 2.6–16. This chapter is first not only because this text is the most frequently cited Pauline passage, but also because the concept of formation that emerges from early Christian use of this passage informs the understanding of formation throughout this study. Within this chapter, it becomes clear that the images and phrases most frequently used from 1 Cor 2 are those of wisdom and what "eye has not seen and ear has not heard" (1 Cor 2.9). Excerpts from this pericope are especially adapted to deal with difficult exegesis and difficult people, as well as to distinguish between different kinds of wisdom. Early Christians drew on the tension in this pericope for a similar strategic purpose: to differentiate between worldly wisdom and the wisdom of God. Through the use of this text, early Christians understand two or three levels of wisdom and define formation as the progression or movement from one level of wisdom to another. As the first chapter concludes, the figure and authority of Paul play a central role in early Christian use of this Corinthian excerpt in a way not entirely dissimilar to the use of Homeric excerpts in Graeco-Roman literary sources.

---

[46] Ian Boxall, *Patmos in the Reception History of the Apocalypse* (Oxford: Oxford University Press, 2013), 14.
[47] Boxall, *Patmos*, 14.
[48] Young, *Biblical Exegesis*, 3–4.

The third chapter focuses on Eph 6.10–17 and emphasises that early Christians are particularly concerned with the images of wrestling, armour, and the fiery darts of the evil one found in this passage. Using the words and images of this second pericope, early Christians are now exhorted in ways that the wisdom described in 1 Cor 2 may be achieved and maintained through actions of prayer, faith, standing firm in the midst of temptation, and putting on the armour of God. Through the use of the images in Eph 6, certain points in the Christian life are identified as times when one is especially vulnerable to attack, weakness, and fear. These times represent liminal moments when the Christian is between sides of the battle, whether joining it for the first time in baptism or within the decisive moment of battle for those facing persecution.

The fourth chapter presents a more pronounced focus on early Christian use of images found within a Pauline text, emphasising the significant connection between exegesis and theology in the process. Using the images of flesh and blood and the kingdom of God as found in 1 Cor 15.50–58, early Christians articulate their developing theology of resurrection. Their focus on 15.50 in particular emphasises the division between flesh and blood and the kingdom of God and the ambiguities in defining each of these elements. Excerpts from this passage are most frequently found in apologetic texts defending different sides of the debate about the form of resurrection.

The focus of the final chapter is on early Christian use of excerpts from Col 1.15–20, where the emphasis is on Christological images and phrases found in the text. These phrases and images are used by early Christians to support theological arguments about the nature of Christ and the relationship between God the Father and God the Son. In the use of this Colossian passage, Christ's identity is as one who is pre-existent and who shares the authority and nature of God, as the head of the church and of humankind. In order to show the hermeneutical and exegetical limits and struggles that accompany early Christian interpretation of this passage, the final section of this chapter extends beyond the time period of this study to explore how the advent of the Arian controversy affected the use of Col 1 in early Christianity.

In order to answer the central question of this project—how did these most frequently used Pauline texts shape and inform early Christian writings? —each chapter provides a variety of excerpts from early Christian writings as described above. These excerpts are selected in order to establish the clearest picture of how early Christian writers used these Pauline texts and how the images and phrases of each excerpt are adapted to a whole range of arguments. This focus leads to a deeper understanding of formation, as well. While this insight into formation was not necessarily a deliberate move by early Christian writers, it can nevertheless be identified in their use of Pauline images and phrases.

Furthermore, while early Christian writers use excerpts from Pauline passages for their own apologetic, exegetical, and theological arguments, they also, through these arguments, enable conclusions to be drawn about their understanding of Paul and of themselves as Christians. Crucial understandings of early Christian identity are discernible from the frequent use of these four passages in early Christian theological arguments. In particular, I conclude that within these writings, Christians are described as ones imbued with wisdom, embattled, raised with Christ at the *eschaton*, and with faith in the one who is fully human, fully divine, pre-existent, and co-creator with God the Father.

Additionally, three striking conclusions were immediately apparent when the four separate chapters were placed side by side. The first is that amongst the preponderance of authors surveyed, four early Christian writers are cited more than any others in what follows: Clement of Alexandria, Irenaeus, Tertullian, and Origen. Others such as Ignatius, Hippolytus, Novatian, Eusebius, and anonymous Valentinian authors also feature. As a consequence of the restrictions outlined by the inductive method used to select principal passages in each chapter, this study gives particular prominence to those early Christian writers who give the most context to their use of Pauline texts. In other words, these select early Christian writers are most frequently engaged within this study because each indicates most clearly within their works that they are referring to something attributed to Paul. This observation is significant for at least two reasons. The first is that the absence of certain authors from these chapters, and especially the absence of a number of heterodox writings, confirms that much the evidence from this time period is fragmentary and numerically insignificant. In some places, this may be due to texts no longer being extant or preserved only in secondary writings but in other places this may suggest that a Pauline text was not only used in contexts of conflict and division. While the words of 1 Cor 15 and Col 1 were embedded in early Christian debates about resurrection and the nature of Christ, this was not the only focus for the use of these texts by early Christians. The second reason that the preponderance of certain authors is significant is that this observation emphasises a limitation of this study. Most significantly, this group of early Christian writers treat Paul in a way that is most accessible for this project while others, whose works are more fragmentary or in many cases, no longer extant, do not.

A second observation, already noted briefly in this introduction, is that theology and the exposition and use of Scripture are essentially one in this time period. As each chapter emphasises through detailed examination, these four passages touch on theological issues that were of critical importance for early Christian writers and central to the formation of their doctrine and the hermeneutics emerging at this time. One of the conclusions drawn by Morgan and based on the use of Homeric texts was that in many places where Homer is cited, his works are not used exegetically or to support a wider argument but rather his name and his writings are used to create an identity for the author as one who is learned and cultured.[49] Similarly, within early Christian writings, Paul is given authority as one who is wise. Consequently, this authority gives weight to early Christian use of his writings on their own, placing their writings within the tradition of the church of which they saw Paul as an integral part.

Additionally, this observation lends context to the question of why early Christians adapted and adopted a variety of hermeneutical tactics in order to ensure that Paul's words supported their own. Just as references to Homer gave weight to the authority of a Graeco-Roman writer as one learned and cultured, so the writings of Paul gave weight to early Christian arguments. In this way, excerpts from these passages are found amongst some of the most controversial theological and interpretative issues of early Christianity: the nature of wisdom and formation; how to stand firm in the face of persecution; the nature of resurrection; and the person and nature of Christ.

The third observation is a practical one regarding how these four passages attributed to Paul were used by early Christians. This observation engages the intersection of theory and practice specifically in the role genre plays in early Christian exegesis. Excerpts from Scripture "functioned in many genres in the patristic period"[50] and overall, these four passages occur within a mix of different genres, especially with early Christian use of 1 Cor 2 and Col 1. However, 1 Cor 15 is used most frequently within apologetic works and Eph 6 is found primarily in paraenetic works, observations which are engaged more fully within this study. Each chapter, therefore, incorporates a concluding section emphasising not only the images and phrases discussed but also exploring the importance of genre and to what extent it shapes the use of the Pauline text and interpretation offered, as well as the interests of the interpreter.

## 1.6 Defining References and Setting Boundaries

Before proceeding with the second chapter, this study must finally address the on-going discussion in biblical, literary, and classical scholarship about the relationship between explicit references to what is now called Scripture and allu-

---

[49] Morgan, *Literate Education*, 77–78.
[50] Young, *Biblical Exegesis*, 4.

sions, references, and echoes of the same texts.[51] Within the survey—excerpts of which are presented in the appendices—the columns listing authors and their works need little clarification; however, the terminology used to describe the relationship between the text and the scriptural passage to which it may refer merits further discussion. When so much of Scripture is a part of the vocabulary of early Christian writers, how do we know whether they are using one word or a series of words from the Pauline epistles or if a possible reference is simply a turn of phrase they have made their own?

While "borrowed material embedded in the flow of a writer's text is a common phenomenon in Antiquity,"[52] early Christian use of a scriptural text is not always a clear-cut, verbatim quotation. Many attempts to identify references in ancient texts require consideration of the author's intention, which, often unspecified, is problematic and one of the many struggles in modern scholarship for categorizing references to Scripture in early Christian writings.[53] Nevertheless, at some point "terminologies must be formulated for these varying kinds of recycled materials."[54] Any study that involves an interpretation of texts, therefore, must address this problem of terminology by determining what, if anything, will be included beyond explicit citations, especially in light of the generic limitations described by Moss at the beginning of this introduction.[55]

As Stanley Porter outlines, current scholarship overlooks questions of definition and terminology because it has failed to develop a "common language" for identifying different ways in which early Christian writers used Scripture in

---

[51] See Choat, "Echo and Quotation," esp. 267–283; Moss, *Other Christs*, 5–7; Richard Hays, *Echoes of Scripture in the Letters of Paul* (New Haven/London: Yale University Press, 1989), 29–32; Naldini, *Il Cristianesimo in Egitto*, 54–56; Bruce F. Harris, "Biblical Echoes and Reminiscences in Christian Papyri," in *Proceedings of the XIV International Congress of Papyrologists, Oxford 24–31, July, 1974* (ed. International Congress of Papyrologists; London: Egypt Exploration Society, 1975), 155–160; Dietrich-Alex Koch, *Die Schrift als Zeuge des Evangeliums: Untersuchungen zur Verwendung und zum Verständnis der Schrift bei Paulus* (Gutenberg: Universität Mainz, 1986); van den Hoek, "Techniques of Quotation," 223–243; Andrew Gregory and Christopher M. Tuckett, "Reflections on Method: What Constitutes the Use of the Writings that Later Formed the New Testament in the Apostolic Fathers?," in *The New Testament and the Apostolic Fathers: The Reception of the New Testament in the Apostolic Fathers* (eds. Andrew Gregory and Christopher M. Tuckett; Oxford: Oxford University Press, 2005), 61–82; esp. 63–68.
[52] van den Hoek, "Techniques of Quotation," 223. See also 228.
[53] For example, Richard Hays finds deeper links between early Christian writings and New Testament texts by elaborately defining both conscious and unconscious intentional echoes of Scripture. See Hays, *Echoes*, esp. 29–32.
[54] van den Hoek, "Techniques of Quotation," 228.
[55] Moss, *Other Christs*, 205n11.

secondary literature.⁵⁶ While some such as Richard Longenecker focus only on "explicit quotations of Scripture that appear in the New Testament," both Porter and Moss argue that this approach is limited and "skews the evidence."⁵⁷ As others have made clear, one "should also bear in mind that ancient ideas of citation and quotation may not always have included our standards of literal quotation and correct attribution."⁵⁸ Furthermore, "with ancient standards of memory, even the most perfect citation will not guarantee that the writer copied it [...] and there is no guarantee the biblical passage is the direct source; a sermon, reading of other literature or hearing the phrase in another way surely can stand between this usage, the words, and the holy text."⁵⁹ Therefore, while a language is needed to describe how early Christian writers used scriptural texts, more often than not this search "depends too much on modern scruples about exact quotation that did not obtain in antiquity, as quotations by Christian writers themselves show well enough."⁶⁰

In order to address these issues of identification, many scholars have created their own classifications to identify references in early Christian and classical texts. Some offer only broad categories of direct or non-direct references, while others offer fine distinctions between different techniques of citation.⁶¹ Helmbold and O'Neil, for example, offer a list of Plutarch's quotations with a brief introduction to highlight problems of identification and terminology. Their list of references is separated into quotations, reminiscences, references, and paraphrases, although the distinction between these terms is not specifically outlined.⁶² Hays develops seven criteria to define "echo" in his book on the use of Scripture in the Pauline epistles, but the detailed and specific nature of his definitions is complex, and as stated above, his reliance on authorial intention both conscious and unconscious is difficult to apply.⁶³ This is a particular chal-

---

**56** Stanley Porter, "The Use of the Old Testament in the New Testament: A Brief Comment on Method and Terminology," in *Early Christian Interpretation of the Scriptures of Israel: Investigations and Proposals* (eds. Craig A. Evans and Jack T. Sanders; Sheffield: Sheffield Academic Press, 1997), 79–97; 80.
**57** Richard Longenecker, *Biblical Exegesis in the Apostolic Period* (2nd ed; Grand Rapids, Mich: Eerdmans, 1999), xvi. See also Porter, "Old Testament in the New Testament," 92; Moss, *Other Christs*, 5.
**58** Choat, "Echo and Quotation," 269.
**59** Choat, "Echo and Quotation," 280.
**60** Gamble, *Books and Readers*, 56.
**61** Porter, "Old Testament in the New Testament," 80.
**62** See William Helmbold and Edward O'Neil, *Plutarch's Quotations* (PhilM 19; Baltimore, Md: American Philological Association, 1959); and van den Hoek, "Techniques of Quotation," 228.
**63** Hays, *Echoes*, 29–32.

lenge since most early Christian writers were steeped in scriptural language and do not reveal to their readers the motivation behind their choice of words.

Ultimately, this study relies on the distinctions and definitions offered by Annewies van den Hoek in her study of Clement of Alexandria's techniques of quotation, and Michael Bird in his study of the reception of Paul in the *Epistle to Diognetus*.[64] Not only are their definitions formulated with regards to writings from the same time period as this project, but each scholar has also attempted to simplify definitions. In the process, they each focus primarily not on authorial intent but on the content and context of each reference in their studies.[65] Acknowledging that "texts can rehearse other texts in a variety of ways,"[66] the selected database of texts in the appendices of this study is divided into three categories: reference, possible reference, and reference not found. Described in greater detail within the appendix, a "reference" is what many scholars might define as a quotation, direct attribution, or paraphrase and has "a considerable degree of literality" and yet it "need not be verbatim in the modern sense."[67] A "possible reference" is a phrase or series of words where similarities between the Pauline passage and early Christian texts can be detected and could be identified as a reference were the context to allow.[68] For passages in this category, conclusions about whether they are a reference to the specific Pauline passage under consideration must necessarily remain provisional. Those texts labelled "reference not found" include texts listed by secondary sources as containing references to Pauline material but in which the corresponding Pauline passage cannot be identified.

Nevertheless, as van den Hoek rightly observes, while terminologies must be formulated and distinctions made, "the forest of quotations should not be hidden by the trees of classification."[69] While indices such as *Biblia Patristica* might suggest that early Christian writers only used individual passages one at a time, by examining the context and content of early Christian writings, it is clear that this is not the case. In fact, one set of passages often serves as a trigger

---

[64] van den Hoek, "Techniques of Quotation," 228–229 and Michael F. Bird, "The Reception of Paul in the *Epistle to Diognetus*," in *Paul and the Second Century* (ed. Michael F. Bird and Joseph R. Dodson; London: T&T Clark, 2011), 74.
[65] See also William L. Petersen, "Patristic Biblical Quotations and Method: Four Changes to Lightfoot's Edition of *Second Clement*" in *Patristic and Text-Critical Studies: The Collected Essays of William L. Petersen* (ed. Jan Kraus and Joseph Verheyden; Leiden: Brill, 2012), 539–566; esp. 562–564.
[66] Bird, "Reception of Paul," 74.
[67] van den Hoek, "Techniques of Quotation," 229.
[68] Bird, "Reception of Paul," 74.
[69] van den Hoek, "Techniques of Quotation," 228.

for another. Angela Christman, who focuses on the unity of the Bible in a study of early Christian reception of excerpts from Ezekiel 1, writes that "early Christian writers display extraordinary sensitivity not only to the particular words of text, but also to the vocabulary of the entire Bible. Thus their interpretation develops, even flourishes, within the linguistic confines of the sacred writings themselves."[70] Part of the examination of the four Pauline passages within this study, therefore, includes attention to other scriptural passages frequently found in close proximity to each pericope. It was clear from the context and content of the references, for example, that excerpts from 1 Cor 2.6–16 with a focus on wisdom are often found in close proximity to excerpts from Prov 8.22 and 1 Cor 3.1–3, while excerpts from Col 1.15–20 with a focus on Christological phrases are often found in close proximity to excerpts from Phil 2.5–11 and John 1.1–18. Consequently, while one pericope may be the focus of a chapter, each chapter also includes "passages most germane to the theological issue under consideration" as they were used by early Christian writers who were "guided by the premise of the bible's unity."[71] Therefore, "some passages receive little attention and some trigger the use of others by connecting simply a word or an image."[72]

## 1.7 Conclusion

With a focus on the use of Paul's most frequently cited texts in ante-Nicene literary sources—1 Cor 2.6–16, Eph 6.10–17, 1 Cor 15.50–58, and Col 1.15–20—the content and context in which these passages occur across a wide spectrum of different early Christian writings is examined in what follows. Through this examination, emerging and varied theological views are identified as early Christians grappled with ideas of formation and wisdom, authority, the nature of resurrection, and the nature of Christ. Cited time and again by early Christians and peppered throughout their works, excerpts from these four passages serve as a focal point for emerging issues, doctrine, and formation—both direct and indirect—in early Christianity. Out of a period described as a "crepuscular zone for the Christian community [...] with 'catholic Christianity' 'developing' but by no means yet

---

[70] Christman, *What Did Ezekiel See*, 159. See also Young, *Biblical Exegesis*, 7, who writes about the unity of Scripture as "a 'dogma' among the Fathers", and Augustine, *Doct.Chr*, 3.27.38 for his description of scriptural exegesis.
[71] Christman, *What Did Ezekiel See*, 98.
[72] Christman, *What Did Ezekiel See*, 98.

shaped,"[73] the quantitative data leading to the discovery of four significant Pauline passages, and engagement with the many contexts in which they occur, allows a qualitative centre to emerge. This study of the most frequently cited Pauline passages raises new questions and conversations within the field of New Testament studies. Moreover, it engenders essential conversations within the burgeoning field of reception history and the study of the effects of a text. The application and adaptation of a methodology from scholars of ancient history to early Christian reception contributes to fruitful reflection on early Christian use of Scripture, the emergence of broader theological topics which characterised early Christianity, and Christian identity itself.

---

**73** Albert C. Outler, "Methods and Aims in the Study of the Development of Catholic Christianity," *SCe* 1 (1981), 7–17; 11.

# Chapter Two:
# 1 Corinthians 2.6–16: Wisdom leads a soul to God[1]

> *But we speak God's wisdom, secret and hidden,*
> *which God decreed before the ages for our glory*
> (1 Cor 2.7)

## 2.1 Early Christian Writers and 1 Corinthians 2[2]

Clement of Rome, writing at the turn of the second century C.E., held Paul's first letter to the Corinthians in high esteem and exhorted his audience to "take up the epistle of the blessed Paul the apostle."[3] Throughout the first three centuries of the Common Era, early Christian writers cite 1 Corinthians more than any of the other epistles attributed to Paul. As Laurence Welborn confirms, "no writing of Paul was so widely read or so highly esteemed in the early church as 1 Corinthians."[4] Amongst early Christian references to the Corinthian epistle, one passage from this letter is used more than any other: 1 Cor 2.6–16. Parts of this pericope are cited at least 690 times by more than 40 different pre-Nicene authors, and excerpts from 1 Cor 2.6–16 may be found in a variety of text types including apologies, commentaries, homilies, and martyrologies.[5]

In the first chapter of this letter, Paul contrasts human and divine wisdom, the latter being seen as foolishness by humankind particularly because it was linked with the folly of the crucified Christ (1.18–24). The themes of contrast and the nature of divine wisdom revealed in the cross are taken up in chapter two. Here, this wisdom, hidden from the powers whether human or divine, catches the powers and principalities off guard as they crucify the Lord of glory and in so doing find themselves not only taken unawares but completely

---

[1] Richard A. Edwards and Robert A. Wild, eds., *The Sentences of Sextus* (TTECL 5; Chico, Calif: Scholars Press, 1981), 37.
[2] Portions of this chapter are published as "A Community of Interpretation: The Use of 1*Corinthians* 2:6–16 by Early Christians" in *Studia Patristica* LXIII (Leuven: Peeters, 2013), 69–80.
[3] Clement of Rome, *1Clem*, 47.1 (*SC* 167).
[4] L.L. Welborn, "'Take up the Epistle of the Blessed Paul the Apostle': The Contrasting Fates of Paul's Letters to Corinth in the Patristic Period," in *Reading Communities, Reading Scripture: Essays in Honour of Daniel Patte* (eds. Gary Phillips and Nicole Wilkinson Duran; Harrisburg, Pa: Trinity Press International, 2002), 345–360; 345.
[5] See Appendix A for details of these references.

routed. Access to that divine wisdom comes through the Spirit, in principle at least, open to all those in Christ, but Paul points forward to a possible distinction between himself and the Corinthians who may claim to know the deep things of God through the Spirit already. This distinction sets up Paul's response to the ethical and practical issues that arise in the rest of the letter.

Scholars such as Kovacs and Mitchell are clear that excerpts from 1 Cor 2 provide "a key to the keys"[6] for understanding the whole of the letter.[7] Nevertheless, for a number of scholars, 1 Cor 2.6–16 is a problematic section of the Corinthian correspondence and much scholarly discourse has been written about the origin and authenticity of this pericope. Bousset and Bultmann, as well as Käsemann and Conzelmann, argue that 2.6–16 is a self-contained unit in which Paul accommodated his understanding of wisdom to contemporary Hellenistic mystery-religions and Valentinian worldviews.[8] Other scholars have reasoned that the character and influence of this pericope is midrashic, Qumranic, or apocalyptic, with some finding similarities between 1 Cor 2.6–16 and Jewish writings such as that of Philo or Jewish Hellenistic wisdom material.[9] Widmann

---

[6] Margaret M. Mitchell, *Paul, the Corinthians, and the Birth of Christian Hermeneutics* (Cambridge: Cambridge University Press, 2010), 57.
[7] Judith Kovacs, "Echoes of Valentinian Exegesis in Clement of Alexandria and Origen: The Interpretation of 1 Corinthians 3.1–3," in *Origeniana Octava: Origen and the Alexandrian Tradition: Papers of the 8th International Origen Congress, Pisa, 27–31 August 2001* (ed. Lorenzo Perrone; Leuven: Peeters, 2004), 317–329; 327.
[8] See Joseph A. Fitzmyer, *First Corinthians* (AB; New Haven: Yale University Press, 2008), 169; Hans Conzelmann, *1 Corinthians* (Hermeneia; Philadelphia: Fortress Press, 1975), 57.
[9] Fitzmyer, *First Corinthians*, 66 and 101; W. Wuellner, "Haggadic Homily Genre in 1 Corinthians 1–3," *JBL* 89 (1970), 199–204; Alexandra Brown, *The Cross and Human Transformation: Paul's Apocalyptic Word in 1 Corinthians* (Minneapolis: Fortress Press, 1995), 36–59; E.E. Ellis, *Prophecy and Heremeneutic in Early Christianity* (Grand Rapids, Mich: Eerdmans, 1978), 213–220; R.B. Gaffin Jr., "Some Epistemological Reflections on 1 Corinthians 2.6–16," *WTJ* 57 (1995), 103–124; Heinz-Wolfgang Kuhn, "The Wisdom Passage in 1 Corinthians 2.6–16 between Qumran and Proto-Gnosticism," in *Sapiential, Liturgical, and Poetical Texts from Qumran: Proceedings of the Third Meeting of the International Organization for Qumran Studies, Oslo 1998* (eds. Daniel K. Falk, Florentino García Martínez, and Eileen M. Schuller; Leiden: Brill, 2000), 240–253; 243–244; Gordon D. Fee, *The First Epistle to the Corinthians* (NICNT; Grand Rapids, Mich: Eerdmans, 1987), 100; R.A. Horsley, "Pneumatikos vs. Psychikos: Distinctions of Spiritual Status among the Corinthians," *HTR* 69 (1976), 269–288; B.A. Pearson, *The Pneumatikos-Psychikos Terminology in 1 Corinthians: A Study in the Theology of the Corinthian Opponents of Paul and Its Relation to Gnosticism* (SBLDS 12; Missoula, Mo: Scholars Press, 1973), 27–37; Ben Witherington, *Jesus the Sage: The Pilgrimage of Wisdom* (Edinburgh: T&T Clark, 1994), 307–314; Friedrich Lang, *Die Briefe an die Korinther* (2nd ed; TZNT; Göttingen: Vandenhoeck & Ruprecht, 1994), 38–41; P. Stuhlmacher, "The Hermeneutical Significance of 1 Cor 2:6–16," in *Tradition and Interpretation in the New Testament: Essays in Honor of E. Earle Ellis* (eds. G.F.

and Walker argue that the pericope is not simply an adaptation but is, in its entirety, an interpolation.[10] As Kovacs and Fitzmyer contend, however, this text is neither an interpolation nor a self-contained unit but is by Paul's own hand and "there is nothing in the passage itself which compels the conclusion that Paul borrowed the antithesis from his opponents."[11]

This modern debate over the authenticity of 1 Cor 2.6–16 is especially important because within this wider pericope, 1 Cor 2.9 is cited in isolation from the rest of the text numerous times by early Christian writers. This is a particularly debated verse, and some of the scholars who argue for the authenticity of this pericope harbour doubts about the authenticity of 1 Cor 2.9.[12] Even Origen attributes 1 Cor 2.9 to the *Apocalypse of Elijah* and Jerome to the *Ascension of Isaiah*,[13] both instances raising questions about whether this singular passage may have been known as part of another source or part of an anthology of quotations, Pauline or otherwise.[14] Nevertheless, even if scholars cannot agree on the origin or

---

Hawthorne and O. Betz; Grand Rapids, Mich: Eerdmans, 1987), 328–347; 330–332; James A. Davis, *Wisdom and Spirit: An Investigation of 1 Corinthians 1.18–3.20 against the Background of Jewish Sapiential Traditions in the Greco-Roman Period* (Lanham, Md: University Press of America, 1984), 54.

**10** Fitzmyer, *First Corinthians*, 169. See also M. Widmann, "1 Kor 2,6–16: Ein Einspruch gegen Paulus," *ZNW* 70 (1979): 44–53; W.O. Walker, "1 Corinthians 2.6–16: A Non-Pauline Interpolation?," *NTS* 47 (1992): 75–94.

**11** Judith Kovacs, "The Archons, the Spirit, and the Death of Christ: Do we need the hypothesis of Gnostic opponents to explain 1 Cor. 2.6–16?," in *Apocalyptic and the New Testament: Essays in Honour of J. Louis Martyn* (eds. Joel Marcus and Marion Soards; JSTS 24; Sheffield: Sheffield Academic Press, 1989), 217–236; 225. Fitzmyer—in line with Lindemann and Murphy-O'Connor—is clear that the myriad of interpretations assuming Paul's accommodation or doubting his authorship is problematic. This passage, Fitzmyer contends, is "neither interpolated nor polemical in tone or style, nor ill-suited to the context" (Fitzmyer, *First Corinthians*, 169. See also A. Lindemann, *Der erste Korintherbrief* [HNT 9/1; Tübingen: Mohr (Siebeck), 2000], 60–61; Jerome Murphy-O'Connor, "Interpolations in 1 Corinthians," *CBQ* 48 [1986]: 81–84), but rather when the verses are analysed, they fit the context and "make up an important paragraph in the letter as a whole, because Paul clarifies in them what he means by real 'wisdom'" (Fitzmyer, *First Corinthians*, 169).

**12** Judith Kovacs writes convincingly against those who claim 1 Cor 2.9 is an interpolation. See Kovacs, "The Archons," 225.

**13** Origen, *Comm.Matt*, 5.29 and Jerome, *Epistle* 57.9. Note that Jerome is not denying Pauline authorship of 1 Cor 2.9 but rather purports to identify the original text from which he claims the apostle is paraphrasing. See also *Ascens.Isa,* 8.11.

**14** See Conzelmann, *1 Corinthians*, 63n70, and Clement of Alexandria, *Les Stromates IV* (trans. Claude Mondésert SJ; SC 463; Paris: Cerf, 2001), 245n2.

authorship of this pericope, they do agree that by the time early Christian writers had a copy of this letter, 1 Cor 2.6–16 was a part of it.[15]

This pericope, in fact, is central to the *Wirkungsgeschichte* (history of effects) of Paul's first letter to Corinth. For Thistleton, 1 Cor 2.6–16 is a "model paradigm" for examining the reception of the Pauline epistles in Christian writing.[16] Alongside Kovacs and Mitchell, Thistleton is one of the few scholars to offer a detailed overview of the reception history of this passage, and within his commentary, he includes an excursus on the "post-history of the text," tracing its use from Irenaeus to Barth.[17] Modelling his approach on that represented within the *EKKNT* series, he briefly gives an overview of the use of excerpts from 1 Cor 2 by a selection of authors, with a particular focus on the nature of the Holy Spirit. While Thistleton recognises that this pericope is "key" in Christian writings up to the present time, he fails to note that one of the reasons scholars of reception history are able to engage this text to such a depth is the frequency of its use across authors and time. In other words, the quantity of excerpts from this pericope by Christian writers enables a more qualitative examination of its reception within early Christian writings.

This chapter indicates major trends of the use of 1 Cor 2.6–16, based on an examination of early Christian writings spread across regions and centuries and composed for a number of different purposes. The number of actual passages from early Christian writers quoted is not exhaustive, but intends to be indicative of the way 1 Cor 2.6–16 is used. Citations similar to the excerpts engaged will be included in the notes throughout the chapter. Through an analysis of the content and context of these references, I found that particular phrases and images from 1 Cor 2 were used consistently across texts and authors. This led to the conclusion that excerpts from this passage are used by early Christian writers in at least three ways: as part of a rhetorical manoeuvre, especially within apologetic discourse; as exegetical evidence for a particular interpretation of Scripture or a theological concept; and as a basis for explaining different kinds of wisdom and concomitantly, different approaches to Christian formation. This chapter, therefore, is comprised of three main sections, focusing on the themes and images drawn from this Corinthian pericope.[18]

---

**15** Walker, "1 Corinthians 2.6–16," 80.
**16** Anthony C. Thistleton, *The First Epistle to the Corinthians: A Commentary on the Greek Text* (NIGTC; Grand Rapids, Mich: Eerdmans, 2000), 285.
**17** Thistleton, *1 Corinthians*, 276–286.
**18** While this approach attempts to explore all of the exegetical options taken by early Christian writers, some references do not fall into these three broad categories such as, for example, when an excerpt is used as part of a list of Pauline passages or in a parenthetical remark. For example,

The use of portions of 1 Cor 2 for apologetical, exegetical, and formative purposes, however, is not the only conclusion that can be drawn from an examination of early Christian writings. With a focus on wisdom and associated phrases from 1 Cor 2, excerpts from this passage are used by early Christian writers to describe and claim the hidden wisdom of God. At the same time, early Christian use of this passage on wisdom informs their understandings of Paul as the custodian and even teacher of this wisdom and, for some early Christian writers, their own self-understanding. The context within which early Christian writers use 1 Cor 2.6–16 offers insight, therefore, into different ways the wisdom and authority claimed by and attributed to Paul may have been a basis for early Christian claims of wisdom and authority within their own teaching and arguments.

## 2.2 Rhetorical Manoeuvres & Apologetic Discourse[19]

Rhetoric is most concisely described as the practical art of deliberation through argument, interpretation, and criticism with the purpose of persuading the other.[20] Early Christian writers relied on such persuasive and at times carefully constructed manoeuvres as part of their apologetic, exegetical, and ethical arguments. Their rhetorical training and its effect on their writing and biblical hermeneutical approaches are well documented by scholars. Margaret Mitchell, for example, is clear that "in ancient rhetorical education students were trained in textual hermeneutics" which was then used in later contexts, debates, and in particular, patristic biblical exegesis.[21] Whether through their own intensive learning or through their encounter with reading and listening to others, early

---

Origen describes a royal official as a "ruler of this age" (*Comm.Jo*, 13.411) and Clement of Alexandria includes 1 Cor 2.7 in a series of Pauline passages (including excerpts from Phil 1, Gal 4, Heb 4, 1 Thess 5, Prov 10 and 29, 1 Cor 4 and 1 Cor 8) which are listed in order to compare Paul's sayings on wisdom with those of the Epicureans and Stoics (*Strom*, 1.55.1). Even so, while they are not included in the body of this chapter, these references may still be found in the survey included as an appendix.

**19** Other examples from early Christian writings include: Clement of Alexandria, *Strom*, 6.68.1–2; Irenaeus of Lyons, *Haer*, 3.2.1; 1.8.4; 1.9.1; Origen, *Cels*, 1.13; 3.20; Pamphilus of Caesarea, *Apol*, 23 and 81; Firmilian of Caesarea, *Cypr*, 9.

**20** Walter Jost and Wendy Olmsted, "Introduction," in *A Companion to Rhetoric and Rhetorical Criticism* (eds. Walter Jost and Wendy Olmsted; Malden, Mass: Blackwell, 2003), xv–xvi; xv.

**21** Mitchell, *Christian Hermeneutics*, 21. Margaret M. Mitchell, "Rhetorical Handbooks in Service of Biblical Exegesis: Eustanthius of Antioch takes Origen Back to School," in *The New Testament and Early Christian Literature in Greco-Roman Context: Studies in Honor of David E. Aune* (ed. John Fotopoulos; *SNT 122*; Leiden: Brill, 2006), 350–367; 353.

Christian writers acquired this highly prized skill and mainstay of Graeco-Roman education.[22] In particular, the protreptic or exhortatory mode of discourse can be discerned within early Christian writings that use 1 Cor 2. This mode is often connected with the idea of persuading others to conversion and moral progression and, in the case of 1 Cor 2, progression from the wisdom of this world to the wisdom of God.[23] Early Christian use of the image of wisdom and the idea of progression from one level of wisdom to another will be taken up and examined in the third section of this chapter.

In a study of Paul's Corinthian correspondence and Christian hermeneutics, Mitchell articulates the view that excerpts from the Corinthian letters and their use by early Christian writers must be closely studied in conjunction with an understanding of rhetorical theories and modes of discourse. While she clarifies that, "no early Christian author of the first generations tries to systematize"[24] certain hermeneutical approaches to reading 1 Corinthians, different sides of early debates do systematize "according to particular constraints [...] and for particular goals."[25] Early Christian writers were "like [their] hermeneutical mentor, Paul, constructing a rhetorical argument,"[26] and 1 Cor 2 is one of the primary texts in which they anchor this rhetorical discourse. For early Christian writers, 1 Cor 2.6–16 provides the perfect close to a difficult conversation or theological discussion. To claim that, "we speak God's wisdom, secret and hidden" (1 Cor 2.7) which "no eye has seen nor ear heard" (1 Cor 2.9) is one simple way to avoid being drawn into a complex argument over a difficult theological concept. Moreover, it serves as a claim by which the writer can control the direction of a discussion, persuading those to whom they write that they in fact hold the right interpretation and understanding.

For Eusebius of Caesarea, who writes towards the end of our time period, the words of 1 Cor 2.6–7 not only enable early Christians to "disapprove of deceitful and sophistical possibilities"[27] by speaking God's wisdom, hidden and secret,

---

[22] Kathy Eden, *Hermeneutics and the Rhetorical Tradition: Chapters in Ancient Legacy and its Humanist Reception* (New Haven/London: Yale University Press, 1997), 41. See also Quintilian, *Orat*, 1.8.17 and Rankin, *Clement to Origen*, 6. Examples of ancient protreptic literature include Plato's *Euthydemus*, Aristotle's *Protrepticus*, and Seneca's *Epistle 90*.
[23] See Rankin, *Clement to Origen*, 7–8. See also David E. Aune, "Romans as a *Logos Protreptikos* in the Context of Ancient Religious and Philosophical Propaganda," in *Paulus und das antike Judentum* (eds. M. Hengel and U. Heckel; Tübingen: Mohr [Siebeck], 1991), 91–124; 91–95.
[24] Mitchell, *Christian Hermeneutics*, 45.
[25] Mitchell, *Christian Hermeneutics*, 48.
[26] Mitchell, *Christian Hermeneutics*, 48.
[27] Eusebius, *Praep.ev*, 1.3.5 (*GCS* 43.1).

but this passage also empowers early Christians to "be prepared to give an answer to every one who asks a reason concerning the hope that is in us."[28] While some early Christian writers use 1 Cor 2.6–16 to close down a conversation and distinguish between insiders and outsiders by claiming the secret and hidden wisdom of God, early Christians also use this passage to open up discourse with opponents in order to discredit their assumptions, even drawing on the same language as these opponents. Origen and Clement of Alexandria, for example, assert that one needs to know the language of those they oppose in order effectively to reshape, reapply, and refute it.[29] In particular, Clement makes clear in his discussions of Valentinian ideas that he knows their teaching and is thus keen to refute it, and one of his extant writings is an annotated collection of Valentinian texts, *Excerpts from Theodotus*.[30] On this basis, Kovacs concludes that, "while attempting to rebut Valentinian ideas, Clement takes many of them over by subtly reshaping them and reapplying their terminology."[31]

Early Christian writers draw not only from the language of their named opponents, but also on resources from within Graeco-Roman rhetoric, Hellenistic Judaism, and Middle Platonic arguments. They do this primarily to refute critics of Christianity and to claim its superiority through the establishment of an alternative set of beliefs, practices, and morals.[32] Early Christians, in this way, use excerpts from 1 Cor 2 rhetorically to defend and establish boundaries of the Christian faith, by rendering an account of the hidden wisdom of God they possess, explicating their understanding of this wisdom both to insiders and outsiders, and engaging in conversation with both.[33] While critics of early Christianity thought that the words of 1 Cor 1–2 confirmed their belief that Christians were vulgar and unlearned,[34] early Christians use the same text to counter these accusations and to claim the wisdom of God over that of the world with God as the one who reveals this divine wisdom to those mature in faith.

---

[28] Eusebius, *Praep.ev,* 1.3.6 (*GCS* 43.1).
[29] See Clement of Alexandria, *Strom*, 1.2.19 and Origen, *Hom.Lev*, 7.6.
[30] See Kovacs, "Echoes of Valentinian Exegesis," 317–322.
[31] Kovacs, "Echoes of Valentinian Exegesis," 328.
[32] Richard Norris, "The Apologists," in *The Cambridge History of Early Christian Literature* (eds. Frances M. Young, Lewis Ayers, and Andrew Louth; Cambridge: Cambridge University Press, 2004), 36–44; 36.
[33] See Edwards et al., "Introduction: Apologetics in the Roman World," 1; Grant, *Greek Apologists*, 9; Simon Price, "Latin Christian Apologetics: Minucius Felix, Tertullian, and Cyprian," in *Apologetics in the Roman Empire: Pagans, Jews, and Christians* (eds. Mark J. Edwards, Martin Goodman, and Simon Price; Oxford: Oxford University Press, 1999), 105–130; 116.
[34] Karl Olav Sandnes, *The Challenge of Homer: School, Pagan Poets, and Early Christianity* (LNTS 400; London/New York: T&T Clark, 2009), 105.

Irenaeus, bishop of Lyons in the 2<sup>nd</sup> century and the "most important controversialist and theologian between the apostles and the third-century Origen,"[35] is one of the first to use excerpts from this Corinthian passage in an apologetic discourse.[36] He relies on an excerpt from 1 Cor 2 in his apology *Against Heresies* to claim that many questions must be left unanswered and in the hands of God and thus, he tries to persuade his readers that the challenging questions of his opponents fall into this category. The explanations that his opponents seek from him cannot be given since he writes that,

> as for us, we still dwell upon the earth, and have not yet sat down upon his throne. For although the Spirit of the Saviour that is in him searches all things, even the deep things of God (1 Cor 2.10: *est scrutatur omnia, et altitudines Dei*), yet as to us there are varieties of gifts, differences of services, and varieties of activities (1 Cor 12.4–6); and we, while upon the earth, as Paul also declares, know in part, and prophesy in part (1 Cor 13.9). Since, therefore, we know but in part, we ought to leave all sorts of difficult questions in the hands of the one who, in some measure, bestows grace on us.[37]

For Irenaeus, the world is divided between those who know the deep things of God (1 Cor 2.10) and those who only know in part (1 Cor 13.9). Because full wisdom has an eschatological and other-worldly element beyond this earthly realm and is available only to those endowed with the Spirit of Christ, the answers to his opponents' questions are too lofty to grasp and are best left to those who "speak wisdom" and have "received the Spirit."[38] He continues in the same work,

> For this reason the Apostle declares, we speak wisdom among those who are perfect (1 Cor 2.6: *Sapientiam loquimur inter perfectos*), calling those persons perfect who have received the Spirit of God (*perceperunt Spiritum Dei*) and who through the Spirit [of God] speak in all languages. [. . .] Similarly we also hear of many in the church who the Apostle calls spiritual, who have prophetic charisms, and who through the Spirit speak all languages and bring to light for general benefit the hidden things of humankind and declare the mysteries of God (*et mysteria Dei*; 1 Cor 2.11,15).[39]

---

**35** Robert M. Grant, *Irenaeus of Lyons* (London: Routledge, 1997), 1.
**36** For a study of the influences of rhetorical forms on Irenaeus, see W.R. Schoedel, "Philosophy and Rhetoric in the *Adversus Haereses* of Irenaeus," *VC* 13 (1959), 22–32; 27–28; T.C.K. Ferguson, "The Rule of Truth and Irenaean Rhetoric in Book 1 of *Against Heresies*," *VC* 55 (2001), 356–375.
**37** Irenaeus, *Haer*, 2.28.7 (Translation adapted from *SC* 294 and *ACW* 64).
**38** Irenaeus, *Haer*, 5.6.1 (*SC* 153).
**39** Irenaeus, *Haer*, 5.6.1 (*SC* 153).

Irenaeus is clear that those whom the Apostle calls "spiritual" are those who have access to the wisdom of God and who possess the gifts that enable them to move from knowing only in part to bringing to light the mysteries of God. The content of this wisdom takes on an eschatological nature, using Paul's ambiguous language about wisdom as that which is hidden, secret, and mysterious, revealed only to those who are perfect and who have received the Spirit of God.[40] Irenaeus uses these excerpts from 1 Cor 2 rhetorically to close down conversation with those who do not possess the Spirit. He describes his opponents as those who are not spiritual, which, for him, explains why they "abuse the scriptures by seeking to support their own system out of them."[41] He articulates his own task, in the words of Paul, "to bring to light for general benefit the hidden things of humankind and declare the mysteries of God" to those who have "received the Spirit of God."[42]

It is worth noting that the language of 1 Cor 2 was "fertile ground" for Irenaeus' opponents, especially the Valentinians.[43] While very few references to excerpts from 1 Cor 2.6–16 are found in heterodox and Valentinian texts, Irenaeus "alludes to the teaching of the Valentinian gnostics" and their use of excepts from 1 Cor 2.[44] As Thistleton notes, "Irenaeus cites around sixteen passages to which the Valentinians appeal," and of these, excerpts from 1 Cor 2 are the "most plausible."[45] Thus, Irenaeus had to be very careful rhetorically since his opponents also appealed to the wisdom of 1 Cor 2.6 and argued that they were the true possessors of the hidden wisdom of God.[46] Irenaeus does not avoid the difficult questions and the views of his opponents completely; rather, he closes the conversation with his opponents as he makes clear that they cannot comprehend God's wisdom. From this point, he reframes their questions and shifts the focus so that he might engage more deeply with that which he believes to be the foundational teaching of the church: "one God, one Christ, and one providentially ordered history."[47]

---

[40] Brown, *The Cross*, 33.
[41] Irenaeus, *Haer*, 1.9.1 (Translation adapted from *SC* 263 and *ACW* 55). See Thistleton, *1 Corinthians*, 276.
[42] Irenaeus, *Haer*, 5.6.1 (*SC* 153).
[43] White, *Remembering Paul*, 37.
[44] Thistleton, *1 Corinthians*, 276.
[45] Thistleton, *1 Corinthians*, 276.
[46] Irenaeus, *Haer*, 3.2.1.
[47] Richard Norris, "Irenaeus' Use of Paul in His Polemic Against the Gnostics," in *Paul and the Legacies of Paul* (ed. William L. Babcock; Dallas, Tex: Southern Methodist University Press, 1990), 79–98; 89. See also 84.

Excerpts from 1 Cor 2.6–16 assist Clement of Alexandria, founder of the putative catechetical school in Alexandria[48] and contemporary of Tertullian, in ending a discussion that, in his own words, was "in the way of my writing."[49] In his *Stromata*, he compares the wisdom of God with that of the Epicureans and Stoics and concludes that while the latter might appear to be wise, in reality they are not.[50] He writes:

> Test everything, says the Apostle, and hold fast to that which is good (1 Thess 5.21). He is speaking to those who are spiritual (πνευματικοῖς), who use truth to examine whether what is said simply has the appearance of, or the reality of, truth (1 Cor 2.15). [...] He is writing to chastise those with the appearance of wisdom (δοκησισόφους) and self-understanding without the reality of wisdom (σοφούς).[51]

Clement argues that, "since our tradition is not held in common or open to all, least of all when you realise the magnificence of the word (τοῦ λόγου), then we keep secret the wisdom that is spoken in mystery (1 Cor 2.7: τὴν ἐν μυστηρίῳ λαλουμένην σοφίαν)."[52] However, Clement urges caution since,

> Even now I am careful, as [Scripture] says, about throwing pearls in front of pigs, in case they trample them underfoot and turn to attack you (Matt 7.6). For it is difficult to present arguments which are really pure and lucid and involve the true light to hearers who are like pigs in their lack of education. For there is nothing that appears more ludicrous to the one in the street than these addresses, or [that appears] more marvellous and divinely inspired to those of noble natures [...] for the natural one (ψυχικός) does not receive the gifts of the Spirit of God (τοῦ πνεύματος τοῦ θεοῦ), for they are foolishness to him (1 Cor 2.14).[53]

For Clement, the connection between the Spirit and wisdom that he finds in 1 Cor 2 is crucial as he weaves this passage together with words from Matt 7 to make clear that Paul's words separate the wise and the uneducated, the spiritual and the unspiritual.[54] By "common" faith, Clement holds the view that those who are spiritual and seek the mind of Christ, have access to wisdom that "eye has not seen and ear has not heard" through the Spirit who searches even the "deep

---

**48** See Eusebius, *Hist.eccl*, 5.10.1; 5.11.1; 6.6.1 for passages that connect Pantaenus and Clement to this "school."
**49** Clement of Alexandria, *Strom*, 1.55.3 (*SC* 30).
**50** Clement of Alexandria, *Strom*, 1.50.1–1.53.2.
**51** Clement of Alexandria, *Strom*, 1.53.3–1.54.3 (Translation adapted from *SC* 30 and *FC* 85).
**52** Clement of Alexandria, *Strom*, 1.55.1–2 (Translation adapted from *SC* 30 and *FC* 85).
**53** Clement of Alexandria, *Strom*, 1.55.3–5 (Translation adapted from *SC* 30 and *FC* 85).
**54** For Thistleton, this is not dissimilar to the Platonic understanding that the pure and impure shall not touch. See Thistleton, *1 Corinthians*, 277.

things of God" (1 Cor 2.9–10: τὰ βάθη τοῦ θεοῦ).⁵⁵ Even though his opponents, especially the Valentinians against whom he writes, may have alleged that their tradition offers direct access to Paul's teaching on wisdom, Clement is clear that this claim is false because the content of the wisdom he proclaims is revealed only by God. He distinguishes between the divine wisdom of those who have the Spirit of God and human wisdom with its human origins and values.⁵⁶ In this way, Clement uses 1 Cor 2 effectively to explain that he does not have any obligation to address the heretical concerns of those who he determines are without faith and who lack education. For Clement, because they are without education, they are unable to grasp the most basic and lucid argument and without faith, they do not have "the mind of Christ" (1 Cor 2.16: ὅ ἐστι νοῦς Χριστοῦ).⁵⁷ Once again, this rhetorical move using 1 Cor 2 to disengage with opponents leads to an understanding of the wisdom of God as that which is revealed only to insiders and bestowed by the Spirit. Nevertheless, for Clement, as will be discussed later in this chapter, it is almost impossible to know God directly and to attain complete wisdom. This esoteric and apophatic understanding that comes through most strongly in Book 5 of his *Stromata* is strongly influenced by his opponents who he is clear have "the appearance of wisdom" but lack "the reality" of wisdom, understanding, and knowledge.⁵⁸

Excerpts from 1 Cor 2 may also be found within the apologetic writings of Tertullian, who wrote in the late 2ⁿᵈ century and is known as a master of rhetorical style and the apologetic genre.⁵⁹ Throughout his works, references to the Pauline writings "play a part in the orchestration of an argument intended to be immediately persuasive."⁶⁰ Facing the threat of heretical teaching, and with a particular focus on Marcion, Tertullian uses excerpts from 1 Corinthians as part of his attempt to defend the faith and tradition of the church. According to Tertullian's treatise *Against Marcion*, Marcion accuses the Christian faith of

---

[55] Clement of Alexandria, *Strom*, 5.25.5 (*SC* 278).
[56] Thistleton, *1 Corinthians*, 277. For Clement's knowledge of Greek philosophical schools and use of rhetoric, see Piotr Ashwin-Siejkowski, *Clement of Alexandria: A Project of Christian Perfection* (London/New York: T&T Clark, 2008), especially the third chapter. For a contrasting perspective, see Salvatore Lilla, *Clement of Alexandria: A Study in Christian Platonism and Gnosticism* (Oxford: Oxford University Press, 1971).
[57] Clement of Alexandria, *Strom*, 5.25.5 (*SC* 278).
[58] Clement of Alexandria, *Strom*, 1.54.3.
[59] Oliver O'Donovan and Joan Lockwood O'Donovan, eds., *From Irenaeus to Grotius: A Sourcebook in Christian Political Thought* (Grand Rapids, Mich/Cambridge: Eerdmans, 1999), 23–24.
[60] Robert D. Sider, "Literary Artifice and the Figure of Paul in the Writings of Tertullian," in *Paul and the Legacies of Paul* (ed. William S. Babcock; Dallas, Tex: Southern Methodist University Press, 1990), 99–120; 100.

being filled with enigmas and uses excerpts from 1 Cor 2 to argue for the existence of two gods: a god of this age and a hidden and concealed God.[61] Tertullian disagrees with Marcion's interpretation of 1 Cor 2 and, attempting to reclaim the Pauline text for his purposes against Marcion, argues that the wisdom of God about which Paul writes enables one to understand that God is undivided. He is clear that Paul refers only to one God when he writes,

> We speak the wisdom of God among those who are perfect (1 Cor 2.6: *cuius dei sapientiam loquatur inter perfectos*). It is that God who has confused the wisdom of the wise (*sapientiam sapientium*), who has brought to nought the understanding of the prudent (*prudentiam prudentium*), who has reduced to folly the wisdom of the world (*sapientia mundi*), by choosing its foolish things, and disposing them to the attainment of salvation (1 Cor 1.19–20, 2.6). This wisdom (*sapientiam*), he says, once lay hidden in things that were foolish, weak, and lacking in honour; once also was latent under figures, allegories, and enigmatical types; but it was afterwards to be revealed in Christ, who was set as a light to the Gentiles, by the Creator who promised through the mouth of Isaiah that he would discover the hidden treasures, which eye had not seen (Isa 64.4) [...] but they lay overshadowed with latent meanings, in which the wisdom of God (*sapientia Dei*) was hidden to be brought to light by and among the perfect, when the time should come, but which God ordained before the ages (1 Cor 2.6–7).[62]

For Tertullian, no one can claim fully to know or to describe God's nature, because "no one knows what is in God except the Spirit of God."[63] Tertullian does not explain, therefore, the divine way of wisdom but rather includes himself in the category of those who cannot fully grasp it. Nevertheless, in order to counter Marcion's belief in two ages and two gods based on the words of 1 Cor 2, Tertullian uses the description of wisdom in the same passage to establish a dichotomy not between two gods, but between the wisdom of this world and the wisdom of God. Tertullian maintains that the wisdom of God described in 1 Cor 2, preordained by God before the ages and brought to light amongst those who are perfect, is not the wisdom Marcion claims. Thus, he places himself on the side of God's wisdom over and against Marcion. In a rhetorical manoeuvre similar to other early Christian writers, Tertullian claims that Marcion is wrong without explaining what the wisdom of God is, apart from his clarity that it is not possessed by Marcion. In this way, excerpts from the same passage used by Marcion help Tertullian argue that a divine way of wisdom does exist and that this wisdom allows him, over Marcion, to claim the correct interpreta-

---

61 Tertullian, *Marc*, 5.6.1–2.
62 Tertullian, *Marc*, 5.6.1–6,7 (*CCL* 1; *SC* 483).
63 Tertullian, *Marc*, 1.2 (*CCL* 1; *SC* 365). See Thistleton, *1 Corinthians*, 278.

tion of Paul's writings. Focusing on Paul's words, "we speak the wisdom of God among them that are perfect" (1 Cor 2.6), Tertullian is clear that not everyone is perfect and therefore not everyone, especially Marcion, can understand the wisdom of God.[64] 1 Cor 2.6–16 is used by Tertullian to place Marcion in the category of those who are not perfect and effectively to show that his claims are not only inconsistent, but also impossible.

Origen, a prolific 3rd century theologian, uses 1 Cor 2.6–16 more than any other early Christian in his extensive writings. He uses excerpts from this passage to defend the Christian faith and respond to those who, in his view, pervert it. When Celsus claims that Jesus suffered and could not prevent his own suffering, even if he had desired to do so, Origen points out that Celsus' Jew has misread Matt 26.39 and without any explanation immediately writes that,

> at the present we postpone the discussion of these problems which require a long explanation, which would appropriately be given with the help of the wisdom of God (σοφίας θεοῦ) to those whom Paul called perfect (τελείοις), when he said, but we speak wisdom among those who are perfect (1 Cor 2.6: Σοφίαν δὲ λαλοῦμεν ἐν τοῖς τελείοις). We only make brief mention of the points which are helpful for our present purpose.[65]

Because Origen does not count Celsus amongst those who are perfect, he is able without any further explanation to discount Celsus' argument, creating a dichotomy between Celsus and himself based on the wisdom they possess. God's wisdom for Origen begins with the proclamation of Christ crucified, as the final section of this chapter will show, and this wisdom is necessary in order to understand correctly Christ's suffering and Matt 26. Because Origen is clear that Celsus does not possess this wisdom of God that Origen claims, he is also clear that Celsus's questions are not worth engaging. This move allows Origen to maintain his focus on the discussion at hand—Jesus' passion—without being distracted by his opponent's assumptions and accusations. He appeals to 1 Cor 2 in order to refute both a contrary exegesis of the text itself and the teaching and questioning of Celsus. In the process, he attempts to persuade his readers that the arguments of Celsus, because they are not based in God's wisdom, are outside the realm of that which is worth pursuing.

Origen maintains this dichotomy between two levels of wisdom when he concludes in the same work that one must ask his opponents who agree with Celsus,

---

[64] Tertullian, *Marc*, 5.6.1–2.
[65] Origen, *Cels*, 2.24 (Translation adapted from *SC* 132 and Chadwick).

Did Paul have no idea of any superior wisdom (σοφίαν) when he professed to speak wisdom among the perfect (1 Cor 2.6: ὁ Παῦλος ἐπηγγέλλετο σοφίαν λαλεῖν ἐν τοῖς τελείοις)? [Celsus] would say, in his reckless way, that though Paul professed this claim he knew nothing of wisdom (σοφόν); we would reply to him saying: first understand clearly the epistles (τὰς ἐπιστολάς) of the one who says this, and look carefully into the meaning of each word in them [...] then show both that you have understood Paul's words (τοὺς Παύλου λόγους) and that you can show some to be simple-minded or foolish (εὐήθεις τινὰς ἢ ἠλιθίους).[66]

For Origen, Paul's words about wisdom should themselves serve as proof of the wisdom and glory of God and be a stepping-stone for understanding the basics of the Christian faith. Using the language of 1 Cor 2.6–16, Origen differentiates between those who, like Paul, speak wisdom among the perfect and those who do not speak this wisdom and without understanding are simple-minded and foolish. Origen not only uses a portion of 1 Cor 2 to disengage with his opponent, but he also sets up a hermeneutic for biblical interpretation. He continues in this section of his apology that those devoted "to attentive reading" will admire Paul "who uses an ordinary vocabulary to contemplate great truths."[67] However, those who do not devote themselves to such reading cannot possess this wisdom of which Paul speaks and therefore they, in Origen's words, "appear ludicrous."[68] In this way, Scripture itself takes on a role in the revelation of the wisdom of God through the Spirit and with this, Origen describes, albeit fleetingly, a hermeneutic of biblical interpretation emerging from Scripture itself.[69]

Early Christians, therefore, use the words of 1 Cor 2 in order to extract themselves both from difficult questions and from complex and, in their view, unnecessary discussions with opponents. They use the dichotomy found in this passage between the wisdom of this world and the wisdom of God to support their claims that the wisdom of God is only available to those who are "perfect" and is only revealed by the Spirit. Setting themselves against their opponents, early Christian writers claim that they are the ones who have access to this divine wisdom revealed by God and effectively end any conversation with opponents in order to move on with their argument. Their focus is not only on wisdom but on the dichotomies between the perfect and the foolish, the spiritual and the unspiritual, that Paul describes. These divisions, like the different levels of wisdom, further support early Christians in their arguments as they claim the side of the perfect and the spiritual and close off any opportunity for debate or discussion.

---

66 Origen, *Cels*, 3.20 (Translation adapted from *SC* 136 and Chadwick).
67 Origen, *Cels*, 3.20 (Translation adapted from *SC* 136 and Chadwick).
68 Origen, *Cels*, 3.20 (Translation adapted from *SC* 136 and Chadwick).
69 See Thistleton, *1 Corinthians*, 279, and Mitchell, *Christian Hermeneutics*, 1–17.

## 2.3 Exegesis of difficult texts[70]

1 Corinthians 2 is used not only to engage difficult opponents, but also to interpret difficult scriptural texts. This pericope is a lens through which many early Christian writers exegete Scripture, especially in their homilies and commentaries. In particular, excerpts from 1 Cor 2.6–16 are used by early Christians to explain difficult texts about the creation of the world, the incarnation and resurrection of Christ, the glory of God, and the consummation of all things in the fullness of time.

Clement of Alexandria uses 1 Cor 2 alongside passages from Colossians and Matthew to grapple with the parable of the leavened bread in Matt 13.33. He relates the hidden elements of this parable to Christ who is hidden in mystery, concealed from those who are not perfect (1 Cor 2.6–8). As he writes in his *Stromata*:

> And was it not this which the prophet meant when he ordered unleavened cakes to be made, suggesting that the truly sacred mysterious word, with respect to the unbegotten and his powers, should be hidden? In confirmation of these things, in the epistle to the Corinthians the Apostle plainly says, but we speak wisdom among those who are perfect, but not the wisdom of this world or of the rulers of this world, that come to nought, but we speak the wisdom of God hidden in mystery (1 Cor 2.6–7: σοφίαν δὲ λαλοῦμεν ἐν τοῖς τελείοις, σοφίαν δὲ οὐ τοῦ αἰῶνος τούτου οὐδὲ τῶν ἀρχόντων τοῦ αἰῶνος τούτου τῶν καταργουμένων· ἀλλὰ λαλοῦμεν θεοῦ σοφίαν ἐν μυστηρίῳ, τὴν ἀποκεκρυμμένην). And again elsewhere he speaks of the recognition of the mystery of God in Christ, in whom all the treasures of wisdom and knowledge are hid (Col 2.2–3) [...] and now, by the parable of the leaven, the Lord makes visible the concealment for he says, the kingdom of heaven is like leaven, which a woman took and hid in three measures of meal, till the whole was leavened (Matt 13.33).[71]

Using 1 Cor 2 to exegete this passage from Matthew, Clement writes that it "plainly" tells the reader that "the wisdom of God hidden in mystery" must remain concealed until the fullness of time. The eschatological edge of the text prevents anyone from having full wisdom. Clement does not exegete this passage any further, since only by the "power of the word" given to those who are perfect can one know the wisdom of God. Here the wider context of Book 5 of Clement's *Stro-*

---

[70] See also Clement of Rome, *1Clem*, 34, 35; *2Clem*, 11; *Ep.virg*, 1.9.4; Irenaeus of Lyons, *Haer*, 5.6.1; Clement of Alexandria, *Paed*, 1.37.1; *Quis.div*, 23.3; *Prot*, 10.94.4; Hippolytus, *Consumm*, 44.1; *Haer*, 6.29, 7.14, 5.22, 6.19, 5.21, 5.19, 5.3; Tertullian, *Res*, 26.1; Origen, *Comm.Jo*, 10.288; *Comm.Matt*, 14.6; *Fr.Luc*, fr.140; *Comm.Cant*, 1.5; *A.Petr*, 39; *Evan.Thom*, 17; *A.Thom*, 1.36; *Orat.Paul*, 9; *M.Polyc*, 2.3; *M.Fruct*, 3.3; Justin the Gnostic, *Bar*, 124; Eusebius of Caesarea, *Mart.Pal*, 48.
[71] Clement of Alexandria, *Strom*, 5.80.4–81.1 (GCS 52; SC 279).

*mata* is important and especially the two major, interrelated themes of esoterism and apophatic theology. Throughout Book 5, and as seen in the excerpt just quoted, the wisdom of God, acquired through Scripture, is deliberately hidden and only realised by those who have the "power of the word" and the help of the Spirit to uncover it. Moreover, Clement also hints at the impossibility of knowing God directly, at least until the fullness of time. In this way, his opponents who claim both the wisdom of God through the same Scripture and a knowledge of God directly are challenged and, in his view, routed.[72]

Clement is clear therefore, that, based on the words of 1 Cor 2, Christ is revealed as the one in whom all wisdom and knowledge are hidden and this wisdom is what "draws to itself secretly and invisibly everyone who receives it" and "brings [the] whole system into unity."[73] Furthermore, Clement suggests that his opponents use portions of 1 Cor 2 not only to make false claims to knowledge, but also to argue that his own teaching and exegesis, which does not claim full knowledge and wisdom, "involved an inferior way of salvation."[74] While he takes Valentinian exegesis seriously, he also firmly holds that it is misguided.[75] Here he offers a glimpse at the importance of spiritual exegesis, incorporating elements from Greek philosophy to ponder Scripture in ways that go beyond a simple reading. Only by studying Scripture with the help of the Spirit and the recognition of God in Christ, can one receive the wisdom and knowledge hidden in Christ and be saved. Against the claim of his opponents that they possess a higher wisdom, Clement claims an even higher wisdom, hidden by God and described in 1 Cor 2.6.

Origen also uses 1 Cor 2.6–16 to exegete scriptural passages on God's hidden wisdom and glory. In his *Commentary on Romans,* Origen relies on excerpts from 1 Cor 2 to discuss Romans 8.18–25 and to describe a future glory which is "far greater and loftier than the firmament which can be seen with eyes."[76] In an attempt to understand Paul's writing on suffering and pain in Romans 8, Origen continues that even if Paul "sustains every manner of punishment that can be inflicted either within human nature or without" and even if,

---

**72** With gratitude to Judith Kovacs for her suggestions on this section and especially the importance of the wider context of Book 5 in Clement's *Stromata*.
**73** Clement of Alexandria, *Strom,* 5.80.7 (*SC* 279).
**74** Kovacs, "Echoes of Valentinian Exegesis," 322.
**75** While Clement is clearly arguing against a heterodox and, most likely, Valentinian opponent, very few references to 1 Cor 2.6–16 are found in heterodox texts with only three possible references in Clement's *Excerpts from Theodotus* and fewer than 20 references in anonymous texts and fragments.
**76** Origen, *Comm.Rom,* 7.5.11 (*SC* 543).

in this extremely short span of life, someone endures things worse than these, and suffers affliction in everything (2 Cor 4.8), and is tormented in mind and body; and should he compare these things both to the future glory that will be revealed to the saints, and to the things that eye has not seen nor ear heard nor has entered the human heart (1 Cor 2.9: *quae oculus non vidit nec auris audiuit nec in cor hominis ascendit*), then one can understand why Paul has said with great sagacity, for I consider that the sufferings of this time are not worth comparing with the coming glory that will be revealed to us (Rom 8.18). For there is indeed nothing that can be found worth comparing to the future glory.[77]

Confronted by Paul's writing on suffering in this section of Romans, the words of 1 Cor 2.6–16 allow Origen to rest in the reality that all has not yet been revealed by God and that when Paul writes about "the suffering of this time," this suffering is incomparable with the glory of God revealed in the fullness of time. For Origen, this bigger eschatological picture of God's wisdom and glory is crucial. Gorday cautions that Origen's exegesis of Paul cannot be understood apart from the "larger picture of Origen's anti-Gnostic polemic" and his aim "to defend the whole salvation-historical picture of God, in which scripture [...] is full of obscurities intended to point the pious reader to a true perception of divine mysteries."[78] Therefore, when Paul talks about "the suffering of this time," Origen can take comfort in the eschatological reality that this suffering, while real, is not the final word.[79] Origen, however, cannot describe what the future glory entails and thus it is embodied by the hidden nature of God and God's wisdom that he finds in the words of 1 Cor 2. For Origen, the simple reading of a biblical passage was usually not sufficient for adequate understanding and interpretation. Thus, in order to come to terms with Paul's suffering, he uses the words of 1 Cor 2 about the wisdom of God hidden in mystery in order to lead his readers to a correct reading of Romans 8. For Origen, understanding Romans 8 is not simply about right interpretation but it is also about future hope and salvation.[80] Therefore, in his exegesis of Romans, Origen uses 1 Cor 2.6–16 both to focus on the glory of God and the difficult language of suffering and pain employed by Paul, and to "interpret spiritual things with spiritual things" (1 Cor 2.14) and lead his readers one step closer to salvation.

Origen's exegetical approach using excerpts from 1 Cor 2 is again encountered in his *Commentary on John*, where he uses the dichotomy between the wis-

---

77 Origen, *Comm.Rom*, 7.4.2–7.4.6 (Translation adapted from *SC* 543 and *FC* 104).
78 Gorday, "Paulus Origenianus," 145.
79 Origen, *Comm.Rom*, 7.4.2–7.4.6.
80 Gorday, "Paulus Origenianus," 153. See also Karen Jo Torjesen, *Hermeneutical Procedure and Theological Structure in Origen's Exegesis* (PTS 28; Berlin/New York: De Gruyter, 1985), 7–106. For a discussion of getting Paul "right," see White, *Remembering Paul*, 164–165.

dom of this world and of God to explicate the Johannine text of the Samaritan woman at the well (John 4.13–14). Origen transforms 1 Cor 2 "into a definitive appeal to the authorial intent of the words of Jesus in the Gospel [...] while also casting Paul as their definitive interpreter."[81] He begins by making clear that not everyone can understand the hidden wisdom of God when he writes,

> Now all are not permitted to examine the things that are beyond that which is written (1 Cor 4.6: τὰ ὑπὲρ ἃ γέγραπται). Unless you have become like them, you may be reproved and hear the word, seek out the things that are too high for you, and search not into things beyond your ability (Sir 3.21). But if we say that some know that which is beyond what is written, we do not mean that these things can be known to all. [...] And the things that eye has not seen (καὶ ἃ ὀφθαλμὸς οὐκ εἶδεν) are beyond the things that are written, and the things that ear has not heard (καὶ ἃ οὖς οὐκ ἤκουσεν) cannot be written (1 Cor 2.9). The things, too, that have not entered the human heart (καρδίαν δὲ ἀνθρώπου) are greater than the well of Jacob (1 Cor 2.9). These things are made manifest from the well of water springing up into eternal life for those who no longer have a human heart, but who are able to say, we have the mind of Christ (1 Cor 2.16: Ἡμεῖς δὲ νοῦν Χριστοῦ ἔχομεν) that we may know the things that have been given to us by God (1 Cor 2.12: εἰδῶμεν τὰ ὑπὸ τοῦ θεοῦ χαρισθέντα ἡμῖν), which also we speak, not in the teachings of human wisdom (διδακτοῖς ἀνθρωπίνης σοφίας), but in teachings of the Spirit (1 Cor 2.13: διδακτοῖς πνεύματος).[82]

Origen's use of 1 Cor 2 to set up his hermeneutic for reading Scripture, as briefly described at the end of the previous section, is especially clear in this excerpt. Before he engages the text directly, he tells his reader what he is about to do using both the words of 1 Cor 4.6 and 1 Cor 2.6–16. For Mitchell, Origen is picking up on a biblical hermeneutic given directly by Paul himself: not to go beyond that which is written (1 Cor 4.6).[83] In this way, Origen's exegesis of John 4 serves "as a hermeneutical guide to reading a pastiche of verses from 1 Corinthians 2"[84] so that the mind of Christ (1 Cor 2.16) must be present for the hermeneutist to know the things given by God (1 Cor 2.12) not through human wisdom but the Spirit. The content of wisdom is only revealed by God in Christ through the Spirit and depends on the one receiving the wisdom and a movement in him or her from human wisdom to divine.

When Origen reads John 4, therefore, he immediately sees within the text the dichotomy between two waters: the water of the well of Jacob and the water Jesus gives springing up to eternal life. Based on his exposition of 1 Cor 2 and not going beyond what is written, Origen focuses on the different kinds of

---

81 Mitchell, *Christian Hermeneutics*, 52–53.
82 Origen, *Comm.Jn*, 13.32–37 (Translation adapted from *SC* 222 and *FC* 89).
83 Mitchell, *Christian Hermeneutics*, 35.
84 Mitchell, *Christian Hermeneutics*, 52. See also Origen, *Princ*, 4.2.3.

water and applies the levels of wisdom from 1 Corinthians directly to his interpretation of the Johannine gospel. Thus, he continues,

> The scriptures are introductions, therefore, called the well of Jacob. Once they have now been accurately understood, one must go up from them to Jesus, that he may freely give us the well of water springing into eternal life. [...] For some who are wise in the scriptures (τὰς γραφὰς σοφοί) drink as Jacob and his sons. But others who are simpler and innocent (ἁπλούστεροι καὶ ἀκεραιότεροι), the ones called sheep of Christ, drink as the livestock of Jacob, and others, misunderstanding the scriptures and maintaining certain irreverent things in their understanding of them, drink as the Samaritan woman drank before she believed in Jesus.[85]

For Origen, using the exegetical hermeneutics found in 1 Cor 2 and applying them to this excerpt from John 4 creates, according to Mitchell, the "quintessential expression of the limits of the literal."[86] While Origen advocates clearly that interpretation should not go beyond that which is written, at the same time he offers the caveat that this is only the case for those who do not have the mind of Christ and who do not know the hidden wisdom of God. In this way, "the more majestic and divine parts of the mysteries of God"[87] are only discerned beyond what is written by those who "are wise in the scriptures" and therefore "drink as Jacob and his sons."[88] Origen describes Scripture as an introduction, the basic well of Jacob for his livestock and the first step in acquiring divine wisdom. This is placed in contrast to the water of Jesus attained only by those who are wise with the hidden wisdom of God. Deeper wisdom is possible and can be known by those who have the mind of Christ, but how to attain this wisdom and detailed descriptions of it remain hidden, beyond the basic "introductions."

Once again, the divisions between the wisdom of this world and the wisdom of God become the point of focus for early Christian writers in their use of this Corinthian pericope and their claim that a deeper level of theological understanding exists. Using these contrasting ways of knowing to engage not only with difficult opponents but also with difficult scriptural texts, early Christians place the revelation of this greater level of secret and hidden wisdom as one of the ultimate goals of Christian life and faith. Therefore, how early Christians understood this wisdom, how they might acquire it, and the progression from one level of wisdom to another, are the focus of the final section of this chapter.

---

85 Origen, *Comm.Jn*, 13.37–39 (Translation adapted from *SC* 222 and *FC* 89).
86 Mitchell, *Christian Hermeneutics*, 36.
87 Mitchell, *Christian Hermeneutics*, 35.
88 Origen, *Comm.Jn*, 13.38–39 (*SC* 222). Mitchell argues, as she reads this passage from Origen, that the water of Jesus "is extra-textual" (Mitchell, *Christian Hermeneutics*, 36).

## 2.4 Wisdom and formation

While excerpts from 1 Cor 2.6–16 are used rhetorically to counter difficult challenges to the Christian faith and exegetically to illuminate difficult passages of Scripture, the persistent use of this passage by early Christian writers to differentiate between the wisdom of this world and the wisdom of God is the focus of this final section. The different wisdoms that early Christian writers identify in 1 Cor 2.6–16—the wisdom of this world, the wisdom of the rulers of this world, and the wisdom of God—provide a foundation for their theological understandings of wisdom and formation. Led by the use of 1 Cor 2 in early Christian writings, the focus of this section is less on the content of wisdom, and more on how this wisdom is acquired and how Scripture may be interpreted and taught in order to move a Christian from one level of wisdom to another.[89]

1 Cor 2 is a central passage with which Clement of Alexandria discusses wisdom and formation. He uses language from this pericope to advocate two different ways of teaching, depending upon whether those being taught are mature in wisdom or new to faith. He reacts to his opponents reading of 1 Cor 2 which claims a clear distinction between ordinary Christians and spiritual elect, especially as they place themselves in the latter category over and against him. Clement offers a different exegesis of this text, arguing that his opponents do not have the higher wisdom they claim and advocating two different kinds of Christian wisdom and formation.[90] In a discussion about enigmatic passages and parables found in Scripture, Clement writes that "the noble Apostle" says,

> But we preach, as it is written, saying what eye has not seen and ear has not heard and has not entered into the human heart, what God has prepared for those who love him (1 Cor 2.9: ἃ ὀφθαλμὸς οὐκ εἶδεν καὶ οὖς οὐκ ἤκουσεν καὶ ἐπὶ καρδίαν ἀνθρώπου οὐκ ἀνέβη, ἃ ἡτοίμασεν ὁ θεὸς τοῖς ἀγαπῶσιν αὐτόν). For God has revealed it to us by the Spirit. For the Spirit searches all things, even the deep things of God (1 Cor 2.10: ἡμῖν γὰρ ἀπεκάλυψεν ὁ θεὸς διὰ τοῦ πνεύματος· τὸ γὰρ πνεῦμα πάντα ἐρευνᾷ, καὶ τὰ βάθη τοῦ θεοῦ). For he knows the spiritual one (πνευματικόν) and the gnostic one (γνωστικόν) as the disciple of the Holy Spirit dispensed by God, which is the mind of Christ (νοῦς Χριστοῦ). But the natural person (ψυχικός)

---

[89] For Stroumsa, this is a novel conclusion since he argues that for Greek philosophical schools such as that of the Stoics, "the idea of conversion to wisdom plays a role" but "not the process of conversion itself" (Guy G. Stroumsa, "*Caro salutis cardo:* Shaping the Person in Early Christian Thought," *HR* 30, no. 1 (1990), 25–50; 28). See also Gerhard B. Ladner, *The Idea of Reform: Its Impact on Christian Thought and Action in the Age of the Fathers* (Cambridge, Mass: Harvard University Press, 1959).
[90] See Kovacs, "Echoes of Valentinian Exegesis," 321–323.

does not receive the things of the Spirit, for they are foolishness to him (1 Cor 2.14: μωρία γὰρ αὐτῷ ἐστιν).⁹¹

As discussed in the last section on exegesis, for Clement, some things, the wisdom of God included, must remain hidden until revealed by the Spirit which alone enables a person to move from foolishness to knowledge, from fear to faith.⁹² Those who have the Spirit have what Clement understands Paul to describe as the mind of Christ and are thus imbued with the wisdom of God revealed by the Spirit. Those, however, who did not know the Spirit, do not possess this revealed wisdom and are thus no more than fools. The Spirit enables the movement to a higher level of wisdom. Kovacs writes that using the dichotomies in 1 Cor 2, Clement offers a "divine pedagogy" that "leads the individual Christian through two distinct stages, as the simple believer moves to a more complete apprehension and application of the truth."⁹³

Clement not only distinguishes between levels of wisdom, but also emphasises how important it is for Christians to grow in wisdom and to move from "simple faith" to an understanding of "what eye has not seen and ear has not heard" (1 Cor 2.9) by means "of Scripture [which] inspires fuller intelligence."⁹⁴ Edwards clarifies that,

> by knowledge or *gnōsis*, Clement did not mean the pursuit of a liberal education in contempt of Biblical teaching and the inheritance of faith; rather he meant the study of Christian doctrine and the scriptures with all the tools that could be supplied by Gentile learning, in order that the doctrines might be better understood and the commandments more perceptively obeyed.⁹⁵

As Clement reflects in *On the Pedagogue*, the role of the teacher—whose model is Christ, the divine pedagogue—is to speak of that which is good, which is "what ear has not heard nor has entered into the heart" (1 Cor 2.9).⁹⁶ Nevertheless, as the giver of all good, God is the one to whom students are directed as the pedagogue, Christ, reveals "the scriptures themselves in a compendious form, setting forth bare commands, fitting them to the time of guidance, and turning

---

91 Clement of Alexandria, *Strom*, 5.25.1–26.1 (SC 278).
92 Judith Kovacs, "Clement of Alexandria," in *Early Christian Thinkers: The Lives and Legacies of Twelve Key Figures* (ed. Paul Foster; Downers Grove, Ill: Intervarsity Press, 2010), 68–84; 79.
93 Kovacs, "Clement of Alexandria," 79–80.
94 Clement of Alexandria, *Strom*, 5.40.1–2 (SC 463).
95 Mark J. Edwards, *Origen against Plato* (Aldershot: Ashgate, 2002), 19.
96 Clement of Alexandria, *Paed*, 3.86.2 (SC 158).

over the interpretation of them to the teacher (τῷ διδασκάλῳ)."⁹⁷ Through revelation by God and assisted by Christ himself, one may ponder the scriptures in ways that go beyond a simple reading and progress toward greater wisdom. Clement once again is clear that higher and hidden wisdom consists in spiritual exegesis of Scripture.⁹⁸ The responsibility of the teacher, therefore, is to lead one to deeper knowledge and wisdom by means of faith and through Scripture.

To describe how this movement toward knowledge and wisdom works practically, Clement uses the image of a ship sailing into the heavenly harbour. He writes in his *Exhortation* that a student must not be enticed and led astray by the wisdom of this world, which he compares to the Sirens, but rather must,

> sail (παράπλει) past the song [...] the *logos* of God (ὁ λόγος ὁ τοῦ θεοῦ) will be your pilot, and the Holy Spirit will bring you to the heavenly harbour, then you will behold (κατοπτεύσεις) my God and will be initiated into these holy mysteries, and you will enjoy the hidden secrets of heaven, the things carefully guarded to me, which ear has not heard (ἃ οὔτε οὖς ἤκουσεν), which are prepared for the heart (ἐπὶ καρδίαν ἀνέβη) whose home is in God (1 Cor 2.9).⁹⁹

Drawing on the language of wisdom within 1 Cor 2, this image of sailing and progression to God is, for Clement, the image of how one grows in wisdom and faith and ultimately how one is introduced to the holy mysteries which "no eye has seen nor ear has heard, nor has entered into the human heart" (1 Cor 2.9). Clement relies on 1 Cor 2 to emphasise the eschatological nature of the wisdom of God, with the understanding that some Christian teachings ought to be kept secret and will be revealed only to those who have been adequately prepared to grasp such wisdom.¹⁰⁰ While education, and even education in Greek philoso-

---

**97** Clement of Alexandria, *Paed,* 3.86.2–87.2 (Translation adapted from *SC* 158 and *FC* 23).
**98** See earlier comments on *Strom* 5.
**99** Clement of Alexandria, *Prot,* 118.4 (*SC* 2); note that in this particular excerpt from *Exhortation,* the subject is particularly difficult to identify. Cyril of Jerusalem, who writes after the time period of this project, offers a similar nautical image when he writes that "each teacher interprets the scriptures according to ability in order to provide the safest course according to the blessed apostle Paul who says, about these things we also speak, not in words taught by human wisdom, but taught by the Holy Spirit, comparing spiritual things with spiritual (1 Cor 2.13). Thus we act like travellers or voyagers, who having one goal for a very long journey, though hastening on with eagerness, yet by reason of human weakness are wont to touch in their way at diverse cities or harbours" (Cyril of Jerusalem, *Catech,* 17.1 [Translation adapted from Reischl and *NPNF* 7]).
**100** Denise Kimber Buell, *Making Christians: Clement of Alexandria and the Rhetoric of Legitimacy* (Princeton, NJ: Princeton University Press, 1999), 74. See also John Behr, *Asceticism and An-*

phy, enables this movement in wisdom, it is knowledge of Scripture, whose understanding is revealed by the Spirit and wise teachers, that guides one to the secret and hidden wisdom of God. Ultimately, formation for Clement "is not a matter of intellect alone; it also addresses the heart and soul of the student and seeks to form his character."[101] The revelation of wisdom by God through the Spirit, therefore, is for those who live in love and not fear and who, guided by the Spirit and words of Scripture, progress to greater levels of wisdom and the holy mysteries of God.

Origen considers 1 Cor 2.6–16 to be particularly significant in his defence and exposition of a spiritual interpretation of Scripture. While Origen adopts a different approach from Clement, his conclusions are similarly based on the distinctions he finds between levels of wisdom described by Paul in this Corinthian passage. He argues for a three-fold wisdom based on his understanding that Paul clearly distinguished between three different kinds of wisdom.[102] Origen writes,

> The holy Apostle, wishing to teach us some great and hidden truth with respect to science and wisdom, says, in the first epistle to the Corinthians, we speak wisdom among them that are perfect; yet not the wisdom of this world, nor of the princes of the world, that come to nought, but we speak the wisdom of God hidden in a mystery, which God ordained before the world for our glory, which none of the princes of the world knew, for had they known it, they would not have crucified the Lord of glory (1 Cor 2.6–8: *Sapientiam autem loquimur inter perfectos; sapientiam vero non huius mundi neque principum huius mundi, qui destruuntur, sed loquimur Dei sapientiam in mysterio absconditam, quam praedestinavit Deus ante saecula in gloriam nostram, quam nemo principum huius mundi cognovit. Si enim cognovissent, numquam Dominum maiestatis crucifixissent*). In this passage, wishing to describe the different kinds of wisdom (*sapientiarum*), he writes that there is a wisdom of this world (*sapientiam huius mundi*), and a wisdom of the princes of this world (*sapientiam principum huius mundi*), and another wisdom of God (*Dei sapientiam*).[103]

In his commentaries and homilies, Origen proceeds from this distinction between types of wisdom that he finds in 1 Cor 2 to differentiate both between members

---

*thropology in Irenaeus and Clement* (OECS; Oxford/New York: Oxford University Press, 2000), 133.

**101** Judith Kovacs, "Divine Pedagogy and the Gnostic Teacher according to Clement of Alexandria," *JETS* 9 (2001), 3–25; quote from Ismo Dundenberg, *Beyond Gnosticism: Myth, Lifestyle, and Society in the School of Valentinus* (New York: Columbia University Press, 2008), 23. See also Kovacs, "Echoes of Valentinian Exegesis," 324–325.

**102** In some places Origen advocates a two-fold wisdom and in others a three-fold division. This inconsistency emphasises the reality that for Origen, the focus is not on the divisions but the progression and movement from one level to another. See Kovacs, "Echoes of Valentinian Exegesis," 329n53.

**103** Origen, *Princ*, 3.3.1 (*GCS* 22). See also 4.2.4.

of a community and between different approaches to formation. In Paul's speaking "wisdom to some as to the perfect, to others as the foolish" (1 Cor 2.6–13),[104] he discerns that some members of the community are therefore perfect and taught in one way, while others are foolish and taught in a different way. In other words, whereas Paul, "speaks wisdom (*sapientiam*) to some as to the perfect, to others as to the foolish, he claims to know nothing at all except Christ Jesus and him crucified (1 Cor 2.2,6). Whereas he teaches some out of the law and the prophets, others he convinces by signs and wonders."[105] Just as different levels of wisdom may be discerned using 1 Cor 2, so excerpts from this passage may also be used to describe different levels of teaching in order to address those at each level of wisdom. The perfect are instructed by Paul in a different way from the foolish. Furthermore, Origen contrasts the content of teaching the perfect with that of teaching the gospel of Jesus Christ and him crucified, which Origen sets forth as the most basic instruction. He, like Paul, must begin by claiming nothing but Jesus Christ and him crucified in order to begin to move from foolishness to perfection and from the wisdom of this world and of the rulers of this world to the wisdom of God. The content of this wisdom begins with the crucified Christ.

Origen, however, not only discerns three types of wisdom based on the words of this Corinthian passage, but also uses this tripartite division to describe the very makeup of the people being taught as three-fold: "body, soul, and spirit."[106] He interprets the distinctions he finds in 1 Cor 2 even further when he then applies this three-fold division to wisdom, teaching, and the makeup of humankind, and to the interpretation of Scripture itself, which he argues also takes three different forms.[107] Thus, Origen connects his understanding of wisdom, formation, and Scripture using the language of 1 Cor 2.[108] In a lengthy passage of *First Principles*,[109] he makes this connection clear when he writes that,

---

**104** Origen, *Comm.Rom*, 1.13.3–5 (SC 532).
**105** Origen, *Comm.Rom*, 1.13.3 (Translation adapted from SC 532 and FC 103).
**106** This is a rather anti-Platonist move for Origen, advocating that the body and not the soul is made up of three-parts.
**107** Origen, *Princ*, 4.2.4 (SC 268/269). See also 3.3.1.
**108** Kovacs notes that Origen applies this understanding not only to the whole of 1 Corinthians, but also to how he understands Paul's other letters so that "Paul has reserved his more advanced teaching for other letters, especially *Romans* and *Ephesians*, and that he intends *1 Corinthians* as a preparation for the study of those letters" (Kovacs, "Echoes of Valentinian Exegesis," 327). See also Origen's comments on 1 Cor 4 in Origen, "Fragment of 1 Corinthians XVIII," in *JTS 9*, ed. Claude Jenkins (1908): 231–247, 353–373, 500–514; 354.
**109** O'Keefe calls this passage Origen's "large macrotheory of interpretation" (John J. O'Keefe, "Scriptural Interpretation," in *The Westminster Handbook to Origen* [ed. John Anthony McGuckin; Louisville, Ky: Westminster/John Knox, 2004], 193–197; 194).

one must write the thought (*νοήματα*) of the sacred writings in a threefold way upon one's own soul (*ψυχήν*), so that the one who is twofold may be edified by what is like the flesh of the Scripture (*τῆς οἰονεὶ σαρκὸς τῆς γραφῆς*), this name being given to the obvious interpretation; while the one who has made some progress may be edified by its soul, as it were; and the one who is perfect and like those mentioned by the Apostle, we speak wisdom among the perfect; yet a wisdom not of this world, nor of the rulers of this world, which are coming to nought, but we speak the wisdom of God, hidden in mystery, which God ordained before the world for our glory (1 Cor 2.6, 7), for this one may be edified by the spiritual law (Rom 7.14) which has a shadow of the good things to come (Heb 10.1). For just as a person is put together from body, soul, and spirit (*ὁ ἄνθρωπος συνέστηκεν ἐκ σώματος καὶ ψυχῆς καὶ πνεύματος*), so in the same way is Scripture, which has been prepared by God to be given to humankind for salvation.[110]

As Mitchell clarifies, this threefold mapping of the interpretation of Scripture—described by Paul, expounded by Origen, and attributed to 1 Cor 2.6–8—allows the language of 1 Corinthians to be "pressed into the service of the hermeneutical theory in a slightly different way: flesh, soul, and spirit are not three types of people *per se*, but they are three elements of which Scripture itself is composed."[111] For Origen, the hermeneutical levels he suggests for interpreting Scripture mirror the different types of wisdom he finds in 1 Cor 2 and therefore, these levels inform how people are taught Scripture based on their level of wisdom and knowledge. Origen understands that the "structure of Scripture is exactly that of the nature of human beings and of the whole universe, a threefold hierarchy of body (or letter), soul, and spirit, so that biblical passages are to be viewed as open in principle to interpretation on all three levels."[112] For Origen, therefore, the "purpose of Scripture is the formation of the soul"[113] so that through Scripture and beginning with its teaching of Christ crucified, the Christian may move from one level of wisdom to another and come to know and assimilate the saving doctrine of God that Scripture contains. Furthermore, Origen is clear that an "obvious" interpretation of Scripture[114] is only one way to understand a text and using the different levels of wisdom that he finds in 1 Cor 2, suggests other ways of interpreting Scripture. As other chapters of this study will make clear, this distinction will become increasingly important, especially in the midst of various theological controversies when the "obvious" interpretation

---

110 Origen, *Princ*, 4.2.4 (Translation adapted from Görgemanns and *SC* 268/269).
111 Mitchell, *Christian Hermeneutics*, 53.
112 Gorday, "Paulus Origenianus," 152–153.
113 Torjesen, *Hermeneutical Procedure*, 43.
114 Origen, *Princ*, 4.2.4.

is no longer sufficient to sustain the positions held by proto-orthodox Christian writers.

While Origen sets out the most basic instruction as the claim of Christ and him crucified, he continues in his homilies to use portions of 1 Cor 2 to describe how one moves from one level of wisdom to another and what the teaching that enables this movement contains. In a *Homily on Leviticus*, Origen uses the words of Leviticus to describe how Paul teaches different people at different levels of wisdom, in order to explicate the content of this teaching. He focuses, in particular, on a comparison between the high priest and Paul, writing that the high priest in Leviticus,

> uses certain clothes while he is in the place for sacrifices and others when he goes out to the people. Paul, the wisest of the high priests and the most skillful of the priests (*Paulus scientissimus pontificum et peritissimus sacerdotum*), used to do this. When he was in the assembly of the perfect (*perfectorum*) or, as it were, placed in the holy of holies and having put on the robe of perfection (*et stola perfectionis*), he used to say, we speak wisdom among the perfect yet not the wisdom of this world, nor of the princes of this world, that come to nought; but we speak the wisdom of God hidden in mystery which none of the princes of this age knew. For had they known it, they would not have crucified the Lord of glory (1 Cor 2.6–8: *sapientiam loquimur inter perfectos, sapientiam autem non huius mundi neque principum huius mundi, qui destruuntur; sed loquimur Dei sapientiam in mysterio absconditam, quam nemo principum huius saeculi cognovit. Si enim cognovissent, numquam Dominum maiestatis crucifixissent*). But nevertheless, after all these things, going out to the people, he changes his robe, and puts on another one, greatly inferior to that one. And what does he say? I determined to know nothing else among you except Jesus Christ and him crucified (1 Cor 2.2: *Nihil aliud inquit iudicavi me scire inter vos nisi Iesum Christum, et hunc crucifixum*). You see, therefore, how this most learned priest when he is within, among the perfect ones (*perfectos*) as in the holy of holies, uses one robe of doctrine, but when he goes out to those who are not capable he changes the robe of the word and teaches lesser things. [...] Thus, Paul knew how to change robes and to use one with the people, another in the ministry of the sanctuary.[115]

As in *First Principles*, Origen is clear that the perfect are instructed by Paul in a different way from the foolish, as he contrasts the content of teaching to the perfect with that of teaching the most basic instruction of Jesus Christ and him crucified. To emphasise this difference, Origen points to Paul himself as a teacher who changes roles and "robes" as he teaches people with different levels of wisdom within his community. Using the images of clothing and specifically the robes of the high priest from Leviticus, Origen describes the difference between

---

[115] Origen, *Hom.Lev*, 4.6 (Translation adapted from *GCS* 29 and *FC* 83). See also, Origen, *Hom.Num*, 6.1.2–3 for a similar description.

the robe of the word for the simple, which he equates to the word of the cross and Christ crucified (1 Cor 1.18–2.4), and the robe of doctrine for those who are able to grasp the wisdom of this word, hidden in mystery. With the ultimate goal being progress in wisdom to the hidden wisdom of God, Origen advocates that the content of teaching as both word and ultimately doctrine is necessary for moving those he teaches to different levels of wisdom and knowledge. Different kinds of teaching are essential in order to address those who possess different kinds of wisdom. Origen describes this clearly in his *Commentary on Romans*, as well, where he writes that,

> the Apostle, who not only preaches but also teaches (*qui non solum praedicet sed et doceat*), makes known the general designation of his task. Indeed, he will preach (*praedicet*) the simple faith (*simplicem fidem*) to those to whom he says I determined to know nothing else among you except Christ Jesus and him crucified (1 Cor 2.2: *nihil enim aliud iudicaui me scire inter uos nisi Christum Iesum et hunc crucifixum*); but he would teach (*doceat*) those to whom he was saying but we speak wisdom among the perfect (1 Cor 2.6: *sapientiam autem loquimur inter perfectos*). Here it is shown that he has, to be sure, conveyed the sound of the preaching to the former but to the latter he has discussed the wisdom of God (*sapientiam Dei*) through words.[116]

For Origen, one begins with preaching the most basic instruction of the crucified Christ and moves to teaching the wisdom of God hidden in mystery. In other words, adapting the distinctions he makes in his *Homily on Leviticus*, one preaches the word and one teaches the doctrine. In this way, 1 Cor 2 was highly valued by Origen for "its role in the comprehensive divine pedagogy—God's plan for training all people up to himself."[117] Despite the central place this Corinthian passage holds for Origen, he is not concerned with the exact details of the content of the teaching that would move a Christian from one level of wisdom or scriptural understanding to another, except that it must begin with Christ crucified. While his opponents may claim that Christianity is for the simple-minded and see his focus on basic instruction and levels of wisdom as a weakness of the Christian faith, for Origen this is one of its great strengths, that the scriptures are accessible to all from the simple to the most advanced.[118]

On a more personal level, Origen applies these words from 1 Cor 2 and his understanding of Paul as teacher of word and doctrine to his own teaching, writing that he also must adapt his teaching accordingly, guided by Christ. He writes that in the words of 1 Cor 2, "Paul speaks also to me, in order that I not build up

---

116 Origen, *Comm.Rom*, 8.6.5 (Translation adapted from *SC* 543 and *FC* 104).
117 Kovacs, "Servant of Christ," 161.
118 See Rankin, *Clement to Origen*, 135–136.

in a careless fashion, since I know that on that day the fire will test the quality of the work which I have built."[119] In this way, Paul "functions as an example" for Origen and "conforms to the needs and circumstances of the author."[120] This connection between 1 Cor 2 and Paul may be seen beyond Origen, as well, where in a number of texts, early Christians not only focus on Paul's wisdom as they adapt 1 Cor 2, but they also describe him as an Apostle, a preacher of truth, and a teacher.[121] The fact that early Christians say something about Paul himself in their use of 1 Cor 2 is not surprising, especially when we consider the conclusions of rhetorical and historical-critical studies that the interpreter of a text always brings bias to an interpretation, especially the bias of his or her own self-understanding and situation.[122] Clement of Alexandria and Origen led a catechetical school in Alexandria, and Tertullian was a trained rhetorician and some suspect may have even taught in a Graeco-Roman educational context before converting to Christianity. Their perceived treatment of Paul, therefore, as a teacher of wisdom, is not extraordinary.

Returning to this specific example from Origen, 1 Corinthians 2 gives him, as one who identifies as a teacher himself, a way of understanding wisdom and formation in terms of moving people from one level of wisdom to another through Scripture and the guidance of the Spirit. At the same time, Paul's words are not "just calling for a spiritual reading and justifying it," but now Paul himself is "*exemplifying in his very person* what a spirit-filled reading looks like."[123] Paul is the "definitive spiritual interpreter"[124] who shows Origen the ways he must preach and teach in order to engage people with different levels of knowledge and of wisdom, leading them from the simple truth of Jesus Christ and him crucified to the secret and hidden wisdom of God.

---

**119** Origen, *Comm.1Cor*, 15.18–20 (Jenkins). See also Kovacs, "Servant of Christ," 170–171.
**120** James W. Aageson, *Paul, the Pastoral Epistles, and the Early Church* (Library of Pauline Studies; Peabody, Mass: Hendrickson, 2008), 1–2.
**121** See *1Clem*, 5.5–7; Tertullian, *Mart*, 3; *Scorp*, 1; 7; *Marc*, 3.14; Irenaeus, *Haer*, 4.41.4; Origen, *Hom.Lev*, 4.6.
**122** L.T. Johnson and W.S. Kurz SJ, *The Future of Catholic Biblical Scholarship: A Constructive Conversation* (Grand Rapids, Mich: Eerdmans, 2002), 269–270. See also Hans-Georg Gadamer, *Truth and Method* (trans. Joel Weinsheimer and Donald G. Marshall; 2nd ed; London/New York: Continuum, 2004); Joseph W. Trigg, *Origen: Bible and Philosophy in the 3rd Century* (Atlanta, Ga: John Knox, 1983), 173.
**123** Mitchell, *Christian Hermeneutics*, 52 (italics original).
**124** Mitchell, *Christian Hermeneutics*, 53.

## 2.5 Conclusions

1 Corinthians 2.6–16, with its tension between the hidden and the revealed, the wisdom of this world and the wisdom of God, was used by early Christian writers to determine difficult theological questions and exegete difficult scriptural texts, and as a way to exit discussion with their opponents in order to discredit the opponents' arguments and expose their heresies. Each approach and use of this passage relies on 1 Cor 2.6–16 for a similar strategic purpose: to differentiate between worldly wisdom and the wisdom of God. This focus on different levels of wisdom allows for a variety of exegetic and apologetic moves, where God's wisdom, hidden and revealed, helps early Christians make sense of difficult questions and texts. Furthermore, this focus on different kinds of wisdom allows for different approaches to Christian formation and teaching, so that those who have some wisdom and knowledge of Scripture, revealed by the Spirit, are taught in one way and those ignorant and without faith in another.

The images and phrases associated with wisdom from 1 Cor 2.6–16 were picked up by early Christian writers and applied to a range of theological arguments. Rhetorically, "God's wisdom, secret and hidden" (1 Cor 2.7) and the wisdom which "eye has not seen nor ear heard" (1 Cor 2.9) are phrases used by early Christian writers in order to make clear that in their writings, they hold the right interpretation of Scripture and the right understanding of an argument. While neat divisions between insiders and outsiders on the basis of knowledge is not possible, that 1 Cor 2 allows early Christians to emphasise different ways of knowing and levels of wisdom, however ambiguous at times, sets up a dualism that problematises any claims to already possess full wisdom in this world. Early Christians use excerpts from 1 Cor 2 with a particular focus on the language of wisdom they find within it, in order rhetorically to close down conversation with those who they argue do not possess this wisdom, revealed by God and the Spirit. This focus, however, is not only on wisdom but also on the dichotomies that early Christians detect within 1 Cor 2 between the wisdom of God and of the world, and between the spiritual and the unspiritual. These divisions function within early Christian apologetic arguments where Christians claim that they fall on the spiritual side of God's wisdom, while their opponents are the ones who have only the wisdom of the world and are thus unspiritual.

These divisions in 1 Cor 2 are also applied to early Christian exegesis, especially when encountering difficult scriptural passages about the glory of God, suffering, the nature of Christ, and the consummation of the world. The different levels of wisdom that early Christians find in this Corinthian passage—the wisdom of this world, of the rulers of this world, and of God—are equated with levels of scriptural understanding and interpretation, especially within the writings of Origen. These distinctions enable them to claim a greater level of wisdom and with that, a deeper theological understanding of the scriptural text that is "beyond that which is written" (1 Cor 4.6). 1 Corinthians 2 is therefore used by early Christians for a variety of exegetical purposes, but particularly by Origen as he describes his own hermeneutical approach to scriptural interpretation. With this approach, Origen determines that only those who possess the wisdom of God have access to deeper understandings of Scripture, but everyone must begin with the basic teaching of the word of Christ crucified in order to progress in wisdom to greater understanding. In this way, Origen with other early Christian writers, problematises systems which claim to already know everything because the understanding of formation and of wisdom that emerges from their use of this passage implicitly demands a continuity and a journey of knowing without an obvious terminus. Thus, Origen can succinctly conclude that when interpreting Scripture,

> however far one may advance in his investigations, and how ever great the progress one may make by unremitting study, assisted even by the grace of God, and with his mind enlightened, one will not be able to attain to the end of those things which are the object of his inquiries. Nor can any created mind in any way deem it possible to reach full comprehension; but after having discovered certain of the objects of its research, it sees again others which still have to be sought out.[125]

The language of progress and levels of wisdom that early Christians find in 1 Cor 2 are not only adapted to support their rhetorical and exegetical arguments but also influences their understanding of formation and how this wisdom is acquired. The wisdom of God, which is the wisdom to which early Christians aspire, is acquired by the Spirit, through knowledge of Scripture, and, at times, with the help of a good preacher and Spirit-filled teacher who are able to preach and teach the basic word of Christ crucified and thus help guide Christians from one level of wisdom to another. This is further confirmed when one recognises, as well, that excerpts from 1 Cor 2 frequently extend to include excerpts from 1 Cor 3.1–3 and the dichotomy between spiritual milk and solid food. Here, the movement from one level of wisdom to another in 1 Cor 2 is emphasised by including the movement from milk to solid food, with both images describing a progression from foundational elements to something of much greater sustenance.[126] The understanding that the goal of Christian life and faith is to move from the wisdom of this world to knowledge of the hidden wisdom of God, influ-

---

[125] Origen, *Princ*, 4.3.13 (*SC* 268/269).
[126] For example, see Clement, *Strom*, 5.65.1–66.1; Kovacs, "Servant of Christ," 147–171.

ences not only an early Christian understanding of formation but also suggests a definition of formation as the movement from one level of wisdom to another. The objective of the teacher, preacher, and writer is to persuade and encourage the Christian in their progress towards attaining the wisdom of God. This conclusion arises from early Christian use of 1 Cor 2 where, with many identifying as teachers themselves, they engage the divisions and dichotomies within this passage between hidden and revealed, spiritual and unspiritual, and the wisdom of this world and of God.

This focus on formation as the movement from one level of wisdom to another is crucial not only for early Christian use of this Corinthian passage, but also for this project as a whole. Understanding teaching and formation in pre-Nicene Christianity is an almost impossible task. Nevertheless, the prominence of 1 Cor 2 and related rhetoric about human and divine wisdom is found throughout what are now defined as proto-orthodox and heterodox texts. Both claim access to a different kind of wisdom that is hidden and secret. For both, as well, this wisdom has its foundation in another world and is used essentially to close off dialogue with others by claiming to know that which is hidden from the world and the rulers of this world. This counter-cultural stance by early Christians who claim the wisdom of God over the wisdom of this world leads to two further reflections on 1 Cor 2.6–16 and its use within early Christian writings.

The first is to focus once again on the importance of the divisions detected by early Christians in the words of 1 Cor 2 and their connection to early Christian identity. That is, these divisions lead early Christians to identify with one side of the divide over the other. They are determined to place themselves on the side of those who are wise, filled with the Spirit, and who have access to the hidden wisdom of God. Early Christian use of 1 Cor 2 and their focus on wisdom therefore emphasises how they understand themselves as Christian: as those imbued with the wisdom of God.

This identity as those who have the wisdom of God, determined by early Christians through their use of 1 Cor 2, leads to a second reflection about the authority this self-understanding gives to early Christians. While the authority of Scripture offers a framework within which debates between early Christian writers could take place, the authority of Paul himself offers a similar place around which debate and inquiry could occur. The ultimate question was not whether Paul was right since Paul's rightness is implicit in his authority, rather the question that remains is who has the wisdom to interpret and understand his writings and the hidden wisdom of God he proclaims. The different sides of early Christian disagreements each sought to claim and re-claim Paul as a figure of authority in their rhetorical, apologetic, and exegetical works. Beneath the arguments of early Christian writers, a subtle interplay of authorities appears as they appeal to the authority of the Pauline texts to ground their arguments, and use Paul's authority as a writer, teacher, and apostle to bolster their own. The wisdom claimed by each author both to persuade and to defend is the hidden wisdom to which Paul refers in 1 Cor 2.6–7 and each writer is eager to claim possession of this wisdom against his opponents. Early Christian writers do not readily extend an invitation to plunge into this "wisdom, secret and hidden" (1 Cor 2.7), but rather, they use the very existence of this wisdom to demonstrate that the argument of an opponent cannot stand.[127] As illustrated in this chapter, early Christian use of 1 Cor 2 places Paul into the role of a custodian and even teacher of wisdom whose words equip them in their arguments. In 1 Cor 2, Paul makes a pronouncement out of the depths of his wisdom, not with explicit and detailed knowledge, but as one with knowledge of the Spirit and thus the higher, hidden things of God. In this way, Paul stands as one with wisdom who is the "theologian-in residence" for early Christians "speaking the truth of the apostolic tradition into the current discussion" and developing concerns of the day.[128]

This authority attributed to Paul, however, is not just as a teacher who knows the wisdom of God, but it also derives from his very name and his writings. Thus, early Christians who claim Paul as "the Apostle" and "my Apostle" rather than "Apostle to the heretics,"[129] claim the identity of one who is wise. The introductory chapter mentioned that one of the conclusions from the survey of Homeric texts in Graeco-Roman literary sources was that Homer's works were not necessarily used exegetically or to support a wider argument but rather to create an identity for the author as one who is learned and cultured.[130] Similarly, Paul is cited in early Christian discourse not necessarily as one who represents culture and learning, but as one who represents spiritual knowledge, wisdom, and progress. Thus, early Christian use of Paul's writings on wisdom and especially the words and images they find in 1 Cor 2 connect their identity with his. Early Christians in their very use of Paul, attempt to harness the authority of the apostle to endow their own writings with authority, power, and, ultimately, the wisdom of God in Christ.

Questions remain about the content of wisdom, teaching, and formation, and exactly how early Christians were moved from one level of wisdom to another, be that by preaching Christ crucified, knowledge of doctrine, the Spirit, or spi-

---

**127** Paul's language about wisdom is itself ambiguous at times where he denies speaking words of wisdom (1 Cor 2.4), speaks words of wisdom among the perfect (2.6), and yet this wisdom is the hidden wisdom of God (2.7). See Brown, *The Cross*, 33.
**128** Blackwell, "Paul and Irenaeus," 196. See also Kovacs, "Servant of Christ," 169–170.
**129** See Tertullian, *Marc,* 3.5.4.
**130** Morgan, *Literate Education*, 77–78.

ritual, even philosophical, exegesis. The minds of early Christian writers and what texts they may or may not have had before them are not known, so these questions will remain beyond what eye has seen and ear has heard. Clearly, 1 Cor 2.6–16 is a significant passage for early Christians; it sets an ideal goal for early Christians as they strive to move those less knowledgeable in the faith and scriptures from one level of wisdom to another. At the same time, it provides an ideal response to opponents of the faith from whom wisdom is hidden. By studying how this text was used across many different writers and genres, one may better understand how early Christians used excerpts from Scripture to form rhetorical and exegetical arguments. More than this, early Christian use of 1 Cor 2 offers a glimpse at how they understood formation and how, as teachers themselves, they understood and defended their entire enterprise of faith modelled on Paul, the one who has attained the perfect wisdom of God.

# Chapter Three:
# Ephesians 6.10–17: spiritual armour...to wage a spiritual war[1]

> *the spiritual forces of wickedness in the heavenly places*
> (Eph 6.12)

## 3.1 Early Christian Writers and Ephesians 6

Considered to be "one of the most influential documents in the Christian church"[2] and the Pauline epistle which exercises "the most influence on Christian thought and spirituality,"[3] the letter to the Ephesians is the first New Testament book to be called "Scripture" in early Christian writings.[4] For many scholars, this letter represents the quintessence of Paul's thought and theology, summarizing some of the central themes in his writings: Christian unity, suffering, pneumatology, and eschatology.[5] However, with no mention of a place name in many early manuscripts, the Ephesian epistle attributed to Paul does not appear to be addressed to one particular congregation but to a group of churches.[6] Some scholars even conclude that because of its summative features, this letter has "no setting and little obvious purpose."[7] Moreover, alongside uncertainty about the letter's community, purpose, and setting, like Colossians the authorship of Ephesians engenders much debate over whether it is authentically by

---

1 Tertullian, *Marc,* 4.20.
2 Harold W. Hoehner, *Ephesians: An Exegetical Commentary* (Grand Rapids, Mich: Baker Academic, 2002), 1.
3 Raymond E. Brown, *An Introduction to the New Testament* (ABRL; New York: Doubleday, 1997), 620.
4 Polycarp, *Phil,* 12.1 ("As it is expressed in these Scriptures [*scripturis*]", *SC* 10)
5 Hoehner, *Ephesians*, 106; C.H. Dodd, "The Mind of Paul: Change and Development," *BJRL* 18 (1934): 3–44; 24–25; F.F. Bruce, "St. Paul in Rome, Part 1," *BJRL* 46, no. 2 (1964): 326–345; 333. For contrast, Muddiman offers six points of theological difference between the Pauline corpus and Ephesians (John Muddiman, *A Commentary on the Epistle to the Ephesians* [BNTC; London: Continuum, 2001], 18–19).
6 References to Ephesus are omitted from P⁴⁶, ℵ, B, 6, and 1739. See M. Jeff Brannon, "'The Heavenlies' in Ephesians: A Lexical, Exegetical, and Conceptual Analysis" (PhD Diss; University of Edinburgh, 2010), 8.
7 Muddiman, *Ephesians*, 12. See also Hoehner, *Ephesians*, 97.

Paul.[8] Nevertheless, early Christian writers assume Paul penned the letter[9] and even "the great majority of scholars who argue for deutero-Pauline authorship still maintain that Ephesians was written in and stands in the Pauline tradition."[10]

The letter to the Ephesians is important for the church for many reasons, not least because Paul summons the recipients of the letter "to unity and holiness of life,"[11] which is modelled by the unity of Christ and exhibited in the corporate life of the church, built on the foundation of the apostles and prophets.[12] The unity of the church and of Christians with one another is one of the overarching themes of the letter, serving as the basis for moral exhortation and encouragement. Because of the letter's exhortative tone, and because no single event or crisis can be discerned as the specific occasion for its composition, scholars describe Ephesians as a homily, as well as a theological tract, a wisdom discourse, an early Christian hymn, and even a baptismal or Eucharistic liturgy.[13] Despite the importance of the Ephesian letter to the church, one of the most cited Pauline passages in early Christian writings is important for a reason beyond the unity expounded within this letter: its imagery. Excerpts from Ephesians 6.10–17 are used more than 450 times by at least 40 different pre-Nicene authors with a particular focus on the spiritual forces of wickedness and the images of fiery

---

**8** Hoehner addresses the assumption that scholars are primarily against Pauline authorship and demonstrates with an elaborate chart that scholars through the 20th century are equally divided on the issue of Ephesian authorship (Hoehner, *Ephesians*, 9–20). I find Muddiman's position on Ephesian authorship compelling as he argues (with Boismard) that Ephesians is the composition of a later follower of Paul who has edited and expanded a genuine Pauline letter. Muddiman gives convincing evidence for an early post-Pauline dating of Ephesians, based both on the dependence of Johannine literature and the Petrine letters on Ephesians, and on the much accepted dependence of Ephesians and Colossians (Muddiman, *Ephesians*, 2–47; see also M.-É Boismard, *L'énigme de la Lettre aux Éphésiens* [EBib 39; Paris: J. Gabalda, 1999], 9–16).
**9** See Irenaeus, *Haer*, 5.2.3, 1.3.1, 1.8.4–5, 5.2.36; Tertullian, *Marc*, 5.17; Clement of Alexandria, *Strom*, 4.65; *Paed*, 1.18; Origen, *Cels*, 3.20. See also Josef Schmid, *Der Epheserbrief des Apostels Paulus: seine Adresse, Sprache und literarischen Beziehungen* (BibS(F) 22; Freiburg: Herder, 1928), 18 and 19n1.
**10** Brannon, "The Heavenlies," 7. See also Alan F. Segal, *Paul the Convert* (New Haven: Yale University Press, 1990), 69.
**11** Muddiman, *Ephesians*, 12.
**12** Hoehner, *Ephesians*, 98–100.
**13** Hoehner, *Ephesians*, 74–76 and 94–102 for a history of scholarship and description of the variety of views regarding the purpose and genre of Ephesians. See also R.R. Williams, "The Pauline Catechesis," in *Studies in Ephesians* (ed. F. L. Cross; London: Mowbray, 1956), 89–96; Martin Kitchen, *Ephesians* (London: Routledge, 1994), 112–128; Andrew T. Lincoln, *Paradise Now and Not Yet: Studies in the Role of the Heavenly Dimension in Paul's Thought with Special Reference to his Eschatology* (SNTS 43; Cambridge: Cambridge University Press, 1981), 136–137.

darts, wrestling, and armour found in the passage.¹⁴ Engaging in a wide-ranging examination of early Christian writings, this chapter offers a profile of the use of images from Eph 6.10–17 and indicates some of the major trends of their reception and use.¹⁵ While excerpts from Eph 6 may be found in a variety of genres and early Christian texts, they appear consistently within exhortatory works such as homilies, treatises, and commentaries. The Graeco-Roman cultural context in which many early Christian lived and wrote was saturated with military language and images and, at times, overshadowed by the threat of persecution. The language and images of Ephesians 6, therefore, provides an obvious reference point by which early Christian writers could encourage those enduring hardship as it describes the evil with which a Christian may contend on both a personal and a cosmic level.

Early Christian focus on images of weapons, wrestling, and warfare from Eph 6 is not insignificant, since this focus occurs in a culture where military images had a "tremendous effect" on all aspects of life.¹⁶ George Caird argues that the idea of spiritual forces of wickedness (Eph 6.12) and their subjugation by Christ "is built into the very fabric of Paul's thought."¹⁷ Even though in passages like Col 2.15, Christ is understood as the victor on the cross, according to Eph 6.12, the spiritual forces of wickedness "are still operative, and the Christian must wrestle with them; they still hold the whole creation in bondage to futility."¹⁸

---

**14** See Appendix B for details of these references. One text included in Appendix B which only appears two times in this survey is *The Hypostasis of the Archons*, which refers to the images in Eph 6.12, in particular. This Nag Hammadi text, dated in the third century C.E., is an anonymous tractate offering an esoteric interpretation of the first six books of Genesis and proclaims the reality of archontic rulers (see Roger Bullard and Bentley Layton, "The Hypostasis of the Archons (II, 4)" in *The Nag Hammadi Library* [ed. James M. Robinson; New York: HarperCollins, 1988], 161–169).
**15** Passages with similar content are cited in the notes to indicate the breadth of the materials consulted.
**16** Adolf Harnack, *Militia Christi: The Christian Religion and the Military in the First Three Centuries* (trans. David McInnes Gracie; Philadelphia: Fortress Press, 1981), 20; and Ramsay MacMullen, *Soldier and Civilian in the Later Roman Empire* (HHM 52; Cambridge, Mass: Harvard University Press, 1963), 164. The language of warfare and, in particular, the putting on of armour may also be found in 1 Thess 5.8, Wis 5.17–18, and Isa 59.17–21. While some scholars such as Thomas Neufeld discern a trajectory through these three texts that leads to Eph 6, early Christian writers do not appear to make such connections, as the examination of their use of Eph 6 in this chapter will confirm (Thomas R. Neufeld, *"Put on the Armour of God": The Divine Warrior from Isaiah to Ephesians* [Sheffield: Sheffield Academic Press, 1997], 151–156).
**17** George B. Caird, *Principalities and Powers: A Study in Pauline Theology* (Oxford: Clarendon Press, 1956), viii–ix.
**18** Caird, *Principalities*, ix. See also Rom 8.20.

Consequently, many early Christian writers take up the images of Eph 6, reflecting not an endorsement of warfare but rather the application of this language to Christian life and thought in a world permeated by war and constant military presence.[19]

One of the central themes appearing time and again when early Christians use excerpts from Eph 6 is the understanding that at certain points in the Christian life, one is especially vulnerable to attack by the spiritual forces of wickedness: in times of persecution and at the time of baptism. Both represent liminal and decisive moments in the life of faith, and early Christians use images from Ephesians 6 to admonish Christians not to turn away from God when they encounter struggle and temptation in the course of their daily life. In this way, the images of wrestling, fiery darts, and armour of God are used by early Christian writers to focus on individual and communal struggles, enabling them to adapt excerpts from this passage in a variety of contexts and arguments. The images of the spiritual forces of wickedness (Eph 6.12) and fiery darts of the evil one (Eph 6.16) are used to describe the many kinds of assault—both superhuman and inner-human—that the Christian might face. Images of wrestling (Eph 6.12) and armour (Eph 6.11, 14) are then adapted to describe how one might stand firm against these forces of evil. More specifically, early Christian writers connect spiritual forces of wickedness with temptation, passions, persecution, and martyrdom and the location of the battlefield on which these spiritual forces are found —both within and without—depends greatly on the context. Even today, the phrase "spiritual forces in the heavenly places" from Eph 6 is the subject of much scholarly debate since neither Paul nor "any one else in the first century had developed a logical system of demonology."[20] Nevertheless, this did not pre-

---

**19** Paul Erdkamp, ed. *A Companion to the Roman Army* (Oxford: Blackwell, 2011), 66.

**20** Caird, *Principalities*, x. The focus of scholarship on Eph 6.12 is especially on the phrase, "in the heavenly places" (ἐν τοῖς ἐπουρανίοις/ *in caelestibus*), since this phrase occurs only fives times in New Testament writings, all of which are in Ephesians (Eph 1.3; 1.20; 2.6; 3.10; 6.12). Scholars are divided on the origin of this phrase, attributing it to a philosophical framework, as well as to a unique aspect of Pauline eschatology. Nevertheless, within early Christian writings, this phrase from Eph 6 is used less than 20 times outside the writings of Origen. See Wilfrid L. Knox, *St. Paul and the Church of the Gentiles* (Cambridge: Cambridge University Press, 1939), 190; Timothy B. Cargal, "Seated in the Heavenlies: Cosmic Mediators in the Mysteries of Mithras and the Letter to the Ephesians," in *SBLSP 1994* (ed. Eugene H. Lovering Jr.; Atlanta: Scholars Press, 1994), 804–821; 820; Andrew T. Lincoln, "A Re-Examination of "the Heavenlies" in Ephesians," *NTS* 19 (1973); 473–482; Ernst Käsemann, "Epheserbrief," in *Die Religion in Geschichte und Geganwart: Handwörterbuch für Theologie und Religionswissenschaft* (ed. Hans von Campenhausen; Tübingen: Mohr, 1958), 517–520; 518–519; Martin R. Pope, "Studies in Pauline Vocabulary," *ExpTim* 22 (1911): 552–554; H. Odeberg, *The View of the Universe in the*

vent early Christian writers from adapting this text to describe forces of evil. Christians have a long and intense history of interest in such forces, which shows as they draw from wide range of other texts to support their concepts of evil and spiritual forces. These influences include Jewish angelology, Graeco-Roman cosmology, and Hellenistic philosophy.[21] Moreover, the rabbinic concept of *yetzer* as an inclination within the soul and the Platonic view of evil within the soul with one part of the soul in conflict with the other,[22] provide touchstones for early Christians as they sought within this "shared cultural atmosphere"[23] to use the images and words from Eph 6 to describe the conflicts they faced as Christians. Furthermore, this emphasis on Eph 6 also points to an emerging anthropology as early Christian writers attempt to discern how the spiritual forces of wickedness and human action are related.[24]

---

*Epistle to the Ephesians* (Lund: Gleerup, 1934), 8 – 20; Chrys C. Caragounis, *The Ephesian Mysterion: Meaning and Content* (ConBNT 8; Lund: Gleerup, 1977), 150 – 152; Michael E. McGough, "An Investigation of 'ΕÔΥΡΑΝΙΟ˜ in Ephesians" (PhD Diss; New Orleans Baptist Theological Seminary, 1987), 2 – 14; 28 – 29; 95 – 96; Horacio E. Lona, *Die Eschatologie im Kolosser- und Epheserbrief* (Würzburg: Echter Verlag, 1984), 297 – 298; 428 – 448; W. Hall Harris III, "'The Heavenlies' Reconsidered: Οὐρανός and Ἐπουράνιος in Ephesians," *BSac* 148 (1991); 72 – 89; 73 – 76, 85 – 89; Brannon, "The Heavenlies," 15 – 31.
**21** See Andrew T. Lincoln, *Ephesians* (WBC 42; Dallas, Tex: Word Books, 1990), 20; Ernest Best, *A Critical and Exegetical Commentary on Ephesians* (ICC; Edinburgh: T&T Clark, 1998), 105 – 110; Caragounis, *Ephesian Mysterion*, 41 – 45, 147; Harris, "'The Heavenlies' Reconsidered," 73 – 74; Odeberg, *View of the Universe*, 7 – 8; A. van Roon, *The Authenticity of Ephesians* (Leiden: Brill, 1975), 213 – 215; F.F. Bruce, *The Epistles to the Colossians, to Philemon, and to the Ephesians* (NICNT; Grand Rapids, Mich: Eerdmans, 1984), 254; Rudolf Schnackenburg, *Ephesians: A Commentary* (Edinburgh: T&T Clark, 1991), 51; Jean-Noël Aletti, *Saint Paul, Épître aux Éphésiens* (EBib 42; Paris: J. Gabalda, 2001), 56; Wesley Carr, *Angels and Principalities: The Background, Meaning, and Development of the Pauline Phrase* hai archai kai hai exousiai (Cambridge: Cambridge University Press, 1981), 96; John G. Gibbs, *Creation and Redemption: A Study in Pauline Theology* (Leiden: Brill, 1971), 130 – 131. See also Christopher Rowland and Christopher R. A. Morray-Jones, *The Mystery of God: Early Jewish Mysticism and the New Testament* (Leiden: Brill, 2009), 601 – 609 who suggest that the writer of Ephesians was deeply rooted in the transformational mysticism of the Jewish Shiur Koma, which in turn is the source for the cosmological language in Eph 6.
**22** Ishay Rosen-Zvi, *Demonic Desires: "Yetzer Hara" and the Problem of Evil in Late Antiquity* (Philadelphia: University of Pennsylvania Press, 2011), 34 – 35.
**23** Rosen-Zvi, *Demonic Desires*, 37.
**24** The relationship between cosmology and anthropology is crucial to note as this chapter explores the connection early Christians make between tangible forces in the Christian life and forces of wickedness in the heavenly places. In this way, for example, the early rabbinic concept of the evil entity of the *yetzer* as an external force upon the soul functions in a similar way to the spiritual forces of wickedness which lead humankind into sin and away from God (see Rosen-Zvi, *Demonic Desires*, 35 – 37 and *Sifre Deut,* 45). For further discussion of cosmology and an-

Early Christians, however, not only draw from other traditions and philosophies, but also from within their own tradition as the images of armour, wrestling, and warfare in Eph 6 trigger connections with other texts attributed to Paul, especially excerpts from 2 Cor 10 and 1 Thess 5. Within these texts, similar images of battle and struggle may be discerned and, at times, early Christians conflate and combine these passages within their arguments.[25] The language of exhortation and images of struggle complement the chapter on 1 Cor 2 and the use of this passage by early Christians to encourage progression from one level of wisdom to another. Focusing once again on images found within the text, early Christians use excerpts from Ephesians to determine how this wisdom can be maintained as they exhort others to stand firm, equipped with the full armour of God in Christ, and not to flee from their faith. This chapter begins first by distinguishing what the spiritual forces of wickedness are according to early Christian writers and then is divided into three further sections, focusing on the images of fiery darts, wrestling, and armour of God as they are used and adapted in a range of early Christian texts.

## 3.2 Spiritual Forces of Wickedness (Eph 6.12)[26]

Excerpts from Eph 6.10–17 may be found at the heart of early Christian exhortation which concerns the liminal moments when one is especially vulnerable to attack by the spiritual forces of wickedness. In times of persecution and at the moment of baptism, in particular, early Christians discern that one is most susceptible to "spiritual forces hidden from ordinary perception—forces both diabol-

---

thropology see Geurt Hendrik van Kooten, *Cosmic Christology in Paul and the Pauline School: Colossians and Ephesians in the Context of Graeco-Roman Cosmology, with a new synopsis of the Greek texts* (WUNT 171; Tübingen: Mohr [Siebeck], 2003); Stroumsa, "*Caro salutis cardo,*" 35–37; Jean Daniélou, *A History of Early Christian Doctrine: The Origins of Latin Christianity* (vol. 3; London Darton, Longman & Todd, 1977).

**25** It is interesting to note that for early Christians, the images and language of Eph 6 are more often associated with other scriptural references to battle and warfare than to other scriptural references to heavenly places. Thus, early Christian writers refer to 2 Cor 10.3–5 and 1 Thess 5.8–9 in close proximity to Eph 6.10–17 approximately 66 times; whereas Eph 1.3, 1.20, 2.6, and 3.10, are each used fewer than 20 times and almost all of these references fall within the works of Origen. For an exception, see Tertullian, *Marc,* 5.18, where Eph 3.10 and 6.12 are connected.

**26** See also Ignatius, *Eph,* 13; Irenaeus, *Haer,* 1.5.4; Tertullian, *Marc,* 5.18; Origen, *Or,* 29.2; *Hom.Exod,* 4.7–9; 5.5; *Hom.Ezech,* 13.1.7–8; Eusebius, *Hist.eccl,* 10.4.58; *Praep.ev,* 5.3.1; 7.16.4; Cyprian, *Pat.* 12.12.

ical and divine."²⁷ Drawing on the divisive language of Eph 6 and an understanding of the Christian as one who is embattled, times of persecution and baptism epitomise moments when the Christian is between sides of the battle. Essentially, times of persecution represent decisive moments in the battle while the time surrounding baptism represents the moment when Christians join the battle for the first time. In persecution, the temptation to flee from faith and succumb to the spiritual forces of wickedness in order to preserve one's earthly life is strong. At baptism, one embodies the Christian identity publicly, sealed by the Holy Spirit, and this time of shifting allegiance is also a time when the new Christian is vulnerable to encounters with the spiritual forces of wickedness trying to draw them away from faith. Using the language and images of Eph 6, early Christian writers offer exhortatory words to those facing persecution and the newly baptised in order to prevent both from turning away from faith in God through Jesus Christ as they encounter struggle and temptation.

The spiritual forces of wickedness as found in Eph 6.12 take many different forms for early Christian writers as they seek to describe the makeup of these forces and to determine how a Christian is to stand firm or even fight against them. While the focus is primarily on liminal moments when a Christian is especially vulnerable to these forces, early Christian writers are also concerned to address those at all levels of faith. Thus, they also use excerpts from Eph 6 to enjoin all Christians to take up the armour of God and stand fast as they encounter struggle and temptation in the course of daily life.

Clement of Alexandria, for example, uses excerpts from Eph 6 to equate spiritual forces of wickedness with the passions that act within a person and lead to disobedience and sin. The words of Eph 6.12 help him to clarify how serious the threat of the passions is when he writes that, "our philosophy says that all passions (τὰ πάθη) are impressions on the soul (ἐναπερείσματα τῆς ψυχῆς) which is malleable and yielding, and, like signatures of the spiritual powers (τῶν πνευματικῶν δυνάμεων) whom our wrestling is against (Eph 6.12: ἡ πάλη ἡμῖν)."²⁸ For Clement, the Ephesian language of spiritual forces of wickedness best describes the category of these passions which place Christians over and against God. The

---

[27] Elaine Pagels, "Ritual in the *Gospel of Philip*," in *The Nag Hammadi Library after Fifty Years, Proceedings of the 1995 Society of Biblical Literature Commemoration* (eds. J.D. Turner and A. McGuire; NHS 44; Leiden: Brill, 1997), 280–291; 283. Pagels includes Ignatius, Justin Martyr, Tatian, Tertullian, Athenagoras, and Origen as those who connect baptism and spiritual attack. See also Stroumsa, "*Caro salutis cardo*," 44; and Everett Ferguson, *Baptism in the Early Church: History, Theology, and Liturgy in the First Five Centuries* (Grand Rapids, Mich: Eerdmans, 2009), 359.

[28] Clement of Alexandria, *Strom*, 2.20.109 (translation adapted from GCS 52 and FC 85).

battleground where Christians contend with these passions is the soul, and they must wrestle to keep the soul free from the internal imprints of the spiritual forces of evil. Clement's language is reminiscent of the Stoic understanding of passions imprinting the soul, even though for Clement the "source of these imprints [...] is not the senses as in the philosophical account, but external spiritual powers."[29] Similar to Epictetus, Clement sees the soul's task as one of distinguishing between false impressions and true, between the spiritual forces of wickedness and God.[30] Nevertheless, "Clement adds a new twist"[31] through his understanding of this destructive activity as the work of the spiritual forces of wickedness, who remain outside humankind even while leaving their impression.[32] The battle, therefore, is both inner-human and superhuman and takes place on two levels, within the person and without, so that the Christian who "obtains mastery in these struggles and overthrows the tempter, menacing as it were, with certain contests, wins immortality."[33] This contest with the spiritual forces is not only about impressions on the soul but also affects salvation.[34]

For Clement, the spiritual forces of wickedness and their destructive nature must be countered and rejected so that the soul may not be harmed. He writes, therefore, that the Christian must,

> put on the armour of God, that we may be able to stand against the wiles of the devil (Eph 6.11: ἐνδύσασθαι οὖν δεῖ τὴν πανοπλίαν τοῦ θεοῦ πρὸς τὸ δύνασθαι ἡμᾶς στῆναι πρὸς τὰς μεθοδείας τοῦ διαβόλου), since the weapons of our warfare are not physical, but have divine power to destroy strongholds, cast down arguments and every lofty thing which exalts itself against the knowledge of God, and bring every thought into captivity under the subjection of Christ, says the divine Apostle (2 Cor 10.3–5). There is no doubt a need of one who shall, in a worthy and discriminating manner, treat the things from which passions arise, such as riches and poverty, honour and dishonour, health and sickness, life and death, toil and pleasure. For in order that we may treat indifferently the things that are ethically indifferent, we need within us great powers of discrimination, since we have been previously corrupted by much weakness, and ignorantly enjoyed a distortion from bad training and nurture.[35]

---

29 Rosen-Zvi, *Demonic Desires*, 38.
30 David Brakke, *Demons and the Making of the Monk: Spiritual Combat in Early Christianity* (Cambridge, Mass: Harvard University Press, 2006), 41. Epictetus, *Diatr*, 2.18.27: "the true athlete is the one who exercises himself against such impressions."
31 Behr, *Asceticism and Anthropology*, 148.
32 Rosen-Zvi, *Demonic Desires*, 38.
33 Clement of Alexandria, *Strom*, 7.3 (translation adapted from *GCS* 17 and *SC* 428).
34 This language is reminiscent of baptism as the moment when the spiritual forces of wickedness can no longer place their signature on a soul that has been claimed and sealed by Christ.
35 Clement of Alexandria, *Strom*, 2.20.109 (translation adapted from *GCS* 52 and *FC* 85).

The spiritual forces against which Christians struggle are thus described by Clement as the strongholds and lofty thoughts that place themselves over and against God. Clement notes the dichotomy present with any language of battle and is clear that in order for the Christian to remain on the opposing side of these spiritual forces, the Christian must live differently and rise above the things from which passions arise, including the conditions of wealth, health, and pleasure.[36] Thus, for Clement, a Christian progresses toward perfection only as the Christian is separated from passion. As he writes above, bad training and ignorance allow these passions to be indulged and to enter into the human soul, but good training and knowledge, as seen in his use of 1 Cor 2 as well, allow one to progress toward perfection.

The danger of passions and the spiritual forces of wickedness is so great, however, that in this context Clement introduces *apatheia*, the Stoic ideal of freedom from emotion.[37] For Clement, *apatheia* is a perfected state achieved by Christ who was completely free from passions, and thus achieving *apatheia* is related to achieving perfection, apart from the spiritual forces of wickedness that affect and mutate the soul.[38] As the chapter on 1 Cor 2 established, one of Clement's main concerns was the progression of the Christian in faith and wisdom. Once again, his concern with progression is emphasised in his exhortation to withstand the evil forces of wickedness so that one may, free from these spiritual forces, move toward perfection and thus God.[39] The language of Eph 6 offers Clement a category—spiritual forces of wickedness—with which he can emphasise the serious threat the passions pose to the soul and place the goal of *apatheia* and freedom from passions within the context of battle. The ultimate goal for Clement is to "carry on" fighting against the spiritual forces of wickedness until they ultimately give up and succumb, "in admiration of the victors."[40]

For Tertullian, the spiritual forces of wickedness are not necessarily the passions that threaten the soul but are equally physical forces represented by those

---

[36] Peter Karavites, *Evil, Freedom, and the Road to Perfection in Clement of Alexandria* (Leiden: Brill, 1999), 37.
[37] Clement of Alexandria, *Strom*, 6.9.74. See also *Strom*, 2.9.45; 2.18.81; 7.3.13; Behr, *Asceticism and Anthropology*, 196–197 n61; Judith Kovacs, "Saint Paul as Apostle of *Apatheia*: Stromateis VII, Chapter 14," in *The seventh book of the Stromateis: proceedings of the Colloquium on Clement of Alexandria (Olomouc, October 21–23, 2010)* (eds. Matyáš Havrda, Vít Hušek, and Jana Plátová; VCSup 117; Leiden: Brill, 2012), 199–216; 208.
[38] See Clement of Alexandria, *Strom*, 6.9; 7.84; 7.86; Kovacs, "Apostle of *Apatheia*," 211 (especially note 57); and Behr, *Asceticism and Anthropology*, 217.
[39] Clement, *Strom*, 6.9.74; 1.10.49; 2.10.46; 7.1.4. See Behr, *Asceticism and Anthropology*, 195–199.
[40] Clement of Alexandria, *Strom*, 2.20.109 (SC 38).

whom he deems to be heretic, especially his opponents who tamper with the words of Scripture. The spiritual forces of wickedness described in Eph 6.12 are working in, or through, his heretical opponents and pose a similarly potent threat to faith and knowledge of Christ. Thus, Tertullian writes that Valentinus,

> laid violent hands on [Scripture] with a no less shrewd bent of mind than Marcion. Marcion openly and nakedly used the knife, not the pen, since he cut the scriptures to suit his argument, whereas Valentinus spared them, since he did not invent scriptures to suit his argument, but argument to suit the scriptures; nevertheless, he took away more and added more by taking away the proper meaning of each particular word, and by adding arrangements of systems which have no existence. These are the natures of the spiritual wickednesses with which we wrestle (Eph 6.12: *ingenia de spiritalibus nequitiae cum quibus luctatio est nobis*).[41]

Tertullian adds that "no one therefore should doubt either that spiritual wickedness (*spiritalia nequitiae*) from which heresies derive have been sent by the devil, or that heresies are not far removed from idolatry, since they belong to the same author and handiwork as idolatry."[42] The image of spiritual forces of wickedness that Tertullian finds in Eph 6 serves a similar function as it did for Clement, offering a category into which he can place what he finds to be egregious misinterpretation of Scripture by his opponents and thus a metaphorical way of talking about their wickedness.[43]

For Origen, an understanding of the Christian as one who is embattled is clear within his homilies where he focuses on images from Eph 6. Within these writings, the Christian is one who constantly resists the spiritual forces of wickedness and shields the self from the fiery darts of evil. These forces assume both an inner-human and superhuman form, attacking the Christian from within and without. Using language similar to that found with his use of 1 Corinthian 2, Origen describes two levels of struggle with spiritual forces of wickedness. He writes that,

> the battle of Christians is twofold. Indeed, for those who are perfect such as Paul and the Ephesians, as Paul himself says, it was not a battle against flesh and blood, but against

---

[41] Tertullian, *Praescr*, 38–39 (*SC* 46). This text is used by some scholars to argue that as early as Valentinus, a collection of New Testament writings called "Scripture" existed. See Lee Martin MacDonald, *The Origin of the Bible: A Guide for the Perplexed* (London: T&T Clark, 2011), 162.
[42] Tertullian, *Praescr*, 40 (*SC* 46).
[43] Novatian draws a similar conclusion in his *Spectacles*, writing of those who misinterpret Scripture that, "it would have been far better for such people to lack knowledge of the scriptures, than to read them in such a manner" since the words of Scripture "are misinterpreted by them as so many incentives for the practice of vice" (Novatian, *Spect*, 2.4; *FC* 67).

principalities and powers, against the rulers of darkness here in this world, against the spiritual forces of wickedness in the heavenly places (Eph. 6.12: *non est pugna adversus carnem et sanguinem, sed adversus principatus et potestates, adversum mundi hujus rectores tenebrarum harum, adversus spiritalia nequitiae in coelestibus*). But for those who are weak and those not yet mature, the battle is still waged against flesh and blood, for they are still assaulted by carnal faults and weaknesses.[44]

Setting up a dichotomy between those who are perfect and mature and those who are weak and immature—language highly reminiscent of 1 Cor 2.6–8—Origen places the two sides that he finds in Eph 6 into this frame. His interpretation situates the perfect in a battle against the principalities and powers, the rulers of darkness, and the spiritual forces of wickedness, and the weak in a battle against flesh and blood. Yet all of these forces are tangible for Origen, whether visible or invisible, and each has the power to exploit those who are ignorant and not yet mature as well as those who are wise and, in the language of 1 Cor 2, perfect.[45] For Origen, the spiritual forces of wickedness are real superhuman powers that threaten the Christian on the journey of faith. The further the Christian progresses toward perfection and God, the more intense the level of attack by spiritual principalities and powers.[46] For those less mature in the faith; however, the attack is very present in carnal temptation and failings.[47] Within this scheme, "struggles against the temptation of the flesh are more elementary than struggles against demonic temptation."[48] The ultimate battle for Origen is not one of bodily strength against sins which "arise from natural desires of the body, such as hunger, thirst, or sexual desire," but "spirit contends against spirit, according to the saying of Paul that our overarching struggle is against principalities and

---

[44] Origen, *Hom.Jos*, 11.4 (translation adapted from *SC* 71 and *FC* 105).
[45] Origen, *Princ*, 3.2.1–2. Within many of these texts, a strong psychological and psychaogogical element exists concerning the effect of these spiritual forces on the soul. Ishay Rosen-Zvi finds remarkable connections between "Origen's account of the demonic assault and the way the rabbis narrate the saga of the *yetzer*—the dynamic of its entry to humans, its mental destructiveness and the religious war against it" (Rosen-Zvi, *Demonic Desires*, 40). Dale Martin, on the other hand, reads Origen as part of "broader shifts in the intellectual culture of the period" with regards to cosmic and moral hierarchies, shifts he also finds in Porphyry and Iamblichus. Dale B. Martin, *Inventing Superstition: From the Hippocratics to the Christians* (Cambridge, Mass: Harvard University Press, 2004), 188–189.
[46] Harnack recognised a shift or progress in the writings of early Christians as a whole and writes that as more martyrologies and ascetical writings were produced, the images of battles against sin and the evil desires of the flesh decreased in comparison to images of battles with demons working through persecutions and the activities of heretics (Harnack, *Militia Christi*, 62–63).
[47] See also Origen, *Hom.Num*, 1.5.
[48] Kovacs, "Servant of Christ," 160. See also Origen, *Princ*, 4.3.12.

powers and the rulers of the darkness of this world (Eph 6.12: *adversum principatus et potestates et mundi huius rectores tenebrarum nobis imminere certamen*).'[49] For Origen, one engaged in this struggle must always be in the "the process of perfection by which the Christian trains himself to be invulnerable to the attacks of the devil."[50]

The spiritual forces of wickedness offer a category of interpretation by which early Christians could discuss the struggles they encountered both within and without. Their encounters with passions and temptation, sin, misinterpretation, and persecution, were likened to confrontations with the forces of evil described in Eph 6. The forces of wickedness are both tangible powers of temptation and passions whose attack results in an internal battle, while at the same time they are also extra-human forces such as sin and cosmic powers whose attack results in an external battle, especially when engaging with the wickedness of another. This can especially be seen when Origen and Clement and their use of this Ephesian passage are examined together. For Origen, these spiritual forces of evil, rulers, and authorities take on a superhuman quality as he advocates for the real and tangible existence and influence of these powers on the lives of the Christian.[51] For Clement, the spiritual forces are primarily limited to and almost demythologised as an internal battle with the passions and temptations that attack the soul from within. Nevertheless, even the significant difference that appears to emerge between Clement and Origen is not absolute. In other words, even for Origen, the only way to be totally free from these forces and the fiery darts of evil is to be free from passions. For both Origen and Clement, therefore, images from Ephesians 6 personify evil acts and forces which work both within the person and without.

From this understanding, not only Clement and Origen but other early Christian writers also adopt a range of images from the surrounding Ephesian text—wrestling, fiery darts, and armour—to describe the influence and consequence of encounters with these spiritual forces. Their concern was not only to emphasise that the spiritual forces of wickedness represented real dangers, capable of inflicting wounds and leading one away from faith and God, but also to establish that through faith, wisdom, and right instruction a Christian could stand firm against these forces. In this way, Christians were offered tools and encouragement so that they might not be as susceptible to the forces of wickedness as the faithless, the weak, and those led astray by false and uninformed teaching.

---

[49] Origen, *Princ*, 3.2.6 (*SC* 268).
[50] Kovacs, "Servant of Christ," 161. See also Origen, *Princ*, 3.2.4.
[51] See Origen, *Princ*, 1.5–7.

## 3.3 Fiery Darts of the Evil One (Eph 6.16)[52]

In a highly militarised culture, the plight of the soldier and the elements of armour would have been familiar to many. Thus, early Christians would have been aware that the particular panoply described by Paul is comprised almost entirely of defensive weapons, to be used only for close combat and standing firm in formation. One of the few offensive weapons to feature in Eph 6.10–17 is found not within the armour of God but is a weapon of attack used by the forces of wickedness: the fiery darts of the evil one. The image of these darts is picked up by early Christians in a similar way to the spiritual forces of wickedness as they use both images to describe the attacks Christians face and against which they must stand firm.

The Valentinian author, whose writings make up much of Clement of Alexandria's *Excerpts of Theodotus*, uses the image of fiery darts particularly within the context of baptism[53] and as such, offers a glimpse of Valentinian use of Eph 6 in his writings.[54] As already mentioned above, baptism is one of the liminal moments when a person is most vulnerable to attack by the spiritual forces of evil. At this time, when Christians join the battle for the first time, Theodotus focuses on Jesus himself who faced temptation and had to fend off the fiery darts of evil after his own baptism. Clement cites the Valentinian author, writing that,

> even the Lord after baptism was troubled like we are and was first with beasts in the desert. Then, when he had prevailed over them and their ruler as if already a true king, he was served by angels. For he who ruled over angels in the flesh was rightly served by angels. Therefore, we must put on the armour of God (Eph 6.12: Δεῖ οὖν ὡπλίσθαι τοῖς κυριακοῖς ὅπλοις) and keep body and soul invulnerable, armour that is able to quench the darts of the devil (Eph 6.16: ὅπλοις σβέσαι τὰ βέλη τοῦ διαβόλου δυναμένοις), as the Apostle says.[55]

---

52 See also Origen, *Comm.Eph*, 3.
53 Clement and the Valentinians may not have held the same understanding of baptism. For example, Kovacs notes that while some Valentinians denigrated the church's baptism against a higher spiritual baptism, for Clement, the baptism offered by the church was perfect. Because Jesus was not deficient when he was baptised and needed no additional teaching to become perfect, so also the church's baptism conveys perfection without additional *gnosis* (Kovacs, "Echoes of Valentinian Exegesis," 321; and Clement of Alexandria, *Paed*, 1.6.30.1–2).
54 See Ferguson, *Baptism in the Early Church*, 318–319; Eric Francis Osborn, "The Bible and Christian Morality in Clement of Alexandria," in *The Bible in Greek Christian Antiquity* (ed. Paul M. Blowers; Notre Dame, Ind: University of Notre Dame Press, 1997), 112–130; 115–116; see also Clement, *Prot*, 11.116.
55 Clement, *Exc.Theod*, 85 (SC 23); note that following Sagnard's source analysis in his *Extraits de Théodote*, this excerpt appears to be from an otherwise unknown Valentinian author. See François Louis Sagnard, *Extraits de Théodote* (SC 23; Paris: Cerf, 1948), 36. Cyril of Jerusalem

Just as Christ was attacked by the darts of the devil immediately after his baptism, so the Christian needs the armour of the Lord in order to keep alert and quench these darts, as well. The darts that Theodotus finds in Eph 6 provide an image to describe the temptations faced by Christ in the desert which is expanded to include all Christians so that they, too, might prevail over trouble. This connection between temptations of the flesh and baptism for Theodotus is particularly significant because it allows him to uphold the adoptionist view that separates the fleshy Jesus from the divine Christ.[56] Baptism, therefore, is not only the moment when Christians acquire the armour of God, but it is also the moment when Christ is joined to Jesus.[57] For the Valentinians, baptism even for Jesus entailed putting on Christ and thus the armour of God acquired by Christians in baptism as protection from the fiery darts of temptation is the same protection and redemption first given to Jesus in his baptism.

Origen especially favours the image of fiery darts found in Eph 6 and the inner-human element that he sees in this image to describe the struggles and attacks Christians face. He writes that through certain acts by a person,

> room is made for the devil, so that, if he enters our heart one time, he will either gain possession of us, or at least will pollute our soul, if he does not obtain full mastery over it by casting on us his fiery darts (*ignita sua iacula*); and by these we are sometimes deeply wounded, and sometimes only set on fire. Seldom and in only a few instances are these fiery darts quenched so they cannot find a place to wound: when one is able to be covered with the strong and powerful shield of faith (Eph 6.16: *ignita iacula restinguuntur [...] cum quis munitissimo et validissimo scuto fidei*).[58]

The image of fiery darts from Eph 6 offers Origen a way to describe all the elements that wound and pollute the soul and lead the Christian astray. In other words, these external forces do not result in an external battle with superhuman powers but an internal battle within the body and the soul with powers that are both superhuman and inner-human. He describes these darts both as evil

---

also uses images from Eph 6 to write that Jesus, after his baptism, "went forth and vanquished the adversary" (*Mystag*, 3.4).

[56] Clement, *Exc.Theod*, 73.1–3 (again, this is most likely the Valentinian author, see Sagnard, *Théodote*, 36). See also Pagels, *Gnostic Paul*, 128–129; Emily J. Hunt, *Christianity in the Second Century: The Case of Tatian* (RECM; New York: Routledge, 2003), 42; Ismo Dundenberg, "The School of Valentinus," in *A Companion to Second Century Christian Heretics* (eds. Antti Marjanen and Petri Luomanen; Leiden: Brill, 2005), 64–99; 80–81.

[57] Clement, *Exc.Theod*, 22.6. See also *Exc.Theod*, 24.1 and the description by Cerinthus in Irenaeus, *Haer*, 1.26.1. Both of these selections from *Excerpts of Theodotus* are attributed by Sagnard to the Valentinian author (see Sagnard, *Théodote*, 33).

[58] Origen, *Princ*, 3.2.4 (SC 268).

thoughts and even passions and as the teachings of his opponents. Origen sounds a pessimistic note as he writes that more often than not, the fiery darts leave a mark before they are quenched. This suggests that one of the reasons this image of the fiery darts is used so frequently by Origen is because of the reality that even if the spiritual forces of wickedness are overcome, they still leave a wound. This language of woundedness leads Origen to incorporate medical terminology into his argument, as he seeks to find a way to heal the wounds inflicted. As such, writing against Celsus, Origen describes his own task as teacher as trying to "extract each dart (βέλος) which wounds him who is not completely fortified by the whole armour of God (Eph 6.13, 16: πάντῃ πεφραγμένον τῇ πανοπλίᾳ τοῦ θεοῦ) and to apply a rational medicine (λογικὸν φάρμακον) to cure the wounds inflicted by Celsus, which prevents those who listen to his words from remaining firm in the faith."[59] For Origen, wisdom and especially teachers play a central role in the acquisition of protection and strength in the struggle against evil. He writes that faithful teachers, "rout countless demons" as they "take up the helmet of salvation, and the sword of the spirit, which is the word of God, by every prayer and supplication (Eph 6.17–18: *et galeam salutaris accipite, et gladium spiritus, quod est verbum Dei, per omnem orationem et obsecrationem*).'[60] The divisions Origen finds in the images of attack from Eph 6 influence his own writings as he seeks to protect those to whom he writes from the wounding words of heresy and to provide healing to those who have been affected and led astray by the irrational arguments of his opponents.

Origen attaches language both of suffering and of healing to the wounds inflicted by the fiery darts and the spiritual forces of wickedness, and this language appears throughout his exhortatory writings where he describes how these forces can take control like an illness. He writes that leprosy "flourishes in inflammation" and that one must "see, therefore, if the inflammation is not in

---

**59** Origen, *Cels*, 5.1 (translation adapted from *SC* 227 and Chadwick). See also Origen, *Comm.Cant*, 3.8 where Origen looks at the fiery darts from a different perspective, as darts not only from the evil one but also darts from God of wisdom, might, and justice which cause a very different kind of wound. Apart from this excursus by Origen, the darts with which one is afflicted are not those of God—wisdom, might, and justice—leading to salvation but darts of the wicked one—fornication, greed, and avarice—which harm the soul. See also Origen, *Hom.Exod*, 1.5.
**60** Origen, *Hom.Lev*, 16.7 (*FC* 83). Although the sword is the one offensive weapon mentioned in the Ephesian armour and is the metaphor upon which Origen focuses in this homily—also drawing on the language of Heb 4 and Rev 19—this sword is not used to attack the enemy but is what enables the believer to stand firm in the midst of attack, confident, as Ephesians suggests, in the word of God and steeped in prayer (see Hoehner, *Ephesians*, 853). See also Origen, *Hom.Jos*, 3.1; 5.2–3 and *Comm.Jo*, 6.10.

every soul which receives fiery darts of the evil one (Eph 6.16: *iacula maligna ignita*)."[61] Connecting the inflammation of leprosy to the fiery darts of Eph 6, Origen concludes that a soul which is not inflamed with faith is infected and blemished by sins and other darts of temptation. This language of inflammation and illness also leads Origen to pronounce that those who have succumbed to an attack by the fiery darts of evil are spiritually epileptic, writing that they have "been cast down by the spiritual forces of wickedness in the heavenly places (Eph 6.12: καταβαλλομένους ὑπὸ τῶν ἐν τοῖς ἐπουρανίοις πνευματικῶν τῆς πονηρίας), and are often ill at the time when the passions attack their soul, at once falling into the fire of burnings.'[62] The language of fire and attack in Eph 6 leads Origen to connect those who are spiritually ill—having fallen prey to the deceit of the world and the fiery inner-human passions of lust—with an attack by forces of wickedness. Ephesians 6 and its images of fiery darts add a dramatic element to Origen's declaration that those who succumb to this attack are spiritually unhealthy and weak. Thus, because the spiritual forces of wickedness are the primary cause of all sin and human suffering for Origen, the only way to resist these evil powers and the wounds caused by the fiery darts of evil is to be free from passions, protected by the shield of faith, and to be "healthy in temperance and the other virtues."[63] For Origen, one "would never be able by himself to overcome an opposing power" and thus it is only "by divine assistance"[64] and his own teaching, over and against that of his opponents, that one can move toward healing.[65]

Within his homilies and commentaries, Origen adapts the image of fiery darts not only to describe the wounds and illness caused by an attack but also to describe what forms these fiery darts might take. Thus, those who attack with "the fiery darts of evil (Eph 6.16: *iacula maligni ignita*)" by "which the soul

---

61 Origen, *Hom.Lev*, 8.8.1–2 (*FC* 83).
62 Origen, *Comm.Matt*, 13.4 (Translation adapted from *ANF* 9 and *SC* 162).
63 Origen, *Comm.Matt*, 13.4 (*SC* 162).
64 Origen, *Princ*, 3.2.5 (*SC* 268). See also Rosen-Zvi who describes how "several rabbinic statements and prayers regarding the *yetzer* present the very same picture of the never-ending struggle as the most fundamental religious mission entrusted to humankind. [...] In both cases the basic metaphor is that of war" (Rosen-Zvi, *Demonic Desires*, 40). He continues that "the detailed resemblance between Origen's account of the demonic assault and the way the rabbis narrate the saga of the *yetzer* [...] is striking" (40).
65 Origen not only self-identifies as a teacher, but sees this identification in terms of Christ's own identity. See Origen, *Comm.Jo*, 32.256 and 32.287 where alongside excerpts from Eph 6, Christ himself is called "teacher."

that is not covered by the shield of faith (Eph 6.16: *scuto fidei*) is wounded unto death,"⁶⁶ have an arsenal of darts in various forms:

> some of fornication, others of greed and avarice; and with these they wound as many as they can. They also have javelins of boasting and vainglory. But all these are very subtle, so that the soul scarcely perceives that she has been pierced and wounded by them, unless she is wearing the armour of God and standing watchful and unmoved against the shrewdness of the devil, covering herself always with the shield of faith (Eph 6.13, 16: *induta est armis Dei et stat vigilans et immobilis adversus astutias diaboli scuto semet ipsam fidei per omnia contegens*) and taking care to leave no part of her body naked of faith. And however many spears the demons have fashioned, even though they be fiery, even though they blaze with the flames of lusts and the fires of vices, if they find her mind fortified by faith, this complete faith extinguishes them all.⁶⁷

The images of Eph 6, to which Origen adds javelins, personify what he considers to be the evil acts and forces of people and the protection that faith can provide. The flames and fires of lust and vice can only be extinguished by faith, and Origen sees his task as making the soul aware of these dangers so that she may not be wounded by the fiery darts of evil. The language and images of warfare and combat add a sense of urgency to Origen's words as he sets forth the very identity of the Christian as one who is embattled, constantly under attack from the fiery darts of the evil one.

The image of fiery darts of the evil one, similar to the spiritual forces of wickedness, is used by early Christians to describe the spiritual struggles and wounds with which Christians are afflicted. The form of these darts is ambiguous and early Christians describe them primarily as temptations and the fires of passions and lust, especially the temptations faced immediately following baptism and upon joining the battle for the first time. In this way, the fiery darts of Eph 6 add to the milieu of attack and combat in which early Christians live and, especially for Origen, allow them to emphasise the harmful potential of the struggles encountered.

---

66 Origen, *Comm.Cant*, 3.8 (*PG* 13).
67 Origen, *Comm.Cant*, 3.8 (translation adapted from *PG* 13 and *ACW* 26). See also *Hom.Num*, 25.1.5.

## 3.4 Wrestling: For our struggle is not against flesh and blood (Eph 6.12)

Wrestlers in the ancient world were considered "models of discipline and virtue in certain philosophical systems"[68] as the plight of the wrestler required much training and preparation in order to engage an opponent. Wrestling is an individual endeavour, depending almost entirely on strength and skill, and wrestling contests would have been a part of Graeco-Roman social life and community. In this context, spiritual forces of wickedness are also understood in early Christian writings through the medium of a wrestling contest, where the language of wrestling from Eph 6 is used to describe the struggle and encounter with evil.[69] The ways that early Christians use the image of wrestling, as well as that of armour in the next section of this chapter, is more varied than the images of evil explored above. However, just as the spiritual forces of wickedness embodied both an inner-human and superhuman element, so the images of wrestling and armour take on a dualistic nature.

Tertullian, for example, focuses on the image of a boxer or cestus player to describe the spiritual struggles encountered by Christians. For Tertullian, the struggles against the spiritual forces of wickedness, especially those encountered through the discipline of fasting, are comparable to the struggles of a wrestler. He writes that,

> To them [cestus-players] bodily ambition is sufficient where strength is necessary; and yet they also strengthen themselves by xerophagies. But ours are other strengths and other powers, just as our contests are other; we whose wrestling is not against flesh and blood, but against the powers of the world, against spiritual malice (Eph 6.12: *non est luctatio adversus carnem et sanguinem, sed adversus mundi potestates, adversus spiritalia ma-*

---

**68** Robin M. Jensen, *Baptismal Imagery in Early Christianity: Ritual, Visual, and Theological Dimensions* (Grand Rapids, Mich: Baker Academic, 2012), 64. See also Epictetus, *Diatr,* 1.24.1–2; 3.15.1–13; 4.4.11–13.
**69** One example of this image, although it does not explicitly use Eph 6.12, is found in the martyrological text of Perpetua and Felicity where Perpetua envisions her martyrdom in terms of physically wrestling a large Egyptian, interpreted by many to represent the forces of wickedness described by Paul. See *Martyrdom of Perpetua and Felicitas,* 10.1–14 (Herbert Musurillo, ed. *The Acts of the Christian Martyrs: Introduction, Texts, and Translations* [OECT; Oxford: Clarendon Press, 1972], 116–119); also Victor Saxer, "The Influence of the Bible in Early Christian Martyrology," in *The Bible in Greek Christian Antiquity* (ed. Paul M. Blowers; Notre Dame, Ind: University of Notre Dame Press, 1997), 342–374; 352–353; and for a similar example, *Barn,* 4.9; 20.1.

## 3.4 Wrestling: For our struggle is not against flesh and blood (Eph 6.12)

*litiae*). Against these it is not by flesh and blood, but faith and spirit that enables us to make a firm stand.[70]

The words of Eph 6.12 enable Tertullian to contrast the physical demands of a wrestler who prepares himself for a contest in flesh and blood with the spiritual demands of a Christian who prepares for a contest in faith and spirit. The image and discipline of a wrestler, including a wrestler's strict eating habits, supports Tertullian's exhortation to fasting, which might be considered equally strict but the purpose of which is to engage a different kind of opponent. Tertullian adapts the language of division between spiritual and physical and between flesh and spirit that he finds in Eph 6 in order to address the physical and spiritual elements of the practice of fasting with images that could be more broadly understood. Moreover, because wrestling is an individual contest where much of the preparation is physical and psychological, Tertullian uses this image to exhort the individual Christian to fasting and taking on a discipline of preparation not dissimilar to that of a wrestler.

While in his treatise on fasting Tertullian remarks sarcastically that "an overfed Christian will be more desirable to bears and lions than to God,"[71] his more serious point is that the spiritual forces of wickedness described in Eph 6.12 are more likely to attack one who is weak, immoral, and undisciplined than one who has discipline like a wrestler.[72] Fasting, for Tertullian, is not just about food but is a practice by which the Christian may prepare for a contest against spiritual forces. Thus, his exaggerated rhetoric about fasting using the language of Eph 6 is not simply a concern for control over the passions of gluttony and desire but a concern for the soul and the preparation and discipline that will enable it to overcome the spiritual forces of wickedness. For Tertullian, the spiritual forces of wickedness cannot be reduced to passions and temptations, nevertheless, only by overcoming passions and temptation will one be able to engage the spiritual forces of wickedness and stand firm in faith. As he is clear elsewhere, the Christian wrestles in a "spiritual war against spiritual enemies in a spiritual campaign and spiritual armour to be fought completely on a spiritual level (*bellum spiritale adversus spiritales hostes spiritali militia et spiritalibus armis spiritaliter debellaturus esset*)."[73]

---

[70] Tertullian, *Jeiun*, 17.7–8 (*CSEL* 20).
[71] Tertullian, *Jeiun*, 17.9 (*CSEL* 20).
[72] See David Rankin, *Tertullian and the Church* (Cambridge: Cambridge University Press, 1995), 182; Karl Olav Sandnes, *Belly and Body in the Pauline Epistles*, (SNTSMS; Cambridge: Cambridge University Press, 2002), 224.
[73] Tertullian, *Marc*, 4.20 (*SC* 456).

Origen also takes up the image of wrestling when he tries to describe not the individual endeavor of the Christian against evil, but how Christ himself enables the Christian to withstand the spiritual forces of wickedness. Origen is clear that one "would never be able by himself to overcome an opposing power, except by divine assistance."[74] This statement triggers two images of wrestling for Origen: the description of wrestling in Eph 6 and the story of Jacob wrestling with the angel in Gen 32. He writes,

> the angel is said to have wrestled with Jacob. Here, however, I understand the writer to mean, that it was not the same thing for the angel to have wrestled with Jacob, and to have wrestled against him; but the angel that wrestles with him is the one who was present with him in order to secure his safety, who, after knowing his moral progress, additionally gave him the name of Israel. In other words, he is with him in the struggle and assists him in the contest [...] Finally, Paul has not said that we are wrestling with principalities or with powers, but against principalities and against powers (Eph 6.12: *nobis esse luctamen cum principibus vel cum potestatibus, sed adversum principatus et adversum potestates*). And hence, although Jacob wrestled, it was unquestionably against some of those powers which Paul declares resist and contend with humankind, and especially with the saints.[75]

Origen focuses on an important distinction between whether one is wrestling with and whether one is wrestling against an opponent. He claims that the image of wrestling in Eph 6 is different from that in Gen 32 because in Eph 6 the Christian is wrestling *against* real and dangerous powers of evil whereas in Gen 32, the wrestler is wrestling *with* God and is assisted in the struggle. Origen continues that, unlike the story of Jacob, the wrestling described in Eph 6 is not

> carried on by the exercise of bodily strength, and the arts of the wrestling school, but spirit contends against spirit (*sed spiritui adversum spiritum pugna est*), according to the saying of Paul that our overarching struggle is against principalities and powers and the rulers of the darkness of this world (Eph 6.12: *adversum principatus et potestates et mundi huius rectores tenebrarum nobis imminere certamen*).[76]

In this struggle, therefore, Origen is clear that one cannot vanquish the powers and principalities or wrestle against them unless one is assisted by God, who as in the story of Jacob, "is with him in the struggle and assists him in the contest."[77] Moreover, Origen applies the discipline and preparation that one learns

---

74 Origen, *Princ*, 3.2.5 (*SC* 268).
75 Origen, *Princ*, 3.2.5 (*SC* 268).
76 Origen, *Princ*, 3.2.6 (*SC* 268).
77 Origen, *Princ*, 3.2.5 (*SC* 268).

as part of the art of wrestling to the Christian life, convinced that the struggle Christians face is not simply of a physical nature but spiritual. Thus, Origen suggests that the Christian must exercise spiritual strength and learn the arts of spiritual wrestling, for which the Lord is the primary example and source of assistance.

For Tertullian and Origen, the spiritual forces of wickedness are real and tangible powers in the life of a Christian and the physical image and act of wrestling that they find in Ephesians 6 enables them to address how one must grapple with these spiritual forces. Wrestling allows them to address the temptations a Christian must resist and to emphasise the spiritual preparation and discipline demanded of the soul so that it might successfully contend with forces of evil. While wrestling is an individual endeavour, Origen in particular is clear that the Christian does not undertake a stance against the spiritual forces alone but that this wrestling can only be engaged *with* Christ *against* the spiritual forces. Wrestling, however, is not the only image early Christians find in Ephesians 6 to describe how one is to withstand the spiritual forces of evil. For early Christians, the location of the struggle against evil is not only in the sports ring, but may also be found on the battlefield. Therefore, another image that plays a significant part in early Christian writings about the spiritual forces of evil is that of the armour of God (Eph 6.11; 13–17).

## 3.5 Take up the whole armour of God (Eph 6.11 and 6.13)[78]

The image from Eph 6 taken up most frequently by early Christian writers is that of the armour of God. Within the panoply described by Paul, which is comprised almost entirely of defensive weapons, the only offensive weapon is the sword. Nevertheless, this weapon is also used defensively and not for long-range offensive fighting (as opposed to projectile weapons such as darts and spears, for instance). How early Christians adapt and expand this panoply, both with words from 2 Cor 10 and with additional offensive weapons of battle, will be noted in this section. Early Christian writers use the image of the armour of God in a wide range of texts, and this section is divided into two main parts to establish what the armour of God represents in early Christian texts and to discuss the different ways this image from Eph 6 was used throughout their writings.

---

**78** See also Clement of Alexandria, *Strom*, 4.7; Origen, *Comm.Cant*, 3.8; *Princ*, 3.2.4; *Fr.Jer*, 2; *Cels*, 8.34; 8.55; *Hom.Gen*, 4.6; 8.10; *Comm.Jo*, 32.19; 32.287; *Comm.Matt*, 11.9; Methodius, *Res*, 3.2.2; and *Didas.Silv*, 94.33–95.12; 96.6–15.

### 3.5.1 What is the armour of God?

Just as early Christians defined the spiritual forces of wickedness in varying ways —from passions and temptations to heretical scriptural interpretation—so too they offer a variety of ways to understand the armour of God. Baptism, prayer, faith, wisdom and education all feature as an interpretation of this armour as early Christians attempt to describe the life one must lead in order to quench the fiery darts of evil and prevail in their stance against the spiritual forces of wickedness.[79] Moreover, some early Christians contend that Christ himself is the armour of God put on by the Christian and that, no matter the action of the Christian, ultimately Christ has won the battle.

**Baptism**[80]
Ignatius is one of the first to use an excerpt from Eph 6 and he does so while encouraging those enduring persecution to work together and not to turn from their faith in Christ. This is only possible, however, when Christians are protected by faith, love, endurance, and the armour of God which for Ignatius is acquired through baptism. Thus, he writes that Christians must "let your baptism stand fast as your armour; faith as a helmet; love as a spear; endurance as a full armour (Eph 6.13, 17: τὸ βάπτισμα ὑμῶν μενέτω ὡς ὅπλα, ἡ πίστις ὡς περικεφαλαία, ἡ ἀγάπη ὡς δόρυ, ἡ ὑπομονὴ ὡς πανοπλία)."[81] Using the language of Eph 6, Ignatius equates baptism with the armour of God, exhorting Christians to allow it, alongside faith, love, and endurance, to act as their protection against spiritual attack. He adapts the language of Eph 6 to include a spear of love, a weapon not found in the Pauline panoply and a decisively offensive weapon. Because of this adaptation, some scholars raise questions about whether this is a reference to Eph 6 or a common Christian typos of the time.[82] However, it is also possible

---

[79] Origen and Methodius also include purity and chastity as ways to acquire the armour of God. In his Ephesians commentary, Origen writes that one "who has restricted his sexual activity and no longer serves it but strives for immortality has girded his loins with truth" (Origen, *Comm.Eph*, 3 [Gregg; Heine]; also *Mart*, 43[ACW 19]) and one who "is attacked neither in his passion nor in his desire" is the one who "remains pure in heart by having put on the breastplate of justice which has been forged for him by God" (*Comm.Eph*, 3). Similarly for Methodius, the armour of God is acquired primarily by those who keep themselves pure by "flying on the heavenward wings of virginity" (Methodius, *Symp*, 8.12 [SC 95]).

[80] See also Tertullian, *Mart*, 3; *Praescr*, 2; Cyprian, *Ep*, 10.2.

[81] Ignatius, *Polyc*, 6.2 (LCL 24).

[82] Other texts from this time period mentioning similar lists of armour include: Polybius, Wis 5.18–22 (each with different spiritual designations), Isa 59 and 1 Thess 5.8. See Jerome Mur-

that Ignatius, who knew of Paul and his letters, was eager to connect the language of Ephesians with that of 1 Thess 5, relating baptism to the Christian qualities of faith, love, and hope (or endurance for Ignatius). Nonetheless, the use of this language and Ignatius' equation of baptism with the armour of God, "indicates a realistic conception of the benefit imparted by baptism."[83]

Origen also connects the image of armour in Eph 6 with baptism, writing that as soon as one is baptised and has "tasted the mysteries of the heavenly host and [has] been restored by the bread of life, we are incited to battle by the apostolic war-trumpet."[84] For Origen, this means the Christian must obey the call of Paul who,

> with a powerful voice, calls out to us saying, put on the armour of God, so that you may be able to stand firm against the shrewdness of the devil (Eph 6.11: *induite vos arma Dei, ut possitis stare adversus astutias diaboli*). He does not permit us to be concealed any longer under the wings of those giving the nourishment of milk. Instead, he summons us to the fields of combat. It is said, put on the breastplate of love and receive no doubt the helmet of salvation, but also, the sword of the spirit and above all, the shield of faith on which you may be able, it says, to extinguish all the fiery darts of the evil one (Eph 6.14, 17, 16: *inquit vos loricam caritatis et galeam nihilominus salutis accipite, sed et gladium inquit spiritus et super omnia scutum fidei, in quo possitis ait omnia iacula maligni ignita exstinguere*).[85]

The connection between Eph 6 and baptism is essential for Origen as he uses Paul's language to describe the importance and challenges of baptism. He makes explicit that the threat to those being baptised is not only the spiritual forces of wickedness, but death itself as he equates martyrdom with baptism. Origen even writes in his treatise on martyrdom that "martyrdom is named a baptism" and incites his readers to "consider the baptism of martyrdom."[86] Both martyrdom and baptism offer the same benefits of salvation and protection for those who stand firm.[87] Here, the Christian is summoned from the protection

---

phy-O'Connor, "Who Wrote Ephesians?," *TBT* 8 (1965): 1201–1209; 1207; Lincoln, *Paradise*, 164–165.
**83** Ferguson, *Baptism in the Early Church*, 210; and William Schoedel, *Ignatius of Antioch: A Commentary on the Letters of Ignatius of Antioch* (Hermeneia; Philadelphia: Fortress Press, 1990), 276.
**84** Origen, *Hom.Judic*, 6.2 (translation adapted from *FC* 119). See also 4.11 and 5.2–3.
**85** Origen, *Hom.Judic*, 6.2 (translation adapted from *FC* 119).
**86** Origen, *Mart*, 30. See also Tertullian, *Bapt*, 16.1; *Pud*, 22.4–10; *Scorp*, 6; Origen, *Comm.Matt*, 16.6; Cyprian, *Fort*, Pr.4; *Ep*, 73.21.1–2; 73.22.2; and Eusebius, citing an unknown source of Origen in *Hist.eccl*, 6.4.3.
**87** Origen, *Mart*, 30 (translation from *ACW* 19). See also *Rom* 6.3–4. Origen also connects Jesus' passion as a martyrdom with baptism, based on the language he finds in Luke 12.50

of the "wings" and the nourishment of milk (language reminiscent of 1 Cor 3) to take up the armour given in baptism and stand firm against evil. Even though baptism, like martyrdom, is an act done to the individual Christian, putting on the armour of God in baptism joins the Christian with a community of those standing firm against the fiery darts of the evil one, having been summoned to the fields of combat.

**Prayer, Faith, and Wisdom**[88]
While the image of the armour of God from Eph 6 is equated by some early Christians with the act of baptism done to the Christian, this same image is also compared with acts of prayer, faith, and growth in wisdom accomplished by the Christian. For Clement of Alexandria, therefore, the armour of God may be compared with wisdom and courage. He writes that,

> the only man of courage is the gnostic, who knows both present and future things; along with these, also knowing, as I have said, the things which are in reality not to be dreaded. Because, knowing vice alone to be hateful and destructive of that which contributes to knowledge, protected by the armour of the Lord, he makes war against it (Eph 6.11, 13: τοῖς ὅπλοις τοῦ κυρίου).[89]

While, according to Clement, vices and passions make up the spiritual forces of wickedness that one must stand against, the virtue of courage is one of the ways Christians fight against the forces of evil. This courage is acquired, moreover, through knowledge of what one must not fear. Only by knowing what is hateful and destructive, can one stand against these things without fear, protected by the armour of God, which here Clement equates with knowledge. As Clement's use of 1 Cor 2 emphasised, knowledge and wisdom enable a Christian to progress in faith toward perfection with God and thus knowing what is not to be feared

---

and Mark 10.38 (see *Comm.Jo*, 6.56; *Comm.Matt*, 16.6; *Hom.Judic*, 7.2; Pamela Bright, "Origenian Understanding of Martyrdom and its Biblical Framework," in *Origen of Alexandria: His World and His Legacy* [eds. Charles Kannengiesser and William L. Petersen; Notre Dame, Ind: University of Notre Dame Press, 1988], 180–199; and Michael M. Winter, *The Atonement* [London: Geoffrey Chapman, 1995], 58–59). Note that even though baptism is only directly mentioned once in the Ephesian epistle (4.5), Rowland and Morray-Jones connect the language of putting on the armour of God with that of baptism, stating that "it is widely recognized that this exhortation, the martial imagery of which has both biblical and post-biblical Jewish antecedents, may have originated in the baptismal-catechetical tradition" (Rowland and Morray-Jones, *The Mystery of God*, 600).
**88** See also Clement of Alexandria, *Strom*, 4.7; Novatian, *Cib*, 1.1; Origen, *Pasch*, 1.38.
**89** Clement of Alexandria, *Strom*, 7.65.1–6 (SC 428).

allows the Christian to make the crucial progression from fear to love protected by this armour.[90]

Tertullian equates the armour of Eph 6 not with knowledge but with prayer, writing that the Christian must put on "the armour of prayer (*armis orationis*)" because "prayer is the bulwark of faith, our defensive and offensive armour against the enemy who is watching us on every side."[91] In order to be protected from the spiritual forces of wickedness and the fiery darts of evil, Tertullian is clear that one must put on this armour in order "to pray at every time and place (Eph 6.18: *omni in tempore et loco orare*)."[92] Combining the images that he finds throughout Scripture on prayer and using the images of armour and battle drawn from Eph 6, Tertullian offers a "theology of prayer" that "is built from every part of the Bible and reflects his understanding of an economy of salvation which finds its consummation in Christ."[93]

For Origen, prayer, which he understands as the direction of one's mind to God,[94] is an essential element in the struggle against evil. He describes the struggle of the Christian as "a prayer battle"[95] that is

> not against flesh and blood, but against the principalities and powers, against the rulers of the darkness of this world, against the spiritual forces of wickedness in the heavenly places (Eph 6.12: *non einem nobis certamen est adversum carnem et sanguinem, sed adversum principatus et potestates adversum mundi huius rectores tenebrarum adversum spiritalia nequitiae in caelestibus*). And it is certain that just as they all oppose the faith and resist piety, just as they are contrary to righteousness and truth and everything good, so they no doubt resist and are opposed to prayer.[96]

Origen uses the images and language of Eph 6 to equate the struggle against the spiritual forces of wickedness to a battle in prayer.[97] Prayer assists in the struggle

---

90 van den Hoek compares Clement's connection between courage and fear with that of Philo. See Annewies van den Hoek, *Clement of Alexandria and his use of Philo in the Stromateis: An Early Christian Reshaping of a Jewish Model* (Leiden: Brill, 1988), 74; and Philo, *Virt*, 1.1–4.
91 Tertullian, *Or*, 29.4 (Translation adapted from *CSEL* 20 and *FC* 40).
92 Tertullian, *Or*, 24.1 (*CSEL* 20).
93 Eric Francis Osborn, *Tertullian, First Theologian of the West* (Cambridge: Cambridge University Press, 1997), 150.
94 Origen, *Comm.Rom*, 10.3. See also Origen, *Hom.Exod*, 11.4.
95 Origen, *Comm.Rom*, 10.15.2 (*SC* 555).
96 Origen, *Comm.Rom*, 10.15.2 (Translation adapted from *SC* 555 and *FC* 104).
97 In one of his *Homilies on Judges*, Origen once again uses a significant portion of Eph 6, writing that "the holy Apostle equips the soldiers of God with weapons appropriate to wars of this kind, by saying, therefore, stand clothed with the breastplate of righteousness and having girded your loins in truth; moreover, receive the helmet of salvation and the sword of the Spirit; indeed,

and serves as the armour of God, enabling one to stand firm and proclaim with Paul that "I have fought the good fight, I have completed the race (2 Tim 4.7)."[98] Origen is clear that victory over the spiritual forces of wickedness is obtained "not by javelins of iron but by the weapons of prayers" which enable the Christian to stand firm.[99] Prayer for Origen is just as tangible as the spiritual forces of wickedness and a battle waged in prayer is just as real and effective as physical, military battle.[100] Thus, defending Christians who refuse to engage in physical combat for the emperor, Origen writes to Celsus that Christians offer "a divine help, putting on the whole armour of God (Eph 6.12: πανοπλίαν ἀναλαμβάνοντες θεοῦ)" because "though they keep their right hands clean, Christians fight through their prayers to God on behalf of those doing battle in a just cause [...] raising a special army of piety through our petitions to God."[101] In this way, Origen uses images from Eph 6 to acknowledge two levels of on-going encounter where the spiritual battle engaged by prayer is just as effective, if not more so, than physical combat within the world. While the emperor's soldiers take up armour to fight physical enemies, Christians are tasked with the greater battle of standing firm in spiritual battle against spiritual enemies on behalf of all who "battle in a just cause."[102]

### 3.5.2 Taking up the armour of God[103]

Clement of Alexandria uses the image of the armour of God to describe how Christians are to combat the spiritual forces of wickedness: peacefully. He taps into a cultural understanding of peace in order to instruct others in their struggle with the spiritual forces. He writes,

---

in all things take up the shield of faith upon which you can extinguish the fiery darts of the evil one (Eph 6.14,17,16)" (*Hom.Judic*, 9.1 [*FC* 119]).
**98** Origen, *Comm.Rom*, 10.15.3 (*SC* 555). Because of his exhortation that one may fight against the spiritual forces of wickedness and acquire the armour of God through prayer, scholars such as Harnack credit Origen as being the father of the concept of the ascetic as the true Christian combatant, carrying on an incessant battle against the attacks of distraction and sin (See Harnack, *Militia Christi*, 49; also Guy G. Stroumsa, *Hidden Wisdom: Esoteric Traditions and the Roots of Christian Mysticism* (SHR 70; Leiden: Brill, 2005), 158).
**99** Origen, *Hom.Judic*, 9.1 (translation from *FC* 119).
**100** See also Origen, *Hom.Jos*, 18.11; 11.11.
**101** Origen, *Cels*, 8.73 (translation adapted from *SC* 150 and Chadwick).
**102** Origen, *Cels*, 8.73 (*SC* 150).
**103** Origen, *Comm.Rom*, 2.5.3; *Hom.Exod*, 3.3; 5.5; Novatian, *Cypr*, 2.5.2 (or Cyprian, *Ep*, 31.25).

> Let us arm ourselves completely in peace, putting on the breastplate of righteousness and taking the shield of faith, and putting on the helmet of salvation, and let us sharpen the sword of the Spirit, which is the word of God (Eph 6.14–16: Ἐξοπλισώμεθα εἰρηνικῶς, ἐνδυσάμενοι τὸν θώρακα τῆς δικαιοσύνης καὶ τὴν ἀσπίδα τῆς πίστεως ἀναλαβόντες καὶ τὴν κόρυν τοῦ σωτηρίου περιθέμενοι καὶ τὴν μάχαιραν τοῦ πνεύματος, ὅ ἐστι ῥῆμα θεοῦ, ἀκονήσωμεν). So the apostle of peace (ὁ ἀπόστολος εἰρηνικῶς) commands.[104]

Clement ironically combines images of peace with the command to take up armour and prepare to stand fast in battle, arguing that Christians have been "educated not for war but for peace."[105] In other words, "the training of the individual and his Christian education could succeed only if they took place in an environment concerned with the achievement of peace and serenity,"[106] even though he contrasts this language of peace with the images of military preparation and training in order to describe the educational process.

Clement's clarification that the armour of God must be taken up peacefully alongside the divisive language of Eph 6 where the Christian is understood to be one who is always fighting against something, would have fit well with the culture in which he writes. Simply stated, the connections between images of peace and those of armour would not have been foreign to those Clement addresses. As Rankin writes, "the Greco-Roman world was deeply disturbed, even terrified, by the prospect of civil strife, disorder and anarchy, and accorded a high value to the qualities of peace, order and harmony."[107] Early Christians in the Roman Empire would have been surrounded by the ideals of *pax Romana*, a peace achieved only by actively subduing—and at times instructing and converting—all enemies. For Clement, this combination of language of peace and combat was not unique to Rome but was that which Christ achieved in his death on the cross. Therefore, Christians must follow his example when facing temptation and struggle, equipped with the armour of God and guided by the words of the apostle of peace.[108]

Tertullian also uses the image of the armour of God as a part of his injunction to Christians facing persecution that they are not to flee from their faith. He writes that Paul,

---

104 Clement of Alexandria, *Prot*, 2.20.4 (Translation adapted from *LCL* 92).
105 Clement of Alexandria, *Paed*, 1.12 (*SC* 70).
106 Gerardo Zampaglione, *The Idea of Peace in Antiquity* (Notre Dame, Ind: University of Notre Dame Press, 1973), 250. See also John Ferguson, *Clement of Alexandria* (New York: Twayne Publishers, 1974), 64; and Rev 19.16 and Gal 3.27, which may also have been on Clement's mind alongside the Eph 6 image of armour.
107 Rankin, *Clement to Origen*, 2.
108 See Klaus Wengst, *Pax Romana and the Peace of Jesus Christ* (trans. John Bowden; London: SCM, 1987).

commands us to stand steadfast (Eph 6.13: *stare immobiles*), certainly not to act an opposite part by fleeing, and to be girt (*accinctos*) not to play the fugitive or oppose the gospel. He points out weapons too, which persons who intend to run away would not need. And amongst these the shield, by which you may be able to quench the darts of the devil (Eph 6.16: *inter quae et clipeum, quo possitis tela diaboli extinguere*), when doubtless you resist him and sustain his assaults in their utmost force.[109]

For Tertullian, Eph 6 reinforces his point that Christians are to stand firm and not turn from their faith for why would Paul mention armour if it were not to be used for resisting evil? Moreover, Tertullian notes that in 1 Thess 5.14, Paul "calls us to support the weak" and yet "not when they flee, for how can the absent be supported by you?"[110] It is not by chance that Tertullian, thought to be the son of an army centurion,[111] chooses to single out the shield, since he would have known that this part of the Pauline panoply is the most communal of the armour named. For the shield to be effective, one must stand firm in formation with others, flanking one another and protecting each other by the placement of the shield.[112] Therefore, the shield is most effective not for an individual soldier, but for a company of soldiers. Tertullian's focus on the armour of God and his use of this particular image, highlights that he is not only describing how to resist evil but is also emphasising community. The injunction to stand firm has a communal function, since only those who do not flee and who take up the armour of God are able to support and comfort one another in their struggle against evil.[113]

---

[109] Tertullian, *Fug*, 9.2 (translation adapted from Bulhart and *FC* 40).

[110] Tertullian, *Fug*, 9.1 (translation adapted from Bulhart and *FC* 40).

[111] Harnack, *Militia Christi*, 52.

[112] By the second and third centuries, the most commonly known and utilised shield is the phalanx, which is used in formation and not for individual combat. One of the few exceptions to this assumption in Graeco-Roman literature is the Homeric hero who often has a phalanx shield and fights an individual battle.

[113] Tertullian connects the taking up of military weapons and the call to military service with the military oath, the *sacramentum* (*pistis* in Greek). The Roman soldier's oath was "not to flee the battlefield or to abandon their place in the battle-line" except to recover a weapon, save a friend, or strike an enemy (Erdkamp, *Roman Army*, 57; also Livy, 22.38.2 – 5; Christine Mohrmann, "Sacramentum dans les plus anciens texts Chrétiens," HTR 47 [1954]: 141 – 152; and Adolf Kolping, *Sacramentum Tertullianeum: Erster Teil* [Regensberg: Münster, 1948], 21 – 43, 77 – 95). Some scholars equate this military oath with the Christian oath to the Lord at baptism and others compare it to the oath of a philosophical student never to disobey God, as does Epictetus (Epictetus, *Diss*. 1.14.13 – 17; 3.24.95 – 99; see also Hilarius Edmonds, "Geistlicher Kriegsdienst: Der Topos der *militia spiritualis* in der antiken Philosophie," in *Militia Christi: die christliche Religion und der Soldatenstand in den ersten drei Jahrhunderten*, [ed. Adolf Harnack; Darmstadt: Wissenschaftl Buchgesellschoft, 1963]: 133 – 162; Edgar Krentz, "Paul,

## 3.5 Take up the whole armour of God (Eph 6.11 and 6.13) — 85

Nevertheless, while the plight and work of one wearing armour may be communal, Tertullian elsewhere takes a different tone when he focuses not on the image of the shield in Eph 6, but that of the sword. Using language from both Ephesians and Revelation, he writes that,

> the apostle John in the Apocalypse describes a sharp two-edged sword as proceeding from the mouth of God (Rev 1.16), exceeding sharp, and this has to be understood as the divine word, doubly sharp in the two testaments of the Law and the Gospel, sharp with wisdom, directed against the devil, arming us against the spiritual forces of wickedness (Eph 6.12: *adversus hostes spiritales nequitiae*) and all concupiscence, and cutting us off even from our dearest for the sake of God's name. But if you refuse to acknowledge John, you have Paul, a teacher (*magistrum*) you share with us, who girds our loins with truth and with the breastplate of righteousness, and shoes our feet with the preparation of the gospel of peace, not war, and bids us to take up the shield of the faith, that by it we may be able to quench all the fiery darts of the devil, and the helmet of salvation, and the sword of the spirit, which is, he says, the word of God (Eph 6.14–17: *praecingentem lumbos nostros veritate et lorica iustitiae et calciantem nos praeparationem euangelii pacis, non belli, adsumere iubentem scutum fidei, in quo possimus omnia diaboli ignita tela extinguere, et galeam salutaris et gladium spiritus, quod est, inquit, Dei sermo).*[114]

The image of the sword as the word of God connects excerpts from Revelation and Ephesians for Tertullian, even as he draws upon other parts of the armour described in Eph 6. However, the striking element of this connection between Ephesians and Revelation is not his focus on the aggressive image of the sword but rather the passive nature of how this sword and the whole armour of God are acquired. In Revelation, Tertullian is clear that the sword proceeding from Christ's mouth is what arms Christians against the spiritual forces of wickedness. In Ephesians, it is Paul who does the girding, shodding, and bidding to take up the helmet, shield, and sword. The passive way by which these items are acquired offers a contrast to his focus on the image of wrestling from this same Ephesian pericope and his exhortation not to flee but stand firm, both of which require action from the Christian on an individual and communal level. Here, Tertullian engages the spiritual forces of wickedness on another level where through Paul's teaching of truth, righteousness, the gospel of peace, and faith,

---

Games, and the Military," in *Paul in the Greco-Roman World: A Handbook* [ed. J. Paul Sampley; Harrisburg, Pa: Trinity Press International, 2003], 344–383; 348). Tertullian refers to *sacramentum* in many of his writings, especially when speaking about the armour of God and the oath of baptism, as do Cyprian and Arnobius after him. See Tertullian, *Mart*, 3; *Praescr*, 20; *Cor*, 2; *Idol*, 19; *Scorp*, 4; *Bapt*, 1.1 and *Marc*, 1.28.3; Cyprian, *Ep*, 10.1–2; 28.1–2; 54.1; Arnobius, *Disp.Nat*, 2.5; Origen, *Hom.Jos*, 4.1; 5.3; *Hom.Lev*, 1.4.6; *Hom.Judic*, 9.1.
**114** Tertullian, *Marc*, 3.14 (translation adapted from *SC* 399 and Evans).

the Christian is clothed with the armour of God and is able to withstand any assaults of spiritual forces.

Both Origen and Cyprian focus on the image of the armour of God within their writings, but add a different twist by equating this armour with Christ. In other words, putting on the armour of God is putting on Christ, language reminiscent of Romans 13.14.[115] Origen writes that,

> it is possible to say that the whole armour of God is Christ so that putting on the whole armour of God is identical to putting on the Lord Jesus Christ (Eph 6.11: πανοπλίαν εἶναι τοῦ Θεοῦ τὸν Χριστόν, ὥστε ταὐτὸν εἶναι τὸ ἐνδύσασθε τὴν πανοπλίαν τοῦ Θεοῦ τῷ ἐνδύσασθε τὸν Κύριον Ἰησοῦν Χριστόν; and Rom 13.14). For if the truth is a girdle and righteousness is a breastplate, and the Saviour is the truth and righteousness (Eph 6.14; John 14.6; 1 Cor 1.30: ζώνη μέν ἐστιν ἡ ἀλήθεια θώραξ δὲ ἡ δικαιοσύνη, ὁ σωτὴρ δέ ἐστιν ἡ ἀλήθεια καὶ ἡ δικαιοσύνη) then it is clear that the Saviour is the girdle and the breastplate. And parallel to these, he would be the preparation of the gospel of peace, and the shield of faith, and the helmet of salvation, and the sword of the Spirit, which is the word of God (Eph 6.15–16: αὐτὸς ἂν εἴη ἡ ἑτοιμασία τοῦ εὐαγγελίου τῆς εἰρήνης καὶ ὁ τῆς πίστεως θυρεὸς καὶ ἡ τοῦ σωτηρίου περικεφαλαία καὶ ἡ τοῦ πνεύματος μάχαιρα, ὅπερ ἐστὶ ῥῆμα Θεοῦ), the word which is living, effective, and sharper than any two-edged sword (Heb 4.12). What other kind of whole armour of God (πανοπλίαν Θεοῦ) can one conceive to be meant, which one who will resist the wiles of the devil (τὰς μεθοδείας τοῦ διαβόλου) must put on, than the virtue which is Christ? When one has put Christ on in all his aspects, he will be sufficient to stand against all the wiles of evil [...] he will not be wounded by the darts of injustice (Eph 6.16: τῶν βελῶν τῆς ἀδικίας).[116]

Even in the midst of persecution, Christ as the full armour of God "constantly stands by and never, at any time, deserts us or hastens to leave."[117] The armour of God that one puts on to withstand these evil forces is Christ himself, who has already faced persecution and death at the hands of the spiritual forces of wickedness. Therefore, when Origen writes that "the Apostle, just as a military leader gives an order to the soldiers of Christ saying, put on the armour of God, so that

---

115 See Cyprian, *Ep*, 55.8–9 (*ad Thibaris*) where he also expands the defensive armour described in Eph 6 to include protection for the eyes, ears, brow, and tongue. Ultimately for Cyprian, the action to which he exhorts Christians is not to fight but "to embrace the Lord himself, hereafter to receive from the Lord the reward of heavenly crowns" (*Ep*, 55.9). Moreover, as Origen (*Princ*, 3.2.5) and Cyprian (*Ep*, 60) are both clear, Christians fight not as individual soldiers, but with Christ himself and as a whole community together. See also Daniélou, *Latin Christianity*, 34, 50–3 and Ronald E. Heine, "Cyprian and Novatian," in *The Cambridge History of Early Christian Literature* (eds. Frances M. Young, Lewis Ayers, and Andrew Louth; Cambridge: Cambridge University Press, 2004), 152–160; 156.
116 Origen, *Comm.Eph*, 3 (translation adapted from Gregg and Heine).
117 Origen, *Hom.Jos*, 1.5 (*SC* 71). Also *Princ*, 3.2.1.

you may be able to stand firm against the shrewdness of the devil (Eph 6.11: *Induite vos arma Dei, ut possitis stare adversus astutias diaboli*),"[118] he is telling Christians to put on Christ. For Origen, Christ is not simply an example, nor is he one who, like Paul, girds a Christian for battle; Christ is now the very armour that they wear.[119] This exhortation, therefore to put on the armour of God in Eph 6 offers an image of putting on Christ that applies to all Christians. However, Origen specifically targets those who are not wise in their faith but who as "babes and sucklings in Christ" may not have a teacher to "defend themselves against the shrewdness of the devil and the attacks of spiritual forces of evil."[120] In this way, since the armour of God is something which clothes all Christians, they are clothed with Christ and thus, even the weakest are able to withstand attacks by the spiritual forces of wickedness because Christ himself will defend them.

For Eusebius, the image of the armour of God and the war-laden language of Eph 6 enables him to concentrate not on the challenges facing early Christians but on Christ's defeat of the spiritual forces of wickedness that has already taken place. Eusebius writes that in his death and resurrection, Christ has

> destroyed the thousands and ten thousands of enemies that had ruled for so long, some fighting on his right hand some on his left, rulers and powers, and those too who are called world-rulers of this darkness and spiritual powers of wickedness (Eph 6.12: κοσμοκράτορας τοῦ σκότους τούτου, τά τε πνευματικὰ τῆς πονηρίας); he thus proved, that they were quite powerless and ultimately with the word of his mouth, frightened away far from him the devil himself, their instigator of evil. He went through and trampled on every power opposed to him, he offered himself as a target for those who wished to attack and tempt him, and as none were able to resist him, he won salvation for humankind.[121]

---

**118** Origen, *Hom.Jos*, 15.1 (translation adapted from *SC* 71 and *FC* 105).
**119** While no scholar appears to suggest this, the language surrounding this use of Eph 6 by Origen gives the armour of God an apotropaic function with Christ serving to protect the Christian from evil forces of wickedness. Were prayer and baptism a kind of talisman for early Christians, equipping them to ward off the spiritual forces of wickedness? One Pauline passage that does appear to have been used in this way, but is also not mentioned by scholars, is Rom 8.31 ("if God is for us, who can be against us?"). According to the comprehensive survey of early Christian use of Pauline texts with which this project began, Rom 8.31 is only cited in early Christian writings seven times and only by Eusebius and Origen; however, it is cited at least 15 times in early Christian epigraphy, particularly on door lintels. Because the rest of this pericope (Rom 8.30–39) is used by early Christians to address suffering, persecution, and to exhort Christians to strength in the midst of suffering, is it possible that Christians were using 8.31 to protect their homes and themselves from harm and persecution? Or, is this excerpt a widely known apotropaic saying with which Paul is familiar and incorporates into his own writing?
**120** Origen, *Comm.Cant*, 2.3 (*PG* 13; *ACW* 26).
**121** Eusebius, *Dem.ev*, 9.7 (translation adapted from *GCS* 23 and Ferrar).

For Eusebius, the armour of God is not something acquired by the Christian nor is the armour Christ himself rather, Christ is the one who is soldier and warrior, taking the initiative against the spiritual forces of wickedness and winning salvation for all. With Christ as the actor against and victor over evil, the Christian assumes a more passive role, for Christ is the one who has already defeated the forces of wickedness. So Eusebius writes elsewhere that Christ himself was,

> extinguishing the menaces of the tyrants by his champion's valour, and manifestly and clearly showing, that neither fire, nor steel, nor even fierce wild beasts, were able to subdue his victorious servants, for he had girded them with the armour of righteousness, and strengthening them with victorious and invincible armour, he made them despise death (Eph 6.11).[122]

The focus is not on the actions that the Christian must take against the spiritual forces of wickedness but the end result: salvation for all by the death and resurrection of Christ. Eusebius uses the images both of the spiritual forces of wickedness and the armour of God, given by Christ the victor, to emphasise that even martyrs take on a passive role as neither Paul nor teachers but Christ himself girds early Christians with armour and ultimately gives them victory over death.

Early Christian use of the Ephesian image of the armour of God to exhort Christians to stand fast against the spiritual forces of evil offers a glimpse of the emerging Christology and ecclesiology at this time. For early Christian writers, the role of Christ in the lives of Christians as they encounter evil and suffering is essential. Whether the focus of these images is to follow the example of Christ, to put on Christ, or to withstand evil with the sure and certain knowledge that Christ has already defeated it and won salvation, in each description Christ is always superior to the spiritual forces of wickedness. Moreover, in the later writings of this period, the language of Christ as victor emerges alongside the understanding of an on-going battle on two levels, especially within the writings of Origen and Eusebius.

### Excursus: Some Challenges

By delving into how excerpts from Eph 6.10 – 17 were adopted by early Christians, one is confronted both by consistent themes of use and also by the various ways this Ephesian passage was adapted within an argument. This variety, as well as

---

122 Eusebius, *Mart.Pal*, 5 (The longer recension of this text, where this quote is found, is only extant in Syriac. The translation used is William Cureton, *Martyrs of Palestine: English & Syriac* [London: Williams and Norgate, 1861]).

## 3.5 Take up the whole armour of God (Eph 6.11 and 6.13)

the focus on images and phrases found in Eph 6, is especially significant because it presents a challenge to some of the modern interpretations and theological assumptions about Eph 6 and its use by early Christians. In particular, early Christian use of Eph 6 brings into question the assumption by some scholars that early Christians understood this pericope as an active and aggressive text. Walter Wink, for example, offers three significant volumes on the role of the "powers" in biblical texts,[123] with the aim of describing all New Testament powers "*in their most comprehensive sense*, understanding them to mean both heavenly *and* earthly, divine *and* human, good *and* evil powers."[124] In his survey of New Testament texts, Wink does not provide any examples of the powers used in this comprehensive sense but rather offers separate examples of different powers within different contexts.[125] Wink is concerned to show how powers are demythologised, especially within the letter to the Ephesians, so that they are not out in the cosmos but "actual physical, psychic, and social forces at work in us, in society, and in the universe"[126] and at the heart of institutions both corporate and religious.[127] He seeks to draw out the meaning of scriptural texts such as Eph 6 and their reference to powers, and through these texts, to challenge the powers of contemporary institutions. For Wink, the armour described in Eph 6 and, in particular, the exhortation to withstand the spiritual forces of wickedness is not a defensive stance but a command to engage with these powers and counter them.[128] However, the conclusions offered by this chapter's engagement with the use of the same Ephesian text by early Christian writers do not fully agree.

The panoply described in the Ephesian pericope is primarily comprised of defensive armour. The language of attack and actual combat against the spiritual forces of wickedness, therefore, enters into early Christian writings only when the focus is either on the one offensive weapon mentioned—the sword—or when early Christians combine this passage with words from 2 Cor 10 to counter and destroy the forces of evil. Moreover, the powers that early Christians equate with the forces of wickedness are not only the tangible powers of temptation and

---

[123] Walter Wink, *Naming the Powers* (1984), *Unmasking the Powers* (1986), and *Engaging the Powers* (1992).
[124] Walter Wink, *Naming the Powers: The Language of Power in the New Testament* (Philadelphia: Fortress Press, 1984), 39 (italics original).
[125] See Clinton E. Arnold, *Ephesians, Power and Magic: The Concept of Power in Ephesians in Light of its Historical Setting* (SNTSM 63; Cambridge: Cambridge University Press, 1989), 49 for a critique of Wink with examples from Col 2, Rom 8, and 1 Cor 15.
[126] Wink, *Naming the Powers*, 62.
[127] Walter Wink, *Engaging the Powers: Discernment and Resistance in a World of Domination* (Minneapolis: Fortress Press, 1992), 6.
[128] Wink, *Naming the Powers*, 165.

passions, but spiritual forces which are often very personal in their nature as sin, distraction and doubt, that threaten to mould and harm the soul.[129] In this way, early Christian use of Eph 6 expands Wink's conclusions about the nature of the battle to include a defensive and passive stance, which is the primary stance early Christians are exhorted to take against the spiritual forces of wickedness.

Another scholar presenting an aggressive and confrontational understanding of the reception of Eph 6 is Thomas Neufeld. Neufeld understands Eph 6 as the end point of a trajectory of texts about the divine warrior beginning with Isa 59, and he reads Eph 6 as a forceful exposition of power. He writes that within Eph 6 "the image of the warrior is intentionally painted in aggressive and confrontative colours"[130] and he identifies this hostility not only as people and institutions as does Wink, but as the spiritual powers in heavenly places with which Christians must hostilely engage.[131] Neufeld creates a trajectory of the divine warrior from Isaiah to Ephesians, with this warrior embodying a peaceful overtone at the beginning and becoming more hostile at the end.[132] This level of aggression and hostility, however, is not supported by early Christians in their use of Eph 6 and their focus on the individual images offered in the text in order to exhort Christians to stand firm rather than to fight and conquer. Christ is the one, in later ante-Nicene texts, who fights the battle while Christians

---

[129] Against Wink, *Naming the Powers*, 104–105.

[130] Neufeld, *Armour of God*, 155.

[131] Other scholars find parallels between Eph 6 and the battle imagery in the War Scroll from Qumran. While this might be important background for understanding the text, the weapons and battle in 1QM are explicitly not spiritual but physical and thus it is difficult to see how this could be a parallel to or background for the spiritual nature of the language in Eph 6, which is clear that the battle is not "against blood and flesh (Eph 6.12)." See Géza Vermès, *An Introduction to the Complete Dead Sea Scrolls* (London: SCM, 1999), 40; Géza Vermès, *The Complete Dead Sea Scrolls in English* (Rev. ed.; London: Penguin Books, 2004), 163; Lincoln, *Paradise*, 165; and Lincoln, *Ephesians*, 437–438, who each claim some parallels or background influence in 1QM. This is against Arnold, *Ephesians, Power and Magic*, 109–110; Von N. Kehl, "Erniedrigung und Erhöhung in Qumran und Kolossä," *ZKT* 91 (1969): 380–389; and Brannon, "The Heavenlies," 207–208.

[132] Neufeld, *Armour of God*, 155–156. This proposed trajectory supports the conclusions of Harnack that the use of Eph 6 and the language of battle shifted from images of sin and desire to images of battles with demons to language of physical holy war. However, for Harnack this shift happened not within the texts themselves but within their reception up to the 5th century (Harnack, *Militia Christi*, 62–63). This understanding pushes back against the idea of a trajectory between texts and Neufeld's suggestion of an influence by Isa 11, 52, and 59 on Eph 6. For more on this influence, see Thorsten Moritz, *A Profound Mystery: The Use of the Old Testament in Ephesians* (Leiden: Brill, 1966), 178–212; Peter Thomas O'Brien, *The Letter to the Ephesians*, (PNTC; Grand Rapids, Mich: Eerdmans, 1999), 456–482; Arnold, *Ephesians, Power and Magic*, 108–109.

take the more passive role of standing firm. These texts do not exhort the Christian to physical battle even when steeped in military language but rather exhort the Christian to stand firm and not to flee from their faith in the face of danger, both spiritual and physical. These conclusions challenge the sweeping proposals of Wink and Neufeld concerning Eph 6 since early Christian writers do not necessarily share their interpretation of this text and understanding of the powers even as they applied the same images from Eph 6 to their own community and context.[133]

The profile of the use of Eph 6.10–17 by early Christian writers presented in this chapter also challenges assumptions by some scholars concerning the emerging doctrine of atonement. First made popular by Gustav Aulén, these assumptions posit that early Christians, when writing about suffering and the saving act of Christ, focused primarily on the cross and in particular on Col 2 and the realised eschatology of a battle already won.[134] Aulén holds that both Paul and early Christian writers have "the same dualistic outlook, the same idea of conflict and triumph; of powers of evil under which mankind is in bondage; of the victory over them won by Christ come down from heaven—that is, by God Himself come to save."[135] For Aulén, Col 2.15 is the central New Testament text exemplifying the Christus Victor understanding of atonement, which he identifies as the classic view that was dominant amongst early Christian writers.[136] The essential aspect of this "classical" approach is "the idea of the Atonement as a divine conflict and victory; Christ—Christus Victor—fights against and triumphs over the evil powers of the world, the 'tyrants' under which mankind is in bondage and suffering, and in Him God reconciles the world to himself."[137]

While this idea of Christ as victor over death is important for an early Christian understanding of salvation, it is only one image among many as this chap-

---

133 This critique is strengthened by early Christian use of other texts that use both the phrase ἐν τοῖς ἐπουρανίοις and τὰ στοιχεῖα τοῦ κόσμου in early Christian writings (Eph 3.10; 2.6 and Col 2.8). See Clement of Alexandria, *Strom*, 4.7; 7.3; Tertullian, *Marc*, 5.18; Origen, *Cels*, 7.46; 5.44; *Princ*, 3.2.4–6; Methodius, *Symp*, 3.6; *Res*, 3.2.1–2. This critique only compares the early reception of Eph 6 with the later reception in Wink and Neufeld and does not claim to have discovered the original meaning of this Ephesian passage.
134 See Lincoln, *Paradise*, 166–170. See also Gustaf Aulén, *Christus Victor: An Historical Study of the Three Main Types of the Idea of the Atonement* (trans. A.G. Hebert; London: SPCK, 1931), 82.
135 Aulén, *Christus Victor*, 82.
136 Aulén, *Christus Victor*, 70.
137 Aulén, *Christus Victor*, 4.

ter's examination of Eph 6—and, later in this study, Col 1—demonstrates.[138] The comprehensive survey of early Christian texts with which this project began highlights a further challenge to Aulén's conclusion and his focus on early Christian use of Col 2.15 to describe his classical view of the atonement. Compared with Eph 6, Col 2.15 is scarcely used by early Christians, occurring only six times outside the works of Origen.[139] Moreover, one of the differences between these texts—Col 2 and Eph 6—is their eschatological emphasis.[140] Van Kooten summarises these differences writing that, in Ephesians "as opposed to Col 2.8–10 and 2.15 where Jesus Christ already led the principalities and powers in triumph, the decisive triumph over the physical cosmos is not yet and the war continues."[141] In this way, that Eph 6 is used exponentially more in early Christian writings than Col 2 serves as a challenge to our understanding of the Christology, ecclesiology, and even eschatology of early Christians compared with assumptions today about the dominance within early Christian theology of Christus Victor.

Early Christian writers in their use of Eph 6 do not confine themselves to one way of understanding Christ's actions, especially when standing against the powers of evil. So Christ is described as the example to imitate, as the one whom the Christian embodies, and even, with Aulén, as the one who claims ultimate victory. The predominant emphasis in early Christian use of the images found in Eph 6 is an exhortation for the Christian to be in Christ, putting on the armour of God, and standing firm in faith. Christ's saving act and Christ's standing firm with and within the Christian are the result of God's gracious activity in Christ and are appropriated through faith.

---

**138** Against Aulén, for example, early Christian use of Col 1 and its description of Jesus Christ as first-born from the dead was not primarily to emphasise Christ's triumph over evil on the cross but, as Irenaeus is clear, to emphasise the doctrine of recapitulation so that Christ takes on all stages of life, and even death, in order to redeem and save it (Irenaeus, *Haer*, 2.22.4). Nevertheless, Blackwell briefly connects Aulén's understanding of Christus Victor with Irenaeus' understanding of recapitulation through the Adam-Christ typology found in Rom 5 and 1 Cor 15. See Blackwell, "Paul and Irenaeus," 201.
**139** Colossians 2.15 may be found once each in Anon, *Prologue Monarchiani*; *M.Apollon*; Hippolytus, *Ben.Is.Jac*,1; *Pasch*, 55.1; Melito, *Pass;* Novatian, *Trin*, (21.9), as well as 43 times in the writings of Origen. Interestingly, although Aulén dedicates a chapter to the writings of Irenaeus and atonement, Col 2.15 does not appear to have been directly cited by Irenaeus in his works.
**140** See Brannon, "The Heavenlies," 207; Lincoln, "Re-Examination," 475–482.
**141** van Kooten, *Cosmic Christology*, 192.

## 3.6 Conclusions

The images of spiritual forces of wickedness, the fiery darts of the evil one, wrestling, and the armour of God within Eph 6.10 – 17 shape early Christians and their writings. Through the medium of exhorting Christians to stand firm against spiritual attack and struggle, these images represent the challenges of temptation, passions, doubt, and heretical teachings, as well as the struggles of those especially vulnerable to attack in the liminal times of persecution and baptism. The images of spiritual forces of wickedness and of fiery darts of the evil one are each used to describe the threats that Christians inevitably face and from which they must defend themselves. The images of wrestling and of the armour of God each offer a way for Christians to counter these threatening forces of evil, and are used by early Christian writers as they encourage and exhort others to stand firm with Christ against evil with ethical injunctions to action, such as prayer, baptism, scriptural study, and increased faith and wisdom. Thus, the images of Eph 6 serve to form both the understanding of the Christian as one who is embattled, as well as the emerging understanding of baptism and persecution as times of heightened vulnerability and attack, spiritually and, in the case of martyrdom, physically.

The language of battle and armour found in Eph 6 led early Christians to draw on texts with similar images such as Revelation, 2 Corinthians, Hebrews, and Romans, and to connect these texts in their works to support their arguments and exhortations. As the images from Eph 6.10 – 17 are adapted, expanded, and applied within a wide range of early Christian writings, each of these images is ensconced by a dualistic understanding of the world which plays out on at least three levels. The first is the very nature and context of battle into which the images from Eph 6 fall. In a highly militarised culture, the images of forces of wickedness, darts of the evil one, wrestling, and armour of God all suggest a dichotomy between sides, one fighting against the other. The second is the realisation that the forces encountered by early Christians take not only two sides, but two forms: encounters with flesh and blood and encounters with spiritual forces of wickedness and evil. Within this embattled context, Christians pick out two images from Eph 6 to describe how the Christian is to stand firm against each form of these forces: by wrestling and by putting on the armour of God. These images and actions offer two different approaches in terms of physicality and the nature of the encounter. A wrestling contest is a physical encounter requiring physical preparation, and even though early Christians are clear that they mean spiritual wrestling with a spiritual opponent, the image is a physical one. Moreover, wrestling is an individual encounter with another and thus the image focuses on the endeavour of the individual Christian in his or her plight against the forces of evil. In contrast, putting on the armour of God and especially the panoply described in Eph 6 suggests taking a defensive stance with defensive armour in a combative setting. The images of the panoply, connected with faith, righteousness, truth, and peace, point to a realm beyond the physical. Moreover, the endeavour of a soldier at this time would have been a communal endeavour, so that Christians would have to work together in formation in order for the armour to be fully effective.

Finally, the images of wrestling and armour include both a passive and an active element in early Christian interpretation, further emphasising the dichotomy found throughout this text. Wrestling, as described by Origen, is actively against the forces of wickedness but also passively with Christ as he stands with and supports the Christian in the contest. Similarly, the armour of God is taken up in order actively to stand firm against the forces of wickedness and to quench the fiery darts of evil while at the same time, Christ is the armour of God put on by the Christian and ultimately he has won the battle.

However, even with a strong Christological element, one of the primary foci of early Christian use of excerpts from Eph 6.10–17 is ethical as early Christians strongly emphasise not what Christ has done but what a Christian must do to progress in wisdom and faith. The ethical focus on what Christians can do to acquire the armour of God and remain steadfast in the face of evil leads early Christian writers to embrace a tone of encouragement with those to whom they write. It is no surprise, therefore, that Eph 6 is most frequently found in exhortative writings such as homilies, commentaries, and instructive treatises since the nature of these texts allows early Christians to engage with the ethical and practical implications of spiritual attack in the lives of Christians. Because these writers assume that terms such as prayer, knowledge, wisdom, and spiritual practices such as fasting need little explanation, one can assume as well that many of these texts were addressed to those already attempting to live a life of Christian belief and practice.

In terms of formation, the ethical injunctions offered by early Christians using the images of Eph 6 have an obvious formational element as the role of the teacher is upheld and supported in a number of early Christian works. As some of these texts emphasise, teachers play an active and crucial role in enabling Christians to stand firm in their encounter with the forces of wickedness. Clement and Origen, for example, advocated that the more advanced a Christian was in faith and in wisdom, the more fierce the attacks would be, not by powers of flesh and blood but by powers in the heavenly places.[142] As Christians prog-

---

[142] Origen, *Princ*, 3.2.3–4; Clement of Alexandria, *Prot,* 11.116.

ress in their faith and wisdom, therefore, they not only encounter greater and more demanding attacks, but they are also equipped to assist and form those who are weak and vulnerable in the battle.[143] This movement emphasises different levels of combat and encounter with spiritual forces of wickedness and an emerging ecclesiology within early Christian writings. Ephesians 6 serves as a peg upon which early Christians can hang exhortations not only to individual Christians but also to the Christian community and those who teach within it. The Christian teacher described alongside the images of Eph 6, therefore, is the one who follows the example of Christ to offer healing and deeper knowledge of Scripture, and who girds the Christian with the armour of God.

The use of these Ephesian images in texts of exhortation and teaching further highlights the formative role that excerpts from Eph 6 have in early Christian writings. This formative aspect is particularly crucial in times of transition and of increased vulnerability for Christians, especially when facing persecution and preparing for baptism. In the chapter on 1 Cor 2, images of the Pauline text were used to identify Christians as those imbued with wisdom who are encouraged and exhorted to progress from one level of wisdom to another in their journey of faith. With Eph 6, early Christians are now exhorted in ways that such wisdom may be achieved and maintained, through prayer, faith, standing firm in the midst of temptation and fear, and putting on the armour of God. For early Christians, the spiritual forces of wickedness in the heavenly places were both within and without the person, not only as tangible powers of temptation and passions but also as superhuman forces that challenged the Christian in faith and prayer and threatened to lead them astray and away from God.

Attacks by the spiritual forces of wickedness and the fiery darts of the evil one in a variety of forms are inevitable in the Christian life. Early Christians mix the images of Eph 6 and in the process emphasise the ecclesiological conclusion that the Christian life is messy and divided. The military images in Eph 6, however, ultimately help Christians to see how they might keep faith and stand firm, no matter how powerful and strong the opposition, even when they need the help of armour, teachers, one another, and Christ himself as they progress toward greater wisdom and ultimately salvation in God. The different levels of wisdom described by early Christian use of 1 Cor 2 is especially bolstered by the language of war and battle in Eph 6, which doesn't just describe the movement from one level to another but the movement from one side to the other. The time of vulnerability in the middle of these two sides, therefore, is cru-

---

**143** See also Kovacs, "Servant of Christ," 159–160; Osborn, "Bible and Christian Morality," 115.

cial and early Christians must hold fast to the wisdom and love of God in these liminal moments in order to stand firm and claim the side against the forces, powers, and principalities of evil and wickedness. Thus, an understanding of what it means to be Christian expands through early Christian use of Eph 6 to include not only an understanding of one instilled with wisdom, but also one embattled and standing firm with Christ against forces of wickedness and evil in the many forms that they take.

# Chapter Four:
# 1 Corinthians 15.50–58: Resolve me of all ambiguities[1]

> *Flesh and blood cannot inherit the kingdom of God*
> (1 Cor 15.50)

## 4.1 Early Christian Writers and 1 Corinthians 15

As observed in the second chapter, early Christians held Paul's first letter to the Corinthians in high esteem, referring to this letter more than any of the others attributed to Paul. While excerpts from 1 Cor 2 constitute the most cited pericope from this epistle, a second frequently used passage falls within the confines of the same letter: 1 Cor 15.50–58. Parts of this pericope are referred to at least 350 times by more than 35 pre-Nicene authors.[2] In particular, early Christians focus on the dichotomous images and phrases within this passage as well as the ambiguous language used by Paul to describe resurrection. Thus, they adopt phrases such as perishable and imperishable, mortal and immortal, and flesh and blood and the kingdom of God, and use these phrases most frequently in the context of arguments about resurrection and its form.

In the penultimate chapter of this letter, Paul offers "a concise summary" of his gospel (15.1–11) "followed by the most detailed treatment in the New Testament of the general resurrection at the end of time."[3] Here, Paul addresses a specific problem in the Corinthian community, namely that some Christians claim "there is no resurrection of the dead" (15.12). Nevertheless, this part of the letter is not addressed to dissenters, but to the whole community as Paul tries to reconcile the Corinthians with one another. The theme of resurrection, both of Christ and of all the dead, and the theme of Christ's defeat of the opposing powers are both emphasised with the result that ultimately "God may be all in all" (15.28).[4] Within this context, Paul attempts to explain the continuity and discon-

---

[1] Christopher Marlowe, *The Tragical History of Dr Faustus*, Act 1, Scene 1, Line 79.
[2] See Appendix C for details of these references.
[3] Judith Kovacs, ed. *1 Corinthians: Interpreted by Early Christian Commentators*, (ECCS; Grand Rapids, Mich: Eerdmans, 2005), 242. See also Judith Kovacs, "1 Corinthians," in *The Oxford Handbook of the Reception History of the Bible* (eds. Michael Lieb, Emma Mason, and Jonathan Roberts; Oxford: Oxford University Press, 2011), 136–148; 146.
[4] Fee, *Corinthians*, 741.

tinuity between the present body and the resurrection body, offering a "paradoxical description of the resurrection body as a 'spiritual body'" (15.44).[5] Beginning with the phrase in 15.50 that "flesh and blood cannot inherit the kingdom of God," this text and the images within it figure frequently in early Christian debates about Christology and about what happens to the body after death.

Unlike the other passages I engage in this study, scholars generally agree that 1 Cor 15 is authentic to Paul.[6] Instead of concentrating on authorship, therefore, the focus of scholarship on this passage tends to emphasise theories about the cause of division in the Corinthian community and the identity of Paul's opponents who say there is no resurrection of the dead (15.12).[7] Asher suggests that within modern scholarship, as many as "seven distinct positions that attempt to identify Paul's opponents and their accompanying doctrines" exist.[8] What this conclusion highlights, however, is not simply the existence of many theories of identity but that Paul's language about his possible opponents, the divisions potentially caused, and the exact nature of resurrection is vague and ambiguous. Given the ambiguities of Paul's language, interpreters from the earliest Christians to modern scholars hold conflicting positions on these issues, especially resurrection.[9] As Rowan Greer makes clear, "competing theological views stood at

---

[5] Kovacs, *1 Corinthians*, 243. See also Jeffrey R. Asher, *Polarity and Change in 1 Corinthians 15: A study of metaphysics, rhetoric, and resurrection* (HUT 42; Tübingen: Mohr [Siebeck], 2000), 47–58.

[6] Even though scholarly consensus holds that 1 Cor 15 is a Pauline composition, the placement of this chapter is debated. Schmithals, for example, posits that 1 Cor 15 did not fall between chapters 14 and 16 but was in a different Pauline letter to the Corinthian community which he (Schmithals) calls "Letter A" (Walter Schmithals, *Gnosticism in Corinth: An Investigation of the Letters to the Corinthians* [Nashville: Abingdon Press, 1971], 91–92).

[7] Asher, *Polarity and Change*, 31n1. See also Margaret M. Mitchell, *Paul and the Rhetoric of Reconciliation: An Exegetical Investigation of the Language of Composition of 1 Corinthians* (HUT 28; Tübingen: Mohr [Siebeck], 1991), 175–177.

[8] Asher, *Polarity and Change*, 32. See 32–48 for descriptions of these seven positions.

[9] See Christopher M. Tuckett, "The Corinthians Who Say 'There is No Resurrection of the Dead' (1 Cor 15,12)," in *The Corinthian Correspondence* (ed. R. Bieringer; Leuven: Leuven University Press, 1996), 251–261; 258; Martinus C. de Boer, *The Defeat of Death: Apocalyptic Eschatology in 1 Corinthians 15 and Romans 5* (JSNTSup 22; Sheffield: JSOT Press, 1988), 93–140; Lincoln, *Paradise*, 64–67; Thistleton, *1 Corinthians*, 1174–1176; Richard B. Hays, *First Corinthians* (IBC; Louisville, Ky: John Knox Press, 1997), 252; Fitzmyer, *First Corinthians*, 539–540; Dale B. Martin, *The Corinthian Body* (New Haven: Yale University Press, 1995), 106; Roy A. Harrisville, *1 Corinthians* (ACNT; Minneapolis: Augsburg, 1987), 247; Conzelmann, *1 Corinthians*, 252; C. F. D. Moule, "St Paul and Dualism: The Pauline Conception of Resurrection," *NTS* 12, no. 2 (1966): 106–123.

the heart of the ancient church's attempts to explain its sacred writings"[10] and thus, "theological disputes in the early church were largely arguments about how rightly to describe" and interpret Scripture.[11]

Because early Christians primarily adopt the images and phrases from 1 Cor 15.50–58 to talk about resurrection, this chapter is divided not by the use of specific images, phrases, or themes within the text but chronologically by author.[12] As in previous chapters, while the actual number of passages selected for review may not be exhaustive, the passages selected are representative of the ways early Christian writers engage 1 Cor 15.50–58.[13] What became increasingly clear when compiling the survey of Pauline texts is that early Christian writings which use this Corinthian pericope overwhelmingly focus on 1 Cor 15.50. The separation in this verse between flesh and blood and the kingdom of God causes early Christians much trouble as they struggle to reconcile the words of this passage with their arguments for and against the resurrection of the flesh.[14]

The focus on 1 Cor 15 in early Christian writings about resurrection takes place within a culture and time in which understandings of the soul, body, flesh, and spirit took different forms, including Graeco-Roman philosophical, Jewish, and Valentinian and "gnostic" views. Thus, when early Christians use the phrase flesh and blood from 1 Cor 15.50, the flesh and blood to which they refer has at least four meanings: the elements that make up the

---

[10] Rowan A. Greer, "Applying the Framework," in *Early Biblical Interpretation* (eds. James L. Kugel and Rowan A. Greer; *LEC*; Philadelphia: The Westminster Press, 1986), 177–199; 185.
[11] Greer, "Applying," 195.
[12] Athenagoras cites Paul only once, using 1 Cor 15.53 in *Res* 18. This reference is not included in what follows as this chapter opted for authors who gave a fuller context to their use of 1 Cor 15. However, Athenagoras' use of 1 Cor 15 serves as a marker within some early Christian debates on resurrection, and his remarks are often cited alongside those of Irenaeus and Tertullian. For a full discussion of Athenagoras' understanding of resurrection in these terms, see Claudia Setzer, *Resurrection of the Body in Early Judaism and Early Christianity: Doctrine, Community, and Self-Definition* (Boston: Brill Academic Publishers, 2004), 86–98.
[13] Passages with similar content are cited in the notes to indicate the breadth of the data consulted. For example, references to this passage may be found in Clement of Alexandria, *Strom*, 2.20; 3.17; Novatian, *Trin*, 10; and Eusebius, *Dem.ev*, 4.12.
[14] Early Christians do use other Pauline texts about resurrection in their writings, but not as frequently as 1 Cor 15.50–58. For example, 1 Thess 5.1–10 occurs 70 times; 1 Thess 4.13–18 occurs 131 times; Col 2.9–15 may be found just over 150 times; Col 3.1–4 may be found more than 90 times; Rom 6.4–11 occurs just over 200 times; and 2 Cor 5.1–5 approximately 110 times. Moreover, these references are found in texts ranging from Valentinian works to Irenaeus, Tertullian to Origen, and Clement of Alexandria to Eusebius.

human body,[15] Christ's human body and nature,[16] Christ's bodily presence in the elements of the Eucharist,[17] and the words and deeds associated with the body and especially the flesh.[18] Early Christians embrace the range of these meanings as they use excerpts from 15.50–58 and try to grasp the full substance and meaning of the phrases within this text to support their own writings. Early use of 1 Cor 15, as this chapter will show, is thus not as much about exegetical method "but the theological function of interpretation."[19] The use of phrases and images from 1 Cor 15.50–58, therefore, enables early Christians to engage with the theology of resurrection, while at the same time grappling with the ambiguous nature of scriptural interpretation and the theological issues that such interpretation raises.

Resurrection was a hot topic in the first few centuries of Christianity, so much so that debates about resurrection "stood at the centre of the storm in the second century" and "at no time in the long history of Christianity has the resurrection of the dead been so much debated as during that period."[20] Nevertheless, in a survey of the idea of bodily resurrection in the ancient world, Wright finds little trace of any concept of the afterlife apart from an immortal but disembodied soul.[21] Stroumsa concludes that resurrection was "a doctrine slower to

---

**15** See, for example, Irenaeus, *Haer*, 5.1.4; Tertullian, *Res*, 49; Origen, *Princ*, 2.10.2–3 and *Fr.Ps*, 1.5; Peter of Alexandria, *Res* (Syriac), 4.4.
**16** See Irenaeus, *Haer*, 5.13.1; 5.14.1–2; Tertullian, *Res*, 49; Pamphilus, *Apol*, 128.
**17** See *Evan.Phil*, 56.26–57.21; Irenaeus, *Haer*, 5.2.2–3.2.
**18** See Irenaeus, *Haer*, 5.13.3–5; 5.9.4; 5.14.4; Tertullian, *Res*, 49.11; and *Marc*, 5.14.
**19** Greer, "Applying," 184.
**20** W.C. van Unnik, "The Newly Discovered Gnostic Epistle to Rheginos on the Resurrection, I and II," *JEH* 15, no. 2 (1964): 153–167; 154–156. See also, James Carleton Paget, "Marcion and the Resurrection: Some Thoughts on a Recent Book," *JSNT* 35, no. 1 (2012): 74–102; 97; Outi Lehtipuu, "'Flesh and Blood Cannot Inherit the Kingdom of God:' The Transformation of the Flesh in the Early Christian Debates Concerning Resurrection," in *Metamorphoses: Resurrection, Body and Transformative Practices in Early Christianity* (eds. Turid Karlsen Seim and Jorunn Økland; Berlin: Walter de Gruyter, 2009), 147–168; 147–148; Gunnar af. Hallström, *Carnis resurrectio: The Interpretation of a Credal Formula* (CHL 86; Helsinki: Societas Scientiarum Fennica, 1988), 9–11; Setzer, *Resurrection of the Body*, 74–75.
**21** N. T. Wright, "Jesus' Resurrection and Christian Origins," *Greg* 83, no. 4 (2002): 615–635; Plato, "Phaedrus," 64CE, 64C; Cicero, *De Re publica*, 6.24.26; Craig S. Keener, *1–2 Corinthians* (NCBC; Cambridge: Cambridge University Press, 2005), 122; Seneca, *Dial*, 12.11.6; Heraclitus, *Ep*, 9; Wis 9.15–16. For a survey of texts which discuss corporeal resurrection, see Claudia Setzer, "Resurrection of the Body in Early Judaism and Christianity," in *The Human Body in Death and Resurrection* (eds. Tobias Nicklas, et al.; Berlin: Walter de Gruyter, 2009); 1–12; 2–5; Setzer, *Resurrection of the Body*, 6–20; George W.E. Nickelsburg, *Resurrection, Immortality, and Eternal Life in Intertestamental Judaism and Early Christianity* (2nd ed; HTS 56; Cambridge,

emerge fully in Jewish thought but already well established in the first Christian century."[22] Therefore, resurrection was "one point on the spectrum of Jewish beliefs about life after death,"[23] and Jewish views about resurrection varied. While some texts suggest an individual, bodily resurrection, others focus on the restoration of Israel. Wisdom 3.7–8, for example, suggests a bodily resurrection of the righteous whose souls are in the hand of God, while Philo holds a more Platonic view of "disembodied bliss for the immortal soul."[24] Some, such as the Sadducees, denied any possibility of resurrection while others, such as the Pharisees, held some form of belief in resurrection after death.[25] Wright concludes his survey with the assertion that early Christian views of resurrection "clearly belonged within the Jewish spectrum, not the pagan one, but were also clearly different."[26] The emerging doctrine of resurrection in Christian thought was different from other views of resurrection at this time not only because of its focus on Christ's resurrection but also because of the Christian anthropology that emerges from a belief in bodily resurrection. Described as "Christianity's greatest contribution to philosophy,"[27] the early Christian concept of the self, of humankind made in the

---

Mass: Harvard University Press, 2006); and Alan F. Segal, *Life after Death: A History of the Afterlife in the Religions of the West* (New York: Doubleday, 2004).

**22** Stroumsa, "*Caro salutis cardo*," 37. See also Oscar Cullman, *Immortalité de l'âme ou Résurrection des morts?* (Paris: Delachaux & Niestlé 1956). The concept of resurrection of the dead emerges in Jewish thought only in the time immediately before the advent of Christianity, with Dan 12.2 often cited as the one pre-Christian mention of it ("Many of those who sleep in the dust of the earth shall awake, some to everlasting life, and some to shame and everlasting contempt" [Dan 12.2]). Some also find mention of resurrection in Isa 25.8; 26.19; Ps 49.15; Os 6.1–3; 13.14; and Ezech 37.1–14, and eschatological resurrection in *2Macc* 7.14; *1Enoch* 51.1; 91.10–11; 103.4; and *T.Benj*, 19.8–10 (Wright, "Jesus' Resurrection," see 616–621). Fitzmyer argues, however, that most of these are figurative references to the restoration of Israel at a future time (see Fitzmyer, *First Corinthians*, 560–561). Setzer counters this, writing that "metaphors only work if they have something to do with the way people think and live. It makes no sense to employ such metaphors, even poetically, for a people with no sense of an afterlife" (Setzer, "Resurrection of the Body," 3). Also, Keener, *1–2 Corinthians*, 122.

**23** Wright, "Jesus' Resurrection," 619.

**24** Wright, "Jesus' Resurrection," 619.

**25** See Mark 12.18; Matt 22.23; Luke 20.27; Acts 4.1–2; 23.6–8; Josephus, *B.J*, 2.8.14 and *A.J*, 18.1.3; Methodius, *Res*, 1.12. Resurrection has even been described as an incentive to martyrdom, as found in Maccabees (See *2Macc* 7; see also *M.Poln*, 14.2; *M.Paul*, 4; *M.Pion*, 21.4).

**26** Wright, "Jesus' Resurrection," 621. See also Stroumsa, "*Caro salutis cardo*," 36.

**27** G. Florowsky, "Eschatology in the Patristic Age: An Introduction," in *Studia Patristica I: Texte und Untersuchungen zur Geschichte der Altchristlichen Literatur* (vol 2; Berlin: Akademie, 1957), 235–250; 249. Quote from Stroumsa, "*Caro salutis cardo*," 36.

image of God, and of identity even after death which included the body and the soul were all radical concepts in the first and second centuries.²⁸

## 4.2 The Valentinians and their Influence²⁹

Anonymous pre-Nicene Christian texts, especially those associated with the Valentinians, rely on excerpts from 1 Cor 15.50–58 in the course of their arguments and offer an example of how this passage was used by some of the earliest Christian writers. Within the Nag Hammadi codices, excerpts from 1 Cor 15.50–58 are cited at least ten times in eight different works,³⁰ and feature in arguments that separate the flesh from immortality, advocate the triumph of spirit over flesh, and contend that immortality and resurrection can be realised in the present. According to White, "some of the language of the Pauline corpus was fertile ground for the Valentinians," and this is especially true of 1 Cor 15.³¹ In fact, according to Clement's Valentinian author Theodotus, Paul was the "Apostle of the resurrection (ὁ Παῦλος ἀναστάσεως Ἀπόστολος)."³² At stake in these texts is an argument for realised eschatology, the "fundamental issue of what it means to be a human being,"³³ and the role of the flesh in the composition of the body, especially in its resurrected state. Each of these arguments is prompted by the words of 1 Cor 15. It is important to note that the Valentinians and others who many scholars label

---

**28** Stroumsa, "*Caro salutis cardo*," 35–37.
**29** In his *Dialogue with Trypho*, Justin Martyr writes that "I and others who are straight thinking Christians on all things, understand that there will be a resurrection of the flesh (Justin Martyr, *Dial*, 80.5 (Goodspeed): σαρκὸς ἀνάστασιν)." This is the earliest mention in an extant Christian writing of the resurrection of the flesh. For Justin, this belief creates a boundary, dividing real Christians who believe in the resurrection from all others. While he does not specifically mention 1 Cor 15 in this context, he was familiar with the epistle and Setzer posits that the boundaries he creates with resurrection belief skirts "the problems caused by Paul's ambiguity in 1 Cor 15 about the raising of spiritual bodies" and about flesh and blood (Setzer, "Resurrection of the Body," 5). Thus, while Justin does not directly cite 1 Cor 15.50, part of his understanding of resurrection could have been influenced by it.
**30** *The Prayer of Paul; The Apocryphon of James; The Gospel of Truth; The Treatise on the Resurrection; The Gospel of Philip; The (Second) Apocalypse of James; The Teachings of Silvanus; Trimorphic Protennoia*. See also the list in Pheme Perkins, "Gnosticism and the Christian Bible" in *The Canon Debate* (eds. Lee Martin McDonald and James A. Sanders; Peabody, Mass: Hendrickson, 2002), 355–371; 368–369.
**31** White, *Remembering Paul*, 37.
**32** Clement of Alexandria, *Exc.Theod*, 23 (SC 23).
**33** Karen L. King, *What is Gnosticism?* (Cambridge, Mass: Belknap Press of Harvard University Press, 2003), 213.

as heretical, were no less Christian than those who opposed them, especially in the first few centuries of Christianity when "the situation is still fluid and the issues not yet always clear-cut."[34] Nevertheless, a notion of *haeresis* clearly existed as early as the New Testament (for example, 1 Cor 11.19 and 2 Pet 2.1), and even though the post-Nicene content of orthodoxy had not yet been formulated, there was still a concept of what constituted heresy.[35] The question, however, was who had the authority to pronounce and determine what counted as such. Irenaeus, for example, described his opponents as those who "believe the same things and have the same doctrine, yet we call them heretics (*haereticos*)."[36] So also Tertullian writes of his interpretation of Scripture, "I say that Marcion's is adulterated. Marcion says the same of mine."[37] As Behr makes clear, categories such as orthodoxy and heresy "are applicable only (if at all) retrospectively, and should not influence unbiased research into the earlier periods during which the boundary lines are still being erected."[38]

The *Treatise on the Resurrection* is a second century Nag Hammadi text from the Codex Jung and is thought to be a "didactic and apologetic letter by an unnamed master to one of his pupils, a certain Rheginos."[39] In a section outlining a Christological foundation for resurrection, using language similar to that found in 1 Cor 15.54, the author writes that,

> the Saviour swallowed up death (1 Cor 15.54) [...] having swallowed the visible by the invisible, and he gave us the way of our immortality. When the perishable puts on the imperishable, and the mortal puts on immortality, then shall come to pass the saying that is written, death is swallowed up in victory (1 Cor 15.54) so that what is mortal may be swallowed up by life. He will swallow up death forever [...] The saying is sure, if we have died with him, we shall also live with him; if we endure, we shall also reign with him (2 Tim 2.11–12a); now if we are manifest in this world wearing him (Rom 13.14; Col 3.10), this is the spiritual resurrection which swallows up the psychic in the same way as the fleshly. It is sown a physical body, it is raised a spiritual body (1 Cor 15.44). If there is a physical body, there is also a

---

**34** Robert McL. Wilson, *The Gospel of Philip* (London: Mowbray, 1962), 4. See also Robert L. Wilken, "Diversity and Unity in Early Christianity," *SCe* 1 (1981): 101–110; 103–104.
**35** With gratitude to Mark Edwards and Judith Kovacs for their clarifying suggestions on proto-orthodoxy and heresy.
**36** Irenaeus, *Haer*, 3.15.1 (*SC* 211).
**37** Tertullian, *Marc*, 4.4.1 (*SC* 456).
**38** Behr, *Asceticism and Anthropology*, 16.
**39** See Harold W. Attridge, ed. *Nag Hammadi Codex 1 (The Jung Codex)*, NHS 22–23 (Leiden: Brill, 1985), 128; *Rheg*, 43.25–26; 44.22; 47.3; 49.10–11. See also Bentley Layton, "Vision and Revision: A Gnostic View of Resurrection," in *Colloque international sur les texts de Nag Hammadi* (ed. Bernard Barc; *BCNH 1*; Quebec: Les Presses de l'Université Laval, 1981), 190–217; 201; van Unnik, "Gnostic Epistle to Rheginos," 146; and Malcolm Lee Peel, *The Epistle to Rheginos: A Valentinian letter on the Resurrection* (NTL; London: SCM, 1969).

spiritual body. When the perishable puts on the imperishable, and the mortal puts on immortality, then shall come to pass the saying that is written, death is swallowed up in victory (1 Cor 15.54).⁴⁰

Focusing on the dichotomies in 1 Cor 15 of perishable and imperishable, mortal and immortal, the author claims that by swallowing up death, Christ dissociates from the corruptible world. As Attridge observes in this Christocentric description of resurrection, there are no references to God the Father in the entire letter, "Christ raises himself!"⁴¹ Therefore, in Christ alone resurrection is possible, and as the author states, "the world is illusion" but resurrection "is real" and even in an apparent contradiction with 15.50, "fleshly."⁴² Here the stress is on resurrection as a symbol and as already present to the extent that the author can ask: "why do you not consider yourself as risen?"⁴³ This resurrection is spiritual and manifest in the world already. The dualistic natures of the world and of humankind, as emphasised in 1 Cor 15, are highlighted in the text's focus on the mortal and perishable nature—the psychic and the fleshly—which are both swallowed up in the spiritual resurrection.⁴⁴ Moreover, this language of dualism points to an understanding of the Christian as one who suffers and rises with Christ and who can look forward to a spiritual resurrection not only in the future, but right now for those who have put on Christ and, in the language of 1 Cor 15.53–54, immortality and imperishability. Setzer suggests, therefore, that resurrection and the focus on the dichotomy between corruption and incorruptibility,

---

**40** *Rheg*, 45.14–end. *The Treatise on the Resurrection* is written in Subachmimic Coptic. This study relies on the translation of this text, on which many scholarly texts and articles also rely, by Peel as found in Attridge, *The Jung Codex*, 147–157. It also recognises that Bentley Layton offers a translation of this text in Bentley Layton, *The Gnostic Treatise on Resurrection from Nag Hammadi* (Atlanta, Ga: Scholars Press, 1979).
**41** Attridge, *Nag Hammadi*, 132.
**42** *Rheg*, 48.15 and 27. Opponents of this view are clear that the "flesh is not illusory" (Tertullian, *Marc*, 5.14) and rely heavily on excerpts from Phil 2.7 and Rom 8.3 to argue that even if Christ took on the likeness of sinful flesh, he did so to redeem flesh by its substance, even as his own flesh is free from sin. See also Origen, *Comm.Rom*, 6.12 and C. Murray-Jones, "Paradise Revisited (2 Cor 12.1–12)," *HTR* 86 (1993): 265–292. Excerpts from Phil 2 also fall amongst the most frequently cited Pauline passages in early Christian writings, occurring more than 565 times. Because the use of this text is similar to that presented in our chapter on Col 1, a separate examination of the use of Phil 2 in early Christian writings does not feature in this study.
**43** *Rheg*, 49.22. See also Moule, "Paul and Dualism," 112.
**44** The *Apocryphon of James* and *Letter of Peter to Philip* hold similar anthropological and Christological views and argue that it is the spiritual soul which will rise to life with God at the resurrection. For discussion of the connection between Valentinian theology and middle-Platonic thought, as well as the major schools of Valentinian thought, see Einar Thomassen, *The Spiritual Seed: The Church of the "Valentinians"* (Leiden: Brill, 2008), 492–494.

perishable and imperishability, acts as "a symbol that aids and maintains the construction of community. It helps forge identity in facing the powerful Greco-Roman culture beyond its borders, and shores up group membership within the group. Like any rich symbol, it reaches beyond itself. It carries with it a set of essential ideas about God, the world, and humanity."[45]

Another anonymous Nag Hammadi text which uses the images and phrases of 1 Cor 15.50–58 is the *Gospel of Philip*. This text is a third century Valentinian collection of statements about ethics and sacraments which is not clearly organised and in which "the line of thought is rambling and disjointed."[46] New Testament phrases may be found throughout this text with excerpts from 15.50–58 occurring in at least two places, particularly to support a realised view of resurrection.[47] The *Gospel of Philip* suggests that the only reason other Christians espouse bodily resurrection is because they fear nakedness and existence apart from a physical body. In other words,

> some are afraid that they may rise naked: because of this they wish to rise in the flesh and [they] do not know that it is those who wear the [flesh] who are naked. Flesh [and blood shall] not inherit the kingdom [of God] (1 Cor 15.50). What is this which will not inherit? This which is on us. But what is this, too, which will inherit? It is that which belongs to Jesus and his blood. Because of this he said, he who shall not eat my flesh and drink my blood has not life in him (John 6.53). He who has received these has food and drink and clothing. I find fault with the others who say that it will not rise. Both of them are at fault.[48]

---

[45] Setzer, "Resurrection of the Body," 6.
[46] Wesley W. Isenberg, "Gospel according to Philip," in *Nag Hammadi Codex II, 2–7: Together with XIII, 2\*, Brit. Lib. Or.4926 (1), and P.Oxy.1, 654, 655* (ed. Bentley Layton; NHS 20; Leiden: Brill, 1989), 131–215; 131–132. Pagels relies on Schenke to clarify that even though this text was compiled from a variety of sources, "the whole is governed by a quite specific spirit" and thus one may speak of the author's viewpoint when referring to the content of this text (see Pagels, "Ritual," 281; and H.M. Schencke, "Das Evangelium nach Philippus," in *Neutestamentliche Apokryphen in deutscher Übersetzung* [ed. Wilhelm Schneemelcher; Tübingen: Mohr (Siebeck), 1987], 1.148–173). Dates for this text vary from the second century to the early fourth century (see Lehtipuu, "Flesh and Blood," 152n30).
[47] Scholars are clear that the Valentinians, and in particular the author of the *Gospel of Philip*, likely knew Paul's letters to the Romans, 1 and 2 Corinthians, Galatians, and Philippians from which he explicitly quotes. This does not mean other letters were unknown to the author (Wilson, *The Gospel of Philip*, 7; Pagels, *Gnostic Paul*, 3). Grant also claims to have discerned references to Ephesians, Thessalonians, Colossians, and Hebrews (Robert M. Grant, "The Mystery of Marriage in the Gospel of Philip," *VC* 15 [1961]: 129–140).
[48] Layton, *Gospel of Philip*, 56.26–57.21. Like *The Treatise on the Resurrection*, the *Gospel of Philip* is a Coptic text and this study relies on the translation provided by Layton in Bentley Layton, ed. *The Gnostic Scriptures: A New Translation with Annotations and Introductions* (ABRL;

Words from 1 Cor 15.50 are used by the *Gospel of Philip*—possibly the only direct citation of this text in Valentinian writings—to set up a series of questions about resurrection which support a denial of resurrection of the flesh and promote the body as a garment to be discarded.[49] Both John 6.53 and 1 Cor 15.50 use the language of flesh and blood, and the author of the *Gospel of Philip* connects the phrases in these texts to support the claims both that flesh and blood will not inherit the kingdom of God and that the flesh and blood that will inherit the kingdom of God is that of Jesus.[50] Balancing these two references to flesh and blood, resurrection is described as an experience in this present world of the sacrament, so that, in the words of John's Gospel, those who have not partaken of the flesh and blood of Jesus have no life in them.[51] Presenting the situation to be much more complex than a rejection or acceptance of the doctrine of bodily resurrection, the *Gospel of Philip* takes a position between these two possibilities, arguing that resurrection is available to Christians in the sacrament of the Eucharist.[52] The subject of rising for the *Gospel of Philip* is the flesh and blood of Jesus and therefore, the author concludes that one should not have any fear about rising naked, because those who have received Jesus in the sacrament are clothed with his flesh and blood.[53] Resurrection understood in this way could be "spiritual and immediate, that is, understood metaphorically rather than as an eschatological, actual resurrection of the body."[54] Engaging one of the main points of contention involving 1 Cor 15.50 and its interpretation, the *Gospel of Philip* uses the distinction between flesh and blood and the kingdom of God to support an understanding of flesh as secondary to the spirit and soul.

---

New York: Doubleday, 1995). For Tertullian's reply to this argument about nakedness, see *Res*, 42.

**49** The language used is similar to that of 2 Cor 5.1–10, but the exchange of garments in the *Gospel of Philip* is not a direct exchange as described in 2 Cor 5 but the putting on of one over another as an additional garment as described in 1 Cor 15 (Moule, "Paul and Dualism," 119–120). See also White, *Remembering Paul*, 38.

**50** A.H.C. van Eijk, "The Gospel of Philip and Clement of Alexandria: Gnostic and Ecclesiastical Theology on the Resurrection and the Eucharist," *VC* 25 (1971), 94–120; 98. See also *Rect.fide*, 5; Wilson, *The Gospel of Philip*, 88–89. For one of the most recent studies of the sacraments in Valentinianism, see Thomassen, *Spiritual Seed*.

**51** Kathy L. Gaca and L.L. Welborn, *Early Patristic Readings of Romans* (New York: T&T Clark, 2005), 116.

**52** Mark Jeffrey Olson, *Irenaeus, the Valentinian Gnostics, and the Kingdom of God (A.H. Book V): The Debate about 1 Corinthians 15.50* (Lewiston, NY: Mellen Biblical Press, 1992), 32–33.

**53** See van Eijk, "The Gospel of Philip," 96.

**54** Stroumsa, "*Caro salutis cardo*," 41.

Based partly on the words found in 1 Cor 15.50, the author of the *Gospel of Philip* tries to hold a balance between a notion of a future spiritual resurrection when the body will be discarded and a concept of resurrection in this present world through the sacrament. Ultimately, however, while one may partake of the flesh and blood of the sacrament in this world, resurrection is not corporeal but spiritual as determined by the words of 1 Cor 15.50 that "flesh and blood cannot inherit the kingdom of God." Nevertheless, a spiritual state of resurrection cannot be attained without receiving the sacrament of Christ's flesh and blood. Only through the flesh and blood of Christ can one experience the resurrection in this life and enter the kingdom of God after death, and thus the author of the *Gospel of Philip* writes that, "those who say they will die first and then rise are in error. If they do not first receive the resurrection while they live, when they die they will receive nothing."[55]

Excerpts from 1 Cor 15.50–58 and especially 1 Cor 15.50, therefore, serve to support the Valentinian view that flesh and blood could not inherit the kingdom of God and that the resurrection may be realised already, manifest in this world through Christ. The words of 1 Cor 15.50 about flesh and blood and the kingdom of God divide the authors of both the *Treatise on the Resurrection* and the *Gospel of Philip* from those who believe in corporeal resurrection, and who, according to the *Gospel of Philip*, are not Christian at all.[56] Therefore, the conclusions drawn from 1 Cor 15 are not only anthropological and Christological but "ultimately had to do with Christian identity and the issue of who may rightfully claim to be a Christian."[57]

---

**55** *Evan.Phil*, 73.1–4. See also *Evan.Phil*, 56.15–19 and 66.16–20; and Heracleon in Origen, *Comm.Jo*, 19.3; 20.7; 13.11–25. Note that some scholars argue that the Valentinians and others like them revere Paul as a gnostic initiate himself and "claim his letters as a primary source of gnostic theology" (Pagels, *Gnostic Paul*, 1. See also Hippolytus, *Haer*, 5.7.14; Irenaeus, *Haer*, 1.8.2–3; 3.2.1–3.3.1). However, as Brown clarifies, "Paul is more likely a source for the first articulations of Christian Gnosticism than a borrower from such traditions" (Brown, *The Cross*, 64).
**56** *Evan.Phil*, 67.9–27; 64.22–27.
**57** Lehtipuu, "Flesh and Blood," 168. Nielsen writes that within early Christian writings, "Pauline influence appears not only very often but also at crucial points where the actual definition of Christianity is at stake" (Charles Merritt Nielsen, "The Epistle to Diognetus: Its Date and Relationship to Marcion," *AThR* 52 (1970): 77–91; 88).

## 4.3 Irenaeus of Lyons[58]

The seriousness with which Irenaeus takes Valentinian exegesis in his own writings confirms the magnitude and urgency of the debate concerning interpretation of 1 Cor 15.50–58.[59] Valentinian appeals to 1 Cor 15 "eventually forced the hand of proto-orthodox defenders of the faith" who saw that they "needed to reclaim these particular Pauline passages for their own side."[60] While the *Gospel of Philip* claimed that those who believe in a corporeal resurrection are not Christian,[61] for Irenaeus, those who do not believe in resurrection of the flesh present an argument that he sees "not simply as a denial of the humanity of Jesus, but as a denigration of the flesh, which [...] is increasingly seen as the instrument of salvation itself."[62] Irenaeus dedicates the fifth book of his *Against Heresies* to refuting the claim that bodily resurrection is not possible because of the inherent evil of the material and fleshly world. Irenaeus "directs his refutation primarily against the disciples of Valentinus, a leading gnostic teacher at Rome, but he also mentions Marcion and many others, claiming to refute all heresies at once."[63] With a particular focus on his opponents' interpretation of 1 Cor 15.50, Irenaeus is clear that,

---

[58] This chapter does not engage with the writings of Clement of Alexandria, but it is interesting to note briefly his use of this Corinthian text. In particular, with the exception of one excerpt in his *Stromata* (Book 4), Clement only considers 1 Cor 15.50–58 in his *On the Pedagogue*. This is striking given—as the rest of this chapter establishes—the importance of this text for his predecessors such as some of the Valentinians and Irenaeus, and his followers such as Origen. Clement writes in *Paed*, 43.2–3 that "by flesh he [Paul] means allegorically the Holy Spirit, for it is by him that the flesh has been made; by blood he indicates to us mysteriously the *logos*, for as overflowing blood the *logos* has been shed upon our life; the Lord is the mixture of both, the food of the little ones [...] the milk [...] by whom alone the little ones are nursed." Thinking back to the connection Clement makes between teaching and solid food and milk based on his interpretation of 1 Cor 2–3 (Chapter 2), one could suggest, although this would need further exploration, that for Clement the teaching of resurrection in flesh and blood is something only for beginners in the faith. This is mentioned with gratitude to Judith Kovacs for noticing Clement's use of this text in the survey and offering a number of constructive questions and suggestions based on this observation.
[59] Kovacs, "Echoes of Valentinian Exegesis," 322.
[60] White, *Remembering Paul*, 37.
[61] *Evan.Phil*, 67.9–27; 64.22–27.
[62] G.W. MacRae, "Why the Church Rejected Gnosticism," in *Jewish and Christian Self-Definition* (ed. E.P. Sanders, *et al*; London: SCM Press, 1980–1982): 126–133; 133.
[63] Setzer, *Resurrection of the Body*, 125 and Irenaeus, *Haer*, 2.31.1. Olson writes with surprise that "one would expect the major exegetical battles to be fought over gospel terrain. Instead, the key verse is Pauline" (Olson, *Irenaeus*, 6).

among the other truths proclaimed by the Apostle, there is also this one, that flesh and blood cannot inherit the kingdom of God (1 Cor 15.50: *caro et sanguis regnum Dei hereditare non possunt*). This is the passage which is adduced by all the heretics (*omnibus haereticis*) in support of their folly, with an attempt to annoy us, and to point out that the handiwork of God is not saved.[64]

Irenaeus is particularly concerned that his opponents use this excerpt from Paul "without having understood the Apostle's meaning, or examined critically the force of the words, but holding fast to the mere expressions by themselves, they die in consequence of their influence, overturning, as far as in them lies, the entire dispensation of God (*universam dispositionem Dei*)."[65] For Irenaeus, his opponents' interpretation of 1 Cor 15.50 does not work because of its understanding of flesh apart from the kingdom of God. Redefining the phrase "flesh and blood," he argues that Paul was not speaking literally when he wrote "flesh and blood will not inherit the kingdom of God."[66] For Irenaeus, flesh and blood refer not only to the physical nature of humankind and to the sacrament of the Eucharist, but by flesh and blood Paul also means those who reject God's Spirit and who do not have the Spirit of God within them. He writes,

> In order that we may not lose life by losing that Spirit which possesses us, the Apostle, exhorting us to the communion of the Spirit (*ad Spiritus communicationem*), has said according to reason in those words already quoted, that flesh and blood cannot inherit the kingdom of God (1 Cor 15.50: *quoniam caro et sanguis regnum Dei possidere non possunt*). Just as if he were to say, do not err; for unless the word of God (*verbum Dei*) dwells within and the Spirit of the Father is in you, and if you shall live frivolously and carelessly as if you were only this flesh and blood, you cannot inherit the kingdom of God.[67]

While his opponents use 15.50 to conclude that Paul really meant physical flesh and blood cannot inherit the kingdom of God and is therefore inferior to the divine nature and spirit, Irenaeus takes an opposing view. Drawing from a range of texts—including excerpts from Romans 8, Phil 3, Gal 5, and 2 Cor 3 and 4—Irenaeus argues that 15.50 refers both to the physical nature of the flesh and to those who partake in immoral works of the flesh.[68] Instead of interpreting flesh and blood as the physical attributes of the resurrection body, which cannot partake in the kingdom of God, Irenaeus equates flesh and blood to actions of

---

64 Irenaeus, *Haer*, 5.9.1 (*SC* 153; Roberts).
65 Irenaeus, *Haer*, 5.13.2 (*SC* 153).
66 Irenaeus, *Haer*, 5.13.3 (*SC* 153).
67 Irenaeus, *Haer*, 5.9.4 (translation adapted from *SC* 153 and Roberts).
68 Blackwell, "Paul and Irenaeus," 198.

frivolous and careless living. Living a life without recognising God as Father, Word, and Spirit is living a life only by flesh and blood and as such, separate from the Spirit, one cannot inherit the kingdom of God. Irenaeus argues that the views of his opponents lead to an interpretation of 1 Cor 15.50–54 which is not logical for they "allege that this passage refers to the flesh strictly so called and not to fleshly works, as I have pointed out."[69] Thus, he is clear that they

> must either allege that the Apostle contradicts his own opinion regarding the saying flesh and blood cannot inherit the kingdom of God (1 Cor 15.50: *quantum ad illud caro et sanguis regnum Dei possidere non possunt*) or they will again be forced to make wicked and crooked interpretations of all the sayings in order to twist and alter the sense of the words.[70]

In this way, Irenaeus turns a simple phrase—flesh and blood—into an ethical injunction, reading beyond what is written to enjoin Christians to live not as if the Spirit is separate from flesh and blood but as if all of life is integrated. In other words, the spiritual elements of life have an ethical and practical element which, according to Irenaeus, his Valentinian opponents miss completely in their interpretation of 15.50. For Irenaeus, the salvation of flesh, blood, and soul must include spiritual works.[71] He continues,

> Inasmuch, therefore, as without the Spirit of God (*Spiritu Dei*) we cannot be saved, the Apostle exhorts us through faith and chaste conversation (*fidem et castam conversationem*) to preserve the Spirit of God, lest having become non-participators of the holy Spirit (*sancti Spiritus*), we lose the kingdom of heaven (*regnum caelorum*), and, he exclaims, flesh alone and blood cannot inherit the kingdom of God (1 Cor 15.50: *non posse carnem solam et sanguinem regnum Dei possidere*).[72]

For Irenaeus, the issue when interpreting 15.50 is the contrast between flesh and blood *and* the kingdom of God and the caveat that flesh and blood alone cannot inherit the kingdom of God. By introducing the Spirit into the equation, Irenaeus argues that flesh and blood can indeed be saved. This ethical exhortation to preserve the Spirit of God through "faith and chaste conversation" gives an active role to Christians in salvation with the notion that by living only for flesh and

---

**69** Irenaeus, *Haer*, 5.13.3 (SC 153).
**70** Irenaeus, *Haer*, 5.13.5 (Translation adapted from *SC* 153 and Roberts).
**71** Irenaeus, *Haer*, 5.9.1–4; 5.10–11. See also *Haer*, 5.13.4. In both of these excerpts, Irenaeus also looks to Romans, especially Rom 8.8–15. See also Rolf Noormann, *Irenäus als Paulusinterpret: zur Rezeption und Wirkung der paulinischen und deuteropaulinischen Briefe im Werk des Irenäus von Lyon* (WUNT 2.66; Tübingen: Mohr [Siebeck], 1994), 505 and 508–12; and White, *Remembering Paul*, 160–161.
**72** Irenaeus, *Haer*, 5.9.3 (translation adapted from *SC* 153 and Roberts).

blood, they can lose the kingdom. If the Christian does not engage the Spirit and allows the self only to live by flesh and blood, this one cannot enter the spiritual realm. In this way, Irenaeus confirms that those who interpret 1 Cor 15 by separating flesh and blood from salvation and the spiritual life, deny the reality that flesh itself is an instrument of salvation and the very handiwork of God.[73] Irenaeus' defence of the flesh, therefore, is more precisely a defence of God and God's creation.

Irenaeus, however, also argues that correct interpretation of 15.50 leads not only to an ethical exhortation, but to a Christological one. In a move that exemplifies the way other scriptural passages are called upon by early Christian writers in order to interpret a particularly difficult text, Irenaeus looks to John's Gospel and asks why Jesus would heal the physical bodies of people he encountered in his life and ministry if the flesh were not valued or saved?[74] He asks about those Jesus raised from the dead, "in what bodies did they rise again?"[75] In other words, would Christ have performed miracles such as raising the body of Lazarus if flesh were not saved? Moreover, it is the reality that Christ himself took on flesh and blood that confirms for Irenaeus the integrity and salvation of the flesh. Focusing on the integrity of Christ's human nature, he writes that,

> inasmuch as the Apostle has not spoken against the very substance of flesh and blood that it cannot inherit the kingdom of God (1 Cor 15.50: *carnis et sanguinis dixit Apostolus non possidere eam regnum Dei*), the same Apostle has everywhere adopted the term flesh and blood with regards to the Lord Jesus Christ, partly indeed to establish his human nature, for he did himself speak of himself as the Son of Man, and partly that he might confirm the salvation of our flesh (*salutem carnis nostrae confirmaret*), for if the flesh were not in a position to be saved, the word of God would not have become flesh (*nequaquam verbum Dei caro factum esset*). And if the blood of the righteous were not to be inquired after, the Lord would certainly not have had blood.[76]

For Irenaeus, a correct understanding of 1 Cor 15 is necessary both to grasp salvation of the flesh and the ethical necessity of the unity of flesh, blood and Spirit, and it is essential for his defence of Christ as both incarnated and resurrected in flesh and blood. In this way, Irenaeus' scriptural interpretation "revolves around defining Christ" so that "all other theological themes such as salvation [...] are subordinated."[77] Therefore, with a focus on 15.50, he continues,

---

[73] Irenaeus, *Haer,* 5.9.1. (*SC* 153).
[74] Irenaeus, *Haer,* 5.13.1 (*SC* 153).
[75] Irenaeus, *Haer,* 5.13.1 (*SC* 153).
[76] Irenaeus, *Haer,* 5.14.1 (translation adapted from *SC* 153 and Roberts).
[77] Greer, "Applying," 185.

this blood could not have been required unless it also had the capability of being saved; nor would the Lord have recapitulated (*recapitulatus*) these things in himself, unless he had himself been made flesh and blood (*caro et sanguis*) after the way of the original formation of man, saving in his own person at the end that which had in the beginning perished in Adam.[78]

The fall of Adam to which Irenaeus refers is therefore part of the process to perfection, the move from corruptibility and mortality to perfection in God who is incorruptible and immortal.[79] Irenaeus concludes that "by no other means could we have attained to incorruptibility and immortality (*incorruptelam et immortalitatem*), unless we had been united to incorruptibility and immortality (1 Cor 15.53: *incorruptelae et immortalitati*)."[80] While the author of the *Gospel of Philip* understood Christ's flesh and blood, as present in the Eucharist, to offer the possibility of a spiritual resurrection to all Christians, Irenaeus understands the resurrection of the flesh and blood of Christ to mean the same resurrection is possible for all humankind. The dignity of the human body is confirmed both by Christ's incarnation and his resurrection. Because Jesus was raised in flesh and blood, so also humankind. The resurrection of the body is not because of the salvific properties of the flesh, nor the actions of the flesh, but because of the salvific actions of God. In other words, "our bodies are raised not from their own substance (*substantia*), but by the power of God (*Dei virtute*)."[81]

Ultimately, it is not the substance of flesh and blood that is at stake for Irenaeus, but salvation. Flesh and blood are agents in salvation but their substance does not determine who and what inherits the kingdom of God, God does. That Christ took on human flesh means, for Irenaeus, that even flesh is saved by Christ's actions. Thus, when Paul speaks about corruption putting on incorruption in 1 Cor 15, the incarnation and resurrection of Christ mean that even death itself is swallowed up in victory.[82] On this basis, Irenaeus argues that the flesh therefore is capable of being saved and will rise from the dead and any suggestion otherwise is to imply that the material world is made by a lesser god.[83] As he writes, "the thing which had perished possessed flesh and blood

---

[78] Irenaeus, *Haer*, 5.14.1 (translation adapted from *SC* 153 and Roberts).
[79] Greer, "Framework," 167. See also Irenaeus, *Haer*, 4.38.
[80] Irenaeus, *Haer*, 3.19.1 (translation adapted from *SC* 211 and *ACW* 65).
[81] Irenaeus, *Haer*, 5.6.2 (*SC* 153).
[82] Irenaeus, *Haer*, 3.16.3.
[83] Irenaeus, *Haer*, 5.1.4.

(*sanguinem et carnem*)" and thus that which is saved must as well.⁸⁴ Irenaeus is clear that the resurrected body is not simply a resuscitated corpse⁸⁵ but rather, as Paul states in 15.53, is immortal and incorruptible and somehow changed. Yet, it is still flesh and blood because, as he writes, Christ "had himself, therefore, flesh and blood (*carnem et sanguinem*), recapitulating (*recapitulans*) in himself not a certain other, but that original handiwork of the Father seeking that thing which had perished."⁸⁶ Therefore, not only in 1 Cor 15 but "in every epistle the Apostle plainly testifies that through the flesh of our Lord and through his blood, we have been saved."⁸⁷ Irenaeus cannot part with his conviction that flesh and blood are essential components of resurrection. The resurrection of flesh and blood that he defends is an essential element for one of his central theological tenets: recapitulation.⁸⁸ His doctrine of recapitulation is at the heart of his theology and integral to his interpretation and his sense of urgency concerning 1 Cor 15.50–54.⁸⁹ If flesh and blood do not inherit the kingdom of God, even in a transformed state, then the integrity of Christ's flesh and thus all human flesh is compromised. Through Christ taking on flesh and being raised in the flesh, those who partake in God's Spirit will be saved, flesh, blood, and all.

For Irenaeus, on the one hand, flesh and blood are understood as fleshy desires and works in need of the Spirit of God and, on the other hand, flesh and blood are essential elements of God's creation and are saved though Christ.⁹⁰ While these two interpretations are seemingly unconnected, they are not for Irenaeus and he writes of Christ's flesh and blood that,

> if flesh and blood are the things which procure for us life, it has not been declared of flesh and blood, in the proper meaning of the terms, that they cannot inherit the kingdom of God (1 Cor 15.50: *non proprie de carne dictum est et sanguine non posse ea possidere regnum Dei*), but to those carnal deeds already mentioned, which, perverting one to sin, deprive him of life.⁹¹

---

**84** Irenaeus, *Haer*, 5.14.2 (*SC* 153). Brian Daley, *The Hope of the Early Church: A Handbook of Patristic Eschatology* (2nd ed; Grand Rapids, Mich: Baker Academic, 2010), 31.
**85** Irenaeus, *Haer*, 5.15.1.
**86** Irenaeus, *Haer*, 5.14.2 (translation adapted from *SC* 153 and Roberts).
**87** Irenaeus, *Haer*, 5.14.3 (translation adapted from *SC* 153 and Roberts).
**88** Recapitulation is "based on the belief that God is so concerned with the physical world and physical human beings that he sent Jesus in a physical body to redeem them all" (Olson, *Irenaeus*, 97). Behr is clear that Irenaeus was concerned to bring together the salvific acts of God in Christ "into one all-embracing divine plan or economy," with Irenaeus being the first to use the term *oikonomia* in such a way (Behr, *Asceticism and Anthropology*, 33).
**89** Greer, "Framework," 165.
**90** Lehtipuu, "Flesh and Blood," 155. See also Irenaeus, *Haer*, 5.2.2.
**91** Irenaeus, *Haer*, 5.14.4 (translation adapted from *SC* 153 and Roberts).

In his interpretation of 15.50, exegesis and theology overlap as Irenaeus offers both an anthropological understanding of the text and the ethical exhortation it engenders, as well as a Christological understanding of flesh and blood by which all are not only saved, but able to be raised in flesh and blood as Christ was. Despite the words of 1 Cor 15.50 that flesh and blood cannot inherit the kingdom of God, Irenaeus concludes that flesh is worthy of salvation. He insists that Christ, as the Word of God made perfect in his incarnation, death, and resurrection, always reveals the power of God which cannot be limited even by flesh and blood.[92] In this way, in his use and interpretation of 1 Cor 15.50, Irenaeus ultimately appeals to his rule of truth which is "the final filter through which Scripture should be interpreted."[93] As Augustine later explains, the rule of truth (or faith) is such that "whatever there is in the word of God that cannot, when taken literally, be referred either to purity of life or soundness of doctrine, [it] should be treated as figurative."[94]

## 4.4 Tertullian[95]

Writing against both the Valentinians and the Marcionites, Tertullian describes 1 Cor 15.50 as "in very truth the gist of the whole question (*reuera totius quaestionis*)"[96] which "our opponents place in the front of the battle."[97] Tertullian therefore focuses almost entirely on the phrases of 15.50 in his use of this Corinthian pericope, but he does so to support a wide range of arguments. Tertullian sees 1 Cor 15.50 as the favourite text for those who deny the resurrection of the flesh. Like those before him, Tertullian holds that resurrection is at the heart of Christian identity as "the essence of this hidden, non-worldly wisdom known only to the few, carrying with it the essential elements of the Christian system."[98] Moreover, like the Valentinians and Irenaeus, Tertullian holds that one's views

---

92 Greer, "Framework," 175.
93 White, *Remembering Paul,* 163. See also John Behr, "Irenaeus on the Word of God," in *Studia Patristica: Papers presented at the 13th International Conference on Patristic Studies held in Oxford 1999* (eds. Maurice F. Wiles and Edward Yarnold; Leuven: Peeters, 2001), 163–167; 167, and Irenaeus, *Haer,* 1.9.4; 1.22.1; 3.2.1; 3.5.1.
94 Augustine, *Doct.Chr,* 3.10.14–16 (*CCL* 32). See Young, *Biblical Exegesis,* 275–277, and Frances M. Young, *The Art of Performance: Toward a Theology of Holy Scripture* (London: Darton, Longman & Todd, 1990), 45–65.
95 See also Tertullian, *Res,* 21.3; 42.1; 42.3; 50.4.
96 Tertullian, *Res,* 49.1 (*CCL* 2).
97 Tertullian, *Res,* 48.1 (*CCL* 2).
98 Setzer, *Resurrection of the Body,* 143. See also Tertullian, *Res,* 22.8–11; 3.6.

on the resurrection can determine "who is a genuine Christian and how one may be recognized."[99] Nevertheless, Tertullian is also aware that the words of Paul in 15.50 are ambiguous in terms of flesh, blood, and resurrection so that no one, and especially not his opponents, can claim fully to understand what Paul meant. Thus, he asks sarcastically, pointing out the folly of such assured conclusions, "is there any now who has risen again, except a heretic (*haereticus*)?"[100]

Like Irenaeus, one of Tertullian's concerns is to define what he thinks Paul means by flesh and blood in 15.50. He does this with a complex description of flesh and blood using the imagery of Adam and Christ found in the verse of 1 Cor 15 immediately preceding 15.50. He writes in his apology against Marcion,

> Let us now discuss the crux of the whole question, the flesh and blood (*carnem et sanguinem*). The way in which these substances (*substantias*) are excluded by the Apostle from the kingdom of God can be understood in light of the preceding passage (1 Cor 15.47–50: *exheredauerit apostolus a Dei regno*). The first man who is from the earth, earthy, that is to say made from mud, refers to Adam. The second man who is from heaven, refers to the Word of God, in other words, Christ, who is still man even though he was from heaven, because he is flesh and soul (*caro atque anima*), that is, what man is and what Adam was.[101]

The distinction between Adam and Christ is not only about flesh and blood and flesh and soul, but, addressing Marcion's question about the separation of flesh, blood, soul, and spirit, is about the attributes and substances of which these elements are comprised. For Tertullian, humankind is not divided into flesh, blood, and spirit, but into two approaches to God: the way of Adam and the way of Christ.[102] Tertullian does not argue that Adam is human and Christ is not. He is clear that both are fully human, made up of flesh, blood, and soul. He is also clear, however, that the orientation of Adam's flesh and blood in disobedience to God led to one outcome and the orientation of Christ's flesh and blood in obedience to God led to another.

Thus, for Tertullian as for Irenaeus, an understanding of flesh and blood involves an ethical dimension. The difference between Adam and Christ is not that of flesh and blood but their approach to God. Because Christ is fully human like Adam, made of the substance of flesh and blood, flesh and blood which is orientated to God can inherit the kingdom of God and be saved. Nevertheless, he

---

**99** Setzer, *Resurrection of the Body*, 143.
**100** Tertullian, *Res*, 22.11 (*CCL* 2). See also *Res*, 24.7.
**101** Tertullian, *Res*, 49.1–21 (*CSEL* 47).
**102** This distinction is similar to the one Moule finds in Pauline texts: the dualism of the will—of obedience and disobedience—which he sees as a moral antithesis rather than one of body and soul, matter and spirit. See Moule, "Paul and Dualism," 107.

continues, "since Marcion entirely refuses to admit the resurrection of the flesh, promising salvation to the soul alone, he makes this a question not of attributes but of substance (*substantiae*)."[103] Tertullian does not believe one can separate the flesh from the soul nor completely discount the flesh and, therefore, even though he reads in 1 Cor 15.50 that flesh and blood cannot inherit the kingdom of God, this is only true if one is identified solely with Adam and not with Christ.[104] As with Irenaeus, right doctrine for Tertullian trumps his opponents reading of the plain sense of the text and ultimately is about the power of God to redeem flesh and blood as Christ did in his resurrection. At stake in this debate is not only the corporeal nature of resurrection, but also the nature of God's power and he "aims his sarcasm at those who doubt the possibility of bodily resurrection, 'your doubts, I believe, would be about the power of God?'"[105]

Nevertheless, while the ethical dimension of Tertullian's concern for the right interpretation of flesh and blood is about one's approach to God, it is also about how the entities of flesh and blood themselves are defined. Thus, apart from his use of Adam and Christ to understand 15.50, Tertullian also offers his own definition of what flesh and blood mean. He writes that the flesh and blood which do not receive the kingdom of God are actually, "the works done in the substance of the flesh, alienating us from the kingdom of God."[106] Flesh and blood are not the elements that make up the corrupted state but they are the subjects of corruption. As with his distinction between Adam and Christ, the disinheritance of flesh and blood found in 1 Cor 15.50 refers only to their works and discipline, not to their substance.[107] Tertullian writes that Paul intended, "flesh and blood cannot attain the kingdom of God (1 Cor 15.50: *caro et sanguis regnum Dei non consequentur*), not passing sentence on the substance (*substantiam*), but on its works (*opera*), and because while still in the flesh we are capable of not committing these, they will be accounted to the guilt not of the substance but of our conduct."[108] In other words, judgement ultimately is not of the physical substance of flesh and blood but the works of flesh and blood

---

[103] Tertullian, *Marc*, 5.10 (translation adapted from *CCL* 1 and Evans). See also *Marc*, 5.14.
[104] See Greer who writes that Christ brings "life by obedience instead of death by disobedience" (Greer, "Framework," 165).
[105] Setzer, "Resurrection of the Body," 7. Tertullian, *Apol*, 48.7.
[106] Tertullian, *Res*, 49.11 (*CSEL* 47).
[107] Daniélou, *Latin Christianity*, 160.
[108] Tertullian, *Marc*, 5.14 (translation adapted from *CCL* 1 and Evans). See also Moule, "Paul and Dualism," 108, where he writes that physical resurrection for Tertullian is ultimately "a moral, not physical or quasi-physical concern."

which lead to its separation and exclusion from the kingdom of God. Marcion's focus on the substance but not the attributes of flesh and blood is a complete misunderstanding of 1 Cor 15.50 for Tertullian. He insists that the focus of 15.50 is first and foremost about the works and attributes of flesh and blood because the question of their substance is not up for debate.

Tertullian's theological need to argue that because Christ took on flesh and was raised in flesh, so too, are all Christians, informs the way he interprets 15.50 and the statement that flesh and blood cannot inherit the kingdom of God. He approaches this text, therefore, in a variety of ways so that whatever approach his opponents take to claim the Pauline words as their own, Tertullian has a counter argument. Therefore, Tertullian reconciles the separation of flesh and blood from the kingdom of God in 1 Cor 15.50 not only by aligning flesh and blood with works and attributes, but also though an exegetical move whereby he separates the kingdom of God from the resurrection. Tertullian offers a close reading of 1 Cor 15.50, arguing that Paul never says flesh and blood cannot be *resurrected*, but that flesh and blood cannot *inherit* the kingdom of God. Thus, resurrection and the kingdom must be two different things. He writes,

> it is not the resurrection that is directly denied to flesh and blood, but the kingdom of God (1 Cor 15.50: *non enim resurrectio carni et sanguini directo negatur, sed Dei regnum*), which is incidental to the resurrection, for there is a resurrection of judgement (John 5.29?) also [...] therefore, while it is in consideration of one's merits that a difference is made in their resurrection by their conduct in the flesh, and not by the substance (*substantiae*) thereof, it is evident even from this that flesh and blood are excluded from the kingdom of God in respect of their sin, not of their substance (*apparet hinc quoque carnem et sanguinem nomine culpae, non substantiae, arceri a dei regno*), and in respect of their natural condition they will rise for judgement, because they rise not for the kingdom (*resurgere in iudicium, quia non resurgant in regnum*). Again, I will say, flesh and blood cannot inherit the kingdom of God (1 Cor 15.50: *caro et sanguis regnum Dei hereditati possidere non possunt*), and justly does the Apostle say this of them considered alone and in themselves, in order to show that the spirit (*spiritum*) is still needed for the kingdom [...] Flesh and blood, therefore, must in every case rise again, equally in their proper quality. But they to whom it is granted to enter the kingdom of God, will have to put on the power of an incorruptible and immortal life (1 Cor 15.53), for without this or before they are able to obtain it, they cannot enter into the kingdom of God. With good reason then flesh and blood as we have already said by themselves fail to obtain the kingdom of God (1 Cor 15.50). But inasmuch as this corruptible, that is the flesh, must put on incorruption and this mortal, that is the blood, must put on immortality (1 Cor 15.53: *corruptiuum istud ab incorruptibilitate, id est caro, et mortale istud ab inmortalitate, id est sanguis*), by the change which is to follow the resurrection, it will for the best of reasons happen that flesh and blood after that change and investiture

will become able to inherit the kingdom of God, but not without the resurrection (1 Cor 15.50).[109]

Resurrection, Tertullian argues, precedes entrance into the kingdom of God and includes the judgement of all.[110] Tertullian uses the words of 1 Cor 15.50–54 to make this claim, because the words of Paul only exclude flesh and blood from the kingdom and not from resurrection. By separating resurrection and entrance into the kingdom of God, Tertullian holds that flesh and blood are included in the resurrection without going against the words of Paul. Thus, he can say of his opponents' interpretations "let us pay attention to the meaning of his words, and the purpose of them, and [his] falsification of Scripture will become evident."[111]

This understanding of resurrection and kingdom separately enables Tertullian to hold together the words from 15.50 and a resurrection of the flesh for all. For Tertullian, "divine justice itself demands the integral resurrection of man."[112] Flesh and blood are an integral part for Tertullian both of the resurrection and of judgement and therefore he writes that a resurrection that does not include flesh and blood is only "half a resurrection" because the full resurrection must include the flesh.[113] He argues that, "if God raises not whole humans, he raises not the dead."[114] This connection between resurrection and judgement gives greater context to the urgency behind Tertullian's concern for a physical understanding of resurrection. He understands that the flesh is the "necessary sphere both of salvation and of judgement"[115] and thus, resurrection in the flesh is necessary for one to be judged fully by God and either deemed worthy to partake in the kingdom of God or not. Tertullian, therefore, is clear that he holds the final trump card against his opponents with this close reading of 1 Cor 15, challenging their assumption that the kingdom of God is the same as resurrection. In this way, he upholds both the integrity of the text and the resurrection of the flesh despite the reality that flesh and blood cannot inherit the kingdom of God. He

---

**109** Tertullian, *Res*, 50.1–4 (*CCL* 2).
**110** If this idea of a "resurrection of judgement" comes from John 5, as suggested above, like those before him (the *Gospel of Philip* used John 6 and Irenaeus used excerpts from John, as well), Tertullian may be using other scriptural texts to make his argument and exegete 1 Cor 15.50.
**111** Tertullian, *Marc*, 5.33 (*CCL* 1).
**112** Stroumsa, "*Caro salutis cardo*," 43. See also Tertullian, *Res*, 56.1–57.6.
**113** Tertullian, *Res*, 2.2 (*CCL* 2). See also Irenaeus, *Haer*, 5.3.1.
**114** Tertullian, *Res*, 57.1 (*CCL* 2).
**115** Moule, "Paul and Dualism," 111. See also *Ap.Bar* l.1–li.10 and Clement of Rome, *2Clem*, 9 for two other early texts connecting resurrection and judgement (110).

turns the tables on his opponents in his accusations that they are really the ones who are reading beyond the text.

For Tertullian, resurrection is not simply a doctrine to be "ambiguously announced and obscurely propounded,"[116] but "the resurrection of the flesh is the Christian's confidence."[117] Using the words of 1 Cor 15, he defends bodily resurrection and the necessity of a material body to endure the full judgement of God. Tertullian's exegesis and theology are the same as he uses 1 Cor 15.50 to support his argument that resurrection of the flesh is possible even if one claims the words of Paul as they are written. His understanding that Christ was truly born, lived, and died in the substance of human flesh means that he can argue for the dignity of the flesh, the power of God to restore the flesh, and a reason for the flesh to be raised for judgement.[118]

## 4.5 Origen[119]

While Irenaeus, Tertullian, and the Valentinians each draw on the words of 1 Cor 15 to counter their opponents whom they deem as "heretics," Origen uses portions of 1 Cor 15.50–58 to counter two different groups who misunderstand resurrection. He writes against those he describes as "heretics" who use excerpts

---

[116] Tertullian, *Res*, 21.3 (*CCL* 2).
[117] Tertullian, *Res*, 1.1 (*CCL* 2).
[118] Everett Ferguson, "Tertullian," in *Early Christian Thinkers: The Lives and Legacies of Twelve Key Figures* (ed. Paul Foster; Downers Grove, Ill: Intervarsity Press, 2011), 85–99; 88. The idea of resurrection for judgement is also reminiscent of John 5.28–29.
[119] One must note that Methodius challenged Origen's interpretation of 1 Cor 15 and his understanding of the resurrection body, writing in his own treatise on resurrection that Origen does not hold an "authentic Christian view of embodiment" (L.G. Patterson, "Who are the Opponents in Methodius' De Resurrectione?," in *Studia Patristica Vol XIX: Historica, Theologica, Gnostica, Biblica et Apocrypha* [ed. E.A. Livingstone; Leuven: Peeters, 1989], 221–229; 228). However, Crouzel and Patterson both argue that Methodius likely had other opponents in mind in his *De Resurrectione* besides Origen (Patterson, "Who are the Opponents," 222; Henri Crouzel, "Les critiques adressées par Methode et ses contemporains à la doctrine origeniste du corps réssuscité," *Greg* 53 [1972]: 679–695). Edwards also counters that Origen's faith in the resurrection of the body alongside his view of the progression of souls and the grace that acts on the living and the dead both "rest on the axiom that body and soul are equally indispensible to the purposes of God" and encompass a part of Origen's theology that Methodius does not fully grasp in his critique (M. J. Edwards, "Origen's Two Resurrections," *JTS* 46, no. 2 [1995]: 502–518; 518). See also Methodius, *Res*, 1.2; 1.5–6; 1.12–13; 2.20; and Caroline Walker Bynum, *The Resurrection of the Body in Western Christianity, 200–1336* (New York: Columbia University Press, 1995), 69.

from 1 Cor 15 to deny any sense of bodily resurrection and he also writes against simple Christians, including earlier church fathers, who in their attempts to advocate bodily resurrection, misunderstand what Paul meant in 1 Cor 15.[120] Both groups, for Origen, misinterpret excerpts from 1 Cor 15 and as a consequence misunderstand resurrection and the form it will take. To the first, he asks, "What is it that is dead? Is it not the body? Therefore, there will be a resurrection of the body."[121] To the second, Origen writes at a much greater length advocating the resurrection of flesh and blood in the transformed state that he finds described in 1 Cor 15.50–58. In this way, especially in his interpretation of 15.50, Origen treads "a middle way between, on the one hand, Jews, millenarian Christians, and pagans who (he thought) understood bodily resurrection as the reanimation of dead flesh and, on the other hand, Gnostics and Hellenists who (he thought) denied any kind of ultimate reality either to resurrection or to body."[122]

In his desire to argue for a bodily resurrection, like those before him Origen cannot ignore the assertion in 1 Cor 15.50 that flesh and blood cannot inherit the kingdom of God. Criticising those who discount this Pauline phrase and advocate a full bodily resurrection, however, he writes that they do so because "they desire after the resurrection to have flesh of such sort that they will never lack the power to eat and drink and to do all things that pertain to flesh and blood (*carnis et sanguinis*), not following the teaching of the apostle Paul about the resurrection of a spiritual body (1 Cor 15.44: *apostoli Pauli de resurrectione spiritalis corporis*)."[123] He is clear that it is "absurd and contrary" to say that the resurrection body "can again be entangled with the passions of flesh and blood (*carnis et sanguinis*), seeing the Apostle manifestly says that flesh and blood shall not inherit the kingdom of God, nor shall corruption inherit incorruption (1 Cor 15.50, *quoniam caro et sanguis regnum Dei non possidebunt, neque corruptio incorruptionem possidebit*)."[124] Because Paul is clear that flesh

---

[120] This understanding of bodily resurrection sparks the question from Celsus, "What sort of person would have any further desire for a body that has rotted?" (Origen, *Cels,* 5.14).
[121] Origen, *Princ,* 2.10.1 (*SC* 253).
[122] Bynum, *Resurrection of the Body,* 64. See also Henri Crouzel, *Bibliographie critique d'Origène* (Instrumenta patristica 8; Steenbrugis: Abbatia s. Petri, 1971); Henri Crouzel, *Origen: The Life and Thought of the First Great Theologian* (trans. A.S. Worrall; San Francisco: Harper & Row, 1989); Henri Crouzel, "La doctrine origenienne du corps ressuscite," *BLE* 31 (1980): 241–266; Jon F. Dechow, *Dogma and Mysticism in Early Christianity: Epiphanius of Cyprus and the Legacy of Origen* (Leuven: Peeters, 1988). For a bibliographic overview of Origen's views of resurrection, see Roukema, "Origen's Interpretation," 329n1–2.
[123] Origen, *Princ,* 2.11.2 (*SC* 253). Here, Origen sounds remarkably like *Evan.Phil,* 56.26–57.21!
[124] Origen, *Princ,* 2.10.3 (*SC* 253).

and blood cannot inherit the kingdom of God in 15.50, Origen looks to what follows in 15.53–54 in order to offer both a challenge and a solution to the interpretation of his predecessors and opponents. He directs his statements at

> some of our own people who either from want of intellect or from lack of instruction introduce an exceedingly low and abject view of the resurrection of the body (*resurrectione corporis*). We ask these men in what manner they think that the psychic body will by the grace of the resurrection be changed and become spiritual; and in what manner they think what is sown in weakness shall be seen as resurrected in strength, and what is sown in dishonour shall rise in glory, and what is sown in corruption shall be transformed into incorruption (1 Cor 15.42: *quomodo quod in infirmitate seminatur, resurrecturum sentiant in virtute, et quod in ignobilitate, quomodo resurgat in gloria, et quod in corruptione, quomodo ad incorruptionem transferatur*).[125]

For Origen, the question is not about whether the body is resurrected but what form this will take, especially when taking seriously the words of 15.50. The opposites that Origen finds in 1 Cor 15.42 and 15.53–54 allow him to argue for a bodily resurrection, but with a body that has been transformed. These dichotomies from 1 Cor 15 support his understanding that there are two types of bodies: spiritual and physical. He tries to hold a balance, writing that the body raised in resurrection is continuous with the physical body in principle, but not in substance,[126] and therefore,

> it is not the same for corruptible nature to put on incorruption and for the corruptible nature to change into incorruption (1 Cor 15.53: Οὐ ταὐτὸν δέ ἐστιν τὸ τὴν φθαρτὴν φύσιν ἐνδύεσθαι ἀφθαρσίαν, καὶ τὸ τὴν φθαρτὴν φύσιν μεταβάλλειν εἰς ἀφθαρσίαν). And we must say the same things also concerning mortal nature, which does not change into immortality (ἀθανασίαν) but puts it on (1 Cor 15.53: ἐνδυομένης δὲ αὐτήν).[127]

---

125 Origen, *Princ*, 2.10.3 (translation adapted from *GCS* 22 and Butterworth).
126 Mark Scott argues that Origen supports some notion of bodily resurrection but "secretly posits the eventual obliteration of the body *after* the resurrection" (Mark S.M. Scott, *Journey Back to God: Origen on the Problem of Evil* [AAR.AS; New York: Oxford University Press, 2012], 122; italics original). Scott explains that for Origen, "In death, we continue to ascend through various gradation of heavenly existence, which requires bodies. He therefore insists on the doctrine of bodily resurrection. But once we complete our journey back to God, bodily existence will no longer be necessary" (122). This is in contrast to Mark Edwards who argues that "Origen envisages no end to corporeality" as the soul "cannot fulfil its lot without embodiment" (Edwards, "Origen's Two Resurrections," 502). See also Origen, *Princ*, 2.10.1 and *Cels*, 1.18–19 where Origen "insists that it is faith in a corporeal resurrection that sets apart the Christian from the Greek" (Edwards, "Origen's Two Resurrections," 503).
127 Origen, *Comm.Jo*, 13.429–430 (translation adapted from *SC* 222 and *FC* 89). Also Origen, *Princ*, 2.10.3.

Here the balance Origen tries to hold between transformation and continuity is clear as he uses 1 Cor 15.53 and the language of "putting on" to describe how the resurrection body does not change, per se, but also is not the same as it "puts on" incorruption and immortality. Origen advocates a transformed, spiritual body based on his understanding of 1 Cor 15 and the progress the body makes from corruption to incorruption.[128] In order to inherit the kingdom of God, one must possess a spiritual body, not by changing into one but by putting one on and progressing from that which is corruptible and mortal to that which is incorruptible and immortal. While flesh and blood cannot inherit the kingdom of God, Origen is clear that a transformed body can. Therefore, for Origen there "will be a time of the resurrection from the dead, when this body which now is sown in corruption, shall rise in incorruption (1 Cor 15.42)."[129]

While it might be easier for Origen, with his opponents, to discard any view of a resurrection body based on the words of 15.50, Origen cannot do this. It is impossible, he writes, "that any other nature than the Father, Son, and Holy Spirit can live without a body [...] for an incorporeal life will rightly be considered a prerogative of the Trinity alone."[130] For Origen, as for others writing before him, a body is necessary for judgement and one can only be judged worthy and put on incorruptibility and immortality if one has a body. The journey to perfection in God, Origen writes, "may require a body, for the sake of moving from place to place"[131] so that

> when the corruptible shall have put on incorruption, and the mortal immortality (1 Cor 15.53: τὸ φθαρτὸν ἐνδύσεται τὴν ἀφθαρσίαν καὶ τὸ θνητὸν τὴν ἀθανασίαν), then shall come to pass what was predicted of old [...] the annihilation of the victory of death, because it had conquered and subjected us to his sway, and of its sting (1 Cor 15.54–55: τῆς νίκης τοῦ θανάτου, καθὸ νικήσας ἡμᾶς ἑαυτῷ ὑπέταξε, καὶ τοῦ ἀπ' αὐτοῦ κέντρου) with which it stings the imperfectly defended soul and inflicts upon it the wounds which result from sin.[132]

Using the dichotomies that he finds in 1 Cor 15, Origen balances the statement that flesh and blood cannot inherit the kingdom of God with the resurrection of the body, which is necessary for judgement and ultimately salvation. Resurrection is not "a sudden resuscitation of the body, since salvation is for [Origen] not

---

128 Also Origen, *Cels*, 5.18–23 and 7.32.
129 Origen, *Princ*, Pr.5 (SC 252).
130 Origen, *Princ*, 2.2.2 (SC 252). Also *Princ*, 1.6.4.
131 Origen, *Cels*, 5.19 (SC 147).
132 Origen, *Cels*, 5.19 (translation adapted from SC 147 and Chadwick).

legal righteousness, but a journey to perfection."[133] He therefore uses the language of 1 Cor 15 to describe the progression from a physical to a spiritual body in the kingdom of God. He writes that "the apostolic teaching is that the soul, having a substance and life of its own, shall, after its departure from this world, be rewarded according to its deserts."[134] Within the body, the soul is both separate from the body and yet "holds the body together, gives it recognizable form, and will actively reassemble it at the resurrection."[135] His anthropology determines his exegesis where the soul and not the body will put on incorruption and immortality, that is, for Origen, "the wisdom and the word, and the righteousness of God which mould, and clothe, and adorn the soul."[136] Origen holds together the body and soul since if both have suffered for Christ, it would be absurd if at the last only the soul were glorified.[137] Thus, it is through the soul that the "very bodies of ours with which we are enveloped may, on account of the word of God and his wisdom (*verbum Dei et sapientiam eius*) and perfect righteousness, earn incorruptibility and immortality" as Paul says, "this corruptible must put on incorruption, and this mortal must put on immortality (1 Cor 15.53: *corruptibile hoc induerit incorruptionem, et mortale hoc induerit inmortalitatem*)."[138]

Resurrection for Origen is a matter "of a profounder and more mystical nature" than almost any other emerging doctrine.[139] Using the words of 1 Cor 15, Origen posits an understanding of the resurrection body in terms of how a spiritual body will inherit the kingdom of God, despite the words of 15.50. The different interpretations that Origen draws out of 1 Cor 15 emphasise not only the ambiguity of Paul's language but also the way Origen reads Scripture, interpreting and adapting it to his theological situation. Thus, while he writes in his *Commentary on John* that the resurrection body does not simply change from mortal-

---

[133] Edwards, "Origen's Two Resurrections," 515.
[134] Origen, *Princ*, Pr.5 (*SC* 252).
[135] Daley, *Hope*, 52. See also, Origen, *Fr.Ps*, 1.5, transl. by Dechow, *Dogma and Mysticism*, 374–375; and Origen, *Princ*, 2.10.2.
[136] Origen, *Princ*, 2.3.2 (*GCS* 22). Here, the language of clothing and adorning is very similar to the idea of "putting on" from 1 Cor 15.53; moreover, the language of Christ as the wisdom of God could have 1 Cor 1.24 and 30 in the background.
[137] See Roukema, "Origen's Interpretation," 337, and Pamphilus, *Apol*, 128.
[138] Origen, *Princ*, 2.3.2 (*GCS* 22).
[139] Origen, *Cels*, 5.19 (*SC* 519, Chadwick). Greer argues that through Origen's use of 1 Cor 15.50–54, one is able to see most clearly "his fundamental distinction between the letter and the spirit, that is, the obvious narrative meaning of the text and its more mysterious spiritual meaning [...] and that the biblical distinction between flesh and spirit, the earthly and heavenly, supplies a warrant for it" (Greer, "Applying," 179).

ity and corruption into immortality and incorruption, against Celsus, using the same Corinthian excerpts, he writes that the resurrected state does involve some change. More precisely, "it is with a secret kind of wisdom that it was said by the Apostle of Jesus, we shall not all sleep, but we shall all be changed, in a moment, in the twinkling of an eye [...] and the dead shall be raised incorruptible and we shall be changed (1 Cor 15.52–53)."[140] He can affirm the Christian view of corporeal resurrection as "worthy of God" and defend a bodily resurrection while at the same time writing that this body is a transformed, spiritual body related to our present body but incorruptible, immortal, and new in appearance.[141]

## 4.6 Conclusions: Resurrection, Hermeneutics, and Formation

The use of excerpts from 1 Cor 15.50–58 within pre-Nicene writings and especially the focus by early Christians on 15.50 highlight some of the controversial issues and ambiguities, both exegetical and doctrinal, at this time. Within the writings of early Christians, the phrases and images from 1 Cor 15.50 and the opposites found in 15.53–54 feature most prevalently. The ambiguities of the phrases and the different ways that they can be interpreted mean that this text is adapted for a wide range of arguments. Moreover, because both the Valentinians and their proto-orthodox opponents use this text, arguments over authority and doctrine happened at the level of hermeneutics and the exegesis of Scripture. Frequently found in texts discussing and defending a theology of resurrection, excerpts from 1 Cor 15 shape early Christian theological and hermeneutical developments more broadly. I have tried to demonstrate through this chapter's examination of the use of portions of 1 Cor 15 how the interpretation of this Corinthian passage affected both understandings of the resurrection of the flesh, and the anthropological, soteriological, and Christological implications of such a position. The conclusions of this chapter, therefore, confirm those of Greer that early Christian use of 1 Cor 15 was "not as much about exegetical method [...] but the theological function of interpretation."[142] Moreover, the ambiguities within this text of what is meant by flesh and blood, the kingdom of God, and putting on imperishability and immortality, allows phrases

---

140 Origen, *Cels*, 5.17 (translation adapted from *SC* 519 and Chadwick).
141 Origen, *Cels*, 5.18–23.
142 Greer, "Applying," 184.

from this Corinthian passage to be adapted to support different sides of the theological argument about resurrection and its form.

Within Valentinian writings, 1 Cor 15.50 is the primary focus when the authors of these texts use excerpts from this Corinthian passage to support a rejection of future resurrection, a confirmation of Christ's resurrection, and the view that apart from Christ, resurrection is spiritual and not corporeal. 1 Cor 15.50 is also a central text for Irenaeus as he defines flesh and blood as the deeds and desires of the flesh and at the same time claims flesh and blood as essential elements of God's creation and, through Christ, the instruments of salvation. For Tertullian, the images and phrases of 15.50–58 support his defence of bodily resurrection and his understanding that a material body is necessary to endure the full judgement of God. Finally, Origen, challenged by the words of 15.50, tries to hold a balance between affirming corporeal resurrection and advocating that this resurrection body will be in a transformed state. The prominence of the use of 15.50 is especially striking as early Christians grapple with how to hold (or not hold) an understanding of bodily resurrection alongside the words that flesh and blood cannot inherit the kingdom of God.

For many, the challenge they find in the words of 1 Cor 15 leads to some complicated exegesis as they both define the meaning of flesh and blood, apart from the human body, to include works and desires and rely on the dichotomies found in 15.53–54 to describe the progress of the body from mortality and perishability to immortality and imperishability. This challenge also leads to a careful reading of the words of 15.50 for those such as Irenaeus and Tertullian, who separate the concepts of resurrection and the kingdom of God, claiming that 15.50 does not exclude flesh and blood from the former. Both of these hermeneutical approaches lead to ethical exhortations, whether through the works of the flesh or through the judgement that will take place before one enters the kingdom of God. Thus, the connection between exegesis and theology includes an ethical element with a concern for how this theology informs the moral and spiritual lives of the Christian.[143] In each use, early Christian writers are challenged by the ambiguity of the words and by different possible interpretations of this text and the theological issues that an interpretation at odds with their own raises. These ambiguities are anthropological, soteriological, and eschatological and include what Paul meant by flesh and blood and the kingdom of God, how the

---

**143** Greer, "Applying," 190–191.

Spirit and judgement each fit into the progression towards the kingdom, and whether the resurrection body is a corporeal or a spiritual one.[144]

The ambiguities that early Christians find in the words and images of 1 Cor 15.50–58 not only influence their interpretation of this passage, but also contribute to the polemical edge often found when they use these words and phrases. One striking element that sets this passage apart from the others engaged in this project is that excerpts from 1 Cor 15 are found primarily within apologetic works. These works, which defend a cause of paramount importance to the writer,[145] are described by Origen as "directed against an alien from the faith, for the sake of those who are still children, tossed to and fro, and carried about with every wind of doctrine (Eph 4.14)."[146] With an issue as central as resurrection to the Christian faith, it is not surprising that most of the instances of early Christian engagement with 1 Cor 15.50–58 occur in works with an apologetic focus. In this context, belief in the resurrection and its correct understanding divided Christians into insiders and outsiders, and the harshness of the polemic within some of the early Christian texts "reveals that deviant interpretations of resurrection–even of resurrection of the flesh–were a real threat for the identity and self-definition of many early Christian groups."[147] The words and images of 1 Cor 15.50–58 provided a point of reference for early Christian writers around which they

---

[144] With 1 Thess 4.15–17 and Rev 20.4–5, excerpts from 1 Cor 15.50–58 serve as the fundamental text for early Christians seeking to discuss the sequence of events and the judgement that would take place at the consummation of the world. Thus, this text is used in such a way that some early Christian writers are described as chiliasts or millenarians when they advocate for an intermediate period between the resurrection of Christ (and sometimes all martyrs; see Rev 20.4) and the resurrection of all others who have died. So the Valentinian use of 1 Cor 15 points to a realised eschatology where resurrection is available here and now while Irenaeus posits a time period of 6000 years during which those who are saved can adjust to their transformed bodies and the "partaking of the divine nature" (Irenaeus, *Haer*, 5.32.1; 5.33–36). See Jean Daniélou, *A History of Early Christian Doctrine: The theology of Jewish Christianity* (vol. 1; London: Darton, Longman & Todd, 1964), 377–404; Daley, *Hope of the Early Church*, 31; 77–78; C. Hill, *Regnum Caelorum: Patterns of Future Hope in Early Christianity* (Oxford: Clarendon, 1992), 5–28; 127–132; 194–95; 249–253; Clementina Mazzucco, "Il millenarismo cristiano delle origini (II–III sec.)," in *Millennium: L'attesa della fine nei primi secoli cristiani. Atti delle III giornate patristiche torinesi* (ed. Renato Uglione; Turin: CELID Editrice, 2002), 145–182; Edwards, "Origen's Two Resurrections," 514. See also Justin Martyr, *Dial*, 80; Irenaeus, *Haer*, 5.32–36; Tertullian, *An*, 58.8 and 55.3; *Mart*, 1; *Marc*, 3.25; Commodianus, *Instr*, 44; and for Origen's opposition to chiliasm see *Princ*, 2.11.2–3.

[145] See Mark J. Edwards, Martin Goodman, and Simon Price, eds., "Introduction: Apologetics in the Roman World" in *Apologetics in the Roman Empire: Pagans, Christians, and Jews* (New York: Oxford University Press, 1999), 1–14; 1–2.

[146] Origen, *Cels*, 5.18 (*SC* 147).

[147] Lehtipuu, "Flesh and Blood," 168.

## 4.6 Conclusions: Resurrection, Hermeneutics, and Formation

could determine the "limits of what was acceptable [...] the warrant not only for what the church was, but also the criterion for what it was allowed to become."[148]

The polemical edge of the writings within which this passage occurs highlights the conclusion that early Christian struggles with the words of this text take place "on several fronts simultaneously," and "it would be an oversimplification to envision only two sides in the debate, say, the promoters of the resurrection of the flesh on the one hand and those of a spiritual resurrection on the other."[149] As Lehtipuu writes, "whether the outsiders could tell the difference, say, between Irenaeus and those whom he calls heretics, is another matter [...] This made the threat of those whose view deviated from that of the author the more dangerous."[150] Even Irenaeus expresses his frustration that his opponents, "speak like us but think otherwise,"[151] "imitate our phraseology,"[152] and take scriptural passages "out of their natural meaning to a meaning contrary to nature."[153] For early Christians, "heresies appeared as the closest, hence, the most immediate and dangerous threat to their emerging collective identity."[154] Therefore, early Christian use of the images of 1 Cor 15 to support their apologetic arguments plays a role in the development of Christian identity.

As the chapter on Col 1 will also explore, the formation of hermeneutical and exegetical interpretations of a passage can develop from situations of conflict, and early Christian use of Paul and his letters is "more than an issue of simple textual interpretation" but merged "with the developing concerns of the day, where the words and ideas of the apostle came to bear on the circumstances and conflicts of the church."[155] This is especially true when the ambiguity of words and ideas in Scripture means that an "obvious" interpretation, in the words of Origen, is inadequate as a solution.[156] Subsequently, early Christian use of 15.50–58 and its anthropological, Christological, and soteriological impli-

---

**148** Leander E. Keck, "Is the New Testament a Field of Study? or, From Outler to Overbeck and Back," *SCe* 1(1981): 19–35; 33. See also Lehtipuu, "Flesh and Blood," 149; Setzer, *Resurrection of the Body*, 134–135; 149–150; Keith Hopkins, "Christian Number and its Implications," *JECS* 6 (1998), 185–226.
**149** Lehtipuu, "Flesh and Blood," 152.
**150** Lehtipuu, "Flesh and Blood," 152.
**151** Irenaeus, *Haer*, 1.Pr.2 (*SC* 263).
**152** Irenaeus, *Haer*, 3.15.1 (*SC* 210).
**153** Irenaeus, *Haer*, 1.9.4 (*SC* 263). See also Tertullian, *Res*, 19.6.
**154** Stroumsa, "*Caro salutis cardo*," 40.
**155** Aageson, *Paul*, 1–2.
**156** Origen, *Princ*, 4.2.4.

cations, defined and refined itself through heresiological polemic.[157] The use of this text apologetically begins with Paul himself, who develops his most detailed discussion of resurrection in 1 Cor 15, responding to those who insist that there is no resurrection of the dead (1 Cor 15.12). Each side of the interpretative struggle about how to understand Paul's words in 1 Cor 15 sought to claim the authority and writings of Paul. Scriptural affirmation and support is so important to early Christian writers, as already seen with their desire to claim Paul as their ally and teacher in the chapter on 1 Cor 2. Nevertheless, with the ambiguity encountered in the writings of Paul concerning resurrection, early Christian writers on all sides "found themselves driven toward one or another mode of biblical 'criticism'—a normative canon within the canon (Marcion), new hermeneutical rules (Irenaeus), allegorical transformations, etc. (Origen)."[158]

The ambiguity found within the Pauline writings on the resurrection body led early Christians such as Irenaeus and Tertullian to make difficult hermeneutical manoeuvres in order to triumph over those whom they saw as drawing incorrect conclusions about the same passage. Because a definitive rebuttal of their opponents is difficult to make on the basis of *sola scriptura*, early Christians mounted ingenious interpretative strategies to support their defence. This is why 1 Cor 15 and other texts engaged in this study are so central to early Christian doctrine and hermeneutics emerging at this time: the "orthodox" are determined to claim the right interpretation of each Pauline text by hermeneutical and exegetical strategies. Early Christians, seeking to claim the authority of Scripture within their theological arguments, found that 1 Cor 15.50–58 posed serious problems to their understanding of resurrection. As a result, they adapted a variety of hermeneutical tactics in order to ensure the words of Paul supported and did not contradict their conclusions, not only about resurrection, but the very make up of Christ and humankind. Scriptural authority, therefore, offered the framework within which early Christian doctrine could emerge and served as the organising principle around which early Christians ordered their argument.[159]

Conclusions about the ways excerpts from 1 Cor 15.50–58 shaped the arguments and hermeneutical strategies of early Christian writers, with a particular focus on the different interpretations of the images and words of the text, lead to two further observations. The first is a challenge to a conclusion in modern

---

157 Stroumsa, "*Caro salutis cardo*," 41.
158 Outler, "Methods and Aims," 11.
159 David Sedley, "Philosophical Allegiance in the Greco-Roman World," in *Philosophia Togata: Essays on Philosophy and Roman Society* (eds. Miriam Griffin and Jonathan Barnes; Oxford: Clarendon Press, 1989), 97–119; 101.

## 4.6 Conclusions: Resurrection, Hermeneutics, and Formation

scholarship, in particular, the recent work of Markus Vinzent. The second is to indicate how this pericope and its use within apologetic works emphasise its role in early Christian formation.

In a recent major study on Christ's resurrection in early Christianity, Markus Vinzent begins with the premise that resurrection is a central idea for Paul, whose understanding of resurrection is most fully developed in 1 Cor 15.[160] Vinzent holds that in the period after Paul and before Marcion, Christ's resurrection "is often obscured, sometimes entirely abandoned, or survives only as one among other testimonies of God's acting."[161] For Vinzent, Marcion is the greatest theologian of the second century and the one who reintroduces resurrection into the centre of the Christian faith. Marcion, he argues, influenced not only the formation of the canon but early Christian thinking in general. Through a rather controversial dating of early Christian writings, with little mention of how controversial some of the dates are, especially for Ignatius, Vinzent demonstrates how early Christians from Ignatius to Melito and Origen were affected and influenced by Marcion's views, especially his views of Christ's resurrection.[162] In other words, the presence, disappearance, and re-emergence of the central place of Jesus' resurrection in early Christian writings are primarily explained by reference to Marcion's influence.[163]

For Vinzent, the focus on Paul and the renewed focus on Christ's resurrection come solely through the central role that Paul's writings played in Marcion's writings and theology. Early Christian reactions to Marcion meant that they were forced to engage with Paul in their arguments.[164] Even those in agreement with Marcion, Vinzent argues, would have engaged Paul since they would have been persuaded to do so by Marcion's writings. Vinzent makes a strong case that Mar-

---

**160** One might argue, however, that Vinzent places Paul's focus on resurrection too central to Paul's argument with the emphasis on the cross, suffering, and death of Christ found throughout the Pauline epistles taking a back seat.
**161** Markus Vinzent, *Christ's Resurrection in Early Christianity and the Making of the New Testament* (Farnham: Ashgate, 2011), 44.
**162** Vinzent, *Christ's Resurrection*, 88–91. Carleton Paget writes in a lengthy review of Vinzent's book that, "Vinzent is reliant upon a kind of mirror-reading, for the majority of the authors whose work he discusses do not explicitly refer to Marcion, and the success of such mirror-reading depends, to some extent, upon the extent to which you have accepted Vinzent's own view about the central importance of Marcion for the developing church (and, of course, his dating of these documents, which is itself in part dependent upon accepting that they are in fact responses to Marcion)" (Carleton Paget, "Marcion and the Resurrection," 76).
**163** Carleton Paget, "Marcion and the Resurrection," 78.
**164** For Vinzent, even the absence of Marcionite influence points to the deliberate avoidance by the author in the work under consideration (see Vinzent, *Christ's Resurrection*, 177).

cion played a significant role in the development of early Christian identities and institutions, and one cannot deny Marcion's possible influence on canonical formation and on early writers such as Valentinus, Justin, Irenaeus, and Tertullian. Nevertheless, is it the case that every Christian writing about Christ's resurrection in this time period relates in some way to Marcion?

It is difficult to argue with Vinzent's conclusions based on the silence of the texts he chooses and the very small number of extant texts between the writings of Paul and Marcion.[165] Nevertheless, this chapter on 1 Cor 15 offers a wider sense of what early Christians were doing when they engaged with one another and the emerging doctrine of resurrection. One of the main problems of beginning with Marcion, as Vinzent does, is that no extant texts from Marcion exist and therefore the survey offered in this chapter, based on the occurrence of Paul in early Christian texts themselves, affords a more secure approach.[166] Moreover, beginning with a Pauline pericope rather than a specific early Christian such as Marcion, this chapter suggests that a single early Christian understanding of 1 Cor 15.50–58 does not exist. An agreed early Christian understanding of resurrection cannot be gleaned from early Christian writings that use the images and words of 1 Cor 15, even from writings well beyond the time of Marcion. Part of the reason for this is that, as this chapter has demonstrated, early Christian concern about resurrection, even just in terms of their use of 1 Cor 15.50–58, emerges for a variety of reasons. They direct their refutations against not only Marcion, but the Valentinians and even one another, claiming to refute all heresies at once.[167] This does not prove that response to Marcion is not primary, but given the patchiness of the evidence and in order not to argue from silence, reconstructions of who influenced and responded to whom are necessarily speculative. If Marcion had not existed, how much of this study of 1 Cor 15 and the application of excerpts from this text by early Christians to support their arguments about resurrection—Christ's and in general—would be difficult to explain?

Early Christian understanding of a theology of resurrection supported by the words and images of 15.50–58 is ambiguous at best. The ambiguity early Chris-

---

**165** See A. Lindemann, *Paulus, Apostel und Lehrer der Kirche* (Tübingen: Mohr [Siebeck], 1999), 295n4 for why definitive conclusions from silence are difficult, especially when considering the importance and significance of Paul and his letters in an early Christian context (Lindemann's focus here is on the 2nd Century). See also Keck, "Field of Study," 32.
**166** Outler argues that it is impossible to determine the "'moment' or series of moments in which Christianity achieved its stabilization of what continued thereafter as an identifiable continuum" and thus would likely take issue with Vinzent's view that Marcion provides the emerging centre around which the Christian doctrine of resurrection develops (Outler, "Methods and Aims," 14).
**167** See Irenaeus, *Haer*, 2.31.1.

tians encountered as they sought to interpret this Pauline text served as a catalyst and focal point of their determination to interpret this text correctly in their theological arguments. The biggest issue they encounter is solving this problem of interpretation both hermeneutically and doctrinally, with a particular focus on what to do with the words of 1 Cor 15.50. The reason for early Christian interest in this text to defend and support their views of resurrection is perhaps not because of Marcion and his influence, but because of the interpretative ambiguity of the Pauline material itself and that it can be adapted and adopted to support arguments on each side of the emerging doctrine of resurrection. Heresy for early Christians is as much about the exegetical problems posed by the Pauline text as it is about the influence of deviants such as Marcion. With Marcion as a part of the reception history of 1 Cor 15.50–58 and the emerging Christian theology of resurrection, the catalyst for early Christian focus on this passage is not necessarily Marcion, but Paul. Paul is the one offering images that can be adapted in multiple ways to support a variety of theological arguments, writing ambiguously about the nature of resurrection, and creating a tension between the words of 15.50 and 15.53–54 that is unresolved. Paul is therefore the focal point for early Christian writings about resurrection which rely on 15.50–58, a history of which Marcion is only a part.

While early Christian use of excerpts from 1 Cor 15.50–58 has the potential to affect modern debates and conclusions such as those of Vinzent, it also plays a role in forming early Christian identity through its high occurrence in apologetic works. Apologists played a central role in the formation of early Christianity, making use of their rhetorical and even philosophical education to serve as mediators between Christianity and other traditions—both religious and philosophical—and to develop and defend ideas within the Christian tradition. The occurrence of this Corinthian passage primarily in apologetic works is not a coincidence, but is central to understanding the use of this passage. This apologetic focus points to the possibility that 1 Cor 15.50–58 played a role in early Christian formation, both directly in terms of the central concepts these writings seek to teach, and indirectly in terms of frightening off those who might form Christians in another way and giving instructions on what not to think and believe.[168] The evaluation of early Christian texts in this chapter suggests that these

---

[168] In this context, orthodox and heterodox shift depending on the perspective of the author. For example, from the Valentinian perspective, Irenaeus is heterodox while from Irenaeus' perspective, the opposite is true. Sedley comments that "In evaluating the arguments on both sides of the debate, it is advisable to start out with a healthy degree of agnosticism as to which party, if either, is in the right" (Sedley, "Philosophical Allegiance," 108). Both parties consider them-

apologies often included the use of philosophical traditions and rhetoric to determine boundaries and convince those who already considered themselves to be Christian about the truths of the Christian faith. While the "implied reader is a non-Christian Roman audience, the reality of Christian apologetic literature was that it was ordinarily written for internal consumption for adherents in order to reinforce beliefs."[169] In other words, most of the works of the apologists from this time period are not likely to have been read outside their communities and the wider church.[170] Even though Tertullian's *Against Marcion* is addressed to Marcion, Marcion himself was dead at the time of writing. The same is true for Origen and his apology against Celsus as well as Methodius in his attack on Origen. In this way, even works addressed to outsiders provided justification and encouragement for those "who would prove to be the principal readers—namely, the insiders."[171] Therefore, one of the fundamental elements of these apologetic texts is the sense of legitimatisation and self-definition they seek to create.[172]

As I have tried to emphasise throughout this chapter which examines early Christian use of 1 Cor 15, this Corinthian text is not simply a proof text. Rather, much is at stake because misinterpretation challenges an entire religious system, self-definition, and the anthropological, eschatological, and Christological doctrines as they emerge and evolve. The ambiguous nature of this text affected how early Christians understood the images and phrases of 1 Cor 15.50–58 and how they engaged with the contradictions found within this pericope. This, in turn, both underscores the hermeneutical and exegetical developments in early Christian writings, and also points to how this Corinthian text may have served "to educate, to offer intellectual fodder, to consolidate, for both new and old members, the experience of belonging—as in some sense all literature does,

---

selves not only to be right and loyal to Paul, but each also labels the other as heretical (108–109).

**169** Bird, "Reception of Paul," 72.
**170** See Edwards, Goodman, and Price, "Introduction," 8–9.
**171** Edwards, Goodman, and Price, "Introduction," 9. As Edwards insists, this is not to underestimate their influence because within the church, "their eloquence would be esteemed both for itself and for the piety that it rendered so conspicuous; small wonder, then, that in each new generation of Christians the most astute apologist is also the most voluminous writer on morals, history, biblical exegesis, and dogmatics" (Edwards, Goodman, and Price, "Introduction," 9).
**172** See Loveday Alexander, "The Acts of the Apostles as an Apologetic Text," in *Apologetics in the Roman Empire: Pagans, Jews, and Christians* (eds. Mark J. Edwards, Martin Goodman, and Simon Price; Oxford: Oxford University Press, 1999), 15–44; 19, and Gregory E. Sterling, *Historiography and Self-Definition: Josephus, Luke-Acts, and Apologetic Historiography* (NovTSup 64; Leiden: Brill, 1991), 382–386.

## 4.6 Conclusions: Resurrection, Hermeneutics, and Formation

and apologetic literature in an even stronger sense."[173] Thus, the use of 15.50–58 repeatedly within an apologetic context emphasises not only early Christian concern for the implications and form of resurrection, but also the formational role of this text for early Christians and their community, doctrine, and scriptural understanding as they sought to establish one way of truth against a myriad of adversarial views and dangers. As early Christians work out their understanding of resurrection, they do so with all of the bluster, polemic, rhetoric and artifice they can as they try to claim the writings of Paul as their own. The urgency with which questions of resurrection are asked and debated reflects the "existential intensity" by which this doctrine emerged and the importance of getting the interpretation of 1 Cor 15 right.[174] As Rajak describes the power of 1 Cor 15 and the enormity of what was at stake in interpreting it correctly, "apologetic became a battle of the books, and also a battle for souls."[175] The right interpretation of this Pauline passage and a right understanding of resurrection was not only about refuting opponents, but was a formational task, shaping the church and those within it.

Thus, formation is central to apologetic, whether the aim is to correct Christians who do not hold the right interpretation of a passage of Scripture such as 1 Cor 15.50–58 or to address a wider theological problem derived from the use of 1 Cor 15. Early Christians use this text within an apologetic context to form, fortify, and correct others in their faith and to claim the authority of the Pauline writings as supportive of their view, no matter the ambiguity they encounter along the way. For early Christians, the images and phrases of 15.50–58 offer not only an interpretative and theological challenge, but in the process emphasise the close connection in early Christian exegesis between Scripture and theology. As they grapple with the meaning of flesh and blood, kingdom, judgement, and progress from mortality and perishability to immortality and imperishability, early Christians do so with a focus on the theology of resurrection and the ethical and soteriological implications of how they define and understand each of the images and phrases involved. In this way, early Christian use of the images and phrases of 1 Cor 15.50–58 shaped not only their theology of resurrection, but the ethical implications of this emerging theology and the

---

[173] Tessa Rajak, "Talking at Trypho: Christian Apologetic as Anti-Judaism in Justin's *Dialogue with Trypho the Jew*," in *Apologetics in the Roman Empire: Pagans, Jews, and Christians* (eds. Mark J. Edwards, Martin Goodman, and Simon Price; Oxford: Oxford University Press, 1999), 59–80; 80.
[174] Stroumsa, "*Caro salutis cardo*," 41–42.
[175] Rajak, "Talking at Trypho," 80.

consequences that a wrong interpretation could have not only for theological argument, but for salvation.

# Chapter Five:
# Colossians 1.15 – 20: There was a time when he was not[1]

> He is the image of the invisible God,
> the first-born of all creation
> (Col 1.15)

## 5.1 Early Christian Writers and Colossians 1

Written in the latter part of the fourth century, the works of Ambrosiaster and John Chrysostom include the first extant commentaries by early Christian writers on Colossians. With commentaries on Romans, the Corinthian correspondence, and Galatians already known at this time, the lack of evidence for an earlier commentary on the Colossian epistle could lead to the assumption that this letter attributed to Paul held a lower status for early Christian writers. Moreover, since modern scholarship does not agree about the status of Colossians as an authentic Pauline composition, the assumption might also be posited that the lack of early commentaries confirms the less authoritative nature of the epistle. Neither of these assumptions is true. While the letter to the Colossians is not cited by early Christian writers as frequently as the other Pauline epistles, one Colossian pericope is amongst the most highly cited Pauline passages in ante-Nicene Christian writings: Col 1.15 – 20. Scattered across early Christian preaching, teaching, apologies, letters, and treatises, excerpts from this pericope are used over 670 times by more than 50 different pre-Nicene authors.[2] Moreover, early Christian writers from Justin Martyr to Methodius, Irenaeus to Eusebius assume Pauline authorship of the Colossian epistle and therefore, any shadows cast by modern

---

[1] Rowan Williams, *Arius: Heresy and Tradition* (2nd ed; London: SCM Press, 2001), 150; Athanasius of Alexandria, *Dep.Ar*, 1.5 – 6; 1.9; 2.37.

[2] See Appendix D for details of these references. Similar to a note in the chapter on early Christian use of 1 Cor 2.6 – 16, one must also mention at the start of this chapter that very few references to excerpts from Col 1.15 – 20 were found in "heterodox" and Valentinian texts. There are only six possible references in Clement's *Excerpts from Theodotus* and fewer than 20 possible references in anonymous texts and fragments. Nevertheless, from the tenor of some early Christian texts, it is clear that some early Christian writers were reacting to what they considered heterodox interpretation of Col 1, especially concerning the body of Christ and perhaps even the myths surrounding how Christ's body was formed at the incarnation (with gratitude to Judith Kovacs for her insights on possible "heterodox" use of Col 1).

scholarship on the authenticity of this letter do not affect the conclusions of this chapter, examining early Christian use of this text.[3]

Addressed to "the saints in Colossae" (Col 1.1), this letter is written to a community that, so far as modern interpreters are aware, Paul did not visit. The exact details of the founding of this Christian community, as well as that of nearby Laodicea and Hierapolis (mentioned in Col 2.1 and 4.13–15), are not known. From the introduction and content, one can assume that the readers of this letter are Christians who have a solid grounding in their faith in and love of God. The tone of the letter is both commendatory and exhortatory, and while opponents or false teachers are in and around the community, Paul does not assume as aggressive a stance in attacking his opponents as found in his letter to the community in Galatia.[4] Immediately following the introductory words to the Colossians, the instructional part of the letter commences with Col 1.15–20, the focus of this chapter and a pericope that many scholars call a "Christ-hymn."[5] This passage sets up the remainder of the letter, establishing the foundational premise that in Christ the entire fullness of God is present and as such, Christ is superior to all other powers and principalities that may exist both on earth and in heaven. Much of the letter that follows is grounded in this dominion of Christ and gives "an exposition of the ways in which the lordship of Christ includes all areas of our life."[6] In other words, "Christ is Lord over all (1:15–20), so his own people should do all in the name of the Lord Jesus (3:17)."[7]

In contrast to the dearth of commentaries on the Colossian epistle by early Christian writers, modern scholars offer an abundance of commentaries and articles which focus on the origin, structure, and content of Col 1.15–20.[8] Despite a

---

[3] Novatian and Origen, for example, introduce excerpts from Col 1.15–20 with the words "when Paul says" (Novatian, *Trin,* 3; Origen, *Princ,* 2.6.1), while Alexander of Alexandria adds a bit more pizzazz to his introduction of a Colossian reference with the words, "the colossally-speaking Paul says" (Alexander of Alexandria, *Ep.Alex,* 6).

[4] Col 2.18–20 is an exception to this statement.

[5] As I will suggest in the concluding section of this chapter, early Christian use of Col 1 challenges this assumed category of "hymn." For an in-depth look at the understanding of "hymn" in early Christian and Graeco-Roman contexts, as well as the influence of patristic reception of two assumed Pauline "Christ-hymns": Col 1.15–20 and Phil 2.5–11, see Benjamin Edsall and Jennifer R. Strawbridge "The Songs we Used to Sing? Hymn 'Traditions' and Reception in Pauline Letters," *JSNT* 37.3 (2015), 290–311; 300–305.

[6] Eduard Lohse, *Colossians and Philemon: A Commentary on the Epistles to the Colossians and to Philemon* (ed. Helmut Koester; Hermeneia; Philadelphia: Fortress Press, 1971), 3.

[7] Lohse, *Colossians,* 4.

[8] A sample of the range of scholarship includes: Robert McL. Wilson, *A Critical and Exegetical Commentary on Colossians and Philemon* (London: T&T Clark International, 2005), 123n1; Lohse, *Colossians,* 41n64; Johannes Lähnemann, *Der Kolosserbrief: Komposition, Situation und*

large number of excurses within modern scholarship on this pericope, very little has been written about its reception by early Christian writers before Chrysostom. Since Col 1.15–20 is one of the most frequently cited Pauline passages in early Christian writings, that early Christian reception has not filtered into more recent debates in order to support developing interpretations of this text is surprising. Lightfoot is one of the few scholars whose commentary on the Colossian epistle, revised for publication in 1890, takes into account the wealth of early Christian references to Col 1.15–20.[9] Referring to patristic use of this passage, Lightfoot lists numerous references to Col 1.15–20 in his commentary, acknowledging that the "history of patristic exegesis of this expression is not without a painful interest."[10] For early Christian writers, Col 1.15–20 offers a veritable goldmine of references to support emerging doctrinal and Christological claims. Apart from Lightfoot, few if any modern commentaries on Colossians make reference to early Christian writings on this text and even then, many commentators simply offer a summary of Lightfoot's work.[11] Modern scholars are anxious to dissect and critique this pericope from a variety of perspectives, often with little consideration for the extensive use of this passage by early Christian writers.[12]

---

*Argumentation* (Gütersloh: Gütersloher Verlagshaus Gerd Mohn, 1971). The pioneering works on this pericope are those of Eduard Norden, *Agnostos Theos: Untersuchungen zur Formengeschichte religiöser Rede* (Stuttgart: B.G. Teubner, 1971), 250–254; Ernst Käsemann, "A Primitive Christian Baptismal Liturgy," in *Essays on New Testament Themes* (ed. Ernst Käsemann; London: SCM, 1964), 148–168; esp. 149–153, and for a completely opposite view (picked up by N.T. Wright) C.F. Burnley, "Christ as the ARXH of Creation," *JTS* 27 (1926): 160–177. Amongst the range of views on this pericope, Mary Rose D'Angelo may be found at one extreme because she views this passage as part of the Wisdom tradition and therefore has retranslated Col 1.15–20 with feminine pronouns: see Mary Rose D'Angelo, "Colossians," in *Searching the Scriptures 2: A Feminist Commentary* (ed. Elisabeth Schüssler Fiorenza; New York: Crossroad, 1993), 313–324; esp. 317–318.

**9** Joseph Barber Lightfoot, *Saint Paul's Epistles to the Colossians and to Philemon: A revised text with Introductions, Notes, and Dissertations* (9th ed.; London: Macmillan, 1890), 144–148. The new *Evangelisch-Katholischer Kommentar* on Colossians, to be published in 2018, and the forthcoming commentary series *Ein patristischer Kommentar zum Neuen Testament* will presumably help to fill this gap significantly.

**10** Lightfoot, *Colossians*, 146.

**11** See Wilson, *Colossians and Philemon*, 135–136.

**12** For example, Matthew Gordley's recent work, with a focus on Col 1.15–20 as a didactic hymn, examines the structural components as well as the Jewish and Graeco-Roman rhetorical elements of the "hymn" without exploring the reception of this text and whether it was received or used as such by early Christians. See Matthew E. Gordley, *Teaching through Song in Antiquity: Didactic Hymnody among Greeks, Romans, Jews, and Christians* (Tübingen: Mohr [Siebeck], 2011). Two recent exceptions to this gap are Michael Peppard, "'Poetry', 'Hymns' and 'Tradition-

This chapter complements Lightfoot's work by examining how early Christians were using Col 1.15–20 with the assumption that this use can lead to a deeper understanding of its early reception and influence on early Christians and their developing doctrines. In particular, I found that excerpts from Col 1 are used to express emerging Christological views and to describe the relationship between the Father and the Son, and that excerpts from this passage are embedded within numerous early Christian writings and arguments. Examining early Christian use of this passage, therefore, also helps to establish a better understanding of its important role in the early formation of Christian doctrine, particularly in the early stages of the Arian controversy.

While the reason for focusing on Col 1.15–20 is because of the high number of references to it by early Christian writers, as in previous chapters, the focus of this chapter is narrowed to a small but representative selection from early Christian writings in order to examine the breadth of how this text was being used.[13] What emerges is that images and phrases from this Colossian pericope are imported into a wide range of contexts and used to support a diversity of discussions and arguments by early Christian writers. This conclusion is supported by the division of the main body of this chapter into two parts in order to establish the different ways that references to this passage in early Christian writings were used: as Christological descriptions to explicate more clearly the person and nature of Christ, and as a text closely connected with at least two other well-known New Testament passages (and concomitantly, also so-called Christological "hymns"): John 1.1–18 and Phil 2.5–11.[14]

## 5.2 Christological Titles and their Implications

Wiles surmises that, "no subject was more central to the hearts and minds of early Christian writers than the subject of the person of Christ" and "the full divinity of Christ and the relation of his divine to his human nature" served as "the

---

al Material' in New Testament Epistles or How to Do Things with Indentations," *JSNT* 30.3 (2008), 319–342 and Edsall and Strawbridge, "Songs we Used to Sing."

**13** As with other chapters of this study, a more comprehensive list of references is cited in the notes throughout to indicate the breadth of material considered.

**14** As noted in the introductory chapter as well as the chapter on 1 Cor 15, excerpts from Phil 2 are also included amongst the most frequently used Pauline passages in early Christian writings, occurring more than 565 times. Because the use of this text is similar to that of Col 1, a separate examination of the use of Phil 2 in early Christian writings does not feature in this study.

themes most ardently and most bitterly discussed."[15] That many titles were ascribed to Jesus—such as those found in Col 1—is a statement few will debate. Eusebius is clear that, when speaking of Christ, myriads of titles are given to him, so much so that, "to him the names of Captain, and great high priest, prophet of the Father, angel of mighty counsel, brightness of the Father's light, only-begotten Son (μονογενῆ τε υἱόν), with a thousand other titles are ascribed in the oracles of the sacred writers."[16] Thus, early Christian writers use "the image of the invisible God" (Col 1.15) to establish that the invisible God the Father may be known through God the Son, the image, thereby allowing God to remain necessarily incorporeal while also being made known. "First-born of all creation" (Col 1.15) is used to argue for the pre-existence of Christ, describing Christ as the one who has been present from the beginning and active as creator. Early Christian writers use "first-born from the dead" (Col 1.18) to describe and defend bodily resurrection and resurrection from the dead in general.[17] "Thrones and dominions" (Col 1.16) is used, particularly by Origen, to describe Jesus as the only and the supreme mediator between humankind and God. Christ as the "head of the body, the Church" (Col 1.18) is used by early Christians to defend their understanding that the Christ who suffered on the cross and died is God the Son, undivided from God the Father. Early Christian writers use the Christological descriptions they find in Col 1 to focus on Christ's pre-existence as one who shares

---

**15** Wiles, *Divine Apostle*, 73. Studies of the development of early Christian Christology embrace a variety of approaches to the subject. Some are diachronic and take an historical approach, examining the process by which phrases about Jesus found in the New Testament were formulated. Other studies focus on New Testament titles given to Jesus, tracing these terms through both pre-Christian and early Christian writings. Others, such as studies of Col 1.15, focus on a particular Christological theme found in the New Testament such as the pre-existence or the begotten nature of Christ and attempt to demonstrate how such a theme is reflected across different New Testament and early Christian writings. See also Frances M. Young, "Prelude: Jesus Christ, foundation of Christianity," in *The Cambridge History of Christianity: Origins to Constantine* (eds. Margaret M. Mitchell and Frances M. Young; Cambridge: Cambridge University Press, 2006), 1–34; 9.
**16** Eusebius, *Laud.Const*, 3.6 (*GCS* 7).
**17** For other examples in early Christian writings where Jesus is described as "first-born from the dead," see: *Ep.Lugd*, 2; Irenaeus, *Haer*, 2.22.4; 3.16.5; 3.22.4; 4.2.4; 4.20.2; 4.24.1; 5.31.2; *Demonst*, 38–40; Hippolytus, *Fr.Reg*, 1; Clement of Alexandria, *Exc.Theod*, 33 (this is most likely the Valentinian author and not Clement; see Sagnard, *Théodote*, 34); Origen, *Comm.-Jo*, 1.108; 1.117–118; 1.121; *Comm.Rom*, 1.6.3; *Comm.Cant*, 1.3; *Cels*, 2.77; *Princ*, 1.3.7; *Hom.Num*, 3.4; *Comm.Ps*, Ps 16.9; Cyprian, *Quirin*, 2.1; Pamphilus, *Apol*, 102; 132; 143; 146; Methodius, *Res*, 1.1.13; 2.1.13; Eusebius, *Hist.eccl*, 5.2.3. This phrase will not be discussed in depth within this chapter because it is especially difficult to determine whether early Christian writers are using Col 1.18 or Rev 1.5 in many of their references to this phrase.

the authority and nature of God, as the head of the church and of humanity, and even as wisdom itself.

### 5.2.1 εἰκὼν τοῦ θεοῦ τοῦ ἀοράτου: "Image of the invisible God"[18]

Early Christian writers use Col 1.15 to describe the invisible and incorporeal nature of God and to consider how God may be known through God's image, Jesus Christ. Their focus on the phrase "image of the invisible God" and especially on the word "image" leads this excerpt to be used in a range of ways across early Christian writings. One of the first to cite this passage at length is Clement of Alexandria. Clement uses part of Col 1.15 in his *Exhortation* for the purpose of ridiculing the Greek deities and disparagingly comparing the work of Greek sculptors, who fashion statues of the gods, with the work of God the Father in creation. He asks the "heathen," to whom his treatise is addressed,

> Who breathed into life? Who bestowed righteousness? Who promised immortality? The creator of all things alone; the great artist and Father has formed us, such a living glory as humankind is. But your Olympian, the image of an image (εἰκόνος εἰκών), greatly out of harmony with truth, is the work of dull Attic hands. For the image of God is his word (Col 1.15: Εἰκὼν μὲν γὰρ τοῦ θεοῦ ὁ λόγος αὐτοῦ), and the genuine son of mind the divine word, the archetypal light of light; and the image of the word (εἰκὼν δὲ τοῦ λόγου) is the true person, the mind which is in humankind, who is therefore said to have been made in the image and likeness of God (Gen 1.27: ὁ κατ᾽ εἰκόνα τοῦ θεοῦ καὶ καθ᾽ ὁμοίωσιν).[19]

With a focus on the word "image," Clement claims that the Olympian Zeus "is only an image of an image," far removed from reality since the statue is an image of the artist's idea and this idea is an image of its object. The divine *logos*, however, is the direct image and Son of God. As Clement argues, to be created in the image of God the Son is to be created not as an "image of an image" but to be created in the very image of God himself.[20] At stake for Clement is the

---

[18] For other examples, see: *Tri.Trac*, 12; *Didas.Silv.* in *The Nag Hammadi Library in English* (eds. James M. Robinson and Richard Smith; Leiden: Brill, 1996), 100–101; 112–113; and Clement of Alexandria, *Exc.Theod*, 7 and 10 (portions of both 7 and 10 are attributed by Sagnard to the Valentinian author; for an analysis of each of these sections, see Sagnard, *Théodote*, 33–36).
[19] Clement of Alexandria, *Prot*, 10.23–26, (translation adapted from *SC* 2 and *LCL* 92).
[20] The use of the phrase, "image of an image," is also found in the works of Philo of Alexandria and his use of Plato to describe both the cosmos and humans as those made after the image of God (εἰκὼν τοῦ νοητοῦ θεὸς αἰσθητός, μέγιστος καὶ ἄριστος κάλλιστός τε καὶ τελεώτατος γέγονεν εἷς οὐρανὸς ὅδε μονογενὴς ὤν; *Tim*. 92c). For Philo, neither the cosmos nor humankind are directly an image of God but the copy of the divine image and as such he writes, "Now if the part is

reality that God the Father alone is the living God who gives life to his image, who in turn takes on the nature and likeness of God. Clement uses this phrase from Colossians to describe how a living image (humankind) implies a living original (God). In the process, he implies not only that the images of pagan gods are not living beings since they are carved by human hands, but also that the pagan gods themselves, therefore, are not living. Connecting the image of the invisible God from Col 1.15 with the image of God found in Genesis, Clement takes "image" to be an entity that expresses or communicates something. Therefore Christ, as the Word of God and image of God's nature and likeness, takes on the very nature and likeness of God.

In the works of Irenaeus, excerpts from Col 1 play a central role in his adaptation of the rhetorical concept of recapitulation (*anakephalaiosis*).[21] Irenaeus utilises this term to argue for the "summing up of all things and all human history under the headship of Christ,"[22] the image of God. With this, he writes that in Christ all things, including the divine plan of salvation, are made complete and can be "summed up" or recapitulated. Irenaeus' understanding of salvation history is "centred on, and culminates in, Christ: what has gone before typifies

---

an image of an image (εἰκὼν εἰκόνος), it is manifest that the whole is so too; [...] the whole creation, this entire world perceived by our sense (seeing that it is greater than any human image) is a copy of the divine image (μίμημα θείας εἰκόνος)" (*Opif*, 25). Not only humankind, but the visible cosmos is "an image of an image," "a copy of the divine image" even as he explains elsewhere that "God's image, the ideal form, and the *logos* itself (εἰκόνι καὶ ἰδέᾳ, τῷ ἑαυτοῦ λόγῳ) are all synonymous entities by which the cosmos was stamped" (*Somn*, 2.45). See Geurt Hendrik van Kooten, *Paul's Anthropology in Context: The Image of God, Assimilation to God, and Tripartite Man in Ancient Judaism, Ancient Philosophy and Early Christianity* (WUNT 232; Tübingen: Mohr [Siebeck], 2008); Behr, *Asceticism and Anthropology*, 139–141; and Philo, *Conf*, 97; *Somn*, 1.139–140; *Spec*, 3.207.

**21** As discussed briefly in the previous chapter on 1 Cor 15, *anakephalaiosis*, meaning a concluding summary, is a term from Graeco-Roman rhetoric first used in a Christian context by Irenaeus, whose understanding "takes its point of departure from Ephesians" 1.9–10 (Greer, "Framework," 169). The concept of recapitulation is a particular focus for Irenaeus concerning the salvation of Adam and the contrast he finds in Paul's writings between Adam and Christ (1 Cor 15.22 and 15.45, for example). Christ not only reversed the effects of the Fall and restored humanity, taking on the same flesh as Adam, but he also retraced every age of all human beings as the "vicarious representative of humanity" (Hans Boersma, *Violence, Hospitality, and the Cross: Reappropriating the Atonement Tradition* [Grand Rapids, Mich: Baker Academic, 2006], 125). See Denis Minns, "Irenaeus," in *Early Christian Thinkers: The Lives and Legacies of Twelve Key Figures* (ed. Paul Foster; Downers Grove, Ill: Intervarsity Press, 2010), 36–51; 47; Grant, *Irenaeus*, 39; and Thomas Holsinger-Friesen, *Irenaeus and Genesis: A Study of Competition in Early Christian Hermeneutics* (JTISup 1; Winona Lake, Ind: Eisenbrauns, 2009), 1–41; and Methodius, *Res*, 1.1.13.
**22** John Behr, "Irenaeus on the Word of God," 163.

its realization in him, as he realizes what will be wrought in those who follow him."[23] Irenaeus writes that God in Christ,

> came to save all through means of himself, all, I say, who through him are born again to God, infants and children and boys and youths and the aged. He therefore passed through every age, becoming an infant for infants, thus sanctifying infants; a child for children, thus sanctifying those who are of this age, at the same time being to them an example of piety, righteousness, and obedience; a youth for youths, becoming an example for them and sanctifying them to the Lord, likewise he was an old man for the aged that he might be a perfect master for all, not merely with respect to setting forth truth, but also with respect to age, sanctifying at the same time the aged also, and becoming an example to them as well. Then at last, he came to death, that he might be the first-born from the dead (Col 1.18 or Rev 1.5: *sit primogenitus ex mortuis*), that in all things he may be pre-eminent, the prince of life, existing before all and going before all.[24]

For Irenaeus, Christ is not only pre-eminent but his death and resurrection lead to the defeat of death because as "image of the invisible God," "head of the Church," and "first-born from the dead," Christ exists before all and goes before all even in death. Christ "simply by recapitulating every age group, sanctified those age groups,"[25] and the life, suffering, and death of Christ serve as an example to Christians in each stage of life.[26] Therefore, when his focus turns to the incarnation and what was accomplished through God taking on human flesh, Irenaeus writes that there is only,

> one God the Father and one Christ Jesus, who is coming throughout the whole disposition (*dispositionem*), and recapitulating all things in himself (*in semetipsum recapitulans*). In this all is a man, the image of God (*plasmatio Dei*) and thus he recapitulated humankind in himself, the invisible becoming visible, the incomprehensible being made comprehensi-

---

**23** Behr, *Asceticism and Anthropology*, 85. See also Irenaeus, *Haer*, 5.36.3.
**24** Irenaeus, *Haer*, 2.22.4 (translation adapted from *SC* 294 and *ACW* 64). Similarly, Origen writes that Christ becomes a youth, an elder, and the first fruits of all creation in order to redeem all (*Hom.Jer*, 1.8.5).
**25** Boersma, *Violence*, 125.
**26** Boersma, *Violence*, 126. While Foster does not discuss Colossians or Irenaeus in terms of polymorphic Christology, Irenaeus offers a possible example of this perspective in his understanding of Christ having taken on all stages of human life in order to save everyone, even in death. For Foster, polymorphic approaches, "like their docetic counterparts [...] are also concerned with transcendence over the physical realm" however, unlike their docetic opponents "the primary interest is a demonstration of the triumph of Jesus over the constraint of death, not a rejection of the material realm itself" (98). In this way, "both docetic and proto-orthodox Christologies were able to use the ability to appear in multiple forms to advance their own perspectives on the nature of the person of Christ" (Paul Foster, "Polymorphic Christology: Its Origins and Development in Early Christianity," *JTS* 38, no. 1 (2007): 66–99; 99).

ble (Col 1.15–16: *et hominem ergo in semetipsum recapitulans est, invisibilis visibilis factus, et imcomprehensibilis factus comprehensibilis*), the impassible becoming capable of suffering, and the Word human, thus recapitulating all things in himself (*universa in semetipsum recapitulans*), so that in the super-celestial, spiritual, and invisible things he might assume supremacy, taking to himself pre-eminence, and constituting himself the head of the Church (Col 1.19: *caput Ecclesiae*), he might draw all things to himself at the proper time.[27]

The word "image" sparks off a series of responses for Irenaeus that focus on the unity of God the Father, the unity of God the Son, and the salvation of all through God in Christ. For Irenaeus, the unity of God the Father affirms the unity of God the Son, the image of God who is fully human and fully divine. Irenaeus is especially concerned to argue that Christ is one—divine and human—and his doctrine of recapitulation holds together this view so that everything human and divine is summed up in Christ. Jesus Christ is not comprised of two parts—a passive, visible part and an impassive, invisible part—but is everything that it is to be God and everything that it is to be human.[28] Therefore, by recapitulating all things in himself, including humankind, "the invisible, incomprehensible, impassible Word becomes visible, comprehensible and passible,"[29] becomes human and, in the process, redeems all.

In his apology against Celsus, Origen uses excerpts from Col 1 and the language of image in a different way as he claims that one mistake easily made by the ignorant, the foolish, and those new to faith, is a failure to see the difference between the image of God (humankind) and God's image (Christ). He writes that,

> Celsus failed to see the difference between what is according to the image of God (Gen 1.27: κατ' εἰκόνα θεοῦ) and of his image (Col 1.15: τῆς εἰκόνος αὐτοῦ), so that he did not realise that God's image is the first-born of all creation (Col 1.15: εἰκὼν μὲν τοῦ θεοῦ ὁ πρωτότοκος πάσης κτίσεως), the very *logos* and truth (ὁ αὐτολόγος καὶ ἡ αὐτοαλήθεια), and further, the very wisdom himself (ἡ αὐτοσοφία) being the image of his goodness, whereas humankind was made according to the image of God (εἰκόνα δὲ τοῦ θεοῦ), and furthermore, every one of whom Christ is head (κεφαλή) is God's image and glory (εἰκὼν καὶ δόξα θεοῦ).[30]

Understanding "image" as an expression of something, Origen uses excerpts from Col 1 and Gen 1 to distinguish between two types of image. While Clement used Col 1 to focus on the nature of God over and against the nature of pagan gods, for Origen the distinction is between the nature of humankind and the na-

---

**27** Irenaeus, *Haer*, 3.16.6 (John Behr, *The Way to Nicaea* [Crestwood, NY: St. Vladimir's Seminary Press, 2001], 126–127 with adaptations).
**28** Behr, *Nicaea*, 125.
**29** Behr, *Nicaea*, 127.
**30** Origen, *Cels*, 6.63 (*SC* 150; Chadwick). See also *Comm.Jo*, 6.49.

ture of Christ. Origen argues that God's image, Christ, is not only differentiated from pagan images but also from humans who are created after him according to the image of God. To be God's image is different and distinct from being made in God's image for God's image, Christ, is that which reveals the otherwise unknowable, invisible, incorporeal God.[31] At stake for Origen is a defense of the incorporeal and invisible nature of God as revealed only in Jesus Christ. He defends this understanding when he writes, in an argument similar to Clement before him, that, "Scripture clearly says that God is incorporeal (ἀσώματον). That is why no one has ever seen God (John 1.18: θεὸν οὐδεὶς ἑώρακε πώποτε) and the first-born of all creation is said to be an image of the invisible God (Col 1.15: εἰκὼν λέγεται εἶναι τοῦ ἀοράτου θεοῦ ὁ πρωτότοκος πάσης κτίσεως), using invisible in the sense of incorporeal."[32]

This use of John 1 and Col 1 together leads Origen to explain in his *First Principles*, how important it is to distinguish between seeing and knowing when speaking about the image of God. This distinction brings to light a different understanding of "image" for Origen, as he tries to describe the identity of God in Christ and how it is that an image may be seen and known. This argument further emphasises his concern for the incorporeal nature of God as he argues that only through God's image, Christ, who is seen, can God be known while remaining incorporeal. He writes,

> See, therefore, if the Apostle does not say the same thing, when, speaking of Christ, he says that he is the image of the invisible God, the first-born of all creation (Col 1.15: *qui est imago invisibilis Dei, primogenitus omnis creaturae*). Not, as some suppose, that the nature of God is visible to some and invisible to others, for the Apostle does not say the image of God invisible to humankind or invisible to sinners (*imago invisibilis Dei hominibus aut invisibilis peccatoribus*), but with unvarying constancy pronounces on the nature of God saying, image of the invisible God (*imago invisibilis Dei*). Moreover, John in his Gospel, saying that no one has seen God at any time (John 1.18), manifestly discloses to all who are capable of understanding, that there is no nature to which God is visible, not as if, he were a being who was visible by nature and merely escaped or baffled the view of a frailer creature.[33]

Origen is particularly concerned with those who assume from the words, "he is the image of the invisible God," that this means God is corporeal. Furthermore,

---

[31] Wiles, *Divine Apostle*, 75–76.
[32] Origen, *Cels*, 7.27 (SC 150; Chadwick). See also *Cels*, 6.69; *Princ*, 1.2.6; *Comm.Jo*, 32.29, and *Hom.Gen*, 1.13 where Col 1.15 is cited with John 14.9 ("He who has seen God has seen the Father").
[33] Origen, *Princ*, 1.1.8 (translation adapted from GCS 22 and Butterworth). See also *Princ*, 2.4.3 for a similar explanation.

he has to balance this phrase with the words of John 1.18 that God cannot be seen. For Origen, Christ as the image of the invisible God holds together this tension and enables him to declare that the invisible God is incorporeal while at the same time God may be seen and known through his image, Christ. Origen is particularly concerned that those against whom he writes do not understand either the nature of God or the nature of God in Christ and in their misunderstanding conclude that his argument is simply that of a frailer creature whose understanding is baffled. For Origen, his opponents are the ones who have not understood the distinction between seeing and knowing and the primary place of Christ in the cosmic hierarchy with God the Father. He therefore continues, "It is one thing to see (*videre*), and another to know (*cognoscere*); to see and to be seen is a property of bodies, to know and to be known is an attribute of intellectual being."[34] The only appropriate attributes of those who have the nature of the deity—the Father and the Son—are those of knowing and being known and one can only know God, incorporeal and invisible, by seeing his image, Jesus Christ.[35] Origen can therefore declare that anyone

> who has understood how we must think of the only-begotten God, the Son of God (μονογενοῦς θεοῦ υἱοῦ τοῦ θεοῦ), the first-born of all creation (Col 1.15: τοῦ πρωτοτόκου πάσης κτίσεως), and how the *logos* became flesh will see that anyone will come to know the Father and maker of this universe by looking at the image of the invisible God (Col 1.15: τὴν εἰκόνα τοῦ ἀοράτου θεοῦ).[36]

Origen's use of Col 1.15 is not to debate what makes Jesus the Son of God, but how it is that Jesus as the image of the invisible God allows God to be known.

For Origen, within this Colossian pericope, "image" is of particular significance where Christ as the image of God makes possible the knowledge of God as God himself becomes visible in Christ, his image. Grillmeier writes, "Christ as image of God is therefore the revelation and the representation of God" and in this way "the cosmological significance of Christ as the image of God comes to the forefront."[37] God is not corporeal but rather, on the contrary, Origen

---

34 Origen, *Princ*, 1.1.8 (*GCS* 22).
35 Origen, *Princ*, 2.4.3.
36 Origen, *Cels*, 7.43 (translation adapted from *SC* 150 and Chadwick).
37 Alois Grillmeier, *Christ in Christian Tradition: From the Apostolic Age to Chalcedon (451)* (trans. John Bowden; London: Mowbray, 1965), 25. Grillmeier also connects Origen's understanding of the words of Col 1.15 as revealing the invisible God through Christ, his image, with Jewish teaching about Wisdom where *sophia* "bears the title *eikōn* of God and represents a heavenly being." He clarifies that where this expression of Hellenistic Judaism is applied to *sophia* rather impersonally, this expression in Paul is "applied to the historical Christ in his total status [...] where Christ is described as mediator of creation" and "the pre-existent Christ

is clear that Col 1.15 holds together the "majesty, unchangability, and invisibility of God with the divinity of the Son" in order to avoid and counter the building consensus of his opponents and their claim that only God the Father possessed full divine attributes.[38]

Novatian, similar to Clement and Origen, uses excerpts from Col 1 in the context of his own concern for whether or not God can be seen. However, Novatian offers a different understanding of "image" and Christ as the "image of the invisible God" with an interpretation closely related to the Christological arguments of Irenaeus and Tertullian.[39] In his treatise on the Trinity, he asks,

> If God cannot be seen, how is it that he was seen [referring to Gen 12.7 and God's appearance to Abraham]? If he has been seen, how is it that he cannot be seen? For John also says, no one has ever seen God (John 1.18). And the apostle Paul says, whom no one has seen or

---

and the divine wisdom of the Jews are one and the same figure" (Grillmeier, *Christian Tradition*, 25). As Fossum writes, however, *sophia* is described not as image of the invisible God but as "an image of God's (perfect) goodness [...] which is not the same thing. It is true that the commentators parallel this representation with the descriptions of Sophia and the Logos as the image of God himself in the works of Philo, but Philo's intermediary is recognized to be a highly complex figure, and so we would have to ask whether Philo actually testifies to the same tradition" (Jarl E. Fossum, "Colossians 1.15–18a in the Light of Jewish Mysticism and Gnosticism," *NTS* 35 (1989): 183–201; 187).

**38** Peter Gorday, ed. *Colossians, 1–2 Thessalonians, 1–2 Timothy, Titus, Philemon* (ACCS NT9; Downers Grove, Ill: Intervarsity Press, 2000), xxvii. Keeping in mind the bigger picture of early Christian Christology emerging at this time, Hurtado writes that the "richness of the NT treatment of Jesus demanded and helped to shape theological and Christological debates of the first five centuries" as Christians in the first few centuries wrestled "intellectually with the problems of how to affirm conscientiously one God while also taking fully seriously the NT emphasis on Jesus' own divine significance and the reality of his participation in human nature" (Larry W. Hurtado, "Christology, NT," in *NIDB* [ed. Katharine Doob Sakenfeld; Nashville, Tenn: Abingdon Press, 2009], 612–622; 622). While Origen is not creating a new Christology, by using the language of "image" from Col 1, he is contributing to and building on an emerging tradition which utilises the Christological formulas of the Pauline epistles and, in particular, Col 1.15–20 as both theological and Christological debates unfold in the first few centuries of Christianity. For more on early Christian Christological developments, see: Christopher M. Tuckett, *Christology and the New Testament: Jesus and his earliest followers* (Edinburgh: Westminster John Knox Press, 2001), 6; Jarl E. Fossum, *The Image of the Invisible God: Essays on the influence of Jewish Mysticism on Early Christology* (NTOA 30; Göttingen: Vandenhoeck & Ruprecht, 1995); Stroumsa, "Caro salutis cardo," 30; Endre von Ivánka, *Plato christianus: la réception critique du platonisme chez les Pères de l'Eglise* (Rev. ed., Théologiques; Paris: Presses universitaires de France, 1990), and on patristic anthropology, see Heinrich Karpp, *Probleme altchristlicher Anthropologie: biblische Anthropologie und philosophische Psychologie bei den Kirchenvätern des dritten Jahrhunderts* (BFCT 44; Gütersloh: C.Bertelsmann, 1950).

**39** See Daniélou, *Latin Christianity*, 3.

can see (1 Tim 6.16). But certainly Scripture does not lie; therefore, God has been seen. Accordingly, this can only mean that it is not the Father who was seen, that is, the one who cannot be seen, but the Son, who is wont both to descend and to be seen, because he descended. He is the image of the invisible God (Col 1.15: *Imago est enim invisibilis Dei*), that our inferior and frail human condition might in time grow accustomed to see God the Father in the image of God (*in imago Dei*), that is, in the Son of God (*in filio Dei*).[40]

Like Origen, Novatian is concerned about the visible nature of the Son and the invisible nature of the Father and how to defend the divine attributes of both God the Father and God the Son. He also has to balance how Scripture can say that God is both seen (Genesis) and not seen (John). Like Origen, he uses the words of Col 1.15 as a loophole that allows him to show that "Scripture does not lie" since Christ as the "image of the invisible God" means that God the Father remains invisible while also being seen in God the Son. However, Novatian is careful to affirm the physical substance of the Son of God as God. He expands exegetically upon an inherited tradition from Justin Martyr, Irenaeus, and Tertullian, arguing that appearances of God in the Old Testament were in fact appearances of the pre-existent Son of God.[41] Where Origen's Hellenistic background does not allow much room for a physical, corporeal, pre-existent God, Novatian reads Col 1.15 differently and, against docetic views of Christ, holds that even before the Incarnation, the pre-existent Son was present in the visions and visitations of the Old Testament to the point that, "it was the Son of God, who is also God, who appeared to Abraham."[42] The description in Col 1.15 of God the Son as the image of the invisible God enables Novatian show that as image, God the Son is not only visible in the Incarnation but is the one who is visible as the divine throughout the scriptural record.[43]

Finally, Eusebius and, just beyond our time period, Cyril of Jerusalem use this Colossian passage and their understanding of "image" to emphasise the undivided nature of God and to argue against the "arrows of heresy."[44] Their focus on this task and their use of Col 1.15 appears to be adaptable, depending on whether they needed to be "anti-Arian [...] to argue for the full divinity of the

---

40 Novatian, *Trin*, 18.1–3 (*CCL* 4; *FC* 67).
41 See also Tertullian, *Prax*, 14.1–4 for a similar argument.
42 Novatian, *Trin*, 18 (*CCL* 4).
43 Daniélou, *Latin Christianity*, 3. See also Tertullian, *Prax*, 14 and 16; Justin Martyr, *Dial*, 56; 60–61; Novatian, *The Trinity, The spectacles, Jewish foods, In praise of purity, Letters* (ed. Russell J. DeSimone; Washington, D.C.: Catholic University of America Press, 1974); and Alan F. Segal, *Two Powers in Heaven: Early Rabbinic Reports about Christianity and Gnosticism* (Studies in Judaism in Late Antiquity 25; Leiden: Brill, 1977).
44 See Cyril of Jerusalem, *Catech*, 4.4 (Reischl; *FC* 64).

Son from before all creation" or "anti-Gnostic [...] to argue for the powerful and full involvement of the Son in the origination, unfolding and renewal of the material universe."[45] Eusebius, in his attempt to show how the "true and only God must be one" with the Son who is "one in being with the Father," uses an everyday understanding of image to explain that,

> For as the image (εἰκών) of a king would be honoured for the sake of him whose character and likeness (τοὺς χαρακτῆρας καὶ τὴν ὁμοίωσιν) it bears, and though both the image and the king (τῆς εἰκόνος καὶ τοῦ βασιλέως) received honour, one person would receive honour, and not two; for there would not be two kings, the first and true one and the one represented by the image, but one in both forms, not only perceived with the eyes, but named and honoured, so I say the only-begotten Son, being the only image of the invisible God (ὁ μονογενὴς υἱός, εἰκὼν ὢν μόνος τοῦ θεοῦ τοῦ ἀοράτου), through bearing his likeness, is rightly called the image of the invisible God (Col 1.15: εἰκών τε ἀνηγόρευται τοῦ ἀοράτου θεοῦ) and is constituted God by the Father himself. Thus he is, with regard to substance, and gives an image of the Father (τὴν εἰκόνα τοῦ πατρός) that grows from his nature but is not something added to him, because of the actual source of his existence. Wherefore he is by nature both God and only-begotten Son (μονογενὴς υἱός).[46]

For Eusebius, this commonplace description of image as a representation, such as an image on a coin, offers an understanding of Christ as the image of God that is different from that of both Clement and Origen.[47] Eusebius uses a metaphor from everyday life not to claim the obvious point that the image on a coin is not living (such as Irenaeus' argument regarding the relationship between "image" and pagan statues) but to defend the position that God is not divided in nature or essence since God the Son—the image—is "constituted God by the Father himself."[48] Image is a representation and not something separated and divided from that which it signifies. Therefore, the concept of "image" that Eusebius discerns in the words of Col 1.15 represents very specific things: guaranteeing value, legitimising commerce, and bestowing authority and value to that for which it is used. The image on the coin is not the same as the emperor's very presence and as such, is representational, and yet the stamped image is what

---

45 Gorday, *Colossians*, xxviii.
46 Eusebius, *Dem.ev*, 5.4.10 (GCS 23; Ferrar). See also Cyril of Jerusalem, *Catech*, 4.4.
47 However, Irenaeus uses a similar illustration to counter the view of his opponents that the invisibility of God means that he was unknown to the creator and to humankind (Irenaeus, *Haer*, 2.6.1 – 2.6.2). Here, Irenaeus also refers to the image of the emperor, such that those who have never actually seen the emperor nevertheless know that he possesses the principle power in the state. Similarly, even though God is invisible, God's power, like the emperor's, is widely known and acknowledged. See also Rankin, *Clement to Origen*, 110 – 111.
48 Eusebius, *Dem.ev*, 4.15 (GCS 23; Ferrar).

gives the coin legitimacy and authority. In this way, the image of God the Father stamped on God the Son gives legitimacy and authority to the Son as the pre-existent co-creator. While Eusebius might not be thinking about this comparison in such detail, his description of image nevertheless offers another understanding of Col 1.15 and more specifically, the use of image in a defense of God the Son as fully divine co-creator.[49]

Early Christians use this portion of Col 1.15 with a particular focus on "image," which can be understood both as something that expresses or makes known the pre-existent Christ and as something that represents the reality of God the Father present in and impressed upon God the Son.[50] "Image of the invisible God," may be found within discussions where early Christians seek to defend God the Father as creator, undivided and incorporeal, while at the same time affirming the lordship of God the Son over all things. Moreover, this phrase is used to help early Christians navigate through the tensions they find within Scripture, especially as they attempt to reconcile the visible incarnate Son of God with the phrase from John 1.18 that God cannot be seen. For different writers, therefore, "image of the invisible God" triggers different images, ideas, and comparisons in a way that is more poetical than argumentative, despite the casting of many of these references within argumentative contexts across treatises and apologies. The wide range of responses in which this excerpt from Col 1 may be found, as well as the diversity of things that the text is used to support and defend, is one of the most fascinating aspects of the use of this portion of Col 1.15–20.

### 5.2.2 πρωτότοκος πάσης κτίσεως: "First-born of all creation"[51]

While a portion of Col 1.15 is used to describe the incorporeal, undivided nature of God known only through God's "image" Christ, Col 1.15 is concomitantly used

---

**49** See Ralph P. Martin, *Carmen Christi: Philippians 2.5–11 in Recent Interpretation and in the Setting of Early Christian Worship* (Cambridge: Cambridge University Press, 1967).
**50** The Christological understandings drawn from Col 1.15 to describe God the Father and God the Son will become increasingly important focal points in the debates of the middle to late 4th century and in particular, the first ecumenical councils.
**51** For other examples in early Christian writings where Jesus is described as "first-born of all creation," see: Justin Martyr, *Dial*, 84; 100; 125; *A.Petr*, 2; Tatian, *Orat*, 5.2; Melito of Sardis, *Pass*, 82; Dionysius of Alexandria, *Fr*, 204–205; 210; *Six*, 3; Irenaeus, *Haer*, 3.16.3; Theophilus, *Autol*, 2.22.1; Tertullian, *Prax*, 5.19.3–5; 7.1; Origen, *Comm.Jo*, 1.118; 1.192; 1.195; 19.20; 28.18; *Comm.Cant*, Pr.; 1.1; 2.1; *Comm.Matt*, 16.8; *Cels*, 2.25; 2.31; 5.37; 6.17; 6.47–48; 6.63–64; 6.69; 7.16; 7.43; 7.65; 7.70; 8.17; 8.26; *Hom.Gen*, 1.13; *Hom.Jer*, 1.8.1; *Hom.Num*,

by early Christians to discuss the pre-existent nature of Christ, as co-creator with God the Father and as incarnate Son. Christ as "first-born of all creation" is singled out by early Christian writers in the service of a wide variety of points and arguments. Their focus, however, on the emerging doctrine of Christ's pre-existence is crucial. By claiming that Christ has been present from the beginning as "first-born of all creation," early Christians offer a defence against accusations that they worship one who has only recently come into being and who has been "born." As both chapters on 1 Corinthians discuss, history and tradition lend authority to argument and therefore, the accusation of novelty with which early Christians grappled is a serious allegation.[52] The final section of this chapter, therefore, extends briefly beyond the ante-Nicene time period in order to examine how the advent of the Arian controversy affected the use of this passage, and especially Col 1.15, in early Christian writings.

For Irenaeus, Christ as the "first-born of all creation" is the one through whom all things were made.[53] He connects Col 1 with John 1, another text frequently used to argue for Christ's pre-existence, in order to describe how God the Son makes all things, visible and invisible. Irenaeus writes that no other "principle nor power nor pleroma" exists apart from God "who, by his Word and Spirit, makes and disposes and governs all things and commands all things into existence."[54] For Irenaeus, this understanding of Christ as "first-born of all creation" needs little explanation or explication because this phrase makes clear that God the Son is one with God the Father in creation through whom all things were made. The words of Col 1 and John 1 say exactly what he needs in order to argue that the eternal God is the one who made all things in the beginning by his Word without "exception or deduction."[55] Irenaeus has become so used to reading John 1 and Col 1 "in a certain way that he cannot see how they could be read differently,"[56] at least until they are read differently by the Arians!

Origen also uses "first-born of all creation" from Col 1.15 to focus on the pre-existent eternal nature of Christ when he argues against Celsus. Celsus claims

---

3.4; Pamphilus, *Apol*, 45; Novatian, *Trin*, 21.1–6; Eusebius, *Dem.ev*, 4.3–4; 5.1; 7.3.14; *Eccl. theol*, 1.38.
52 See Origen, *Cels*, 5.37.
53 Irenaeus, *Haer*, 3.11.1 (*SC* 211). See also Daniélou, *Latin Christianity*, 337–338.
54 Irenaeus, *Haer*, 1.22.1 (translation adapted from *SC* 264 and *ACW* 55).
55 Irenaeus, *Haer*, 1.22.1 (*SC* 264).
56 Sedley, "Philosophical Allegiance," 111.

that Christians worship a creature who has recently come into existence,[57] and Origen is anxious to show that Christ is not novel. He writes that,

> even if, the first-born of all creation (Col 1.15: ὁ πρωτότοκος πάσης κτίσεως) seems to have become man recently, yet he is, in fact, not new on that account. For the divine scriptures know that of all created things, he is oldest, and that to him God said of the creation of humankind, let us make humankind in our image and likeness (εἰκόνα καὶ ὁμοίωσιν).[58]

Making clear his intention to defend Christ as fully God and present with God at the creation of humankind, Origen further emphasises the status of Christ as the "oldest" by connecting Christ with the figure of Wisdom. He uses the words of both Prov 8 and Col 1 to confirm Christ's presence and cosmic role in creation. The pre-existent Christ, eternally generated "before any beginning,"[59] that Origen finds in Col 1 means that everything revealed in creation, especially Wisdom as the "eternal self-expression of God" (Wis 7.26), is made manifest in the person of Christ.[60] Origen asserts that the Son of God,

---

[57] See *Cels*, 6.17, 6.47, 6.64; *Comm.Jo*, 1.18, 19.20, 28.18; *Comm.Matt*, 16.8, for a few examples of this use. See also J.P. Lightfoot, *Colossians*, 142–148, for a detailed list of early Christian use of Col 1.15: "first-born of all creation" and Wiles, *Divine Apostle*, 77–81.
[58] Origen, *Cels*, 5.37 (translation adapted from *SC* 147 and Chadwick). Tertullian makes a similar argument in *Prax*, 1; 8; and 19. One must note that Origen's doctrine of the Word holds together createdness and temporal eternity. For Origen, the Word is created in the image of God and is the one after which all rational beings are made. At the same time, this created Word participates in all aspects of God since the Word was generated or created in eternity. As he writes in *First Principles*, the Word as Wisdom "was generated before any beginning that can be either comprehended or expressed" (*Princ*, 2.1.2, [*SC* 253]). In other words, the createdness of the Word is eternal in the sense that it is a continuous and even atemporal creation or generation.
[59] Origen, *Princ*, 2.1.2, (*SC* 253).
[60] Aidan O'Boyle, *Towards a Contemporary Wisdom Christology: Some Catholic Christologies in German, English, and French 1965–1995* (Vatican City: Gregorian Biblical Institute, 2003), 189–190; see also H. Jaeger, "The Patristic Conception of Wisdom in the Light of Biblical and Rabbinical Research," *StPatr* IV, no. 79 (1961): 90–106; James D. G. Dunn, *The Theology of Paul the Apostle* (Edinburgh: T & T Clark, 1998), 269; John Anthony Dunne, "The Regal Status of Christ in the Colossian 'Christ-Hymn': A re-evaluation of the influence of Wisdom traditions," *TrinJ* 32NS (2011): 3–18 (contra Dunn); Jean-Noël Aletti, *Colossiens 1,15–20: Genre et exégèse du texte: fonction de la thématique sapientielle* (AnBib 91; Rome: Pontifical Biblical Institute, 1981); Gregory E. Sterling, "Prepositional Metaphysics in Jewish Wisdom Speculation and Early Christological Hymns," in *Wisdom and Logos: Studies in Jewish thought in Honor of David Winston* (eds. David T. Runia and Gregory E. Sterling; Atlanta, Ga: Scholars Press, 1997), 217–238; N. T. Wright, "Poetry and Theology in Colossians 1.15–20," *NTS* 36 (1990): 444–468. For those urging caution when referring to the Wisdom Tradition and Colossians, see Robert Morgan, "Jesus Christ, The Wisdom of God (2)," in *Reading Texts, Seeking Wisdom: Scripture and Theology* (eds. David Ford and Graham Stanton; London: SCM Press, 2003),

is termed Wisdom (*sapientia*), according to the expression of Solomon about the person of Wisdom (*ex persona sapientiae*), the Lord created me, the beginning of his ways, among his works, before he made any other thing. Before the ages he founded me. In the beginning, before he made the earth, before he brought forth the fountains of waters, before the mountains were made strong, before all the hills, he brought me forth (Prov 8.22). He is also called first-born (*primogenitus*), as the Apostle has declared: who is the first-born of all creation (Col 1.15: *qui est primogenitus omnis creaturae*). However, first-born (*primogenitus*) is not by nature a different person from Wisdom (*sapientia*), but one and the same.[61]

For Origen, Christ "is wisdom (*sapientia*), and in wisdom there can be no suspicion of anything corporeal."[62] Similar to the way he used the description of Christ as "image of the invisible God," Origen is concerned to defend the incorporeal nature of God, and the equation he makes between Wisdom and Christ as "first-born of all creation" gives him another way to uphold his defence. Col 1.15 lends support to his understanding that God the Son, as the image of God and first-born of all creation, is active in creation with God the Father who remains invisible and incorporeal. The figure of Wisdom in Hellenistic-Jewish literature with which Origen would have been familiar is not that of a divine being apart from the one God; rather, Origen relies on the language of wisdom in order to speak about God the Son alongside God the Father.[63] Combining excerpts from Col 1 and Prov 8, Origen claims that Christ is "*both* to be identified as the divine Wisdom, i.e. none other than the one creator God active in creation and now in redemption, *and* to be distinguished from the Father, not as in dualism whereby two gods are opposed, nor as in paganism where two gods are distinguished and given different (and in principle parallel) tasks."[64] For Origen, the Son as Wisdom and *logos* is therefore "always with God as an effect of the eternal will of God; thus, Origen may say that the Son has no beginning because he began in the Father."[65]

---

22–37; 29; Fossum, *Image*, 13–17; Robert M. Grant, *Jesus after the Gospels: The Christ of the Second Century* (London: SCM, 1990), 32; Segal, *Two Powers*, 220–225.

[61] Origen, *Princ*, 1.2.1 (translation adapted from *GCS* 22 and Butterworth).

[62] Origen, *Princ*, 1.2.6 (translation adapted from *GCS* 22 and Butterworth).

[63] Eusebius also connects the pre-existent Christ, first-born of all creation, with Wisdom when he discusses the divine nature of Christ and draws on excerpts from Col 1 and Prov 8. See Eusebius, *Dem.ev*, 5.1.4–8 and Rebecca Lyman, *Christology and Cosmology: Models of Divine Activity in Origen, Eusebius, and Athanasius* (Oxford: Clarendon Press, 1993), 71–72.

[64] Wright, "Poetry and Theology," 462–463 (italics original).

[65] Lyman, *Christology and Cosmology*, 71. See also Origen, *Princ*, 1.2.9.

**Excursus on *Prayer of Joseph***
The synonymous use of Jesus' name and the title "first-born of all creation" is a particularly interesting phenomenon because of connections made by many scholars between this phrase from Col 1.15 and *Prayer of Joseph*. In a fragment of *Prayer of Joseph*, an early Jewish-Christian text that has been preserved in Origen's *Commentary on John*, the angel Israel is described as the "first-born of all creation."[66] Fossum suggests that the words of Col 1.15 cannot be understood apart from a pre-Christian Jewish tradition, reflected in Philo and found in *Prayer of Joseph*. Early Christians, in his view, would have had this text in mind where the divine glory is a form of the invisible God which was both "first-born" and appeared in throne visions.[67] While Daniélou does not take the argument this far, he does observe that *Prayer of Joseph* and *Ascension of Isaiah* are closely connected "archaic works cherished by the same group of Jewish Christians."[68] Therefore, it is possible that the phrase "first-born of all creation" may include some contextual elements from or references to *Prayer of Joseph*.

The connection between these Jewish-Christian texts and Col 1 is further nuanced by Bauckham who observes that early Christians "very consciously using this Jewish theological framework, created a kind of christological monotheism by understanding Jesus to be included in the unique identity of the one God of Israel."[69] In this manner, scholars such as Fossum and Talbert see *Prayer of Joseph* as a part of the Jewish-Christian tradition where first-born is connected both to Wisdom and to Christ.[70] However, one must be mindful that within the writings of Philo, parallels to this text are found with a slightly different word: πρωτόγονος (as opposed to πρωτότοκος). Because some argue that the form found in Philo is the original form of *Prayer of Joseph*,[71] they also hold that

---

**66** See Origen, *Comm.Jo*, 2.31(25). See also Justin Martyr, *Dial*, 75.3.
**67** Fossum, *Image*, 14–17.
**68** Daniélou, *Jewish Christianity*, 17. For more on why this connection makes sense, see the section of this chapter on "thrones and dominions" and the discussion of how portions of Col 1.16 could also be understood through the lens of the *Ascension of Isaiah*.
**69** Richard Bauckham, *Jesus and the God of Israel: God Crucified and other studies on the New Testament's Christology of Divine Identity* (Grand Rapids, Mich: Eerdmans, 2008), 234.
**70** For an in-depth overview of connections between "first-born" and Wisdom, see Jarl E. Fossum, *The Name of God and the Angel of the Lord: Samaritan and Jewish concepts of intermediation and the origin of Gnosticism* (WUNT 36; Tübingen: Mohr, 1985), 314–318; and C.H. Talbert, "The Myth of the Descending–Ascending Redeemer in Mediterranean Antiquity," *NTS* 22 (1976): 418–440; 418.
**71** H. Windisch, "Die göttliche Weisheit der Juden und die paulinische Christologie," in *Neutestamentliche Studien für G. Heinrici* (eds. A. Deissman and H. Windisch; Leipzig: J.C. Hinrichs, 1914), 220–234; 225n1.

this difference in terminology negates a connection between *Prayer of Joseph* and Colossians and therefore, any conclusions ultimately can only be provisional.

Tertullian understands Christ to be "first-born of all creation" and uses this phrase from Col 1 to argue against Marcion's claim that Christ is a recent creation who exists only as an image and a phantom of flesh. Tertullian writes,

> If Christ is not the first-born of creation (Col 1.15: *christus primogenitus conditionis*), as that Word of the creator by whom all things were made and without whom nothing was made (John 1.3: *omnia facta sunt et sine quo nihil factum est*), if it is not true that in him all things were created, whether in heaven or on earth, visible and invisible, whether thrones or dominions or principalities or powers (Col 1.16: *in caelis et in terris, visibilia et invisibilia, siue throni siue dominationes siue principatus siue potestates*); if all things were not created by him and for him—for it was necessary that Marcion should disapprove of this—then the Apostle could not have so plainly said, and he is before all. For how is he before all, if he is not before all things? How, again, is he before all things, if he is not the first-born of creation (*primogenitus conditionis*), if he is not the Word of the creator?[72]

Like those before him, Tertullian desires to close down any suggestions that Christ is a recent creation and furthermore, any suggestions that Christ is a phantom of flesh. For Tertullian, both of these arguments threaten Christ's divine nature and the indivisibility of God the Father. Tertullian does not expand with much detail upon his understanding of Christ found in Colossians and John, because he is clear that excerpts from these texts state that if God the Son is first-born, then he is necessarily pre-existent, the Word of the Father and creator of all things visible and invisible. From this, he can claim that God the Father is not divided and move on to another point with Marcion.[73] As Bain observes, while Paul is "substantially consulted" by Tertullian throughout his works, Paul is also introduced at times when Tertullian's case has already been made and thus the words of Paul arrive "on the scene as something of a reinforcement

---

[72] Tertullian, *Marc*, 5.19.4 (translation adapted from *CCL* 1 and Evans). Tertullian makes a similar argument in *Prax*, 8 and 19.
[73] Gorday, *Colossians*, 10. For an example just beyond the end of our time period, see Marius Victorinus, *Ar*, 3.F where he builds on Col 1.15, "first-born of all creation," to write that, "this one is begotten as a son, the creation as that which is created. Not that there was another after him, but because he was the first-born of all creatures. Moreover, it says all creatures, both of heaven and earth, visible and invisible. Without a creation therefore, the Son is. Therefore by nature and by begetting, he is Son."

or clinching witness"[74] to emphasise and bring to a conclusion his—in this case Christological—point.

Early Christians use this portion of Col 1.15 to defend Christ's pre-existence and divine attributes against those who argue that Christ has recently been created. Maintaining that Christ as "first-born of all creation" places Christ with God the Father in creation, early Christians use this Colossian passage with excerpts from John 1 and Gen 1 to emphasise Christ's presence from the beginning and eternally before time. Origen adds further emphasis to this claim by connecting Col 1.15 with the description of Wisdom in Prov 8 to suggest that like Wisdom, Christ begins in God and is always with God. Drawing on this language of Wisdom, early Christian use of this portion of Col 1.15 is also reminiscent of similar quotations from early Jewish-Christian texts such as the *Ascension of Isaiah* and *Prayer of Joseph*. Nevertheless, the early Christian defence of Christ in this way, with a focus on placing Christ in the beginning with God but without worrying about the emphasis on Christ as one created by God, serves as an implicit endorsement of what was to become an Arian position, in particular, the understanding of Jesus Christ as a creature who cannot be fully divine.[75]

### 5.2.3 θρόνοι εἴτε κυριότητες: "Thrones and Dominions"[76]

The Colossian phrase, "thrones and dominions and rulers and powers," is also significant for the Christology developing within early Christianity. Early Christians use this particular phrase to focus on the creation of these entities by God

---

**74** Andrew M. Bain, "Tertullian: Paul as Teacher of the Gentile Churches," in *Paul and the Second Century* (eds. Michael F. Bird and Joseph R. Dodson; London: T&T Clark, 2011), 207–225; 209.

**75** In an interpretation and critique of Origen on the created/uncreated nature of God the Son, Patterson offers a sympathetic view of Origen, describing how he was misunderstood both by the Arians and by Methodius (L.G. Patterson, "Methodius, Origen, and the Arian Dispute," in *StPatr* (ed. E.A. Livingstone; Oxford: Pergamon Press, 1982), 912–923; esp. 917–921). See also Jonathan Z. Smith, "The Prayer of Joseph," in *Religions in Antiquity: Essays in Memory of E.R. Goodenough* (ed. J. Neusner; Leiden: Brill, 1970), 253–294; Fossum, "Colossians 1.15–18a," 190; and Daniélou, *Jewish Christianity*, 168. The Arian use of Col 1.15–20 will be engaged in greater depth in the concluding section of this chapter.

**76** For other examples in early Christian writings where Jesus is connected with "thrones and dominions" see: Clement of Alexandria, *Exc.Theod*, 19.4; Hippolytus of Rome, *Noet*, 6; Tertullian, *Marc*, 5.19.4–5; Origen, *Princ.* 1.5.1; 1.5.3; 1.6.2; 1.8.4; 1.7.1; 2.6.1; 2.9.4; 4.30; *Cels*, 4.29; 6.71; *Comm.Jo*, 1.88; 1.108; 10.284; *Hom.Lev*, 7.2; Pamphilus, *Apol*, 45; Eusebius, *Dem.ev*, 7.Pr.

through Christ, whereby they are counted among those things, visible and invisible, in heaven and on earth. However, the use of this Colossian phrase—especially favoured by Origen—is complicated by its possible connection with throne imagery found in *Ascension of Isaiah*, a second-century Christian document.[77] Arguably, *Ascension of Isaiah* offers one of the earliest interpretations of Col 1.16 in the form of an apocalyptic narrative, outlining the subordination of the throne to the Beloved who dwells in the seventh heaven. The sixth chapter of the *Ascension* includes a detailed description of Isaiah's vision and ascent to heaven where he encounters not only God on his throne at the top of the seventh heaven, but also other thrones, a number of which are found throughout this text.[78] These thrones are "very clearly subordinated to God" and scholars argue the text presents a subordinationist Christology.[79] The unique position of God is undisputed in the *Ascension of Isaiah*, while at the same time heaven is portrayed as being "filled throughout with mediatorial beings, each rank of which serves to bridge the gap between God and humanity."[80] While Origen of-

---

[77] Loren T. Stuckenbruck, "Worship and Monotheism in the *Ascension of Isaiah*," in *The Jewish Roots of Christological Monotheism: Papers from the St. Andrews Conference on the Historical Origins of the Worship of Jesus* (eds. Carey C. Newman, James R. Davila, and Gladys S. Lewis; Leiden: Brill, 1999), 70–89; 70. For scholarly literature on *Ascension of Isaiah*, see Paolo Bettiolo et. al., eds. *Ascensio Isaiae. Textus* (Turnhout: Brepols, 1995); Enrico Norelli, ed. *Ascensio Isaiae: Commentarius* (CCA 8; Turnhout: Brepols, 1995); C. Detlef G. Müller, "The Ascension of Isaiah," in *New Testament Apocrypha* (eds. Wilhelm Schneemelcher and R. McL Wilson; Cambridge: Clarke, 1991), 603–620; Richard Bauckham, "The Ascension of Isaiah: Genre, Unity, and Date," in *The Fate of the Dead: Studies on the Jewish & Christian Apocalypses* (ed. Richard Bauckham, NTSup 93; Leiden: Brill, 1998), 363–390; Jonathan Knight, *Disciples of the Beloved One: The Christology, Social Setting and Theological Context of the Ascension of Isaiah* (JSPSup 18; Sheffield: Sheffield Academic Press, 1996); Jonathan Knight, *Christian Origins* (London: T & T Clark, 2009); Segal, *Two Powers*; Jarl Fossum, "Jewish-Christian Christology and Jewish Mysticism," *VC* 37 (1983), 260–287.

[78] *Ascens.Isa*, 7.14, 19, 24, 29, 33; 8.7–10; Richard Bauckham, "The Throne of God and the Worship of Jesus," in *The Jewish Roots of Christological Monotheism: Papers from the St. Andrews Conference on the Historical Origins of the Worship of Jesus* (eds. Carey C. Newman, James R. Davila, and Gladys S. Lewis; Leiden: Brill, 1999), 43–69; 52n19. See also *Ascens.Isa*, 9.24–25; 11.40; and Catherine Playoust, "'Written in the book that I prophesied publicly': The Discernment of Apocalyptic Wisdom According to the *Ascension of Isaiah*," in *SBL Annual Meeting* (http://www.sbl-site.org/assets/pdfs/Playoust.pdf20 November 2006), 6.

[79] Bauckham, "Throne of God," 52n19; Christopher Rowland, *The Open Heaven: A Study of Apocalyptic in Judaism and Early Christianity* (London: SPCK, 1982), 94–111.

[80] Stuckenbruck, "Worship and Monotheism," 74. Thrones of this nature are encountered as heavenly beings in *Testament of Levi* and *Apocalypse of Elijah*, as well. In *Testament of Levi*, the orders within the celestial hierarchy place thrones and powers first, these two being in the highest or seventh heaven. See James D. G. Dunn, *The Epistles to the Colossians and to Phil-*

fers a different hierarchy in his *First Principles* with thrones falling into the second level behind dominions,[81] the possibility that early Christian writers may have been interpreting this theological phrase from Col 1.16—the only occurrence of the phrase "thrones and dominions" in the New Testament—through the lens of early Jewish-Christian cosmological understandings and with documents such as the *Ascension of Isaiah* cannot be neglected. The symbolism of the throne, as the sign of God's absolute sovereignty over the whole creation, was not only a significant symbol in Second Temple Jewish monotheism but also represents an essential characteristic of divine identity.[82] Therefore, once again at stake in early Christian use of this image from Col 1 is the fully divine nature of God the Son. The use of this language of thrones and dominions by early Christian writers draws out "the full consequences of Jesus' exaltation to the divine throne, and deliberately deploy the strongest Jewish theological means of placing Jesus emphatically on the divine side of the line between the one God of Israel and the rest of reality, his creation"[83] and thereby "unequivocally within the unique divine identity."[84]

The *Ascension of Isaiah* is distinct for its time because of its seven-storied cosmology and the disguised descent of Christ.[85] Relating to the use of Col 1.15–20 by early Christian writers, the focus in *Ascension* on the descent and ascent of Christ is of great importance for the developing doctrine of pre-existence, since it explicitly offers some of the logical and narrative elements necessary for understanding this doctrine in later New Testament writings.[86] The resulting relationship in *Ascension of Isaiah* between God the Father and God the Son, between the "Most High" and the "Beloved One," under the influence of Jewish angelology is therefore "an entirely new form of belief which is of great importance for understanding the intellectual development of the earliest Christianity; including, most importantly, the prehistory of the Arian controversy."[87] The narrative of *Ascension* also challenges the assumption that the idea of the pre-existence of Christ found in early Christian writings and especially the writings of

---

emon: *A Commentary on the Greek Text* (Grand Rapids, Mich: Eerdmans, 1996), 92–93; Lightfoot, *Colossians*, 151; *T.Levi*, 3.8; *Ap.Eli*, 1.10–11; and Daniélou, *Jewish Christianity*, 15.
**81** Origen, *Princ*, 1.5.3 and 1.6.2.
**82** Bauckham, "Throne of God," 52–53.
**83** Bauckham, "Throne of God," 66.
**84** Bauckham, "Throne of God," 67.
**85** Jonathan Knight, "The Origin and Significance of the Angelomorphic Christology in the *Ascension of Isaiah*," *JTS(n.s.)* 63, no. 1 (2012): 66–105; 87.
**86** Knight, "Angelomorphic Christology," 88–89. See also Rowland and Morray-Jones, *The Mystery of God*, 165.
**87** Knight, "Angelomorphic Christology," 96.

Paul can only be attributed to Jewish wisdom categories.⁸⁸ In other words, the "traditional assumption of a 'wisdom' influence [...] is too one-sided."⁸⁹

Within this context, early Christian writers, and especially Origen, use the phrase concerning "thrones and dominions" from Col 1.16 to show that Christ is the one and only mediator between God and humanity, despite the existence of many rational beings—angels, thrones, and dominions—between them. While this approach may also be discerned in the works of Marcellus and the later Arians as they claim that God the Son was in fact subordinate to God the Father,⁹⁰ the point made by Origen and others in this time period was not one of subordination but that Christ is fully God even though he is also mediator, the one in and through whom God acts. Wiles clarifies, with both Col 1 and John 1, "in the ante-Nicene period the subordinationist implications of the text are accepted as entirely natural; they appear for the most part to be accepted as something requiring neither to be pressed nor to be explained away."⁹¹ Amongst pre-Nicene writers, subordinationism was "the common position"⁹² and early Christian writers do not have difficulty holding this position, especially when speaking of the relation between God the Son and God the Father in the creation of the world and at its consummation.⁹³

While Origen applies this phrase from Col 1.16 to Christ, he is first concerned with the underlying nature and purpose of these "thrones and dominions" and their creation. Even though the subordination of Jesus is not at stake as an issue for Origen, the subordination of thrones and dominions is. In *First Principles*, he writes that he wants to consider,

> whether those who are called holy principalities (*sancti principatus*) began from the moment of their creation by God to exercise power over some who were made subject to them, and whether these latter were created of such a nature and formed for the very purpose of being subordinate and subject. Similarly, also, whether those which are called powers (*potestates*) were created of such a nature and for the express purpose of exercising power, or whether their arriving at that power and dignity is a reward and dessert of their virtue. Moreover, also, whether those which are called thrones (or seats) (*throni [vel sedes]*) gained that stability of happiness at the same time with their coming forth into being so as to have that possession from the will of the Creator alone; or whether those which are called dominions (*dominationes*) had their dominion conferred on them not as

---

**88** Knight, "Angelomorphic Christology," 97.
**89** Knight, "Angelomorphic Christology," 104–105.
**90** Wiles, *Divine Apostle*, 89.
**91** Wiles, *Divine Apostle*, 88. For a similar argument, see Edwards, *Origen against Plato*, 70.
**92** Rankin, *Clement to Origen*, 136n54. See also Joseph W. Trigg, *Origen* (ECF; New York: Routledge, 1998), 23.
**93** Wiles, *Divine Apostle*, 89.

a reward for their proficiency, but as the peculiar privilege of their creation, so that it is something which is in a certain degree inseparable from them and natural.[94]

Regarding the nature of these thrones and other rational beings, Origen continues, with a clear reference to Paul and a lengthy quote from Col 1.16. He writes,

> the Apostle Paul, moreover, describing created things by species and numbers and orders, speaks as follows when showing that all things were made through Christ saying, and in him were all things created, that are in heaven and that are in earth, visible and invisible, whether they be thrones or dominions or principalities or powers, all things were created by him and in him, and he is before all, and he is the head (Col 1.16–18: *Et omnia in ipso creata sunt, quae in caelis sunt et quae in terra, sive visibilia sive invisibilia, sive sedes sive dominationes sive principatus sive potestates, omnia per ipsum et in ipso creata sunt, et ipse est ante omnes, et ipse est caput*). He therefore manifestly declares that in Christ and through Christ were all things made and created, whether visible, which are corporeal, or whether invisible, which I regard as none other than incorporeal and spiritual powers. But of those things which he had termed generally corporeal or incorporeal, he seems to me, in the words that follow, to enumerate the various kinds, thrones, dominions, principalities, powers, strengths (*throni dominationes principatus potestates virtutes*).[95]

Notwithstanding these great rational beings and however unworthy humanity might seem in comparison, Origen is clear that "though we humans fall short of these beings [some of which are called thrones, others called principalities, and other authorities and powers (Col 1.16)], we have hopes that by living a good life and doing everything according to reason (τὸν λόγον) we may ascend to the likeness of all these."[96] In this way, Col 1.15–18 allows early Christians, and particularly Origen, to emphasise "the immeasurable superiority of Christ over whatever rival might [...] be suggested"[97] as the one who is pre-existent and through whom all things were made. Colossians 1.16 plays a role only as it is pressed into service by Origen to support his claim that Jesus is the one

---

**94** Origen, *Princ*, 1.5.3 (translation adapted from *GCS* 22 and Butterworth).
**95** Origen, *Princ*, 1.7.1 (translation adapted from *GCS* 22 and Butterworth).
**96** Origen, *Cels*, 4.29 (translation adapted from *SC* 136 and Chadwick). See also *Cels*, 3.34. While I have focused on Origen's Christological interpretation in his use of Col 1.16, this text also refers to another major theme in Origen's theology: that human beings can make spiritual progress and ascend through the ranks of the hierarchy of spiritual beings and "ascend to the likeness of all these" (*Cels*, 4.29). This theme relates to the idea of progress discussed in chapter 2 (1 Cor 2) where the human being, by moral purification and progress in knowledge and wisdom, can gradually ascend to God by rising through the various grades of the heavenly hierarchy.
**97** C. F. D. Moule, *The Epistles to Colossians and to Philemon* (Cambridge: Cambridge University Press, 1957), 65–66.

and only mediator between humanity and God. More of a confessional claim than an argument, Origen tries to be clear that in a world with various cosmological hierarchies, from Plato to *Ascension of Isaiah*, Christ as fully human and fully divine is the only one who mediates between God and humanity. Whatever else may exist (or whatever others claim exists) in the intermediate space, using the words of Col 1.16, Origen is clear that Christ is the only one who mediates. Christ is the "image of the invisible God and the first-born of all creation" and thus even though it might seem like Christ exists in an intermediate realm between God the Father and the created world with thrones, dominions, principalities, and powers, the focus remains on Christ's eternal nature.[98]

### 5.2.4 ἡ κεφαλὴ τοῦ σώματος, τῆς ἐκκλησίας: "The head of the body, the Church"

The Christological challenge for early Christian writers is both to describe how Christ is fully human and fully divine, and to determine how the Christ who suffered on the cross and died is God the Son undivided from God the Father. One of the ways early Christians address the latter challenge is through their use of the images found in Col 1.18. Focusing on Christ as the "head of the body, the Church," early Christians such as Clement of Alexandria and, just beyond the ante-Nicene time period, Cyril of Jerusalem offer a play on the word "head" in order to defend God the Son as the head of the church who also suffered and died. Whereas Christ's suffering and death served as a point of attack for many who could not comprehend a God who could suffer and die, Christ as head holds together for early Christians the reality that Jesus Christ was both fully God as head of the Church and fully human on the cross. While some see the moment on the cross as the moment when the divine Christ is separated from the human Jesus, Clement and Cyril argue otherwise.

Clement, for instance, uses this description of Christ to speak both about Christ as head of the church and about the crown of thorns placed upon his physical head. He writes, "for the Lord's crown prophetically pointed to us, who were once barren, who are placed around him through the church of which he is the head (Col 1.18: διὰ τῆς ἐκκλησίας, ἧς ἐστιν κεφαλή)."[99] For Clement, Christ's physical suffering and death serves as a prophetic message that God

---

[98] For a later exposition of this point against the Arians, who used the same argument to show that Christ was part of the created realm, see Marius Victorinus, *Ar*, 1.24 (F). See also Wiles, *Divine Apostle*, 78–80.
[99] Clement of Alexandria, *Paed*, 2.8.73.3 (translation adapted from *SC* 108 and *FC* 23).

the Son, whose physical head was crowned with thorns and suffered on the cross, is the head of the body, the church, undivided from God the Father. The image of head that Clement finds in Col 1.18 allows him to write both about the physical part of the body that the image of a head conjures up as well as head in terms of authority and source, connecting the two in the person of Christ through his physical and his authoritative creative nature as fully human and fully divine.

Just beyond the end of our time period, Cyril of Jerusalem similarly discusses Jesus as the "head" not only in terms of his crown of thorns but Golgotha itself. He asks,

> Who were they then, who prophetically named this spot Golgotha, in which the true head Christ (ἡ ἀληθὴς κεφαλὴ Χριστός) endured the cross? As the Apostle says, who is the image of the invisible God (Col 1.15: ὅς ἐστιν εἰκὼν τοῦ θεοῦ τοῦ ἀοράτου), and a little after, and he is the head of the body the church (Col 1.18: καὶ αὐτός ἐστιν ἡ κεφαλὴ τοῦ σώματος τῆς ἐκκλησία). And again, the head of every man is Christ (1 Cor 11.3: παντὸς ἀνδρὸς ἡ κεφαλὴ ὁ Χριστός ἐστί). [100]

After a list of other Pauline texts which include the word "head" (1 Cor 11.3, Col 2.10), Cyril exclaims, "The head suffered in the place of the skull. O wondrous prophetic appellation. For the very name also reminds you, saying, think not of the crucified as of a mere man; he is the head of all principality and power."[101] Christ whose head was crowned with thorns and who was crucified at the place of the skull, plays a prophetic role for Cyril. The irony that the physical head of the head of the church suffered at the place of the skull confirms for Cyril that God the Son is not a mere man who was crucified but truly is the head of all powers and people. In this way, the prophetic metaphor of the head that both Clement and Cyril find in Col 1 connects the physicality of the crucifixion with the physicality of God the Son as both fully human and fully divine, never giving up his place as head of the church, of humanity, and of all principality and power, even on the cross. Here, once again, the concept of recapitulation which is so important for the emerging Christological theology of this time is present as "the whole of the past and the future, the earthly and the heavenly, is to be contained in Christ, the sovereign head."[102]

---

**100** Cyril of Jerusalem, *Catech*, 13.22–23 (Reischl; *FC 61*).
**101** Cyril of Jerusalem, *Catech*, 13.22–23 (Reischl; *FC 61*).
**102** Grillmeier, *Christian Tradition*, 15.

## 5.3 Close Connections with John 1 and Philippians 2[103]

As stated in the introductory chapter, part of this study includes attention, where possible, to other scriptural passages frequently found in close proximity to each pericope. With a focus on Christological words and images, excerpts from Col 1.15–20 are often connected with two other texts with high Christological views: John 1.1–18 and Phil 2.5–11.[104] Like Col 1, excerpts from John and Philippians are used by early Christians to defend and support their Christological claims. The connection between Col 1.15 and John 1.18 has already been briefly encountered in this chapter as early Christians attempt to reconcile God the Father as incorporeal and unseen with God the Son as fully divine and visible in the Incarnation.

The connection between these three texts is not surprising. As Gordley and Grillmeier argue, "outside of Colossians, Christ's mediating role in creation is explicitly referenced in the New Testament in the Fourth Gospel (1:1–3; 1:10)"[105] and the Christological phrases within John 1 situate it as "the most influential New Testament text in the history of dogma."[106] While Phil 2.5–11 is not always included in this latter category, nevertheless, one of the main reasons these three passages may have been used in close proximity to each other in early Christian texts is because each could be read as ascribing a pre-existent status to Jesus: the one who took on the form of a slave, through whom God created all things, and

---

**103** See also, Origen, *Comm.Jo*, 10.23; Clement of Alexandria, *Exc.Theod*, 19; 43 (a portion of 43 is likely the Valentinian author; see Sagnard, *Théodote*, 35); Novatian, *Trin*, 13.1–2; Eusebius, *Hist.eccl*, 11.19.4; Eusebius, *Dem.ev*, 7.Pr.
**104** Wiles notes that Phil 2 was one of the main texts upon which the docetists relied as they used the text to show that Paul does not directly affirm the humanity of Jesus but only uses words like form, likeness, and fashion to describe his nature (Wiles, *Divine Apostle*, 82–83). Tertullian counters this view directly in *Marc*, 5.20.3–4.
**105** Matthew E. Gordley, *The Colossian Hymn in Context* (WUNT 228; Tübingen: Mohr Siebeck, 2007), 207. Cerfaux does not include Phil 2.5–11 in this category since he understands the Philippian pericope to deal only "with the life of Christ" while the Colossian pericope and others in this category deal "with the mystery of his work" (Lucien Cerfaux, *Christ in the Theology of St. Paul* [trans. Geoffrey Webb and Adrian Walker; New York: Herder & Herder 1959], 370). However, Edwards argues that Phil 2 was used in a similar way to Col 1 to describe Christ as equal to and undivided from God (Phil 2.6), as both human and divine (Phil 2.7), and as one exalted to glory (Phil 2.8–9). See Mark J. Edwards, ed. *Galatians, Ephesians, Philippians* (ACCS NT8; Downers Grove, Ill: Intervarsity Press, 1999), 236–237; see also Edsall and Strawbridge, "Songs we Used to Sing," 11–13.
**106** Grillmeier, *Christian Tradition*, 27.

who reconciles all things to himself.[107] As Hurtado writes, each of these passages ascribe a pre-existent mode to Jesus as one who shares the divine nature, and "celebrate the historic/earthly appearance of Jesus"[108] placing side by side, whether intentionally or not, the pre-existent Son of God and the true and full humanity of Christ.[109] Grillmeier connects the Christological formulas found in these three passages most explicitly when he writes that even if these texts were affected by other influences—in particular, Wisdom teaching and terminology—the Pauline expressions found in Colossians ("image of invisible God") and Philippians ("equality with God" and "form of God") "already point in the direction of the Johannine concepts and terminology and stand on the same theological plane as John does."[110] While one cannot know definitively why early Christian writers used these texts with such regularity in conjunction with one another, the underlying theology of the pre-existent status of Christ within each passage is a significant connecting factor.

Tertullian joins excerpts from Phil 2 and Col 1 when he writes about Christ as undivided and not separated into two beings or forms, human and divine. Against Marcion, who appears to use excerpts from Phil 2 to argue that Christ is not fully human and his flesh only imaginary, Tertullian writes that,

> Of course, the Marcionites suppose that they have the Apostle on their side in the following passage in the matter of Christ's substance (*substantia Christi*), that in Christ there was nothing but a phantom of flesh (*phantasma carnis*).[111] For he says of Christ, that being in the form of God, he thought it robbery to be equal with God; but emptied himself and took upon him the form of a servant (Phil 2.6–7: *quod in effigie Dei constitutus non rapinam existimauit pariari Deo, sed exhausit semetipsum accepta effigie serui*), not the reality, and was made in the likeness of man, not a man, and was found in the form (*figura*) of a man,

---

107 See Edwards, *Galatians*, xxii; Martin, *Carmen Christi*, 111–112; 290–293; Martin Hengel, *The Son of God: The Origin of Christology and the History of Jewish-Hellenistic Religion* (London: SCM Press, 1976); Jack T. Sanders, *The New Testament Christological Hymns: Their Historical Religious Background* (Cambridge: Cambridge University Press, 1971), 77–79; and Markus N. A. Bockmuehl, *A Commentary on the Epistle to the Philippians* (BNTC; London: A&C Black, 1997), 42n130. Bockmuehl writes, scholars "continue to congregate" around Phil 2.5–11 making it—with Col 1.15–20 one might argue—one of the most interpreted texts of the New Testament so much so that "none but the most conceited could claim to have mastered the secondary literature, and none but the dullest would find pleasure or interest in wading through it." With over six hundred texts written to interpret this passage, the "deluge of scholarly debate" is "uncontainable" (115).
108 Hurtado, "Christology, NT," 3.
109 Grillmeier, *Christian Tradition*, 17.
110 Grillmeier, *Christian Tradition*, 32. See also Bauckham, *Jesus and the God of Israel*, 235.
111 For other examples of Marcion's use of *phantasma* to describe Christ's body, see Tertullian, *Carn.Chr*, 1.2; *Marc*, 3.10.11; 4.7.1–5; 5.8.3.

not in his substance (*substantia*), that is to say, his flesh. Just as if to a substance there did not accrue both form and likeness and fashion (*non et figura et similitudo et effigies substantiae*). It is well for us that in another passage [the Apostle] calls Christ the image of the invisible God (Col 1.15: *imaginem Dei invisibilis*).[112]

Tertullian is eager to claim Paul's authority as the Marcionites assume Paul is "on their side." Here, the words concerning form and image connect Phil 2 and Col 1 as Tertullian establishes that these words are Pauline whereas the vocabulary Marcion uses to describe Christ is not. Moreover, Tertullian continues that if Marcion's claim that Christ is only a phantom of flesh and therefore not fully human is true, then an unintended consequence of this position is that Christ is not fully God either. Following a reference to Col 1.15 and arguing that Christ is fully human even as he takes on the form and image of a man, Tertullian writes,

For in both cases the true substance will have to be excluded if form and likeness and fashion shall be claimed for a phantom (*si effigies et similitudo et figura phantasmati uindicabuntur*). But since he is, in the form and image of God (*in effigie et in imagine Dei*), as the Son of the Father, truly God, in the form and image of humankind (*in effigie et imagine hominis*), he has already been judged, as the son of man, to be found as truly man.[113]

Disturbed by Marcion's Christology, Tertullian argues that while Pauline texts such as Col 1 and Phil 2 could support the distinction between God the Father and God the Son, this distinction is superficial. Using Col 1 as a proof text to correct Marcion's misinterpretation of Phil 2, Tertullian seeks to reclaim both passages. The link between Jesus and Christ is crucial for Tertullian's argument. He uses both of these Pauline excerpts to describe the connection between the humanity of Jesus and the divinity of Christ as undivided so that Paul could not have called God the Son, Jesus Christ, obedient unto death, if he had not been made in the image of God and as God, found in the fashion and image of humankind. Moreover, substance (*substantia*) is central to Tertullian's understanding of how the Father and the Son are related to one another. For Tertullian, substance is that which unifies the Father and the Son despite their different forms so that God the Father and God the Son are inseparable in a unity that is "a unity of substance, not a singularity of number."[114] Tertullian also includes

---

112 Tertullian, *Marc*, 5.20.3 – 4 (*CCL* 1). See also Tertullian, *Prax*, 10.
113 Tertullian, *Marc*, 5.20.4 (translation adapted from *CCL* 1 and Evans).
114 Christopher J. Stead, "Divine Substance in Tertullian," *JTS(n.s.)* 14.1 (1963): 46 – 66; 46 and 55. See also Ernest Evans, *Tertullian's Treatise against Praxeas* (London: SPCK, 1948), 38 – 58; Osborn, *Tertullian*, 132; and Tertullian, *Prax*, 25.621.

rhetorical questions directed at Marcion which serve to demonstrate the sarcastic regard with which he held his opponents as he reclaims the language of Col 1 and Phil 2 from Marcion. Here he proclaims that one may, "more easily find a man born without a heart or without brains, like Marcion himself, than without a body, like Marcion's Christ."[115]

The connections made by Origen between excerpts from Col 1, Phil 2, and John 1 are different from those made by Tertullian as Origen stresses both the relationship between God and humankind, made in God's image, and the relationship between God and Christ, his image. Each passage builds upon the other within his argument, using the language of image and form to emphasise the nature of and relationship between God, Christ, and humankind. In one of his *Homilies on Genesis*, Origen writes that,

> God made humankind according to the image of God (*imaginem Dei*) he made him (Gen 1.27). Therefore, what other image of God (*imago Dei*) is there according to the likeness of whose image humankind is made, except our Saviour, who is the first-born of all creation (Col 1.15: *qui est primogenitus omnis creaturae*). [...] For just as one who sees an image of someone, sees him whose image it is, so also one sees God through the Word of God, which is the image of God (Col 1.15: *verbum Dei, quae est imago Dei*). And thus what he said will be true: he who has seen me has also seen the Father (John 1.18: *qui me vidit, vidit et patrem*). Humankind, therefore, is made according to the likeness of his image (*imaginis similitudinem*) and for this reason our Saviour, who is the image of God (*qui est imago Dei*), moved with compassion for humankind who had been made according to his likeness, [...] and came to him, as also the Apostle attests saying, since he was in the form of God, he did not think it robbery to be equal with God, but emptied himself taking the form of a servant, and in appearance found as a man, he humbled himself even to death (Phil 2.6–8: *cum in forma Dei esset, non rapinam arbitratus est esse se aequalem Deo, sed semet ipsum exinanivit formam servi accipiens, et habitu repertus ut homo, humiliavit semet ipsum usque ad mortem*).[116]

As seen earlier with his use of Col 1.15, Origen connects the language of God's image with both Christ and humankind. As he explains: because the Word, as first-born of all creation (Colossians) is in the beginning with God (John), Christ himself is in the beginning as the image and form of God (Colossians and Philippians) and humans are created in the image of Christ. In this way, Christ as the image of God is "moved with compassion" for humanity made according to his

---

**115** Tertullian, *Marc*, 4.10.16 (*CCL* 1; Evans) and Bart D. Ehrman, *Lost Christianities: The Battles for Scripture and the Faiths we Never Knew* (Oxford: Oxford University Press, 2003), 191. See also Géza Vermès, *Christian Beginnings: From Nazareth to Nicaea, AD 30–325* (London: Penguin UK, 2012).
**116** Origen, *Hom.Gen*, 1.13 (translation adapted from *GCS* 29 and *FC* 71).

likeness. For Origen, everything "comes back to Christ as its primary orientation point" so that all of creation is rooted in the beginning, which is in Christ.[117] Therefore, Origen writes that,

> Seeing, then, that all things which have been created are said to have been made through Christ and in Christ, as the Apostle Paul most clearly indicates saying, for in him and by him were all things created, whether things in heaven or things on earth, visible and invisible, whether they be thrones or dominions or principalities or powers (Col 1.16: *in ipso et per ipsum creata sunt omnia, sive quae in caelo sunt, sive quae in terra, visibilia et invisibilia, sive throni sive dominationes sive principatus sive potestates*), all things were created by him and in him (*omnia per ipsum et in ipso creata sunt*); and also in his Gospel, John indicates nothing except the same thing, saying, in the beginning was the Word, and the Word was with God, and the Word was God: the same was in the beginning with God. All things were made by him, and without him was not anything made (John 1.1–3: *In principio erat verbum, et verbum erat apud Deum, et Deus erat verbum; hoc erat in principio apud Deum. Omnia per ipsum facta sunt, et sine ipso factum est nihil*) [...] then, Christ is, as it were, the word and wisdom (*verbum et sapientia*).[118]

Christ as Word and Wisdom embodies the different descriptions of creation in Col 1 and John 1. As human and divine, Christ serves a mediating role for Origen (similar to that described earlier in this chapter with Col 1.18), except now this mediation comes through the language of creation that Origen finds in Colossians and John. In and through Christ as described in Col 1, all things were created and because all things were also created in and through the Word as described in John 1, Christ as co-creator is Word and Wisdom. By connecting Col 1 and John 1 and arguing that they proclaim the same thing, Origen can defend the purpose of creation as good and consistent with the purposes and righteousness of God while holding together, through this language of creation, the tension of the fullness of God present within the human Christ.

Once again, early Christian writers uphold the unity of God the Son as fully human and fully divine by using the language from Col 1, John 1, and Phil 2 to support their claim. Tertullian is clear that language of "image" and "form" do not allow a separation of human attributes from Christ, while Origen focuses on both "form" and "image" to argue that God the Son is equal to God the Father and that the *logos* in the beginning with God is the image of God, Christ. The understanding of Christ as the image and form of God who is in the beginning with God is essential for early Christians, and their adaptation of these three passages

---

[117] Peter Bouteneff, *Beginnings: Ancient Christian Readings of the Biblical Creation Narratives* (Grand Rapids, Mich: Baker Academic, 2008), 115.
[118] Origen, *Princ*, 2.9.4 (translation adapted from *GCS* 22 and Butterworth). See also *Princ*, 2.6.3.

together supports their defence of God as undivided and Jesus Christ as divine and pre-existent.

## 5.4 Concluding Remarks: Why Colossians 1.15–20?

Early Christians use excerpts from Col 1.15–20 within their writings to emphasise what they found to be essential about Christ. For early Christian writers, the pre-existent Christ is present with God the Father from the beginning with a primary role in the creation, sustaining, and reconciliation of all things. Finding themselves challenged by notions of a divided Christ (two natures) and a divided God (Father and Son), early Christian writers use this pericope to support their arguments and in the process to effect the theological developments of the church. While many other understandings of Christ—his ascension or his miracles, for example—could have been used to uphold his divine nature, Col 1 is the passage that early Christians turn to time and again to help them think about and defend the emerging doctrine of Christ's divinity.

The highly charged Christological setting in which excerpts from Col 1.15–20 are found helps to explain the focus on particular phrases and images drawn from the Colossian text. The understanding of Christ as "image of the invisible God," "first-born of all creation," and "head of the church" alongside the images of thrones, dominions, powers, and creation, is apparent throughout early Christian writings as this Colossian pericope is adapted, expanded, and used with other scriptural passages such as John 1.1–18 and Phil 2.5–11. Moreover, connections might also be made not only with other New Testament texts, but Jewish and Jewish-Christian texts such as *Prayer of Joseph* and *Ascension of Isaiah*, as well as the writings of Philo and the rhetorical concept of recapitulation.

A conclusion such as this might not seem very radical, and yet it does offer a challenge to the widespread assumption within modern scholarship that Col 1.15–20 is a "hymn." Michael Peppard notes that "not one source from early Christianity regards any of the passages identified as poems or hymns" and the use of Col 1 in this chapter supports Peppard's claim.[119] As Bart Ehrman is clear and as I have shown throughout this study, early Christian reception of a text such as Col 1 "can tell us a good deal about the history of exegesis and the nature of early Christian theological developments and social conflicts, and the role that these matters themselves played in the transmission of the

---

[119] Peppard, "Poetry," 324.

Christian scriptures."[120] Therefore, it is significant that Col 1 is not treated as a hymn or placed in a liturgical setting within extant ante-Nicene texts. While many scholars are convinced of the hymnic nature of this pericope, this conclusion is not reflected in early Christian use.[121] It is certainly true that Graeco-Roman writers do not always identify the exact genre of texts they use to make an argument. Nevertheless, the lack of positive evidence for the use of Col 1.15–20 as a hymn is a silence that cannot be ignored. It is clear that this pericope is a significant text for early Christian writers through their frequent use of its phrases and the important role it plays in shaping early Christian theology and especially Christology; however, based on patristic evidence, it is difficult to identify Col 1.15–20 as a "hymn" with any degree of confidence.[122]

How Col 1 shaped early Christian writers and writings, therefore, is understood primarily through the ways the images and phrases within it were used and expanded to address a range of Christological and theological arguments. In this way, Christ as "image of the invisible God" is used by early Christians to defend both the invisible and incorporeal nature of God the Father and the corporeal nature of God the Son. "Image" in these texts takes on slightly different meanings to support arguments about the pre-existent Christ and the relationship between God the Father and God the Son. The term holds together the tension found in Scripture between the visible, corporeal nature of the Incarnation of God with the phrase in John 1.18 that God cannot be seen. The phrase "first-born of all creation" is used similarly within texts that focus on creation and God as creator. Also used to support and defend claims of Christ's pre-existence, the focus of early Christians who adapt this excerpt within their argu-

---

[120] Bart D. Ehrman, "The Use and Significance of Patristic Evidence for NT Textual Criticism," in *New Testament Textual Criticism, Exegesis, and Early Church History* (eds. Barbara Aland and Joël Delobel; CBET 7; Kampen: Kok Pharos, 1995), 118–135; 135; see also pages 127–128 and John Anthony McGuckin, "Recent Biblical Hermeneutics in Patristic Perspective: The Tradition of Orthodoxy" *GOTR* 47.1–4 (2002), 295–326; 309.

[121] See Ernst Käsemann, "Eine urchristliche Taufliturgie," in *Exegetische Versuche und Besinnungen* (ed. Ernst Käsemann; vol. 1; Göttingen: Vandenhoeck & Ruprecht, 1960), 34–51; Andrew T. Lincoln, "The Letter to the Colossians," in (*NIB*; Nashville, Tenn: Abingdon Press, 2000), 602–605; Gordley, *Teaching*, 229–230, 268–290.

[122] Early Christian use of excepts from Col 1 and Phil 2 in close proximity to one another, as highlighted in part of this chapter, should not be seen as evidence that they were therefore both recognised as a "hymn," but rather that phrases from each pericope were used to uphold similar Christological arguments. As Bockmuehl confirms in his Philippian commentary, "the existing evidence is too limited to permit any definite conclusions about the specific identification, setting, and use of first-century Christian hymnic texts" (Bockmuehl, *Philippians,* 117). See also Edsall and Strawbridge, "Songs we Used to Sing," 303–305.

ments is on the creative acts of God and on Christ as one who has been present from the beginning and active as creator. The images of "thrones, dominions, principalities, and powers" are especially favoured by Origen in a world with various competing cosmological hierarchies. This phrase, alongside the Christological descriptors before it, is used to support arguments that Christ is both fully human and fully divine, and is the only one who mediates between God and humanity. Christ as "head of the body, the Church" also plays a role in early Christian defence of the divine nature of Christ as the image of head, in particular, is used to defend the understanding that the Christ who physically suffered and died on the cross is God the Son who, with the authority and divine nature of God the Father, is head of all. Col 1.15–20 functions in a variety of contexts and supports the defence of early Christian Christological and theological claims. This multivalent use highlights the plasticity of this Colossian passage as it inspires a range of ideas and conclusions about the person and nature of Christ based on the phrases early Christians find within it.

Nevertheless, as Christological debates and arguments developed throughout this time period, early Christian focus on and defence of Christ's origin and pre-existence is achieved through increasingly complex hermeneutical moves. Early Christians adapted and expanded their interpretation and use of Col 1.15–20 as their opponents exposed the limits of this passage. Seeking to reclaim the words of Paul from opponents who argue that God is divided and Christ is a phantom or a creature, early Christian writers can no longer use the words and images of Colossians alone to support their arguments. This is especially true when their opponents are using the same texts, a problem already emphasised in the previous chapter on 1 Cor 15. Up to this point early Christian writers used the words of Col 1 to argue for the divine and pre-existent nature of Christ and to dismiss the arguments of their opponents without worrying about the implications of the subordination of God the Son to God the Father. This argument no longer works, however, when their opponents claim the same passage to argue that Jesus Christ is not fully divine. In the final section of this chapter, therefore, the time frame of this study is extended to examine more fully how the interpretation and use of Col 1.15–20 shaped early Christian writers and their doctrine, especially as they describe and defend the nature of Christ in one of the first major conflicts facing the early Church: the Arian controversy.

### 5.4.1 Colossians 1.15–20 and the Arian Controversy

As one of the most frequently cited pericopes of the Pauline epistles, Col 1.15–20 contributes greatly to the formation and development of Christological claims, especially on the cusp of the first councils and official creedal statements. This is particularly clear through the ways that the use of Col 1.15–20 is adapted once this pericope becomes the focus of the Arian controversy in the immediate post-Nicene time period. As Lightfoot observes, the Arian controversy "gave a different turn to the exegesis" of Col 1.15–20 as the Arians focused on the expression "first-born of all creation" and concluded from it that God the Son was a created being.[123] With Col 1 situated at the heart of the Arian debate, the emphasis of early Christians on the pre-existence of Christ and the use of this text to defend Christ's divine nature must shift since early Christian interpretation of this Colossian pericope can no longer solve the Christological and hermeneutical problems presented by the Arian claims.

Shortly before 320 C.E., Arius became a leading figure in a Christological controversy that divided the church for most of the fourth century.[124] As Stead remarks, "there is no need to argue the crucial importance of the Arian controversy in the early development of Christian doctrine" since it was from this controversy that the first creedal statement to demand universal assent was formed.[125] Despite scholarly endorsements of the importance of Arius and the Arian movement in the history of Christian writings and doctrine, very little of Arius' own writings have survived. This means that the writings which are extant must be treated with caution and the recognition that "divorced from their own original literary context, they are, in the works in which they are now found, very far from presenting to us the systematic thought of Arius as he himself saw it."[126] According to Williams, "'Arianism' as a coherent system, founded by a single great figure and sustained by his disciples, is a fantasy—more exactly, a fantasy based on the polemic of Nicene writers, above all Athanasius."[127] Nevertheless, while a coherent system might not be entirely definable, some of the beliefs and doctrinal arguments attributed to Arius and his followers are possible to identify.

Essentially, Arius' thesis is that God the Son is a creature, begotten from God the Father and created in time. Consequently, he denies the full divinity of God the Son. Drawing on the same expressions found in Col 1 that early Christian writers used to defend the Son's divinity, especially Christ as the first-born of all creation, Arius argues that it is impossible for God the Son as a created

---

[123] Lightfoot, *Colossians*, 146. See also Hengel, *Son of God*, 155–156.
[124] Williams, *Arius*, 1. For a history of scholarship on Arius and Arianism, see Williams, *Arius*, 2–25.
[125] Christopher Stead, "Arius in Modern Research," *JTS(n.s.)* 45.1 (1994): 24–36; 24.
[126] Williams, *Arius*, 95. See also Charles Kannengiesser, *Athanase d'Alexandrie, évêque et écrivain. Une lecture des traités Contre les Ariens* (Paris: Beauchesne, 1983), 457.
[127] Williams, *Arius*, 82.

being to be both pre-existent and consubstantial with God the Father. This, for Arius, protects the transcendence of God. In his study on the history of Arian thought, Lorenz writes that Arius' main concern is theological, and that Arius presents a Christological picture based on a Jewish-Christian theology of the angelic, high-priest mediator.[128] Arguing from the writings of Arius preserved by Athanasius and Alexander, Lorenz further describes how Arius stands in the tradition of a "*Christologie von unten*"[129] where his primary concern is to uphold the unique dignity of God the Father in the face of attempts unduly to glorify God the Son.[130] At the heart of this debate, however, is not simply Arius' denial of the full divinity of Christ and his advocacy of Christ's nature as that of a creature, but more crucially the fact that Arius and his followers were using Scripture—and especially Col 1.15—to reach these conclusions.[131]

Within their arguments, the Arians relied on scriptural texts that they understood to assert the created nature of Christ, namely Prov 8.22 ("The Lord created me at the beginning of his work") and Col 1.15 ("first-born of all creation"). These passages supported their conclusions about both the unbegotten nature of God the Father and the begotten nature of God the Son, who is the form and image of God. Certainly, pre-existence is an issue for the Arians, just as it was for early Christian writers. Except that the question of Christ's pre-existence was solved by the Arians by denying the full divinity of Jesus Christ, who as a creature and a created being, cannot be of the same substance as God and thus cannot exist with God before being created.[132] Arius agrees with early Christian conclusions that God the Father is necessarily uncreated and unbegotten, and yet, be-

---

[128] Rudolf Lorenz, *Arius judaizans? Untersuchungen zur dogmengeschichtlichen Einordnung des Arius* (Göttingen: Vandenhoeck & Ruprecht, 1979), 119–121. See also Williams, *Arius*, 146–147.
[129] Lorenz, *Arius judaizans*, 124. See also Robert C. Gregg and Dennis Groh, *Early Arianism: A View of Salvation* (London: SCM Press, 1981). One must note that Lorenz's understanding of Arius is not immune to criticism and must be balanced with other views (that of Williams and Stead, for example).
[130] Stead, "Arius in Modern Research," 36.
[131] Were our study to include the Council of Nicaea and the first creedal statement of the church, we would see how these claims by Arius led to the Nicene claim that God the Son is consubstantial (*homoousios*) with God the Father in a move which essentially anathematises the Arian theology we have described, arguing against Arius for the full divinity of the Son, who is distinct from and yet one with the Father. It is not until the later writings of the Cappadocians against the Eunomians (the later followers of Arius) that this is worked out in greater detail as they (Cappadocians) strive to reiterate the divinity of the Son as consubstantial with the Father, even as God remains incorporeal and unbegotten.
[132] Note that even though the Son is a created being for Arius, the Son is also pre-existent to the world.

cause the Son is created and begotten as he finds in the words of Col 1, the Son cannot truly be God.[133] As Arius purportedly wrote, "there was when he [the Son] was not."[134]

Arius' theology is not based on a new understanding of Col 1.15, but rather builds on how this same Scripture had already been used by early Christian writers.[135] Only now, it is used to oppose these earlier works and to claim that the same words from Colossians which early Christians used to defend the divinity of God the Son, actually point to a Christ who is subordinate to God and thus not fully divine. For example, Rebecca Lyman describes how Origen's explanation of the incarnation of the pre-existent divine *logos* is "one of the first constructive Christologies" and yet, at the same time, its subordinationist tendencies and Origen's language concerning the pre-existent Christ "anticipated many problems in later theology regarding the proper union of divine and human nature."[136] While many early Christians had problems neither with the subordination of God the Son in their interpretations of Scripture, nor with seeing Jesus as separate from the Father in an apocalyptic cosmological framework, with the Arian interpretation of Col 1, early Christians like Athanasius must now grapple with the implications of these issues in order to enable the basic insights of the earliest Christological confessions to be expressed aright. These early Christological claims based on an exegesis of Col 1 could no longer by themselves address the Arian claims of Christ as a creature, created and begotten in time. Athanasius cannot fathom how Arius can draw the conclusions he does from Col 1, and yet he also knows that expressing his incredulity will not solve the deeper interpretative issue at stake. He writes against Arius that,

> if the Word (ὁ λόγος) was one of the creatures, Scripture would have said of him, that he is firstborn of the other creatures (πρωτότοκος τῶν ἄλλων κτισμάτων ἐστί). But now since what the sacred writers actually do say is, that he is the firstborn of all creation (Col 1.15: πρωτότοκός ἐστι πάσης τῆς κτίσεως), it is clearly shown that the Son of God is other than all creation and not a creature.[137]

---

**133** Athanasius, *Dep.Ar*, 70 (Opitz; *NPNF* 4). See also *C.Ar*, 2.6–3.1, 3.5–6; and Williams, *Arius*, 97–98.
**134** Williams, *Arius*, 150; Riemer Roukema and Saskia Deventer-Metz, *Jesus, Gnosis and Dogma* (London: T&T Clark, 2010), 184. See also Athanasius of Alexandria, *C.Ar*, 1.5–6; 1.9; 2.37; Khaled Anatolios, *Athanasius* (London: Routledge, 2004), 126.
**135** See Lorenz, *Arius judaizans*, 76–78; and Williams, *Arius*, 86.
**136** Lyman, *Christology and Cosmology*, 69.
**137** Athanasius, *C.Ar*, 1.63.5 (Metzler; *NPNF* 4). See also Anatolios, *Athanasius*, 126. Athanasius cites Col 1.15–20 more than 70 times in his own writings, here using Col 1 to point out Arius' error.

## 5.4 Concluding Remarks: Why Colossians 1.15–20?

To this defence, he also offers what appears to be an "external hermeneutical principle, namely the fundamental otherness of the divine"[138] in order to express the divine nature of Christ: *homoousios*. The problem with Col 1.15 was that the Arians' interpretation of this passage (and Prov 8.22) to defend Christ as creature and not fully divine was entirely plausible, and the problem for Athanasius and his sympathisers is that the basic sense of Col 1.15 leads to Arianism.

Exegetes of the second and third centuries set forth the pre-existent Christ using Col 1 and other related texts in order to defend their understanding of Christ as fully human and fully divine, undivided from God the Father. However, the hermeneutical moves used by the likes of Origen and Tertullian to make Christological claims stressing the ontological unity of Father and Son no longer worked.[139] Athanasius therefore had to take an approach to exegesis which attended to his understanding of the sense of Scripture as a whole as he "sought to reinterpret texts exploited by the opposition in the light of his hermeneutical principles."[140] It is true Athanasius assumes that his expression of the divine nature of Christ is consistent with Scripture, but now—and as this study already encountered with 1 Cor 2 and the hermeneutics of at least two levels of understanding and interpreting Scripture—scriptural texts can only be the beginning point of theological interpretations and weight is not put on the most basic sense of the biblical words at the expense of the rule of faith.[141]

The history of the interpretation of Col 1.15–20 both affects and is shaped by the Arian controversy and early Christian understanding of Jesus Christ, the image of the invisible God and the first-born of all creation. When early Christians wrote about the divine nature of God the Son and the pre-existence of Christ, Col 1.15–20 was one of the main Pauline texts to which they turned. Just as the use of 1 Cor 2 underlined ways early Christians used Paul's writings to think about formation, wisdom, and how to read Scripture, so their reception of Col 1 establishes ways early Christians used Paul's writings to think about the divine nature of Jesus Christ, while at the same time beginning to grapple with the limits of *sola scriptura* in that enterprise.

---

[138] Young, *Biblical Exegesis*, 32. Athanasius, *Decr*, 11.4–6; 10.4–6, 13.
[139] Martin Werner, *The Formation of Christian Dogma: An historical study of its problem* (trans. S. G. F. Brandon; London: A&C Black, 1957), 158.
[140] Young, *Biblical Exegesis*, 37.
[141] Young, *Biblical Exegesis*, 32. See also p40.

# Chapter Six:
# Conclusion

*the treasure of divine meaning*
*is enclosed within the frail vessel of the common letter*[1]

Four of the most frequently cited Pauline passages in early Christian writings shape this enquiry into the pre-Nicene reception of Paul and his letters. Excerpts from these passages are used to support and give authority to a wide range of theological and exegetical arguments, while at the same time early Christian writers claim the authority and wisdom of Paul to give weight to their own words. One of the challenges of any study of early Christian Pauline reception is drawing together, in a way that is both justifiable and coherent, the large number of early Christian writings that use the letters attributed to Paul. Many early Christian works are not translated and some remain unpublished. Moreover, early Christians knew and used a diversity of scriptural texts within their writings and their adaptation is multivalent as they integrated these scriptural texts to support arguments, give authority to theological claims, and to teach. In order to grapple with these challenges, this study adapted a method from scholars of ancient history and, based on a collation of more than 27,000 references to the Pauline letters in ante-Nicene writings, limited its focus to 1 Cor 2.6–16, Eph 6.10–17, 1 Cor 15.50–58, and Col 1.15–20. A significant contribution of this method to the wider discussion of early Christian reception is the identification of these frequently cited Pauline passages. Furthermore, this identification then opened the doors for an examination of the ways each text was used across a range of early Christian writings and, subsequently, enabled conclusions to be drawn about the development and formation of early Christian scriptural interpretation, theological doctrine, and even identity.

The second chapter focused on excerpts from 1 Cor 2.6–16 and how this most frequently cited pericope was used in early Christian writings. Early Christians drew on the tension in this pericope for a similar strategic purpose: to differentiate between worldly wisdom and the wisdom of God. With a focus on the language of wisdom, early Christian writers used excerpts from this passage to distinguish between different levels of wisdom, to describe and claim the hidden wisdom of God, and to inform their understanding of Paul and of themselves as teachers of this wisdom. The distinction between different levels of wisdom within this Corinthian text allowed for different approaches to Christian formation, as

---

[1] Origen, *Princ*, 4.3.13.

formation was defined as the progression or movement from one level of wisdom to another. This understanding of formation shaped not only early Christian interpretation of 1 Cor 2, but also the understanding of formation put forth by this study.

Throughout early Christian writings, rhetoric about wisdom was adapted as early Christians drew on this prominent Corinthian text within their arguments and some of the fiercest theological debates about scriptural interpretation. Both the proto-orthodox and the heterodox claimed access to a different kind of wisdom compared to their opponents. For both, there was a wisdom with its foundation in another world. By identifying with this wisdom, dialogue was closed off with the other as each appealed to the wisdom hidden from the rulers of this age. The images and phrases from 1 Cor 2 described an enigmatic wisdom which Paul and early Christians after him claimed.[2] Early Christians' use of 1 Cor 2 and, consequently, their focus on wisdom enabled an understanding of Christian identity to emerge: Christians are those who are imbued with divine wisdom.

The third chapter focused on Eph 6.10–17 and emphasised that early Christians are particularly concerned with the images of wrestling, armour, fiery darts, and spiritual forces of wickedness. Using the words and images of this second pericope, early Christians are now exhorted in the ways that the wisdom described in 1 Cor 2 may be achieved and maintained through actions of prayer, faith, standing firm in the midst of temptation, and putting on the armour of God. Just as the images of wisdom from 1 Cor 2 led to a counter-cultural stance by early Christians who claimed the wisdom of God over the wisdom of this world, so early Christian use of Eph 6 was counter-cultural as well. Early Christians embraced the familiar language of warfare and used this language from Eph 6 to describe not a physical battle but a spiritual one. As a result, an understanding of formation expanded to include not only the movement from one level of wisdom to another, but also the movement from one side of the battle to the other.

Using the images of Eph 6, early Christians identified certain points in the Christian life when one was especially vulnerable to attack, weakness, and fear. These times represented liminal moments when the Christian was between sides of the battle, whether joining it for the first time in baptism or within the decisive moment of battle for those facing persecution. The images of Eph 6, and especially the dichotomies and divisions associated with the language of warfare, emphasised an understanding of the Christian as embattled. Ethical injunctions to prayer, baptism, faith, purity, and wisdom were offered as concrete ways

---

2 Brown, *The Cross*, 33.

that Christians could maintain faith and stand firm in the face of evil, holding fast to the very wisdom of God to which they were exhorted using the images of 1 Cor 2.

The fourth chapter continued this focus on early Christian use of images within the Pauline letters and in the process, emphasised the significant connection between exegesis and theology. Using the images of flesh and blood, kingdom of God, perishable and imperishable, mortal and immortal found in 1 Cor 15.50–58, early Christians articulated their developing theology of resurrection. While 1 Cor 2 was used to describe different levels of wisdom and Eph 6 to describe opposing sides in the struggle against evil, early Christians used 1 Cor 15 to engage diverse and opposing understandings of resurrection and the doctrinal implications of each. In particular, progress here is no longer between different levels of wisdom or different sides of a battle. Rather, progress is identified as the move from mortality and perishability to immortality and imperishability. Particular focus on 15.50 emphasised the division between flesh and blood and the kingdom of God and the ambiguities in defining each of these elements. As early Christians grappled with the words of 1 Cor 15.50, crucial to the emerging Christian identity was the struggle to affirm the value of flesh and blood as the medium of salvation while accepting its problematic character—both spiritual and somatic—as highlighted in this Pauline passage. This interpretative problem with 1 Cor 15 and the complex exegesis undertaken—both in terms of how flesh and blood were defined and the place of judgement and its relation to the kingdom of God—emerged again in the final chapter on Col 1.15–20 which needed to be rescued from its use by the Arians.

The apologetic nature of the texts in which 1 Cor 15.50–58 was most frequently found offered another dimension to early Christian use of this pericope. Apologetic works shape community, doctrine, and scriptural understanding as they seek to establish one way of truth over and against opposing views. The focus on resurrection within apologetic writings emphasised an understanding of the Christian as one who looks forward to a resurrected body, in whatever form that might take, in the kingdom of God. Such use of 1 Cor 15 underscores one of the reasons that each of the passages engaged in this study was so central to the formation of early Christian doctrine and hermeneutics developing at this time. Each Christian writer claimed the right interpretation of these key Pauline texts by hermeneutical and exegetical strategies. For those seeking to claim the authority of scriptural support within their theological arguments, each of these four texts posed serious problems to ideas concerning wisdom, spiritual forces, the *eschaton*, resurrection, and Christ. As a result, early Christian writers adapted and adopted a variety of hermeneutical tactics in order to ensure Paul's words supported their own, not only about resurrection but about the very constitution and nature of Christ, humankind, and even salvation. Scriptural authority and exegetical debate offered a framework within which early Christian doctrine could emerge and served as the organising principle around which they ordered their arguments.

To be sure, engagement with four of the most frequently cited Pauline texts led to what early Christians believed to be central theological debates at this time. Clement of Alexandria's understanding of teaching and formation, Irenaeus's understanding of recapitulation and the rule of truth, the Valentinian understanding of Eucharistic sacrament and the flesh, Origen's understanding of scriptural interpretation, and Tertullian's understanding of resurrection and the substance of the body all emerged as these four Pauline texts were taken up, adapted, and reworked within early Christian writings. Theology and the interpretation of Scripture were intertwined in this period (as in subsequent periods). The ways in which scriptural interpretation affected and shaped the key theological issues of Christology, anthropology, cosmology, and identity for the earliest interpreters of Paul lends strong evidence to Greer's conclusion that "for early Church fathers, Scripture yielded a theological vision when rightly interpreted. And theological disputes in the early church were largely arguments about how rightly to describe that vision and to define the hero of the story that comprised the vision."[3]

While the fourth chapter on 1 Cor 15 emphasised this focus on theological vision and right understanding described by Greer, the final chapter on the use of Col 1.15–20 in early Christian writings focused almost entirely on the "hero of the story,"[4] Christ. The images and metaphors that early Christian writers found in this final pericope were used to support theological arguments about the nature of Christ and the relationship between God the Father and God the Son. The theological focus on resurrection encountered in early Christian use of 1 Cor 15 expanded in this final chapter to include the person and nature of Christ in his incarnation, suffering, death, and resurrection. From the use of this Colossian passage, Christ's identity was of one who is pre-existent and who shares the authority and nature of God, as the head of the church and of humankind.

Early Christian use of Col 1, however, did not focus on dualistic images and division as discussed in previous chapters, but on images of unity and oneness, especially in Christological arguments. As early Christians were challenged by the notions of a divided Christ and a divided God, excerpts from this text were

---

3 Greer, "Applying," 195.
4 Greer, "Applying," 195.

used to argue for unity in support of their theological conclusions that Christ is one nature, human and divine. Nevertheless, as Christological debates and arguments developed throughout this time period, focus on Christ's origin and pre-existence was achieved through increasingly complex hermeneutical moves as the limitations of this Colossian passage and its ability to support Christological arguments on its own were exposed. Seeking to reclaim the words of Paul from opponents who argued that God was divided and Christ was a phantom or a creature, early Christian writers could no longer use the words and images of Colossians alone to support their arguments. In order to establish the hermeneutical and exegetical effects of this struggle and the intersection between scriptural interpretation and theology more clearly, the final section of this chapter extended beyond the ante-Nicene period to explore how the advent of the Arian controversy affected early Christian use of this passage.

With a focus on four of the most frequently cited passages and an examination of how they shaped early Christians and their writings, each chapter encountered some of the most controversial theological and interpretative issues in early Christianity. Emphasising the close connection between scriptural interpretation and theological doctrines, the issues engaged using these four pericopes included the nature of wisdom, the importance of standing firm in faith, the nature of resurrection and the body, and the nature of Christ. Within this context, study of the use of these Pauline passages highlighted some crucial understandings of early Christian identity; early Christian writers understood themselves to be imbued with wisdom, embattled, raised with Christ at the *eschaton*, and with faith in one who is fully human, fully divine, pre-existent, and co-creator with God the Father. Moreover, the content and context of the use of these four passages offered a fresh understanding of early Christian formation, separate from the attempts of modern scholars to recover early Christian catechesis, school teaching, and pedagogy. As Frances Young argues, formative catechesis and the content of teaching, especially before Nicaea, are almost impossible to determine and define. Nevertheless, this study provided a wider sense of what early Christians were doing when they engaged with one another and with the words of Scripture, and how this engagement, based on their use of four key scriptural passages, contributed to an understanding of early Christian formation.

As early Christians defined and redefined the images and phrases they found within each Pauline pericope to support their theological arguments, this study refined and redefined the concept and content of early Christian formation. The fact that the most highly cited Pauline passage in early Christian writings is Paul's teaching about human and divine wisdom leads to an expanded understanding of formation. The differentiation between levels of wisdom, sides of a battle, and ways of understanding Christ and the progression towards the kingdom of God suggests that early Christians embraced a self-identity in which they were aware that they were different, special, and could sit at odds with the wisdom of this world and the conventions of wider society.

In the chapter on 1 Cor 2, therefore, an understanding of formation emerged as the movement from one level of wisdom to another with the content of this wisdom beginning with the proclamation of Christ crucified and ending with the secret and hidden wisdom of God. In particular, the ways in which Clement of Alexandria and Origen use 1 Cor 2 indicated that formation implicitly demanded progress and a journey of knowing and increasing in wisdom without an obvious terminus. The chapter on Ephesians also included a language of progression. In this chapter, however, progress is depicted not as moving from one level of wisdom to another but, using language of warfare and battle, from one side of the battle to the other. The military images from Eph 6 helped Christian writers encourage the faithful to stand firm as they progressed toward greater wisdom and ultimately salvation in God.

Language of progression was also important for early Christian use of 1 Cor 15 as writers sought to form Christian understanding of the phrase "flesh and blood cannot inherit the kingdom of God (15.50)." The ultimate goal of Christian life and faith through the lens of this pericope was the movement from perishable to imperishable and mortal to immortal, and all of this movement toward the final goal of partaking in the kingdom of God. Within the final chapter on Col 1, the emphasis was not as much on language of journey and progression, but on claiming a right understanding of the nature of Christ using the words of 1.15–20. However, this right understanding was important for formation, since, as the first chapter emphasised, the basic instruction that leads to greater wisdom was that of Jesus Christ and him crucified. Therefore, the focus by early Christians on Christological images and phrases and their determination correctly to describe Christ's nature were essential both to their own understanding and proclamation of Christ crucified and, consequently, to the movement of those to whom they wrote towards the hidden wisdom of God.

Formation finally is not understood here as pedagogy, but as progress from one level—be that faith, knowledge, or wisdom—to another. This understanding emerged from the ways that each passage was engaged and the dichotomies and divisions early Christians found in each. The eschatological elements of not yet achieving full wisdom, perfection, protection from evil, understanding of Christ, and ultimately, the kingdom of God, suggest that Christian identity is wrapped in and shaped by this sense of journey. For early Christian writers such as the Valentinians and others with "gnostic" systems of theology, the terminus of journey and progression could be realised in the present. However, for those writing against them and others claiming what is now called an "orthodox" position, the journey continued on a spiritual and cosmic level beyond the present. Early Christians saw that to attain the level of wisdom they claimed in their writings was to reach a level of wisdom that was unknowable and even hidden from those who did not have the right faith, knowledge, wisdom, and even Spirit. Early Christian use of the images and words of each pericope to set one understanding against another was an attempt to persuade those to whom (or against whom) they wrote that different levels of understanding and ways of being existed, and this act of persuasion was an attempt at formation. This understanding of formation, alongside the methodology on which this study is founded, contributes to an understanding of ways these four frequently cited passages were used to shape early Christians and in the process, Christianity as a system of practice and belief.

However, this study is not without limitations. As the chapter on Col 1 highlighted in its brief engagement with the Arian controversy, each chapter could have expanded into its own project and focused in a more in-depth way on the intersection between the scriptural interpretation and theological implications of each passage as it was used by early Christians. This is particularly the case if the methodological approach of this study, determining and focusing on the most frequently cited passages in a given time period, was applied to the reception of other scriptural texts. What if other passages had been considered and this study included the top ten most frequently cited Pauline pericopes? Would conclusions about what theological and hermeneutical issues were so central to early Christians change if excerpts from a frequently cited Gospel text were included? What if the focus had shifted only to consider those frequently cited texts which are now called "Christ-hymns" such as Phil 2, Col 1, and John 1? Or what if the time frame were extended beyond Nicaea to include the conciliar definitions and ensuing debates? Each of these questions emerges from this project and offers areas for further research and study.[5]

Above all, the use of these four frequently cited Pauline pericopes revealed the diverse theologies and hermeneutical strategies at play in ante-Nicene writings. Contrasting views about wisdom, salvation, resurrection, and Christ's nature demonstrate ways in which ideas about interpretation were formed and emerged in a time when questions of method and theological exposition of Scripture were still unsettled. This study engaged a wide range of texts and

---

[5] Based on this project, a digital database is being produced which will contain all of the writings of Paul which occur in ante-Nicene texts. It will be presented in a searchable, sortable, and accessible form to complement other research tools and enable wider access to and use of these texts, both Pauline and patristic.

the differences between them, tracing the contours and overlap between theology and exegesis in order to examine how these texts shape early Christians and their writings and to determine what was "formation" for the earliest Christian communities. Just as there is no singular way that each of these texts was adapted and used by early Christian writers, so also is there no homogenous view of early Christian interpretation and the effect that Scripture has upon early Christian writings, theology, and ultimately identity as Christian.

# Appendix:
# Introduction

> *the forest of quotations should not be hidden by the trees of classification*[1]

## A.1 Databases

The following appendices include sections from the comprehensive database of Pauline references in pre-Nicene writings. In order to facilitate ease of use, the appendices are organised to correspond with the chapters of this study and are ordered by Pauline passage. These appendices serve both as a resource for readers interested in the large number of references consulted for each chapter and also as a means of greater transparency in the work of this project. Each appendix includes works in Greek, Latin, and a few from the Nag Hammadi library in Coptic. Each entry includes not only the Pauline passage, but also the location of the reference by early Christian author and text. As mentioned in the introduction, sources consulted to create this database included *Biblia Patristica* with updated versions found on *Biblindex*, editions of *Sources chrétiennes* from our time period, series such as *Fathers of the Church*, *CCL*, and *GCS*, and databases such as *Cetedoc* (Latin) and *Thesaurus Linguae Graecae* (Greek).

A column is also included to indicate the relationship between the scriptural passage as presently known and the reference as found in the early Christian text. While Young writes that early Christian writings are so "packed with scriptural allusion, or, if not allusion, language that can be paralleled in scriptural material, that a comprehensive examination is beyond our scope,"[2] the database that follows suggests that a comprehensive examination can begin to yield answers to the character of scriptural allusion. As outlined in the introduction, based on the definitions and distinctions offered by Annewies van den Hoek and Michael Bird, each entry into the database has been divided into three groups: references, possible references, and reference not found.[3]

---

[1] van den Hoek, "Techniques of Quotation," 228.
[2] Young, *Biblical Exegesis*, 222.
[3] van den Hoek, "Techniques of Quotation," 228–229 and Bird, "Reception of Paul," 74.

## A.1.1 Reference (R)

A "reference" is what many scholars might define as a quotation, direct attribution, or paraphrase. It will "have a considerable degree of literality" and yet it "need not be verbatim in the modern sense" but only "follow the source to a considerable extent."[4] A reference may include two to three sentences from the Pauline epistles or only a few words and is identified through the context in which the words or phrases occur, usually entailing a "deliberate lifting of one text into another with some kind of marker to signify the use of a second text."[5] References are most easily identified when the ancient authors tell us they are referring to a scriptural text, although this is not always the case.[6] As Moss describes her own method of surveying quotations from the Gospels in early Christian martyrological texts, if a reference "is discernible in the minds of readers—be they ancient or modern—then this interpretation bears explanation and interpretation."[7]

This way of categorising a reference as something dependent on a specific Pauline epistle enabled me to take into consideration the reality that different authors use different techniques when they quote from or paraphrase Scripture. As I highlighted with some early Christian excerpts in the preceding chapters, some authors combine two passages into one sentence in order to make a point while others use one passage of Scripture to illuminate their understanding of another. In some places an author might rely upon an image or word found in Scripture and in others an author might indicate a reference to a large section of a scriptural text. Many of these references were not specifically engaged within this study because some are "merely passing allusions to the text that shed little or no light on its meaning," others are "quotations that are intended to reinforce a point made on the strength of some other part of Scripture," and still others do not engage the context of the author's argument and appear to be added as a rhetorical flourish.[8] The excerpts from early Christian writings quoted in each chapter fall primarily into this category of "reference," since these texts offers the most concrete examples of the use of a Pauline passage by early Christian writers.

---

4 van den Hoek, "Techniques of Quotation," 229.
5 Bird, "Reception of Paul," 74.
6 van den Hoek, "Techniques of Quotation," 229.
7 Moss, *Other Christs*, 205n11.
8 Gerard Bray, ed. *1–2 Corinthians* (ACCS NT7; Downers Grove, Ill: Intervarsity Press, 1999), xix.

## A.1.2 Possible Reference (PR)

A "possible reference" is a phrase or series of words where similarities between the Pauline passage and early Christian texts can be detected and where it could be identified as a reference were the context to allow. A possible reference offers an "awareness of a second text through its particular choice of subject, language, and grammar" but often "requires a shared knowledge of a second text between the author and reader in order to be discernible."[9] With a possible reference, neither the context nor the content of the surrounding text allows certainty about whether it is a clear reference to and dependent upon Pauline material.[10] These examples, at times, have few literal correspondences to the Pauline texts listed; they instead allude to the text in theme, thought, or through a few words. Some scholars categorise these examples as reminiscences or even echoes, where it can be "difficult to decide whether we are really hearing an echo at all, or whether we are only conjuring things out of the murmurings of our own imaginations."[11] Examples like these cannot be classified as a reference since knowledge of the textual tradition of the author is not available to us, and thus, I have left the verdict open as to whether such examples are a Pauline reference and categorise them as "possible."[12] The placement of texts in this category can be somewhat subjective;[13] nevertheless each appendix offers a consistent categorisation of passages according to the degree to which they rely on Paul. Some of these texts may be found in the main body of this study, but most are only listed in the appendices that follow.

## A.1.3 Reference Not Found (RNF)

The final category of texts, which do not feature in this study beyond the appendices, are identified as "reference not found." This category includes texts listed in secondary sources as containing references to Pauline material but in which,

---

**9** Bird, "Reception of Paul," 74.
**10** Sometimes dependence on Scripture is clear, but not a Pauline passage specifically. This is indicated, for example, in the chapter of Col 1 where it is unclear in places whether "πρωτότοκος ἐκ τῶν νεκρῶν" is Col 1.18 or Rev 1.5.
**11** Hays, *Echoes*, 23. See also van den Hoek, "Techniques of Quotation," 229.
**12** This decision is both a text-critical one and hermeneutical, since our methods and assumptions regarding textual interpretation and cross-referencing differ from those of early Christian writers. See Gadamer, *Truth and Method*, 507–543.
**13** Bird, "Reception of Paul," 74.

upon looking at the context and content of the text, the corresponding Pauline passage cannot be identified or detected. This category also includes the few works listed in *Biblia patristica*, particularly fragments of Origen, which could not be located. These passages remain in the database since some serve as a potential critique, suggesting that the secondary source in which the reference was found is probably incorrect.

The databases which follow are intended to provide a solid foundation for engaging with Pauline references in early Christian writings and a starting point for examining how early Christians were using these texts. The quantitative nature of the excerpts in the following appendices was central for this study; however, this is only the starting point. One of the main contributions of this project to the wider discussion of Pauline reception in early Christian writings is how the *content* of the interpretation of key passages, distilled from these appendices, enables a wide-ranging examination of the ways each text is used and what this use conveys about the development and formation of early Christian interpretation, theological doctrine, and identity.


**Note:** An (*) next to a scriptural text indicates that the Pauline passage falls within a quotation or paraphrase that belongs to another author (a quote within a quote). For example, one excerpt from 1 Cor 2.14 in Origen's *Commentary on John* falls within a much longer phrase that Origen attributes to Heracleon.

# Appendix A: 1 Corinthians 2.6–16

| 1 Corinthians | Early Christian Writer | Early Christian Work | Reference Status |
|---|---|---|---|
| 2.6 | Anonymous | Ep.Apost. 28 | PR |
| 2.6 | | Orat.Paul. | RNF |
| 2.6 | Clement of Alexandria | Strom. 6.65.5 | R |
| 2.6 | | Strom. 6.68.1 | R |
| 2.6* | Cyprian of Carthage | Ep. 75.9 | RNF |
| 2.6 | Eusebius of Caesarea | Comm.Isa. 20 | PR |
| 2.6 | | Comm.Isa. 70 | PR |
| 2.6 | | Comm.Isa. 160 | PR |
| 2.6 | | Comm.Isa. 208 | PR |
| 2.6 | | Comm.Isa. 311 | PR |
| 2.6 | | Comm.Isa. 376 | PR |
| 2.6 | | Comm.Isa. 376 | PR |
| 2.6 | | Comm.Ps. | PR |
| 2.6 | | Comm.Ps. | PR |
| 2.6 | | Comm.Ps. | PR |
| 2.6 | | Comm.Ps. | PR |
| 2.6 | | Comm.Ps. | PR |
| 2.6 | | Comm.Ps. | PR |
| 2.6 | | Comm.Ps. | PR |
| 2.6 | | Comm.Ps. | PR |
| 2.6 | | Comm.Ps. H | PR |
| 2.6 | | Comm.Ps. H | PR |
| 2.6 | | Comm.Ps. H | PR |
| 2.6 | | Dem.ev. 10.8.57 | PR |
| 2.6 | | Dem.ev. 10.8.68 | RNF |
| 2.6 | | Dem.ev. 2.3.101 | PR |
| 2.6 | | Dem.ev. 5.20.8 | PR |

Appendix A: 1 Corinthians 2.6 – 16 — **187**

| 1 Corinthians | Early Christian Writer | Early Christian Work | Reference Status |
|---|---|---|---|
| 2.6 | Eusebius of Caesarea | Dem.ev. 7.1.116 | RNF |
| 2.6 | | Dem.ev. 7.1.64 | RNF |
| 2.6 | | Dem.ev. 9.7.26 | PR |
| 2.6 | | Fr. | RNF |
| 2.6 | | Fr.G.I. 2.2 | PR |
| 2.6 | | Fr.G.I. 3.5 | PR |
| 2.6 | | Fr.G.I. 4.24 | PR |
| 2.6* | | Qu. 1.2 | PR |
| 2.6 | Firmilian of Caesarea | Cypr. 9 | PR |
| 2.6 | Hippolytus of Rome | Comm.Dan. 1.15.5 | PR |
| 2.6 | | Noet. 9.1 | PR |
| 2.6 | Ignatius of Antioch | Eph. 17.1 | PR |
| 2.6 | | Eph. 19.1 | PR |
| 2.6 | Irenaeus of Lyons | Haer. 1.1.17 | R |
| 2.6* | | Haer. 1.8.4 | R |
| 2.6 | | Haer. 3.2.1 | R |
| 2.6 | | Haer. 5.6.1 | R |
| 2.6 | Lactantius | Inst. 5.1.15 | PR |
| 2.6 | Origen of Alexandria | Comm.Jo. 13.241 | R |
| 2.6 | | Comm.Jo. 19.56 | R |
| 2.6 | | Comm.Jo. 6.267 | R |
| 2.6 | | Comm.Matt. 12.30 | PR |
| 2.6 | | Comm.Matt. 12.32 | PR |
| 2.6 | | Comm.Matt. 12.39 | PR |
| 2.6 | | Comm.Matt. 12.39 | RNF |
| 2.6 | | Comm.Matt. 17.23 | PR |
| 2.6 | | Comm.Matt. A 32 | R |
| 2.6 | | Comm.Matt. A 35 | PR |
| 2.6 | | Comm.Rom. 1.13.3 | R |

# Appendix A: 1 Corinthians 2.6–16

| 1 Corinthians | Early Christian Writer | Early Christian Work | Reference Status |
|---|---|---|---|
| 2.6 | Origen of Alexandria | Comm.Rom. 1.16.2 | PR |
| 2.6 | | Comm.Rom. 10.10.2 | PR |
| 2.6 | | Comm.Rom. 10.10.2 | PR |
| 2.6 | | Comm.Rom. 10.5.6 | PR |
| 2.6 | | Comm.Rom. 2.14.14 | R |
| 2.6 | | Comm.Rom. 5.2.6 | R |
| 2.6 | | Comm.Rom. 7.19.2 | R |
| 2.6 | | Comm.Rom. 7.7.4 | R |
| 2.6 | | Comm.Rom. 8.6.5 | R |
| 2.6 | | Comm.Cant. 2.5 | PR |
| 2.6 | | Cels. 1.13 | R |
| 2.6 | | Cels. 2.24 | R |
| 2.6 | | Cels. 3.20 | R |
| 2.6 | | Cels. 3.59 | PR |
| 2.6 | | Cels. 5.32 | PR |
| 2.6 | | Cels. 6.9 | PR |
| 2.6 | | Or. 21.2 | PR |
| 2.6 | | Or. 25.1 | PR |
| 2.6 | | Princ. 1.5.2 | PR |
| 2.6 | | Princ. 2.5.1 | RNF |
| 2.6 | | Princ. 3.2.1 | R |
| 2.6 | | Princ. 3.3.1 | R |
| 2.6 | | Princ. 3.3.1 | R |
| 2.6 | | Princ. 3.3.3 | R |
| 2.6 | | Princ. 4.1.7 | R |
| 2.6 | | Fr.1Cor. 12 | RNF |
| 2.6 | | Fr.1Cor. 43 | PR |
| 2.6 | | Fr.1Cor. 43 | PR |
| 2.6 | | Fr.1Cor. 9 | R |

Appendix A: 1 Corinthians 2.6 – 16 — **189**

| 1 Corinthians | Early Christian Writer | Early Christian Work | Reference Status |
|---|---|---|---|
| 2.6 | Origen of Alexandria | Fr.1Cor. 9 | R |
| 2.6 | | Fr.Luc. 186 | R |
| 2.6 | | Fr.Matt. 153 | PR |
| 2.6 | | Fr.Ps. | PR |
| 2.6 | | Fr.Ps. | PR |
| 2.6 | | Fr.Ps. | PR |
| 2.6 | | Fr.Ps. D | R |
| 2.6 | | Fr.Ps. E 113.21 | RNF |
| 2.6 | | Fr.Ps. E 118.161 | PR |
| 2.6 | | Hom.Ps. 4.10 | RNF |
| 2.6 | | Hom.1 Reg. (28) 10 | PR |
| 2.6 | | Hom.Isa. 3.1 | PR |
| 2.6 | | Hom.Isa. 3.1 | PR |
| 2.6 | | Hom.Jer. 12.12 | PR |
| 2.6 | | Hom.Jer. 7.3 | PR |
| 2.6 | | Hom.Jer. 7.3 | PR |
| 2.6 | | Hom.Jer. 8.8 | R |
| 2.6* | | Hom.Lev. 4.6 | R |
| 2.6 | | Hom.Lev. 4.8 | PR |
| 2.6 | | Hom.Luc. 6.5 | R |
| 2.6 | | Hom.Num. 18.3.2 | PR |
| 2.6 | | Hom.Num. 23.6 | RNF |
| 2.6 | | Hom.Ps. (36) 3.6 | PR |
| 2.6 | | Philoc. 1.11 | R |
| 2.6 | | Philoc. 1.29 | PR |
| 2.6 | Tertullian | Herm. 19.5 | PR |
| 2.6 | | Marc. 5.6.1 | R |
| 2.6 | | Marc. 5.6.2 | R |
| 2.6 – 7 | Clement of Alexandria | Strom. 5.80.4 – 5 | R |

| 1 Corinthians | Early Christian Writer | Early Christian Work | Reference Status |
|---|---|---|---|
| 2.6–7 | Eusebius of Caesarea | Praep.ev. 1.3.5 | R |
| 2.6–7 | Origen of Alexandria | Comm.Jo. 19.56 | R |
| 2.6–7 | | Comm.Rom. 1.13.6 | R |
| 2.6–7 | | Comm.Cant. 1.3 | PR |
| 2.6–7 | | Comm.Cant. 3.14 | PR |
| 2.6–7 | | Cels. 3.47 | R |
| 2.6–7 | | Princ. 4.2.4 | R |
| 2.6–7 | | Fr.1Cor. 27 | R |
| 2.6–7 | | Fr.Rom. 11 | R |
| 2.6–7 | | Fr.Cant. | PR |
| 2.6–7 | | Hom.Exod. 12.4 | R |
| 2.6–7 | | Hom.Gen. 14.4 | R |
| 2.6–7 | | Hom.Num. 6.1.2 | R |
| 2.6–7 | Clement of Alexandria | Strom. 5.65.5–66.1 | R |
| 2.6 or 2.8 | Eusebius of Caesarea | Dem.ev. 7.1.106 | PR |
| 2.6 or 2.8 | | Dem.ev. 8.1.59 | PR |
| 2.6 or 2.8 | | Dem.ev. 9.8.13 | PR |
| 2.6 or 2.8 | Origen of Alexandria | Cels. 8.13 | PR |
| 2.6 or 2.8 | | Cels. 8.36 | PR |
| 2.6 or 2.8 | | Cels. 8.4 | PR |
| 2.6 or 2.8 | | Hom.Luc. 6.4 | PR |
| 2.6–8 | Arnobius of Sicca | Disp.Nat. 1.63 | PR |
| 2.6–8 | Clement of Alexandria | Strom. 5.25.2–3 | R |
| 2.6–8 | Minucius Felix | Oct. 10.5 | PR |
| 2.6–8 | Origen of Alexandria | Cels. 3.19 | R |
| 2.6–8 | | Princ. 3.3.1 | R |
| 2.6–8 | | Princ. 3.3.2 | R |
| 2.6–8 | | Fr.Ps. | PR |
| 2.6–8 | | Hom.Ezech. 13.1.4 | R |

## Appendix A: 1 Corinthians 2.6–16

| 1 Corinthians | Early Christian Writer | Early Christian Work | Reference Status |
|---|---|---|---|
| 2.6–8 | Origen of Alexandria | Hom.Lev. 4.6 | R |
| 2.6–8 | | Hom.Luc. 4.6 | RNF |
| 2.6–8 | | Hom.Num. 6.1.3 | R |
| 2.7 | Anonymous | A.Phil (graeca) 11 | PR |
| 2.7 | Clement of Alexandria | Strom. 1.55.1 | R |
| 2.7 | | Strom. 5.49.2 | PR |
| 2.7 | | Strom. 5.80.7 | PR |
| 2.7 | Eusebius of Caesarea | Mart.Pal. 48 | PR |
| 2.7 | Lactantius | Inst. 5.15.8 | PR |
| 2.7 | | Inst. 6.7.3 | RNF |
| 2.7 | Origen of Alexandria | Comm.1Thess. | R |
| 2.7 | | Comm.Jo. 10.286 | R |
| 2.7 | | Comm.Jo. 10.85 | PR |
| 2.7 | | Comm.Jo. 13.3 | PR |
| 2.7 | | Comm.Matt. 10.5 | PR |
| 2.7 | | Comm.Matt. 12.38 | PR |
| 2.7 | | Comm.Matt. 13.3 | PR |
| 2.7 | | Comm.Matt. 15.28 | PR |
| 2.7 | | Comm.Matt. 17.2 | R |
| 2.7 | | Cels. 3.61 | PR |
| 2.7 | | Princ. 3.3.1 | R |
| 2.7 | | Princ. 3.4.4 | PR |
| 2.7 | | Fr.1Cor. 49 | R |
| 2.7 | | Fr.1Cor. 9 | R |
| 2.7 | | Fr.1Cor. 9 | R |
| 2.7 | | Fr.1Cor. A 49 | R |
| 2.7 | | Fr.Luc. 140 | PR |
| 2.7 | | Fr.Ps. D | R |
| 2.7 | | Fr. C | RNF |

| 1 Corinthians | Early Christian Writer | Early Christian Work | Reference Status |
| --- | --- | --- | --- |
| 2.7 | Origen of Alexandria | Hom.Jer. 12.13 | R |
| 2.7 | Tertullian | Marc. 5.6.1 | R |
| 2.7 | | Marc. 5.6.2 | R |
| 2.7 | | Marc. 5.6.3 | R |
| 2.7 | | Marc. 5.6.6 | PR |
| 2.7 | | Marc. 5.6.9 | PR |
| 2.7–8 | Lactantius | Inst. 5.18.11 | PR |
| 2.7–8 | | Inst. 6.23.15 | PR |
| 2.7–8 | Origen of Alexandria | Comm.Jo. 10.266 | R |
| 2.7–8 | | Comm.Jo. 13.8 | PR |
| 2.7–8 | | Comm.Matt. 13.8 | PR |
| 2.7–8 | | Comm.Ps. A (50) | R |
| 2.7–8 | | Comm.Rom. 4.11.4 | R |
| 2.7–8 | | Comm.Cant. 2.4 | R |
| 2.7–8 | | Princ. 4.2.6 | R |
| 2.8 | Anonymous | Askew. 1.7 | PR |
| 2.8 | | Tri.Trac. 3.65 | PR |
| 2.8 | | Ascens.Isa. 10.11 | PR |
| 2.8 | | Ascens.Isa. 9.14 | PR |
| 2.8 | | Ep.Apost. 28 | PR |
| 2.8 | Arnobius of Sicca | Disp.Nat. 1.53 | PR |
| 2.8 | Clement of Alexandria | Exc.Theod. 5.4 | PR |
| 2.8 | Eusebius of Caesarea | Comm.Isa. 20 | RNF |
| 2.8 | | Comm.Ps. | PR |
| 2.8 | | Comm.Ps. | PR |
| 2.8 | | Comm.Ps. | PR |
| 2.8 | | Comm.Ps. | PR |
| 2.8 | | Comm.Ps. | PR |
| 2.8 | | Comm.Ps. | PR |

Appendix A: 1 Corinthians 2.6–16 — **193**

| 1 Corinthians | Early Christian Writer | Early Christian Work | Reference Status |
|---|---|---|---|
| 2.8 | Eusebius of Caesarea | Comm.Ps. H | PR |
| 2.8 | | Comm.Ps. H | PR |
| 2.8 | | Dem.ev. 2.3.101 | PR |
| 2.8 | | Dem.ev. 5.20.8 | PR |
| 2.8 | | Dem.ev. 7.1.118 | PR |
| 2.8 | | Dem.ev. 7.1.118 | PR |
| 2.8 | | Dem.ev. 7.1.64 | PR |
| 2.8 | | Fr.G.I. 2.2 | PR |
| 2.8 | | Fr.G.I. 4.24 | PR |
| 2.8* | | Qu. 1.2 | PR |
| 2.8 | Ignatius of Antioch | Eph. 17.1 | PR |
| 2.8 | | Eph. 19.1 | PR |
| 2.8 | | Trall. 4.2 | PR |
| 2.8 | Justin Martyr | Qu.resp. 463 | PR |
| 2.8 | | Qu.resp. 488–89 | PR |
| 2.8 | Lactantius | Inst. 5.1.15 | RNF |
| 2.8 | Origen of Alexandria | Comm.Jo. 13.411 | PR |
| 2.8 | | Comm.Jo. 6.267 | R |
| 2.8 | | Comm.Matt. 12.1 | PR |
| 2.8 | | Comm.Matt. 13.11 | RNF |
| 2.8 | | Comm.Matt. 13.6 | RNF |
| 2.8 | | Comm.Matt. 17.11 | PR |
| 2.8 | | Comm.Matt. A 125 | R |
| 2.8 | | Comm.Matt. A 125 | R |
| 2.8 | | Comm.Rom. 1.6.2 | R |
| 2.8 | | Comm.Rom. 7.19.2 | R |
| 2.8 | | Comm.Rom. 7.19.4 | PR |
| 2.8 | | Comm.Rom. 8.8.12 | PR |
| 2.8 | | Princ. 3.2.1 | R |

| 1 Corinthians | Early Christian Writer | Early Christian Work | Reference Status |
| --- | --- | --- | --- |
| 2.8 | Origen of Alexandria | Fr.1Cor. 9 | R |
| 2.8 | | Fr.1Cor. 9 | PR |
| 2.8 | | Fr.Lam. 107 | PR |
| 2.8 | | Fr.Matt. 13 | RNF |
| 2.8 | | Fr.Ps. | PR |
| 2.8 | | Fr.Ps. | PR |
| 2.8 | | Fr.Jer. | PR |
| 2.8 | | Hom.Ps. 4.10 | RNF |
| 2.8 | | Hom.Exod. 5.3 | RNF |
| 2.8 | | Hom.Exod. 8.6 | PR |
| 2.8 | | Hom.Ezech. 13.1.5 | R |
| 2.8 | | Hom.Jer. 18.8 | PR |
| 2.8 | | Hom.Jer. 7.3 | PR |
| 2.8 | | Hom.Jer. 7.3 | PR |
| 2.8 | | Hom.Jer. 8.8 | R |
| 2.8 | | Hom.Luc. 6.5 | R |
| 2.8* | Tertullian | Marc. 5.6.5 | R |
| 2.8 | | Marc. 5.6.5 | PR |
| 2.8 | | Marc. 5.6.7 | R |
| 2.8* | | Marc. 5.6.8 | R |
| 2.8–9 | Anonymous | Orat.Paul. | PR |
| 2.9 | Alexander of Alexandria | Ep.Alex. 1.5 | R |
| 2.9 | Anonymous | Askew. 3.114 | PR |
| 2.9 | | Diogn. 12.1 | PR |
| 2.9 | | A.Thom. 22 | PR |
| 2.9 | | A.Thom. 36 | PR |
| 2.9 | | A.Petr.copt. 39 | PR |
| 2.9 | | Ep.Apost. 21 | RNF |
| 2.9 | | Evan.Thom. (copt.) 17 | PR |

Appendix A: 1 Corinthians 2.6–16 — **195**

| 1 Corinthians | Early Christian Writer | Early Christian Work | Reference Status |
|---|---|---|---|
| 2.9 | Anonymous | M.Polyc. 2.3 | PR |
| 2.9 | | M.Fruct. 3.3 | PR |
| 2.9 | Clement of Alexandria | Exc.Theod. 10.5 | PR |
| 2.9 | Valentinian Author cited by Clement of Alexandria | Exc.Theod. 86.3 | PR |
| 2.9* | Clement of Alexandria | Paed. 1.37.1 | PR |
| 2.9 | | Paed. 2.129.4 | PR |
| 2.9 | | Paed. 3.86.2 | PR |
| 2.9 | | Protr. 118.4 | PR |
| 2.9 | | Protr. 94.4 | PR |
| 2.9 | | Quis.div. 23.3 | PR |
| 2.9 | | Strom. 2.15.3 | PR |
| 2.9 | | Strom. 2.15.3 | PR |
| 2.9 | | Strom. 2.7.3 | PR |
| 2.9 | | Strom. 4.114.1 | PR |
| 2.9 | | Strom. 4.135.3–4 | PR |
| 2.9 | | Strom. 5.40.1 | R |
| 2.9 | | Strom. 6.107.2 | PR |
| 2.9 | | Strom. 6.68.1 | R |
| 2.9 | Clement of Rome | 1Clem. 34.8 | PR |
| 2.9 | | 1Clem. 35.3 | PR |
| 2.9 | Clement of Rome-Pseudo | 2Clem. 11.7 | PR |
| 2.9 | | 2Clem. 14.5 | PR |
| 2.9 | | Ep.virg. 1.9.4 | PR |
| 2.9 | Commodian | Apol. | PR |
| 2.9 | | Instr. 1.27.9 | PR |
| 2.9 | | Instr. 2.13.14 | R |
| 2.9 | Cyprian of Carthage | Ep. 58.10 | PR |
| 2.9 | Eusebius of Caesarea | Comm.Isa. 10 | PR |

| 1 Corinthians | Early Christian Writer | Early Christian Work | Reference Status |
| --- | --- | --- | --- |
| 2.9 | Eusebius of Caesarea | Comm.Isa. 158 | PR |
| 2.9 | | Comm.Isa. 158 | PR |
| 2.9 | | Comm.Isa. 269 | PR |
| 2.9 | | Comm.Isa. 296 | PR |
| 2.9 | | Comm.Isa. 361 | PR |
| 2.9 | | Comm.Isa. 403 | PR |
| 2.9 | | Comm.Isa. 409 | PR |
| 2.9 | | Comm.Ps. | PR |
| 2.9 | | Comm.Ps. | PR |
| 2.9 | | Comm.Ps. | RNF |
| 2.9 | | Marc. 1.1 | PR |
| 2.9 | | Marc. 1.1 | PR |
| 2.9 | | Marc. 2.4 | PR |
| 2.9 | | Marc. 5.23 | PR |
| 2.9 | | Laud.Const. 6.21 | PR |
| 2.9 | | Mart.Pal. 48 | PR |
| 2.9 | | Dem.ev. 5.1.18 | R |
| 2.9 | | Ep.Const. | PR |
| 2.9 | | Fr. | RNF |
| 2.9 | | Fr.Luc. | PR |
| 2.9 | | Fr.Luc. | PR |
| 2.9 | | Hist.eccl. 10.4.70 | PR |
| 2.9 | | Praep.ev. 11.38.7 | PR |
| 2.9 | | Praep.ev. 6.6.67 | RNF |
| 2.9 | | Theoph.fr. 3.40 | PR |
| 2.9 | | Theoph.fr. 5.28 | PR |
| 2.9 | Hippolytus of Rome | David 12.4 | PR |
| 2.9 | | Comm.Dan. 4.59.2 | PR |
| 2.9 | | Univ. 137 | PR |

# Appendix A: 1 Corinthians 2.6–16

| 1 Corinthians | Early Christian Writer | Early Christian Work | Reference Status |
|---|---|---|---|
| 2.9* | Hippolytus of Rome | Haer. 5.24.1 | PR |
| 2.9* |  | Haer. 5.26.17 | PR |
| 2.9* |  | Haer. 5.27.2 | PR |
| 2.9* |  | Haer. 6.24.4 | PR |
| 2.9 | Hippolytus of Rome-pseudo | Consumm. 44 | PR |
| 2.9 | Irenaeus of Lyons | Haer. 5.36.3 | PR |
| 2.9 | Justin the Gnostic | Baruch 29 | PR |
| 2.9 |  | Baruch 33 | PR |
| 2.9 | Methodius of Olympus | Symp. 8.2 | PR |
| 2.9 |  | Res. 1.56.7 | RNF |
| 2.9 |  | Res. 1.56.9 | PR |
| 2.9 |  | Res. 1.58.7 | RNF |
| 2.9 | Novatian | Trin. 7.3 | PR |
| 2.9 | Origen of Alexandria | Comm.Jo. 13.34 | R |
| 2.9 |  | Comm.Matt. 17.33 | PR |
| 2.9 |  | Comm.Matt. A 117 | PR |
| 2.9 |  | Comm.Matt. A 18 | PR |
| 2.9 |  | Comm.Matt. A 28 | R |
| 2.9 |  | Comm.Matt. A 55 | R |
| 2.9 |  | Comm.Rom. 7.4.2 | R |
| 2.9 |  | Comm.Rom. 7.4.6 | PR |
| 2.9 |  | Comm.Rom. 7.5.11 | PR |
| 2.9 |  | Comm.Cant. 1.5 | R |
| 2.9 |  | Comm.Cant. 2.1 | PR |
| 2.9 |  | Or. 27.16 | PR |
| 2.9 |  | Princ. 3.6.4 | PR |
| 2.9 |  | Fr.1Cor. 10 | PR |
| 2.9 |  | Fr.Ezech. B | RNF |
| 2.9 |  | Fr.Ps. | PR |

| 1 Corinthians | Early Christian Writer | Early Christian Work | Reference Status |
| --- | --- | --- | --- |
| 2.9 | Origen of Alexandria | Fr.Ps. E 118.161 | PR |
| 2.9 | | Fr.Cant. | PR |
| 2.9 | | Hom.Jer. 19.15 | PR |
| 2.9 | | Hom.Jer. 19.15 | PR |
| 2.9 | | Hom.Jos. 6.1 | PR |
| 2.9 | | Hom.Judic. 6.4 | PR |
| 2.9 | | Hom.Luc. 9 | RNF |
| 2.9 | | Hom.Num. 23.6.1 | PR |
| 2.9 | | Hom.Num. 26.3.5 | PR |
| 2.9 | | Hom.Num. 28.4.2 | PR |
| 2.9 | | Hom.Num. 9.8.2 | R |
| 2.9 | | Hom.Num. 9.8.2 | R |
| 2.9 | | Hom.Ps. (36) 3.9 | PR |
| 2.9 | | Hom.Ps. (38) 2.2 | PR |
| 2.9 | Tertullian | Res. 26.7 | PR |
| 2.9 | | Spect. 30.7 | PR |
| 2.9 | Theophilus of Antioch | Autol. 1.14 | PR |
| 2.9–10 | Clement of Alexandria | Strom. 5.25.4 | R |
| 2.10 | Anonymous | P.Oxy 17.2074 19.17 | RNF |
| 2.10 | | Evan.Ver. | PR |
| 2.10 | | Od.Sal. 16.8 | PR |
| 2.10 | Arnobius of Sicca | Disp.Nat. 1.63 | RNF |
| 2.10* | Clement of Alexandria | Strom. 4.110.3 | RNF |
| 2.10 | | Strom. 6.166.3 | PR |
| 2.10 | Clement of Rome | 1Clem. 40.1 | PR |
| 2.10 | Eusebius of Caesarea | Comm.Ps. | PR |
| 2.10* | Hippolytus of Rome | Haer. 5.6.4 | PR |
| 2.10 | Ignatius of Antioch | Philad. 7.1 | PR |
| 2.10 | Irenaeus of Lyons | Haer. 2.22.3 | RNF |

Appendix A: 1 Corinthians 2.6–16 — **199**

| 1 Corinthians | Early Christian Writer | Early Christian Work | Reference Status |
|---|---|---|---|
| 2.10 | Irenaeus of Lyons | Haer. 2.28.7 | R |
| 2.10 | | Haer. 4.33.3 | PR |
| 2.10 | Origen of Alexandria | Comm.Jo. 2.6 | PR |
| 2.10 | | Comm.Jo. 20.74 | PR |
| 2.10 | | Comm.Matt. 14.11 | PR |
| 2.10 | | Comm.Matt. 15.31 | PR |
| 2.10 | | Comm.Matt. 16.4 | PR |
| 2.10 | | Comm.Matt. 17.33 | PR |
| 2.10 | | Comm.Matt. A 111 | PR |
| 2.10 | | Comm.Matt. A 20 | PR |
| 2.10 | | Comm.Rom. 3.8.5 | R |
| 2.10 | | Comm.Rom. 3.8.8 | R |
| 2.10 | | Comm.Rom. 8.11.7 | PR |
| 2.10 | | Comm.Rom. 8.13.6 | R |
| 2.10 | | Comm.Rom. 8.13.6 | R |
| 2.10 | | Comm.Rom. 9.3.9 | R |
| 2.10 | | Cels. 6.17 | PR |
| 2.10 | | Or. 2.4 | PR |
| 2.10 | | Pasch. 1.31 | PR |
| 2.10 | | Princ. 1.3.4 | PR |
| 2.10 | | Princ. 2.9.5 | PR |
| 2.10 | | Princ. 4.2.7 | RNF |
| 2.10 | | Princ. 4.3.14 | PR |
| 2.10 | | Princ. 4.3.4 | R |
| 2.10 | | Princ. 4.4.8 | PR |
| 2.10 | | Fr.1Cor. 10 | PR |
| 2.10 | | Fr.1Cor. 10 | PR |
| 2.10 | | Fr.1Cor. 10 | PR |
| 2.10 | | Fr.1Cor. 10 | PR |

| 1 Corinthians | Early Christian Writer | Early Christian Work | Reference Status |
|---|---|---|---|
| 2.10 | Origen of Alexandria | Fr.Ps. F | PR |
| 2.10 | | Fr.Rom. A 31 | PR |
| 2.10 | | Hom.Exod. 12.3 | PR |
| 2.10 | | Hom.Exod. 2.4 | PR |
| 2.10 | | Hom.Exod. 4.2 | R |
| 2.10 | | Hom.Ezech. 1.16.1 | PR |
| 2.10 | | Hom.Ezech. 11.3.3 | PR |
| 2.10 | | Hom.Num. 12.1.5 | PR |
| 2.10 | | Hom.Num. 12.2.4 | PR |
| 2.10 | | Hom.Num. 18.2.2 | PR |
| 2.10 | | Hom.Ps. 4.2 | RNF |
| 2.10 | | Schol.Gen. | RNF |
| 2.10* | Pamphilus of Caesarea | Apol. 82 | R |
| 2.10–16* | Eusebius of Caesarea | H.E. 5.7.8 | PR |
| 2.10, 13 | Clement of Alexandria | Strom. 2.7.3 | PR |
| 2.11 | Cyprian of Carthage-Pseudo | Jud. 1.4 | PR |
| 2.11 | Eusebius of Caesarea | Comm.Ps. | PR |
| 2.11 | | Comm.Ps. | PR |
| 2.11 | Irenaeus of Lyons | Haer. 5.6.1 | PR |
| 2.11 | Origen of Alexandria | Comm.Jo. 32.218 | PR |
| 2.11 | | Comm.Matt. 13.2 | R |
| 2.11 | | Comm.Matt. 14.6 | R |
| 2.11 | | Comm.Rom. 2.9.4 | R |
| 2.11 | | Comm.Rom. 8.13.6 | R |
| 2.11 | | Comm.Cant. Pr | PR |
| 2.11 | | Cels. 4.30 | PR |
| 2.11 | | Or. 1.1 | PR |
| 2.11 | | Dial. 7 | R |
| 2.11 | | Fr.1Cor. 11 | R |

Appendix A: 1 Corinthians 2.6–16 — **201**

| 1 Corinthians | Early Christian Writer | Early Christian Work | Reference Status |
|---|---|---|---|
| 2.11 | Origen of Alexandria | Fr.1Cor. A 47 | PR |
| 2.11 | | Fr.Eph. 21 | PR |
| 2.11 | | Fr.Eph. 28 | RNF |
| 2.11 | | Fr.Ps. E 115.2 | RNF |
| 2.11 | | Fr. 14 | RNF |
| 2.11 | Tertullian | Herm. 18.1 | PR |
| 2.11 | | Marc. 2.2.4 | PR |
| 2.11 | | Prax. 19.2 | PR |
| 2.11 | | Prax. 8.4 | PR |
| 2.11–12 | | Marc. 2.2.6 | R |
| 2.12 | Anonymous | Od.Sal. 6.6 | RNF |
| 2.12 | | Orat.Paul. | RNF |
| 2.12 | Clement of Alexandria | Strom. 5.25.5 | R |
| 2.12 | Clement of Rome-Pseudo | Recog. 3.11.5 | RNF |
| 2.12 | Eusebius of Caesarea | Comm.Ps. | PR |
| 2.12 | Methodius of Olympus | Cib. 5.1–2 | PR |
| 2.12 | Novatian | Trin. 29.20 | R |
| 2.12 | Origen of Alexandria | Comm.Jo. 1.24 | PR |
| 2.12 | | Comm.Jo. 10.172 | PR |
| 2.12 | | Comm.Jo. 13.37 | R |
| 2.12 | | Comm.Jo. 20.6 | PR |
| 2.12 | | Comm.Matt. A 131 | RNF |
| 2.12 | | Comm.Matt. A 39 | PR |
| 2.12 | | Comm.Rom. 9.30.2 | R |
| 2.12 | | Comm.Cant. 1.5 | R |
| 2.12 | | Comm.Cant. 2.4 | R |
| 2.12 | | Comm.Cant. 2.5 | PR |
| 2.12 | | Fr.1Cor. 11 | R |
| 2.12 | | Fr.Cant. | PR |

| 1 Corinthians | Early Christian Writer | Early Christian Work | Reference Status |
|---|---|---|---|
| 2.12 | Origen of Alexandria | Fr.Ps. | R |
| 2.12 | | Hom.Ezech. 2.2.3 | PR |
| 2.12 | | Hom.Gen. 1.17 | R |
| 2.12 | | Hom.Num. 26.3.4 | PR |
| 2.12 | Tertullian | Marc. 4.26.4 | RNF |
| 2.12–13 | Justin Martyr-Pseudo | Coh.Gr. 8.2 | PR |
| 2.12–13 | Origen of Alexandria | Comm.Jo. 13.35 | R |
| 2.12–13 | | Or. 1.1 | PR |
| 2.12–13 | | Princ. 4.2.3 | PR |
| 2.12–13 | | Fr.Ps. | PR |
| 2.12–13 | | Hom.Lev. 5.6.2 | PR |
| 2.12–13,16 | | Philoc. 1.10 | R |
| 2.12–14 | Eusebius of Caesarea | Marc. 1.2 | R |
| 2.12–14 | | Marc. 1.2 | PR |
| 2.12–15 | Origen of Alexandria | Comm.Jo. 20.74 | PR |
| 2.12–15* | | Princ. 1.8.2 | PR |
| 2.12,16 | | Hom.Jos. 9.8 | PR |
| 2.13 | Clement of Alexandria | Paed. 1.6.1 | PR |
| 2.13 | | Strom. 1.87.4–5 | R |
| 2.13 | | Strom. 5.19.3 | R |
| 2.13 | Cyprian of Carthage-Pseudo | Novat. 3.1 | RNF |
| 2.13 | | Jud. 1.3 | PR |
| 2.13 | Eusebius of Caesarea | Comm.Isa. 363 | PR |
| 2.13 | Hippolytus of Rome | Comm.Dan. 3.2.4 | R |
| 2.13* | | Haer. 7.26.3 | R |
| 2.13 | Origen of Alexandria | Comm.Jo. 13.36 | R |
| 2.13 | | Comm.Jo. 13.361 | PR |
| 2.13 | | Comm.Matt. 10.16 | PR |
| 2.13 | | Comm.Matt. 11.18 | PR |

| 1 Corinthians | Early Christian Writer | Early Christian Work | Reference Status |
|---|---|---|---|
| 2.13 | Origen of Alexandria | Comm.Matt. 14.14 | R |
| 2.13 | | Comm.Matt. 16.4 | PR |
| 2.13 | | Comm.Matt. 17.6 | RNF |
| 2.13 | | Comm.Matt. A 52 | PR |
| 2.13 | | Comm.Ps. I-XXV (1) 3 | R |
| 2.13 | | Comm.Rom. 1.14.1 | PR |
| 2.13 | | Comm.Rom. 3.2 | RNF |
| 2.13 | | Comm.Cant. 3.12 | PR |
| 2.13 | | Cels. 4.44 | RNF |
| 2.13 | | Cels. 4.71 | PR |
| 2.13 | | Cels. 7.11 | PR |
| 2.13 | | Pasch. 40 | PR |
| 2.13 | | Princ. 4.3.15 | PR |
| 2.13 | | Fr.1Cor. 11 | R |
| 2.13 | | Fr.Ps. | R |
| 2.13 | | Hom.Exod. 1.2 | PR |
| 2.13 | | Hom.Ezech. 1.2.4 | PR |
| 2.13 | | Hom.Ezech. 1.4.3 | PR |
| 2.13 | | Hom.Ezech. 6.4.2 | PR |
| 2.13 | | Hom.Gen. 2.6 | PR |
| 2.13 | | Hom.Gen. 6.3 | PR |
| 2.13 | | Hom.Gen. 7.4 | R |
| 2.13 | | Hom.Isa. 6.1 | PR |
| 2.13 | | Hom.Jos. 15.1 | R |
| 2.13 | | Hom.Jos. 15.3 | PR |
| 2.13 | | Hom.Num. 16.9 | RNF |
| 2.13 | | Hom.Num. 22.2.2 | PR |
| 2.13 | | Hom.Ps. 1.1 | RNF |
| 2.13 | | Philoc. 2.3 | R |

# Appendix A: 1 Corinthians 2.6–16

| 1 Corinthians | Early Christian Writer | Early Christian Work | Reference Status |
|---|---|---|---|
| 2.13–14 | Eusebius of Caesarea | Marc. 1.3 | R |
| 2.13–14 | Hippolytus of Rome | Prov. | PR |
| 2.13–14* | | Haer. 5.8.26 | R |
| 2.13–14 | Origen of Alexandria | Fr.Pr. | PR |
| 2.14 | Clement of Alexandria | Strom. 1.56.1 | PR |
| 2.14 | | Strom. 5.25.5 | R |
| 2.14 | | Strom. 6.166.3 | PR |
| 2.14 | Eusebius of Caesarea | Praep.ev. 12.7.1 | PR |
| 2.14 | Hippolytus of Rome | Comm.Dan. 3.2.5 | R |
| 2.14* | | Haer. 6.34.8 | PR |
| 2.14* | Irenaeus of Lyons | Haer. 1.8.3 | R |
| 2.14 | | Haer. 5.8.3 | PR |
| 2.14 | Origen of Alexandria | Comm.Jo. 1.3 | PR |
| 2.14 | | Comm.Rom. 2.14.15 | PR |
| 2.14 | | Comm.Cant. 1.3 | RNF |
| 2.14 | | Comm.Cant. 3.1 | PR |
| 2.14 | | Cels. 6.71 | PR |
| 2.14 | | Princ. 2.8.2 | R |
| 2.14 | | Princ. 2.8.2 | R |
| 2.14 | | Princ. 3.6.6 | PR |
| 2.14 | | Fr.1Cor. 11 | R |
| 2.14 | | Fr.1Cor. 8 | PR |
| 2.14 | | Fr.1Cor. A 73 | PR |
| 2.14 | | Fr.Job. | PR |
| 2.14 | | Fr.Luc. 192 | PR |
| 2.14 | | Fr.Ps. A | PR |
| 2.14 | | Fr. F | RNF |
| 2.14 | | Hom.Gen. 10.5 | PR |
| 2.14 | | Hom.Gen. 16.4 | PR |

Appendix A: 1 Corinthians 2.6–16 — **205**

| 1 Corinthians | Early Christian Writer | Early Christian Work | Reference Status |
| --- | --- | --- | --- |
| 2.14 | Origen of Alexandria | Hom.Gen. 7.2 | R |
| 2.14 | | Hom.Jer. 12.1 | PR |
| 2.14 | | Hom.Judic. 5.5 | RNF |
| 2.14 | | Hom.Judic. 5.6 | PR |
| 2.14 | | Hom.Judic. 8.3 | PR |
| 2.14 | | Hom.Lev. 2.2.3 | R |
| 2.14 | | Hom.Luc. 36.1 | PR |
| 2.14 | | Hom.Num. 23.5.2 | PR |
| 2.14 | | Hom.Num. 24.2 | RNF |
| 2.14 | | Hom.Num. 26.4.3 | PR |
| 2.14 | | Hom.Num. 4.3 | RNF |
| 2.14 | Tertullian | Mon. 1.3 | PR |
| 2.14 | | Marc. 2.2.6 | R |
| 2.14 | | Marc. 4.22.5 | PR |
| 2.14 | | Jeiun. 3 | PR |
| 2.14–15 | Irenaeus of Lyons | Haer. 1.1.16 | PR |
| 2.14–15 | Methodius of Olympus | Symp. 8.6 | PR |
| 2.14–15 | | Res. 1.58.7 | PR |
| 2.14–15* | Origen of Alexandria | Comm.Jo. 2.138 | R |
| 2.14–15 | | Comm.Jo. 28.179–80 | PR |
| 2.14–15 | | Comm.Rom. 2.4.2 | PR |
| 2.14–15 | | Comm.Rom. 3.10 | RNF |
| 2.14–15 | | Hom.Judic. 4.4 | PR |
| 2.14–15 | | Hom.Lev. 2.2.4 | R |
| 2.15 | Clement of Alexandria | Paed. 1.37.1 | PR |
| 2.15 | | Strom. 1.50.3 | R |
| 2.15* | Irenaeus of Lyons | Haer. 1.8.3 | R |
| 2.15 | | Haer. 4.33.1 | RNF |
| 2.15 | | Haer. 4.33.15 | PR |

| 1 Corinthians | Early Christian Writer | Early Christian Work | Reference Status |
|---|---|---|---|
| 2.15 | Irenaeus of Lyons | Haer. 4.33.7 | RNF |
| 2.15 | | Haer. 5.10.2 | PR |
| 2.15 | | Haer. 5.6.1 | R |
| 2.15 | | Haer. 5.8.2 | PR |
| 2.15 | | Haer. 5.9.2 | PR |
| 2.15 | Origen of Alexandria | Comm.Jo. 10.28 | PR |
| 2.15 | | Comm.Jo. 10.28 | PR |
| 2.15 | | Comm.Jo. 13.361 | PR |
| 2.15 | | Comm.Jo. 2.138 | R |
| 2.15 | | Comm.Jo. 28.179 | PR |
| 2.15 | | Comm.Jo. 28.181 | PR |
| 2.15 | | Comm.Matt. 16.4 | PR |
| 2.15 | | Comm.Matt. 17.13 | R |
| 2.15 | | Comm.Matt. 17.6 | PR |
| 2.15 | | Comm.Matt. A 19 | RNF |
| 2.15 | | Comm.Rom. 2.14.24 | R |
| 2.15 | | Comm.Rom. 2.4.4 | R |
| 2.15 | | Comm.Rom. 4.8 | RNF |
| 2.15 | | Comm.Rom. 6.7.6 | R |
| 2.15 | | Comm.Rom. 7.6.6 | R |
| 2.15 | | Comm.Rom. 9.36.2 | R |
| 2.15 | | Comm.Cant. 3 | RNF |
| 2.15 | | Princ. 1.8.4 | PR |
| 2.15 | | Princ. 3.6.6 | PR |
| 2.15 | | Fr.1Cor. 11 | R |
| 2.15 | | Fr.1Cor. 18 | PR |
| 2.15 | | Fr.1Cor. A 73 | R |
| 2.15 | | Fr.Ps. E 118.140 | PR |
| 2.15 | | Hom.Exod. 10.4 | PR |

| 1 Corinthians | Early Christian Writer | Early Christian Work | Reference Status |
| --- | --- | --- | --- |
| 2.15 | Origen of Alexandria | Hom.Ezech. 13.1.6 | PR |
| 2.15 | | Hom.Ezech. 4.7.2 | PR |
| 2.15 | | Hom.Jer. A 2.1 (28.1.5) | PR |
| 2.15 | | Hom.Judic. 4.4 | PR |
| 2.15 | | Hom.Judic. 8.4 | PR |
| 2.15 | | Hom.Lev. 7.5.5 | PR |
| 2.15 | | Hom.Num. 2.1.3 | PR |
| 2.15 | | Hom.Num. 27.11.2 | PR |
| 2.15 | | Hom.Num. 27.12 | RNF |
| 2.15 | | Hom.Num. 27.12.2 | PR |
| 2.15 | | Hom.Cant. 2.1.2 | PR |
| 2.15 | | Schol.Gen. | RNF |
| 2.15 | Tertullian | Ux. 2.6.1 | RNF |
| 2.15–16 | Clement of Alexandria | Strom. 1.53.3 | R |
| 2.15–16 | | Strom. 5.25.5 | R |
| 2.15–16 | Origen of Alexandria | Fr.1Cor. A 73 | R |
| 2.15–16 | Tertullian | Prax. 19.2 | R |
| 2.16 | Anonymous | Tri.Trac. 1 | RNF |
| 2.16 | | Didas.Sil. | RNF |
| 2.16 | Commodian | Apol. | RNF |
| 2.16 | Eusebius of Caesarea | Comm.Ps. | PR |
| 2.16 | Hippolytus of Rome | Prov. 41 | PR |
| 2.16 | Origen of Alexandria | Comm.Jo. 1.24 | PR |
| 2.16 | | Comm.Jo. 10.172 | R |
| 2.16 | | Comm.Jo. 10.286 | R |
| 2.16 | | Comm.Jo. 13.35 | R |
| 2.16 | | Comm.Jo. 20.1 | RNF |
| 2.16 | | Comm.Jo. 20.6 | PR |
| 2.16 | | Comm.Matt. 15.30 | PR |

| 1 Corinthians | Early Christian Writer | Early Christian Work | Reference Status |
| --- | --- | --- | --- |
| 2.16 | Origen of Alexandria | Comm.Matt. 17.13 | PR |
| 2.16 | | Comm.Matt. 17.13 | PR |
| 2.16 | | Comm.Rom. 5.10.7 | R |
| 2.16 | | Comm.Rom. 6.9 | RNF |
| 2.16 | | Comm.Cant. 1.5 | R |
| 2.16 | | Cels. 3.21 | PR |
| 2.16 | | Cels. 5.1 | PR |
| 2.16 | | Or. 1.1 | PR |
| 2.16 | | Princ. 4.2.3 | PR |
| 2.16 | | Fr.Ps. | R |
| 2.16 | | Fr.Ps. C | PR |
| 2.16 | | Fr.Ps. C | RNF |
| 2.16 | | Fr.Ps. D | PR |
| 2.16 | | Fr.Cant. | PR |
| 2.16 | | Hom.Exod. 12.1 | R |
| 2.16 | | Hom.Exod. 13.1 | PR |
| 2.16 | | Hom.Ezech. 2.2 | RNF |
| 2.16 | | Hom.Ezech. 2.2.3 | PR |
| 2.16 | | Hom.Gen. 1.17 | R |
| 2.16 | | Hom.Jos. 9.6 | RNF |
| 2.16 | | Hom.Lev. 5.6.2 | PR |
| 2.16 | | Hom.Num. 24.2.4 | R |
| 2.16 | Pamphilus of Caesarea | Apol. 23 | PR |
| 2.16 | Tertullian | Herm. 18.1 | PR |
| 2.16 | | Herm. 45.5 | R |
| 2.16 | | Marc. 5.6.9 | PR |
| 2.16 | | Cor. 4.6 | PR |
| 2.16 | | Scorp. 7.6 | R |

# Appendix B: Ephesians 6.10–17

| Ephesians | Early Christian Writer | Early Christian Work | Reference Status |
|---|---|---|---|
| 6.10 | Origen of Alexandria | Fr.Eph. 32 | PR |
| 6.10 | | Fr.Eph. 33 | R |
| 6.10–12 | | Cels. 8.34 | R |
| 6.11 | Anonymous | Didas.Sil. 94.33–95.12 | PR |
| 6.11 | | Didas.Sil. 96.6–15 | PR |
| 6.11 | | P.Ber.13415 | RNF |
| 6.11 | Valentinian Author cited by Clement of Alexandria | Exc.Theod. 85 | R |
| 6.11 | Clement of Alexandria | Strom. 2.20.2 | R |
| 6.11 | Commodianus | Apol. | PR |
| 6.11 | Cyprian of Carthage | Ep. 55.9 | R |
| 6.11 | Eusebius of Caesarea | Comm.Ps. | R |
| 6.11 | | Hist.eccl. 2.14.6 | PR |
| 6.11 | Methodius of Olympus | Symp. 8.12 | PR |
| 6.11 | | Res. 2.5.2 | R |
| 6.11 | Origen of Alexandria | Comm.Rom. A 9.21.1 | PR |
| 6.11 | | Comm.Cant. 2.3 | PR |
| 6.11 | | Comm.Cant. 3.8 | R |
| 6.11 | | Or. 30.1 | PR |
| 6.11 | | Princ. 3.2.1 | R |
| 6.11 | | Fr.1Cor. A 90 | R |
| 6.11 | | Fr.Eph. 33 | R |
| 6.11 | | Fr.Eph. 33 | R |
| 6.11 | | Fr.Eph. 34 | R |
| 6.11 | | Fr.Ezech. A | PR |
| 6.11 | | Fr.Pr. | PR |
| 6.11 | | Fr.Ps. A | PR |
| 6.11 | | Hom.Jos. 15.1 | R |

| Ephesians | Early Christian Writer | Early Christian Work | Reference Status |
|---|---|---|---|
| 6.11 | Origen of Alexandria | Hom.Jos. 16.5 | PR |
| 6.11 | | Hom.Jos. 9.9 | PR |
| 6.11 | | Hom.Judic. 2.3 | PR |
| 6.11 | | Hom.Judic. 6.2 | R |
| 6.11 | | Hom.Lev. 3.8 | RNF |
| 6.11 | | Hom.Luc. 35 | RNF |
| 6.11 | | Hom.Ps. 1.4 | R |
| 6.11 | Tertullian | Marc. 5.18.12 | PR |
| 6.11 | | Marc. 5.18.6 | PR |
| 6.11 or 13 | Eusebius of Caesarea | Laud.Const. 9.8 | PR |
| 6.11 or 13 | Origen of Alexandria | Cels. 8.73 | PR |
| 6.11 or 13 | | Fr.Ps. | PR |
| 6.11 or 13 | | Fr.Deut. | PR |
| 6.11 or 13 | | Hom.1 Reg. 16 | R |
| 6.11 or 13 | Tertullian | Cult.fem. 2.11.2 | PR |
| 6.11–12 | Cyprian of Carthage | Pat. 12.12 | PR |
| 6.11–12 | Origen of Alexandria | Fr.Eph. 33 | R |
| 6.11–13 | Hippolytus of Rome | David 12.3 | PR |
| 6.11–13 | Origen of Alexandria | Cels. 8.55 | R |
| 6.11–13,14 | Tatian | Orat. 16.7 | PR |
| 6.12 | Anonymous | Bruc. | RNF |
| 6.12 | | Hyp.Arch. 86 | R |
| 6.12 | | Interp.An. 20.22–23 | PR |
| 6.12 | | Interp.An. 6.32 | PR |
| 6.12 | | Trim.Prot. | PR |
| 6.12 | | Didas.Sil. 117.14–16 | PR |
| 6.12 | | M.Apollon. | RNF |
| 6.12 | Arnobius of Sicca | Disp.Nat. 1.53 | RNF |
| 6.12 | Clement of Alexandria | Ecl. 20.1 | RNF |

| Ephesians | Early Christian Writer | Early Christian Work | Reference Status |
|---|---|---|---|
| 6.12 | Valentinian Author cited by Clement of Alexandria | Exc.Theod. 48 | PR |
| 6.12 | Clement of Alexandria | Quis.div. 29 | PR |
| 6.12 | | Strom. 2.20 | R |
| 6.12 | | Strom. 3.16 | R |
| 6.12 | | Strom. 4.7 | PR |
| 6.12 | | Strom. 5.14.2 | R |
| 6.12 | | Strom. 5.14.2 | PR |
| 6.12 | | Strom. 7.3.4 | PR |
| 6.12 | Eusebius of Caesarea | Comm.Isa. 20 | PR |
| 6.12 | | Comm.Isa. 20 | PR |
| 6.12 | | Comm.Isa. 160 | PR |
| 6.12 | | Comm.Isa. 221 | R |
| 6.12 | | Comm.Isa. 221–222 | R |
| 6.12 | | Comm.Ps. | R |
| 6.12 | | Comm.Ps. | R |
| 6.12 | | Comm.Ps. | R |
| 6.12 | | Comm.Ps. | R |
| 6.12 | | Comm.Ps. | PR |
| 6.12 | | Comm.Ps. | PR |
| 6.12 | | Comm.Ps. A | PR |
| 6.12 | | Eccl.theol. 1.12 | RNF |
| 6.12 | | Eccl.theol. 2.20.6 | R |
| 6.12 | | Laud.Const. 2.3 | PR |
| 6.12 | | Dem.ev. 10.8.68 | PR |
| 6.12 | | Dem.ev. 9.1 | PR |
| 6.12 | | Dem.ev. 9.7 | PR |
| 6.12 | | Fr.G.I. 1.14 | PR |
| 6.12 | | Fr.G.I. 3.42 | PR |

| Ephesians | Early Christian Writer | Early Christian Work | Reference Status |
| --- | --- | --- | --- |
| 6.12 | Eusebius of Caesarea | Fr.G.I. 3.5 | PR |
| 6.12 | | Praep.ev. 11.26.7 | R |
| 6.12 | | Praep.ev. 5.2.4 | PR |
| 6.12 | | Praep.ev. 5.3.1 | PR |
| 6.12 | | Praep.ev. 7.16.4 | R |
| 6.12* | | Praep.ev. 13.13.32 | PR |
| 6.12* | | Praep.ev. 13.13.9 | R |
| 6.12 | | Theoph.fr. A | RNF |
| 6.12 | | Theoph.fr. A 1.39 | PR |
| 6.12 | Hippolytus of Rome-Pseudo | Gaium 7 | PR |
| 6.12 | Irenaeus of Lyons | Haer. 1.10.1 | PR |
| 6.12 | | Haer. 1.5.4 | PR |
| 6.12 | | Haer. 1.5.4 | PR |
| 6.12 | | Haer. 2.31.3 | PR |
| 6.12 | Lactantius | Opif. 1.7 | RNF |
| 6.12 | | Inst. 4.30.2 | PR |
| 6.12 | Methodius of Olympus | Symp. 4.4 | PR |
| 6.12 | | Symp. 6.1 | PR |
| 6.12 | | Symp. 8.13 | PR |
| 6.12 | | Res. 1.38.5 | PR |
| 6.12 | | Res. 2.5.2 | R |
| 6.12 | | Res. 3.23.9 | PR |
| 6.12 | Novatian | Cib. 1.5 | PR |
| 6.12 | | Spect. 2.3 | R |
| 6.12 | Origen of Alexandria | Comm.Eph. 122 | R |
| 6.12 | | Comm.Eph. 123 | R |
| 6.12 | | Comm.Eph. 164 | PR |
| 6.12 | | Comm.Eph. 254–60 | R |
| 6.12 | | Comm.Eph. 78 | R |

| Ephesians | Early Christian Writer | Early Christian Work | Reference Status |
|---|---|---|---|
| 6.12 | Origen of Alexandria | Comm.Jo. 10.182 | PR |
| 6.12 | | Comm.Jo. 2.167 | PR |
| 6.12 | | Comm.Jo. 32.256 | PR |
| 6.12 | | Comm.Jo. 32.30 | R |
| 6.12 | | Comm.Jo. 32.31 | R |
| 6.12 | | Comm.Matt. 10.14 | PR |
| 6.12 | | Comm.Matt. 12.13 | R |
| 6.12 | | Comm.Matt. 12.13 | R |
| 6.12 | | Comm.Matt. 13.4 | PR |
| 6.12 | | Comm.Matt. 16.23 | PR |
| 6.12 | | Comm.Matt. 17.2 | PR |
| 6.12 | | Comm.Matt. 17.2 | PR |
| 6.12 | | Comm.Matt. A | PR |
| 6.12 | | Comm.Matt. A | R |
| 6.12 | | Comm.Matt. A | PR |
| 6.12 | | Comm.Matt. A | RNF |
| 6.12 | | Comm.Matt. A | PR |
| 6.12 | | Comm.Rom. A 1.16.4 | R |
| 6.12 | | Comm.Rom. A 1.18.6 | R |
| 6.12 | | Comm.Rom. A 10.15.3 | R |
| 6.12 | | Comm.Rom. A 10.5.7 | PR |
| 6.12 | | Comm.Rom. A 2.5.3 | R |
| 6.12 | | Comm.Rom. A 3.5.3 | PR |
| 6.12 | | Comm.Rom. A 5.1.17 | PR |
| 6.12 | | Comm.Rom. A 7.12.5 | PR |
| 6.12 | | Comm.Rom. A 7.12.6 | R |
| 6.12 | | Comm.Rom. A 7.12.9 | PR |
| 6.12 | | Cels. 8.34 | R |
| 6.12 | | Or. 26.3 | PR |

| Ephesians | Early Christian Writer | Early Christian Work | Reference Status |
|---|---|---|---|
| 6.12 | Origen of Alexandria | Or. 26.5 | PR |
| 6.12 | | Or. 26.5 | PR |
| 6.12 | | Or. 29.2 | R |
| 6.12 | | Pasch. 49 | PR |
| 6.12 | | Princ. 1.5.2 | R |
| 6.12 | | Princ. 1.5.2 | R |
| 6.12 | | Princ. 1.5.3 | R |
| 6.12 | | Princ. 1.6.3 | PR |
| 6.12 | | Princ. 1.6.3 | PR |
| 6.12 | | Princ. 1.8.4 | R |
| 6.12 | | Princ. 3.2.1 | R |
| 6.12 | | Princ. 3.2.3 | R |
| 6.12 | | Princ. 3.2.4 | R |
| 6.12 | | Princ. 3.2.4 | R |
| 6.12 | | Princ. 3.2.5 | R |
| 6.12 | | Princ. 3.2.6 | R |
| 6.12 | | Princ. 3.2.6 | R |
| 6.12 | | Princ. 3.4.1 | R |
| 6.12 | | Princ. A | RNF |
| 6.12 | | Princ. A 2.8.3 | PR |
| 6.12 | | Mart. 48 | PR |
| 6.12 | | Fr.1Cor. 20 | R |
| 6.12 | | Fr.1Cor. 28 | R |
| 6.12 | | Fr.Eph. 33 | R |
| 6.12 | | Fr.Eph. 33 | R |
| 6.12 | | Fr.Eph. 33 | R |
| 6.12 | | Fr.Exod. | RNF |
| 6.12 | | Fr.Jer. 40 | PR |
| 6.12 | | Fr.Lam. | PR |

| Ephesians | Early Christian Writer | Early Christian Work | Reference Status |
|---|---|---|---|
| 6.12 | Origen of Alexandria | Fr.Luc. 195 | PR |
| 6.12 | | Fr.Luc. 197 | R |
| 6.12 | | Fr.Luc. 246 | PR |
| 6.12 | | Fr.Matt. 151 | PR |
| 6.12 | | Fr.Matt. 291 | PR |
| 6.12 | | Fr.Matt. 50 | PR |
| 6.12 | | Fr.Ps. | PR |
| 6.12 | | Fr.Ps. A 141 | PR |
| 6.12 | | Fr.Ps. D | RNF |
| 6.12 | | Fr.Ps. D | PR |
| 6.12 | | Fr.Ps. E | R |
| 6.12 | | Fr.Ps. E 118 | PR |
| 6.12 | | Fr.Rom. 5 | PR |
| 6.12 | | Fr.Rom. B 49 | PR |
| 6.12 | | Fr.Rom. B 52 | R |
| 6.12 | | Fr. | RNF |
| 6.12 | | Fr. D | RNF |
| 6.12 | | Hom.Exod. 11.4 | R |
| 6.12 | | Hom.Exod. 3.3 | PR |
| 6.12 | | Hom.Exod. 4.7 | PR |
| 6.12 | | Hom.Exod. 5.4 | PR |
| 6.12 | | Hom.Exod. 5.5 | R |
| 6.12 | | Hom.Exod. 6.2 | PR |
| 6.12 | | Hom.Exod. 8.3 | R |
| 6.12 | | Hom.Exod. 8.6 | PR |
| 6.12 | | Hom.Ezech. 1.3.9 | PR |
| 6.12 | | Hom.Ezech. 13.1.7 | PR |
| 6.12 | | Hom.Ezech. 13.1.8 | PR |
| 6.12 | | Hom.Ezech. 4.1.14 | PR |

| Ephesians | Early Christian Writer | Early Christian Work | Reference Status |
|---|---|---|---|
| 6.12 | Origen of Alexandria | Hom.Ezech. 7.8.2 | R |
| 6.12 | | Hom.Ezech. 7.9.1 | R |
| 6.12 | | Hom.Ezech. 9.3.3 | PR |
| 6.12 | | Hom.Gen. 15.5 | PR |
| 6.12 | | Hom.Gen. 16.5 | RNF |
| 6.12 | | Hom.Gen. 9.3 | R |
| 6.12 | | Hom.Jos. 1.5 | PR |
| 6.12 | | Hom.Jos. 11.4 | R |
| 6.12 | | Hom.Jos. 11.4 | R |
| 6.12 | | Hom.Jos. 12.1 | R |
| 6.12 | | Hom.Jos. 12.1 | R |
| 6.12 | | Hom.Jos. 12.1 | R |
| 6.12 | | Hom.Jos. 12.3 | RNF |
| 6.12 | | Hom.Jos. 15.1 | R |
| 6.12 | | Hom.Jos. 15.5 | PR |
| 6.12 | | Hom.Jos. 3.1 | PR |
| 6.12 | | Hom.Jos. 5.2 | R |
| 6.12 | | Hom.Judic. 6.6 | R |
| 6.12 | | Hom.Lev. 16.6 | R |
| 6.12 | | Hom.Lev. 9.5 | R |
| 6.12 | | Hom.Luc. 39.5 | PR |
| 6.12 | | Hom.Num. 16.7.11 | PR |
| 6.12 | | Hom.Num. 16.7.5 | R |
| 6.12 | | Hom.Num. 18.4.3 | PR |
| 6.12 | | Hom.Num. 19.1 | RNF |
| 6.12 | | Hom.Num. 19.2.2 | PR |
| 6.12 | | Hom.Num. 25.4.1 | R |
| 6.12 | | Hom.Num. 26.6.2 | R |
| 6.12 | | Hom.Num. 27.12.6 | PR |

| Ephesians | Early Christian Writer | Early Christian Work | Reference Status |
| --- | --- | --- | --- |
| 6.12 | Origen of Alexandria | Hom.Num. 7.5.5 | PR |
| 6.12 | | Hom.Num. 7.5.5 | PR |
| 6.12 | | Hom.Num. 7.6.1 | R |
| 6.12 | | Hom.Ps. 4.2 | R |
| 6.12 | | Hom.Cant. 2.8 | RNF |
| 6.12 | Pamphilus of Caesarea | Apol. 25 | PR |
| 6.12 | Tertullian | Marc. 3.14.3 | PR |
| 6.12 | | Marc. 4.20.4 | PR |
| 6.12 | | Marc. 5.18.12 | PR |
| 6.12 | | Marc. 5.18.13 | R |
| 6.12 | | An. 57.2 | RNF |
| 6.12 | | Fug. 1.5 | PR |
| 6.12 | | Fug. 12.5 | PR |
| 6.12 | | Jeiun. 17.8 | R |
| 6.12 | | Praescr. 39.1 | PR |
| 6.12 | | Praescr. 40.8 | PR |
| 6.12 | | Res. 22.11 | RNF |
| 6.12–17 | Cyprian of Carthage | Ep. 55.8 | R |
| 6.12–17 | | Test. 3.117 | R |
| 6.12,16 | Ignatius of Antioch | Eph. 13 | R |
| 6.13 | Anonymous | Rect.Fide 1.19 | R |
| 6.13 | Eusebius of Caesarea | Comm.Ps. | R |
| 6.13 | | Mart.Pal. 7 | PR |
| 6.13 | | Fr. Luc. | R |
| 6.13 | | Hist.eccl. 2.14.6 | RNF |
| 6.13 | | Laud.Const. 1 | RNF |
| 6.13 | Hermas of Rome | Past. 2.12.2 | PR |
| 6.13 | Methodius of Olympus | Symp. 2.2 | PR |
| 6.13 | | Res. 2.5.2 | R |

| Ephesians | Early Christian Writer | Early Christian Work | Reference Status |
|---|---|---|---|
| 6.13 | Novatian | Bon.pud. 2.1 | PR |
| 6.13 | Origen of Alexandria | Fr.Eph. 34 | R |
| 6.13 | | Fr.Eph. 34 | R |
| 6.13 | | Fr.Exod. A | PR |
| 6.13 | | Hom.Ezech. 2.3.1 | RNF |
| 6.13 | | Hom.Jos. 9.9 | RNF |
| 6.13 | | Hom.Ps. A 1.1 | R |
| 6.13 | Tertullian | Fug. 10.1 | PR |
| 6.13 or 11 | Eusebius of Caesarea | Comm.Ps. B | PR |
| 6.13 or 11 | Origen of Alexandria | Comm.Jo. 32.19 | R |
| 6.13–14 | Eusebius of Caesarea | Mart.Pal. 5 | PR |
| 6.13–14 | | Fr. Luc. | R |
| 6.13–14 | Novatian | Cypr. 31.5.2 | R |
| 6.13–17 | Origen of Alexandria | Comm.Eph. 261–67 | R |
| 6.13–17 | | Comm.Eph. 261–67 | R |
| 6.13–17 | | Hom.Ps. 2.8 | R |
| 6.13–17 | | Hom.Ps. 3.1 | R |
| 6.13–17 | | Hom.Ps. 3.3 | R |
| 6.13–17 | Tertullian | Res. 3.4 | PR |
| 6.13,16 | Anonymous | Rect.Fide 1.19 | R |
| 6.13,16 | Origen of Alexandria | Comm.Jo. 32.19 | R |
| 6.13,16 | | Cels. 5.1 | PR |
| 6.13,17 | Ignatius of Antioch | Polyc. 6 | PR |
| 6.14 | Anonymous | M.Dat. 3 | RNF |
| 6.14 | Clement of Rome-Pseudo | Ep.virg. 2.8.2 | PR |
| 6.14 | Cyprian of Carthage | Ep. 55.9 | R |
| 6.14 | Eusebius of Caesarea | Comm.Ps. | PR |
| 6.14 | | Pasch. 7 | PR |
| 6.14 | | Fr. | RNF |

## Appendix B: Ephesians 6.10–17

| Ephesians | Early Christian Writer | Early Christian Work | Reference Status |
|---|---|---|---|
| 6.14 | Eusebius of Caesarea | Vit.Const. 2.16.2 | PR |
| 6.14 | Hippolytus of Rome | Trad.ap. 42 | RNF |
| 6.14 | Methodius of Olympus | Symp. 8.12 | RNF |
| 6.14 | | Res. 2.5.2 | R |
| 6.14 | Origen of Alexandria | Pasch. 38 | R |
| 6.14 | | Fr.Eph. 33 | R |
| 6.14 | | Fr.Eph. 33 | R |
| 6.14 | | Fr.Eph. 34 | R |
| 6.14 | | Fr.Ezech. A | PR |
| 6.14 | | Fr.Jos. | RNF |
| 6.14 | | Fr.Luc. 156 | RNF |
| 6.14 | | Fr.Ps. | PR |
| 6.14 | | Hom.1 Reg. 16 | R |
| 6.14 | | Hom.1 Reg. 16 | R |
| 6.14 | | Hom.Exod. 4.9 | PR |
| 6.14 | | Hom.Ezech. 6.10.1 | R |
| 6.14 | | Hom.Gen. 4.6 | R |
| 6.14 | | Hom.Gen. 8.10 | PR |
| 6.14 | | Hom.Jos. 3.1 | PR |
| 6.14 | | Hom.Jos. 5.2 | R |
| 6.14 | | Hom.Judic. 6.2 | PR |
| 6.14 | | Hom.Num. 20.1.5 | R |
| 6.14 | | Hom.Num. 25.2.2 | R |
| 6.14 | | Hom.Num. 27.7.1 | PR |
| 6.14 | | Hom.Num. 7.6.1 | R |
| 6.14 | | Hom.Ps. 2.8 | R |
| 6.14 | Polycarp of Smyrna | Phil. 2.1 | PR |
| 6.14 | Tertullian | Marc. 4.20.4 | RNF |
| 6.14 | | Fug. 9.2 | R |

| Ephesians | Early Christian Writer | Early Christian Work | Reference Status |
|---|---|---|---|
| 6.14 | Tertullian | Pat. | RNF |
| 6.14 | | Pat. | RNF |
| 6.14–15 | Anonymous | A.Thom. 147 | PR |
| 6.14–15 | Origen of Alexandria | Hom.Exod. 3.3 | R |
| 6.14–17 | Clement of Alexandria | Protr. 11.116 | R |
| 6.14–17 | Origen of Alexandria | Comm.Eph. 252–53 | R |
| 6.14–17 | | Hom.Judic. 9.1 | R |
| 6.14–17 | Tertullian | Marc. 3.14.4 | R |
| 6.14–17 | | Cor. 1.3 | PR |
| 6.14–17 | | Fug. 9.2 | PR |
| 6.14,17 | Anonymous | M.Fruct. 7.2 | PR |
| 6.15 | Cyprian of Carthage | Ep. 55.9 | R |
| 6.15 | Eusebius of Caesarea | Pasch. 7 | PR |
| 6.15 | Hippolytus of Rome | Ben.Is.Jac. 2 | RNF |
| 6.15 | | Consumm. 46 | R |
| 6.15 | Origen of Alexandria | Pasch. 37 | R |
| 6.15 | | Pasch. 38 | R |
| 6.15 | | Fr.Eph. 33 | R |
| 6.15 | | Fr.Eph. 33 | R |
| 6.15 | | Fr.Eph. 34 | R |
| 6.15 | | Fr.Eph. 34 | R |
| 6.15 | | Hom.Ezech. 6.9.1 | R |
| 6.15 | | Hom.Judic. 8.5 | PR |
| 6.15 | | Hom.Num. 20.1.5 | R |
| 6.15 | | Hom.Ps. 2.8 | R |
| 6.15 | | Hom.Ps. 4.2 | R |
| 6.15–17 | Methodius of Olympus | Res. 2.5.2 | R |
| 6.16 | Anonymous | Rect.Fide 1.19 | R |
| 6.16 | | M.Dat. 3 | RNF |

| Ephesians | Early Christian Writer | Early Christian Work | Reference Status |
|---|---|---|---|
| 6.16 | Anonymous | P.Wurz.3 3 | RNF |
| 6.16 | Valentinian Author cited by Clement of Alexandria | Exc.Theod. 85 | R |
| 6.16 | Clement of Alexandria | Strom. 4.22 | PR |
| 6.16 | Commodian | Apol. | PR |
| 6.16* | Cyprian of Carthage | Ep. 30.6 | RNF |
| 6.16 | | Ep. 55.9 | R |
| 6.16 | Eusebius of Caesarea | Comm.Ps. | PR |
| 6.16 | | Comm.Ps. | PR |
| 6.16 | | Comm.Ps. | PR |
| 6.16 | | Comm.Ps. B | PR |
| 6.16 | | Laud.Const. 7.5 | PR |
| 6.16 | | Fr.G.I. 4.19 | PR |
| 6.16 | | Hist.eccl. 10.4.58 | PR |
| 6.16 | Hippolytus of Rome | David 12.1 | PR |
| 6.16 | | Trad.ap. 42 | RNF |
| 6.16 | Methodius of Olympus | Symp. 2.2 | PR |
| 6.16 | | Sang. 9.6 | R |
| 6.16 | Methodius of Olympus-pseudo | Sym.et Ann. 10 | PR |
| 6.16 | Novatian | Cypr. 30.6.3 | RNF |
| 6.16 | Origen of Alexandria | Comm.Jo. 10.205 | PR |
| 6.16 | | Comm.Jo. 13.402 | PR |
| 6.16 | | Comm.Jo. 13.441 | PR |
| 6.16 | | Comm.Jo. 32.20 | PR |
| 6.16 | | Comm.Jo. 32.24 | R |
| 6.16 | | Comm.Jo. 32.287 | PR |
| 6.16 | | Comm.Jo. 6.10 | PR |
| 6.16 | | Comm.Matt. 11.9 | PR |
| 6.16 | | Comm.Rom. A 1.16.4 | R |

| Ephesians | Early Christian Writer | Early Christian Work | Reference Status |
|---|---|---|---|
| 6.16 | Origen of Alexandria | Comm.Cant. 3.8 | R |
| 6.16 | | Comm.Cant. 3.8 | R |
| 6.16 | | Or. 30.3 | R |
| 6.16 | | Or. 30.3 | R |
| 6.16 | | Princ. 3.2.4 | R |
| 6.16 | | Princ. 4.3.12 | PR |
| 6.16 | | Fr.Eph. 33 | R |
| 6.16 | | Fr.Eph. 35 | R |
| 6.16 | | Fr.Eph. 35 | R |
| 6.16 | | Fr.Exod. A | R |
| 6.16 | | Fr.Jer. 2 | PR |
| 6.16 | | Fr.Lev. | RNF |
| 6.16 | | Fr.Ps. | PR |
| 6.16 | | Fr.Ps. | PR |
| 6.16 | | Fr.Ps. | RNF |
| 6.16 | | Fr.Ps. | RNF |
| 6.16 | | Fr.Ps. A | RNF |
| 6.16 | | Fr.Ps. A | R |
| 6.16 | | Fr.Ps. A | R |
| 6.16 | | Fr.Ps. C | RNF |
| 6.16 | | Fr.Ps. E | R |
| 6.16 | | Fr.Cant. A | RNF |
| 6.16 | | Hom.1 Reg. 16 | R |
| 6.16 | | Hom.1 Reg. 16 | R |
| 6.16 | | Hom.Exod. 1.5 | R |
| 6.16 | | Hom.Exod. 5.5 | R |
| 6.16 | | Hom.Gen. 4.6 | R |
| 6.16 | | Hom.Jos. 12.2 | PR |
| 6.16 | | Hom.Jos. 9.2 | PR |

Appendix B: Ephesians 6.10–17 — **223**

| Ephesians | Early Christian Writer | Early Christian Work | Reference Status |
|---|---|---|---|
| 6.16 | Origen of Alexandria | Hom.Jos. 9.3 | PR |
| 6.16 | | Hom.Judic. 6.2 | R |
| 6.16 | | Hom.Jer. 18.1.2 | PR |
| 6.16 | | Hom.Lev. 8.8 | PR |
| 6.16 | | Hom.Lev. 9.8 | R |
| 6.16 | | Hom.Num. 14.2.10 | PR |
| 6.16 | | Hom.Num. 25.2.2 | R |
| 6.16 | | Hom.Num. 7.6.1 | R |
| 6.16 | | Hom.Num. 8.1.7 | R |
| 6.16 | | Hom.Num. 8.1.7 | R |
| 6.16 | | Hom.Ps. 2.8 | R |
| 6.16 | | Hom.Ps. 2.8 | R |
| 6.16 | | Hom.Ps. 3.3 | R |
| 6.16 | | Hom.Ps. A 1.1 | R |
| 6.16 | | Hom.Ps. A 1.1 | R |
| 6.16 | | Hom.Num. 20.1.5 | R |
| 6.16 | Tertullian | Fug. 3.3 | PR |
| 6.16 | | Fug. 9.2 | R |
| 6.16–17 | Anonymous | Rect.Fide | RNF |
| 6.16–17 | Clement of Alexandria | Strom. 7.11 | PR |
| 6.16–17 | Cyprian of Carthage | Ep. 25.5 (31.5) | PR |
| 6.16–17 | Novatian | Cypr. 31.5.2 | PR |
| 6.16–18 | Eusebius of Caesarea | Laud.Const. 1 | RNF |
| 6.17 | Anonymous | M.Dat. 3 | PR |
| 6.17 | | M.Dat. 3 | RNF |
| 6.17 | Cyprianus Carthage-Pseudo | Comput. 10 | PR |
| 6.17 | Cyprian of Carthage | Ep. 55.9 | R |
| 6.17 | | Ep. 55.9 | R |
| 6.17 | Eusebius of Caesarea | Fr. Pr. | PR |

| Ephesians | Early Christian Writer | Early Christian Work | Reference Status |
|---|---|---|---|
| 6.17 | Hippolytus of Rome | David 12.1 | PR |
| 6.17 | Methodius of Olympus | Symp. 8.12 | PR |
| 6.17 | | Lepr. 8.2 | PR |
| 6.17 | | Lepr. 8.5 | PR |
| 6.17 | Origen of Alexandria | Comm.Matt. 16.4 | RNF |
| 6.17 | | Comm.Matt. A | R |
| 6.17 | | Comm.Matt. A | PR |
| 6.17 | | Comm.Rom. A 7.11.3 | PR |
| 6.17 | | Pasch. 38 | R |
| 6.17 | | Fr.Eph. 33 | R |
| 6.17 | | Fr.Eph. 33 | R |
| 6.17 | | Fr.Eph. 35 | R |
| 6.17 | | Fr.Lam. 104 | R |
| 6.17 | | Fr.Pr. | PR |
| 6.17 | | Fr.Ps. | RNF |
| 6.17 | | Fr.Deut. A | PR |
| 6.17 | | Hom.1 Reg. 16 | R |
| 6.17 | | Hom.1 Reg. 16 | R |
| 6.17 | | Hom.Gen. 4.6 | R |
| 6.17 | | Hom.Gen. 8.10 | PR |
| 6.17 | | Hom.Jos. 15.3 | PR |
| 6.17 | | Hom.Jos. 15.3 | PR |
| 6.17 | | Hom.Jos. 15.6 | R |
| 6.17 | | Hom.Jos. 16.3 | RNF |
| 6.17 | | Hom.Judic. 6.2 | PR |
| 6.17 | | Hom.Judic. 6.2 | R |
| 6.17 | | Hom.Lev. 16.7 | R |
| 6.17 | | Hom.Lev. 16.7 | R |
| 6.17 | | Hom.Num. 13.1.1 | R |

Appendix B: Ephesians 6.10 – 17 — **225**

| Ephesians | Early Christian Writer | Early Christian Work | Reference Status |
|---|---|---|---|
| 6.17 | Origen of Alexandria | Hom.Num. 13.2.2 | PR |
| 6.17 | | Hom.Num. 20.1.5 | R |
| 6.17 | | Hom.Num. 20.5.1 | PR |
| 6.17 | | Hom.Num. 25.2.2 | R |
| 6.17 | | Hom.Num. 7.6.1 | R |
| 6.17 | | Hom.Num. 7.6.1 | R |
| 6.17 | | Hom.Ps. 2.8 | R |
| 6.17 | | Hom.Ps. 3.1 | R |

# Appendix C: 1 Corinthians 15.50–58

| 1 Corinthians | Early Christian Writer | Early Christian Work | Reference Status |
|---|---|---|---|
| 15.50 | Anonymous | Rect.Fide 2 | R |
| 15.50 | | Rect.Fide 5 | R |
| 15.50 | | Rect.Fide 5 | R |
| 15.50 | | Rect.Fide 5 | R |
| 15.50 | | Rect.Fide 5 | R |
| 15.50 | | Diogn. 6.8 | PR |
| 15.50 | | Ap.Jas. fr12 | PR |
| 15.50 | | Evan.Phil. 21 | PR |
| 15.50 | Clement of Alexandria | Paed. 3.37.3 | RNF |
| 15.50 | | Strom. 2.20.125 | R |
| 15.50 | | Strom. 3.17.104 | R |
| 15.50* | Irenaeus of Lyons | Haer. 1.30.13 | PR |
| 15.50 | | Haer. 3.7.1 | PR |
| 15.50 | | Haer. 4.11.1 | RNF |
| 15.50 | | Haer. 5.10.1 | R |
| 15.50 | | Haer. 5.10.2 | R |
| 15.50 | | Haer. 5.10.2 | R |
| 15.50 | | Haer. 5.11.1 | R |
| 15.50 | | Haer. 5.11.2 | R |
| 15.50 | | Haer. 5.12.3 | R |
| 15.50 | | Haer. 5.13.2 | R |
| 15.50* | | Haer. 5.13.3 | R |
| 15.50 | | Haer. 5.13.5 | R |
| 15.50 | | Haer. 5.14.1 | R |
| 15.50 | | Haer. 5.14.4 | R |
| 15.50 | | Haer. 5.19.1 | R |
| 15.50 | | Haer. 5.19.2 | R |

# Appendix C: 1 Corinthians 15.50–58 — 227

| 1 Corinthians | Early Christian Writer | Early Christian Work | Reference Status |
|---|---|---|---|
| 15.50 | Irenaeus of Lyons | Haer. 5.9.4 | R |
| 15.50 | | Haer. 5.9.1 | R |
| 15.50* | | Haer. 5.9.1 | R |
| 15.50* | | Haer. 5.9.1 | R |
| 15.50 | | Haer. 5.9.3 | R |
| 15.50 | | Haer. 5.9.3 | R |
| 15.50 | | Haer. 5.9.4 | R |
| 15.50 | | Fr. Haer. | R |
| 15.50 | Melito of Sardis | Fr. 2.62 | R |
| 15.50 | Methodius of Olympus | Symp. 3.7 | PR |
| 15.50 | | Symp. 3.7 | PR |
| 15.50* | | Res. 1.12.8 | R |
| 15.50* | | Res. 1.22.5 | PR |
| 15.50 | | Res. 1.23.2 | R |
| 15.50 | | Res. 1.61.3 | PR |
| 15.50 | | Res. 1.7.4 | RNF |
| 15.50 | | Res. 2.17.1 | R |
| 15.50 | | Res. 2.17.4 | R |
| 15.50 | | Res. 2.17.9 | R |
| 15.50 | | Res. 2.18.1 | R |
| 15.50* | | Res. 2.18.10 | R |
| 15.50 | | Res. 2.18.4 | R |
| 15.50* | | Res. 2.18.9 | R |
| 15.50 | Novatian | Trin. 10.9 | PR |
| 15.50 | Origen of Alexandria | Comm.Ps. I-XXV A 144 | R |
| 15.50 | | Comm.Rom. A 1.1 | RNF |
| 15.50 | | Comm.Rom. A 5.10.8 | R |
| 15.50 | | Cels. 5.19 | R |
| 15.50 | | Or. 26.6 | PR |

| 1 Corinthians | Early Christian Writer | Early Christian Work | Reference Status |
| --- | --- | --- | --- |
| 15.50 | Origen of Alexandria | Princ. 2.10.3 | R |
| 15.50 | | Fr.Ps. | R |
| 15.50 | | Fr.Ps. C | R |
| 15.50 | | Hom.Jos. 15.6 | PR |
| 15.50 | | Hom.Ps. 143.3 | PR |
| 15.50 | | Hom.Ps. 83.3 | PR |
| 15.50 | Peter of Alexandria | Res.(Syriac) 4.4 | R |
| 15.50 | | Res.(Syriac) 4.4 | R |
| 15.50 | Tertullian | Marc. 5.10.11 | R |
| 15.50 | | Marc. 5.10.15 | R |
| 15.50 | | Marc. 5.12.6 | PR |
| 15.50 | | Marc. 5.14.4 | PR |
| 15.50* | | Carn.Chr. 15.3 | RNF |
| 15.50 | | Res. 48.1 | R |
| 15.50 | | Res. 49.1 | R |
| 15.50 | | Res. 49.12 | R |
| 15.50 | | Res. 49.9 | R |
| 15.50 | | Res. 50.4 | R |
| 15.50 | | Res. 50.5 | R |
| 15.50 | | Res. 50.5 | R |
| 15.50 | | Res. 51.1 | R |
| 15.50 | | Res. 51.4 | R |
| 15.50 | | Res. 51.7 | R |
| 15.50–54 | Hippolytus of Rome | Univ. | PR |
| 15.51 | Anonymous | Rect.Fide 5 | R |
| 15.51 | | Trim.Prot. 40–41 | PR |
| 15.51 | | Trim.Prot. 41 | PR |
| 15.51 | Origen of Alexandria | Comm.Is. 28 | PR |
| 15.51 | | Comm.Matt. A 52 | PR |

| 1 Corinthians | Early Christian Writer | Early Christian Work | Reference Status |
|---|---|---|---|
| 15.51 | Origen of Alexandria | Comm.Ps. I-XXV A 3.6 | PR |
| 15.51 | | Cels. 5.19 | R |
| 15.51 | | Princ. 2.10.3 | R |
| 15.51 | | Fr.1Cor. A 88 | R |
| 15.51 | | Fr.Luc. 199 | R |
| 15.51 | | Fr.Ps. | PR |
| 15.51 | | Fr.Ps. | PR |
| 15.51* | Pamphilus of Caesarea | Apol. 137 | PR |
| 15.51 | Peter of Alexandria | Res.(Syriac) | R |
| 15.51–52 | Origen of Alexandria | Res. 2 | PR |
| 15.51–52 | Hippolytus of Rome | Univ. | PR |
| 15.51–52 | | Univ. | PR |
| 15.51–52 | Methodius of Olympus | Res. 3.12.3 | R |
| 15.51–52 | Origen of Alexandria | Comm.1Thess. | RNF |
| 15.51–52 | | Comm.1Thess. | RNF |
| 15.51–52 | | Comm.Matt. A 52 | PR |
| 15.51–52 | | Cels. 5.17 | R |
| 15.51–52 | | Or. 26.6 | PR |
| 15.51–52 | Pamphilus of Caesarea | Apol. 130 | PR |
| 15.51–52 | Peter of Alexandria | Res.(Syriac) 4.5 | R |
| 15.51–52 | Tertullian | Res. 42.1 | R |
| 15.51–53 | Anonymous | Rect.Fide 5 | R |
| 15.51–53 | Origen of Alexandria | Comm.Matt. A 70 | RNF |
| 15.51–54 | Anonymous | Rheg. 48 | PR |
| 15.52 | | Did. 16.6 | PR |
| 15.52 | | Trim.Prot. 41 | PR |
| 15.52 | | A.Paul. 7.3.24 | PR |
| 15.52 | Clement of Alexandria | Paed. 2.41.4 | PR |
| 15.52 | | Quis.div. 3.6 | PR |

| 1 Corinthians | Early Christian Writer | Early Christian Work | Reference Status |
| --- | --- | --- | --- |
| 15.52 | Commodian | Apol. | PR |
| 15.52 | | Instr. 43–44 | PR |
| 15.52 | Eusebius of Caesarea | Comm.Ps. | PR |
| 15.52 | Hippolytus of Rome | Laz. 8 | R |
| 15.52 | Hippolytus of Rome-pseudo | Consumm. 35 | PR |
| 15.52 | | Consumm. 37 | PR |
| 15.52 | | Consumm. 39 | PR |
| 15.52 | Irenaeus of Lyons | Haer. 5.13.1 | PR |
| 15.52 | Minucius Felix | Oct. 11.2 | RNF |
| 15.52 | Origen of Alexandria | Comm.1Thess. | RNF |
| 15.52 | | Comm.Jo. 20.231 | R |
| 15.52 | | Comm.Matt. 14.10 | PR |
| 15.52 | | Comm.Matt. 14.9 | PR |
| 15.52 | | Comm.Matt. A 138 | PR |
| 15.52 | | Comm.Matt. A 67 | PR |
| 15.52 | | Cels. 2.65 | R |
| 15.52* | | Cels. 5.14 | PR |
| 15.52 | | Cels. 5.17 | R |
| 15.52 | | Princ. 2.3.7 | R |
| 15.52 | | Fr.Ezech. A | PR |
| 15.52 | | Fr.Luc. 228 | PR |
| 15.52 | | Fr.Matt. 500 | PR |
| 15.52 | | Fr.Ps. | PR |
| 15.52 | | Fr.Ps. A 150 | PR |
| 15.52 | | Hom.Jos. 6.4 | R |
| 15.52 | | Hom.Luc. 10.4 | PR |
| 15.52 | Peter of Alexandria | Res.(Syriac) | R |
| 15.52 | Tertullian | Ux. 1.5.3 | PR |
| 15.52 | | Marc. 3.24.6 | RNF |

Appendix C: 1 Corinthians 15.50–58 — **231**

| 1 Corinthians | Early Christian Writer | Early Christian Work | Reference Status |
|---|---|---|---|
| 15.52 | Tertullian | Marc. 5.10.14 | R |
| 15.52 | | Marc. 5.20.7 | PR |
| 15.52 | | An. 55.3 | PR |
| 15.52 | | Res. 51.8 | PR |
| 15.52 | | Res. 57.8 | R |
| 15.52 | Victorinus of Pettau | Comm.Apoc. 20.2 | R |
| 15.52 | | Dec. | PR |
| 15.52–53 | Methodius of Olympus | Res. 1.4.2 | RNF |
| 15.52–53 | Tertullian | Marc. 5.12.2 | R |
| 15.53 | Anonymous | Rect.Fide 5 | R |
| 15.53 | | Rect.Fide 5 | R |
| 15.53 | | A.Paul. | RNF |
| 15.53 | | Ep.Apost. 21 | PR |
| 15.53 | | Ep.Apost. 21 | RNF |
| 15.53 | | P.Ber.13415 | RNF |
| 15.53 | Athenagoras of Athens | Res. 16 | PR |
| 15.53 | | Res. 18 | R |
| 15.53 | Clement of Alexandria | Paed. 1.32.4 | PR |
| 15.53 | | Paed. 1.84.3 | PR |
| 15.53 | | Paed. 2.100.2 | PR |
| 15.53 | | Paed. 3.2.3 | PR |
| 15.53 | Cyprian of Carthage | Mort. 8.8 | PR |
| 15.53 | Eusebius of Caesarea | Comm.Isa. 374 | R |
| 15.53 | | Comm.Ps. | R |
| 15.53 | | Comm.Ps. | PR |
| 15.53 | | Dem.ev. 4.13.10 | PR |
| 15.53 | Heracleon the Gnostic | Jo. fr40 | PR |
| 15.53 | Hippolytus of Rome | Comm.Dan. 2.28.4 | PR |
| 15.53 | Ignatius of Antioch | Tars. 7 | R |

| 1 Corinthians | Early Christian Writer | Early Christian Work | Reference Status |
|---|---|---|---|
| 15.53 | Irenaeus of Lyons | Haer. 3.20.2 | RNF |
| 15.53 | | Haer. 4.38.4 | PR |
| 15.53 | | Haer. 5.1.1 | RNF |
| 15.53 | | Haer. 5.10.2 | R |
| 15.53 | | Haer. 5.13.5 | R |
| 15.53 | | Demonst. 33 | PR |
| 15.53 | Justin Martyr | Apol. 1.19.4 | PR |
| 15.53 | | Res. 10 | PR |
| 15.53 | Methodius of Olympus | Lepr. 10.3 | PR |
| 15.53 | | Res. 2.14.9 | R |
| 15.53 | | Res. 2.15.8 | PR |
| 15.53 | | Res. 2.16.2 | PR |
| 15.53 | | Res. 2.16.6 | PR |
| 15.53 | | Res. 2.17.4 | R |
| 15.53 | | Res. 2.18.10 | R |
| 15.53 | | Res. 2.18.4 | R |
| 15.53 | | Res. 2.18.5 | R |
| 15.53 | | Res. 2.22.2 | RNF |
| 15.53* | | Res. 3.11.4 | PR |
| 15.53 | | Res. 3.16.3 | PR |
| 15.53 | | Res. 3.23.4 | PR |
| 15.53 | Origen of Alexandria | Comm.Eph. 3 | PR |
| 15.53* | | Comm.Jo. 13.418 | PR |
| 15.53 | | Comm.Jo. 13.429 | PR |
| 15.53 | | Comm.Jo. 13.429 | PR |
| 15.53 | | Comm.Jo. 13.430 | PR |
| 15.53 | | Comm.Rom. A 6.1.7 | R |
| 15.53 | | Comm.Rom. A 7.11.3 | PR |
| 15.53 | | Comm.Rom. A 7.3.3 | PR |

| 1 Corinthians | Early Christian Writer | Early Christian Work | Reference Status |
|---|---|---|---|
| 15.53 | Origen of Alexandria | Comm.Rom. A 8.10.8 | PR |
| 15.53 | | Comm.Cant. 2.5 | PR |
| 15.53 | | Cels. 5.19 | R |
| 15.53 | | Cels. 7.32 | PR |
| 15.53 | | Princ. 2.3.2 | R |
| 15.53 | | Princ. 2.3.2 | R |
| 15.53 | | Princ. 2.3.2 | R |
| 15.53 | | Princ. 2.3.3 | R |
| 15.53 | | Hom.Ps. (36) 5.6 | R |
| 15.53 | | Hom.Ps. 15.1 | RNF |
| 15.53 | Peter of Alexandria | Res. 3.1 | R |
| 15.53 | | Res. 3.2 | PR |
| 15.53 | Tatian | Orat. 20.6 | PR |
| 15.53 | Tertullian | Ux. 1.7.1 | PR |
| 15.53 | | Herm. 34.4 | RNF |
| 15.53 | | Marc. 5.10.14 | R |
| 15.53 | | Marc. 5.12.3 | R |
| 15.53 | | Cult.fem. 2.6.4 | PR |
| 15.53 | | Res. 36.5 | RNF |
| 15.53 | | Res. 42.13 | PR |
| 15.53 | | Res. 42.3 | R |
| 15.53 | | Res. 42.5 | R |
| 15.53 | | Res. 42.9 | PR |
| 15.53 | | Res. 51.8 | R |
| 15.53 | | Res. 54.2 | PR |
| 15.53 | | Res. 54.4 | PR |
| 15.53 | | Res. 56.3 | RNF |
| 15.53 | | Res. 57.9 | R |
| 15.53 | | Res. 58.3 | RNF |

| 1 Corinthians | Early Christian Writer | Early Christian Work | Reference Status |
|---|---|---|---|
| 15.53 | Tertullian | Res. 60.4 | PR |
| 15.53 | Theophilus of Antioch | Autol. 1.7 | PR |
| 15.53 | | Autol. 2.27 | PR |
| 15.53 | Victorinus of Pettau | Comm.Apoc. 1.7 | R |
| 15.53 or 54 | Irenaeus of Lyons | Haer. 3.20.2 | PR |
| 15.53–54 | Anonymous | Evan.Ver. 3.20 | PR |
| 15.53–54 | Clement of Alexandria | Paed. 2.109.3 | PR |
| 15.53–54 | Eusebius of Caesarea | Comm.Ps. | PR |
| 15.53–54* | | Marc. 2.3.33 | PR |
| 15.53–54* | | Marc. 2.3.35 | PR |
| 15.53–54 | | Fr. Luc. | PR |
| 15.53–54 | | Fr. W | RNF |
| 15.53–54 | Irenaeus of Lyons | Haer. 2.19.6 | PR |
| 15.53–54 | | Haer. 2.23.7 | PR |
| 15.53–54 | | Haer. 2.29.2 | PR |
| 15.53–54 | | Haer. 3.19.1 | PR |
| 15.53–54 | | Haer. 5.2.3 | PR |
| 15.53–54 | | Haer. 5.3.2 | PR |
| 15.53–54 | | Fr. A | RNF |
| 15.53–54 | Melito of Sardis | Pass. 2–3 | PR |
| 15.53–54 | Methodius of Olympus | Res. 1.61.4 | PR |
| 15.53–54 | | Res. 1.61.4 | PR |
| 15.53–54 | | Porph. 2.2 | PR |
| 15.53–54 | Origen of Alexandria | Or. 25.3 | R |
| 15.53–54 | | Princ. A | PR |
| 15.53–54 | | Fr.Cant. A | RNF |
| 15.53–54 | Peter of Alexandria | Res.(Syriac) 4.5 | R |
| 15.53–55 | | Res.(Syriac) 4.5 | R |
| 15.53–54 | Tertullian | Res. 50.6 | R |

## Appendix C: 1 Corinthians 15.50–58 — 235

| 1 Corinthians | Early Christian Writer | Early Christian Work | Reference Status |
|---|---|---|---|
| 15.53–54 | Tertullian | Res. 51.10 | R |
| 15.53–54 | Victorinus of Pettau | Just. 8 | RNF |
| 15.53–55 | Cyprian of Carthage | Test. 3.58 | R |
| 15.53–55 | Irenaeus of Lyons | Haer. 5.13.3 | R |
| 15.53–55 | Methodius of Olympus | Porph. 3.4–5 | PR |
| 15.53–56 | Origen of Alexandria | Princ. 2.3.2 | R |
| 15.54 | Anonymous | Rheg. 45 | R |
| 15.54 | | Rheg. 45 | PR |
| 15.54 | | Rheg. 48–49 | PR |
| 15.54 | | Rect.Fide 5 | PR |
| 15.54 | | Evan.Ver. | RNF |
| 15.54 | | Od.Sal. 15.8 | PR |
| 15.54 | | A.Achat. 29 | PR |
| 15.54 | | A.Achat. 30 | R |
| 15.54 | Clement of Alexandria | Strom. 4.6.91 | PR |
| 15.54 | Commodian | Apol. | PR |
| 15.54 | Eusebius of Caesarea | Dem.ev. 4.14 | PR |
| 15.54 | | Theoph.fr. A | PR |
| 15.54 | | Qu. 10.3 | PR |
| 15.54 | Heracleon the Gnostic | Jo. fr40 | PR |
| 15.54 | Irenaeus of Lyons | Haer. 1.10.3 | R |
| 15.54 | | Fr. A | RNF |
| 15.54 | Methodius of Olympus | Res. 2.18.11 | R |
| 15.54* | Origen of Alexandria | Comm.Jo. 13.418 | PR |
| 15.54 | | Comm.Rom. A 1.4.1 | PR |
| 15.54 | | Cels. 5.19 | R |
| 15.54 | | Cels. 6.36 | R |
| 15.54 | | Princ. A | PR |
| 15.54 | Tertullian | Res. 47.13 | PR |

| 1 Corinthians | Early Christian Writer | Early Christian Work | Reference Status |
|---|---|---|---|
| 15.54 | Tertullian | Res. 54.3 | PR |
| 15.54 | | Res. 54.5 | R |
| 15.54 | | Res. 61.4 | RNF |
| 15.54–55 | Anonymous | Rect.Fide 2 | PR |
| 15.54–55 | | I.land.70 | RNF |
| 15.54–55 | | P.Oxy.2074 | RNF |
| 15.54–55 | Irenaeus of Lyons | Haer. 3.23.7 | PR |
| 15.54–55 | Origen of Alexandria | Hom.Ps. 140.6 | PR |
| 15.54–55 | Tertullian | Marc. 5.10.16 | R |
| 15.54–56 | | Res. 51.6 | R |
| 15.54–57 | | Pat. | RNF |
| 15.55 | Anonymous | Orac.Sib. 8 | PR |
| 15.55 | | Od.Sal. 15.9 | RNF |
| 15.55 | | P.Argent.5 et 6 | RNF |
| 15.55 | | A.Achat. 30 | R |
| 15.55 | Clement of Alexandria | Paed. 2.74.3 | PR |
| 15.55 | Eusebius of Caesarea | Dem.ev. 10.1.36 | PR |
| 15.55 | Hippolytus of Rome | Pasch. | RNF |
| 15.55* | Lactantius | Inst. 7.20.4 | PR |
| 15.55 | Origen of Alexandria | Comm.Jo. 10.229 | PR |
| 15.55 | | Comm.Matt. A 132 | PR |
| 15.55 | | Comm.Rom. A 5.1.21 | R |
| 15.55 | | Or. 25.3 | PR |
| 15.55 | | Pasch. 48 | PR |
| 15.55 | | Fr.Jer. 54 | PR |
| 15.55 | | Hom.Cant. 2.12 | RNF |
| 15.55 | | Hom.Ps. 114.8 | RNF |
| 15.55 | Tertullian | Cor. 14.3 | PR |
| 15.55 | | Res. 47.13 | PR |

Appendix C: 1 Corinthians 15.50–58 — **237**

| 1 Corinthians | Early Christian Writer | Early Christian Work | Reference Status |
|---|---|---|---|
| 15.55 | Tertullian | Res. 54.5 | R |
| 15.55–56 | Anonymous | M.Marian. | PR |
| 15.55–56 | | M.Mont. | PR |
| 15.55–56 | Eusebius of Caesarea | Dem.ev. 4.12.5 | PR |
| 15.55–56 | Origen of Alexandria | Cels. 5.19 | R |
| 15.55–56 | | Princ. 2.3.3 | R |
| 15.55–56 | | Princ. 3.6.3 | PR |
| 15.55–56 | | Comm.Rom. A 5.3.6 | R |
| 15.56 | Anonymous | A.Achat. 28 | PR |
| 15.56 | Cyprian of Carthage-Pseudo | Sing. 16 | RNF |
| 15.56 | Hippolytus of Rome | Pasch. | RNF |
| 15.56 | Origen of Alexandria | Comm.Rom. A 5.1.21 | R |
| 15.56 | | Comm.Rom. A 5.1.21 | R |
| 15.56 | | Comm.Rom. A 6.1.9 | R |
| 15.56 | | Comm.Rom. A 6.3 | RNF |
| 15.56 | | Fr.Rom. A 31 | PR |
| 15.56 | Tertullian | Marc. 1.22.3 | PR |
| 15.57 | Melito of Sardis | Fr. 2.41 | R |
| 15.57 | Methodius of Olympus | Res. 2.17.3 | R |
| 15.57 | Tertullian | Marc. 5.10.16 | R |
| 15.58 | Anonymous | Ep.Apost. 6 | PR |
| 15.58 | | P.Wurz.3 3 | RNF |
| 15.58 | Origen of Alexandria | Fr. 21 | RNF |
| 15.58 | Polycarp of Smyrna | Phil. 10.1 | PR |
| 15.58 | Tertullian | Fug. 9.2 | RNF |

# Appendix D: Colossians 1.15 – 20

| Colossians | Early Christian Writer | Early Christian Work | Reference Status |
|---|---|---|---|
| 1.15 | Anonymous | P.Oxy.210 | PR |
| 1.15 | | Tri.trac.1 | RNF |
| 1.15 | | Tri.trac.12 | PR |
| 1.15 | | Tri.trac.13 | PR |
| 1.15 | | Tri.trac.15 | PR |
| 1.15 | | Tri.trac.2 | PR |
| 1.15 | | Tri.trac.3 | PR |
| 1.15 | | Tri.trac.3 | PR |
| 1.15 | | Tri.trac.3 | PR |
| 1.15 | | A.Petr.copt. 2 | PR |
| 1.15 | | A.Petr.gr. 2 | PR |
| 1.15 | | A.Thom.A 39 | PR |
| 1.15 | | A.Thom.A 48 | PR |
| 1.15 | | A.Thom.A 60 | R |
| 1.15 | | A.Thom.A 60 | PR |
| 1.15 | | Ap.Jo. 15 | PR |
| 1.15 | | Ap.Jo. 15 | PR |
| 1.15 | | Ap.Jo. B 27 | PR |
| 1.15 | | Didas.Sil. 16.56 | PR |
| 1.15 | | Didas.Sil. 17.5 | PR |
| 1.15 | | Didas.Sil. 22.10 | PR |
| 1.15 | | Evan.Aeg. 4.61.8 | PR |
| 1.15 | | Evan.Aeg. 4.74.17 | PR |
| 1.15 | | Evan.Thom. 83 | PR |
| 1.15 | | Or.Paul | PR |
| 1.15 | | Naass.Ps | PR |
| 1.15 | Clement of Alexandria | Exc.Theod. 19.4 | R |

# Appendix D: Colossians 1.15–20

| Colossians | Early Christian Writer | Early Christian Work | Reference Status |
|---|---|---|---|
| 1.15 | Clement of Alexandria | Exc.Theod. 7.3 | R |
| 1.15 | | Exc.Theod. 8.2 | PR |
| 1.15 | Valentinian Author cited by Clement of Alexandria | Exc.Theod. 33.1–2 | PR |
| 1.15 | | Exc.Theod. 6.2 | PR |
| 1.15 | Clement of Alexandria | Paed. 3.3 | PR |
| 1.15 | | Protr. 9 | PR |
| 1.15 | | Strom. 4.90.2 | PR |
| 1.15 | Clement of Rome-Pseudo | Recog. 3.11.6 | PR |
| 1.15 | | Recog. 3.8.1 | PR |
| 1.15 | | Recog. 3.9.5 | PR |
| 1.15 | Cyprian of Carthage | Test. 2.1 | R |
| 1.15 | Dionysius of Alexandria | Six. 51.10 | PR |
| 1.15 | Dionysius of Rome | Sab. 2 | PR |
| 1.15 | Eusebius of Caesarea | Dem.ev. 4.2 | PR |
| 1.15 | | Dem.ev. 5.1.12 | R |
| 1.15 | | Dem.ev. 5.1.16 | R |
| 1.15 | | Dem.ev. 5.1.21 | R |
| 1.15 | | Dem.ev. 5.1.28 | PR |
| 1.15 | | Dem.ev. 5.1.28 | PR |
| 1.15 | | Dem.ev. 5.1.7 | R |
| 1.15 | | Dem.ev. 5.29.1 | PR |
| 1.15 | | Dem.ev. 5.3.2 | PR |
| 1.15 | | Dem.ev. 5.4.10 | PR |
| 1.15 | | Dem.ev. 5.5.2 | PR |
| 1.15 | | Dem.ev. 5.8.3 | RNF |
| 1.15 | | Dem.ev. 7.2.4 | PR |
| 1.15 | | Dem.ev. 7.3.14 | PR |
| 1.15 | | Eccl.theol. 1.10.5 | R |

# Appendix D: Colossians 1.15 – 20

| Colossians | Early Christian Writer | Early Christian Work | Reference Status |
|---|---|---|---|
| 1.15 | Eusebius of Caesarea | Eccl.theol. 1.20.73 | R |
| 1.15 | | Eccl.theol. 1.20.74 | R |
| 1.15 | | Eccl.theol. 1.20.90 | R |
| 1.15 | | Eccl.theol. 1.20.94 | R |
| 1.15 | | Eccl.theol. 1.9.2 | RNF |
| 1.15 | | Eccl.theol. 2.14 | RNF |
| 1.15 | | Eccl.theol. 2.17 | RNF |
| 1.15 | | Eccl.theol. 2.20.15 | R |
| 1.15* | | Eccl.theol. 2.23.4 | R |
| 1.15* | | Eccl.theol. 2.23.4 | R |
| 1.15* | | Eccl.theol. 2.23.4 | R |
| 1.15 | | Eccl.theol. 2.25 | RNF |
| 1.15 | | Eccl.theol. 2.7.5 | R |
| 1.15 | | Eccl.theol. 3.5.19 | PR |
| 1.15 | | Eccl.theol. 3.6.5 | R |
| 1.15 | | Eccl.theol. 3.7.1 | PR |
| 1.15 | | Ep.Caes. | PR |
| 1.15 | | Hist.eccl. 7.15.15 | PR |
| 1.15* | | Hist.eccl. 7.6 | PR |
| 1.15 | | Marc. 1.1 | RNF |
| 1.15* | | Marc. 1.2.15 | R |
| 1.15* | | Marc. 1.4.30 | R |
| 1.15* | | Marc. 1.4.30 | R |
| 1.15* | | Marc. 1.4.31 | R |
| 1.15* | | Marc. 1.4.31 | R |
| 1.15* | | Marc. 1.4.32 | R |
| 1.15 | | Marc. 2.1 | RNF |
| 1.15* | | Marc. 2.2.4 | R |
| 1.15* | | Marc. 2.3.23 | R |

Appendix D: Colossians 1.15 – 20 — **241**

| Colossians | Early Christian Writer | Early Christian Work | Reference Status |
|---|---|---|---|
| 1.15* | Eusebius of Caesarea | Marc. 2.3.24 | R |
| 1.15* | | Marc. 2.3.3 | R |
| 1.15* | | Marc. 2.3.4 | R |
| 1.15* | | Marc. 2.3.5 | R |
| 1.15* | | Marc. 2.3.6 | R |
| 1.15* | | Marc. 2.3.7 | R |
| 1.15 | | Marc. 2.4 | RNF |
| 1.15 | | Comm.Ps. | PR |
| 1.15 | | Comm.Ps. | PR |
| 1.15 | | Theoph.fr. 1.38 | R |
| 1.15 | | Qu. 14.1 | RNF |
| 1.15 | Hippolytus of Rome | Antichr. 43 | PR |
| 1.15 | | Comm.Dan. 4.11.5 | PR |
| 1.15* | | Haer. 5.10.2 | PR |
| 1.15 | Hippolytus of Rome-pseudo | Helc.Ann. 2 | PR |
| 1.15 | Ignatius of Antioch | Eph. 20 | PR |
| 1.15 | | Tars. 4.2 | PR |
| 1.15 | Irenaeus of Lyons | Haer. 1.1.8 | R |
| 1.15 | | Demonst. 22 | PR |
| 1.15 | | Demonst. 39 | R |
| 1.15 | | Fr. 2 | PR |
| 1.15 | | Haer. 1.10.1 | PR |
| 1.15 | | Haer. 3.16.3 | PR |
| 1.15 | | Haer. 4.21.3 | PR |
| 1.15 | Justin Martyr | Dial. 100.2 | PR |
| 1.15 | | Dial. 125.3 | PR |
| 1.15 | | Dial. 138.2 | PR |
| 1.15 | | Dial. 84.2 | PR |
| 1.15 | | Dial. 85.2 | PR |

# Appendix D: Colossians 1.15–20

| Colossians | Early Christian Writer | Early Christian Work | Reference Status |
|---|---|---|---|
| 1.15 | Lactantius | Inst. 4.11.7 | PR |
| 1.15 | | Inst. 4.6.2 | RNF |
| 1.15 | Melito of Sardis | Pass. 59 | RNF |
| 1.15 | Methodius of Olympus | Cib. 1.4 | PR |
| 1.15 | | Sang. 7.3 | PR |
| 1.15 | | Symp. 3.3 | PR |
| 1.15 | Novatian | Trin. 18.3 | R |
| 1.15 | | Trin. 21.3 | R |
| 1.15 | | Trin. 21.3 | R |
| 1.15 | | Trin. 21.3 | R |
| 1.15 | | Trin. 28.29 | PR |
| 1.15 | Origen of Alexandria | Cels. 2.25 | PR |
| 1.15 | | Cels. 2.31 | PR |
| 1.15 | | Cels. 4.85 | PR |
| 1.15 | | Cels. 5.11 | PR |
| 1.15 | | Cels. 5.37 | PR |
| 1.15 | | Cels. 6.17 | PR |
| 1.15 | | Cels. 6.40 | RNF |
| 1.15 | | Cels. 6.47 | PR |
| 1.15 | | Cels. 6.48 | PR |
| 1.15 | | Cels. 6.63 | PR |
| 1.15 | | Cels. 6.64 | R |
| 1.15 | | Cels. 6.69 | R |
| 1.15 | | Cels. 7.16 | PR |
| 1.15 | | Cels. 7.27 | R |
| 1.15 | | Cels. 7.38 | PR |
| 1.15 | | Cels. 7.43 | PR |
| 1.15 | | Cels. 7.43 | PR |
| 1.15 | | Cels. 7.65 | PR |

# Appendix D: Colossians 1.15 – 20

| Colossians | Early Christian Writer | Early Christian Work | Reference Status |
|---|---|---|---|
| 1.15 | Origen of Alexandria | Cels. 7.70 | PR |
| 1.15 | | Cels. 8.12 | PR |
| 1.15 | | Cels. 8.13 | RNF |
| 1.15 | | Cels. 8.17 | PR |
| 1.15 | | Cels. 8.17 | PR |
| 1.15 | | Cels. 8.26 | PR |
| 1.15 | | Comm.Matt. 10.23 | PR |
| 1.15 | | Comm.Matt. 13.10 | PR |
| 1.15 | | Comm.Matt. 14.7 | PR |
| 1.15 | | Comm.Matt. 15.10 | R |
| 1.15 | | Comm.Matt. 16.8 | PR |
| 1.15 | | Comm.Matt. 17.14 | PR |
| 1.15 | | Comm.Matt. 17.20 | R |
| 1.15 | | Comm.Cant. 1.2 | PR |
| 1.15 | | Comm.Cant. 2.1 | PR |
| 1.15 | | Comm.Cant. 2.1 | PR |
| 1.15 | | Comm.Jn. 1.104 | PR |
| 1.15 | | Comm.Jn. 1.118 | PR |
| 1.15 | | Comm.Jn. 1.175 | PR |
| 1.15 | | Comm.Jn. 1.188 | PR |
| 1.15 | | Comm.Jn. 1.192 | PR |
| 1.15 | | Comm.Jn. 1.195 | PR |
| 1.15 | | Comm.Jn. 1.200 | R |
| 1.15 | | Comm.Jn. 1.28 | PR |
| 1.15 | | Comm.Jn. 1.283 | PR |
| 1.15 | | Comm.Jn. 1.62 | PR |
| 1.15 | | Comm.Jn. 1.80 | R |
| 1.15 | | Comm.Jn. 10.23 | R |
| 1.15 | | Comm.Jn. 10.264 | PR |

## Appendix D: Colossians 1.15 – 20

| Colossians | Early Christian Writer | Early Christian Work | Reference Status |
|---|---|---|---|
| 1.15 | Origen of Alexandria | Comm.Jn. 10.284 | PR |
| 1.15 | | Comm.Jn. 10.286 | PR |
| 1.15 | | Comm.Jn. 10.286 | PR |
| 1.15 | | Comm.Jn. 13.234 | PR |
| 1.15 | | Comm.Jn. 19.10 | PR |
| 1.15 | | Comm.Jn. 19.128 | PR |
| 1.15 | | Comm.Jn. 19.147 | PR |
| 1.15 | | Comm.Jn. 19.154 | PR |
| 1.15 | | Comm.Jn. 2.104 | R |
| 1.15 | | Comm.Jn. 2.16 | R |
| 1.15 | | Comm.Jn. 2.187 | PR |
| 1.15 | | Comm.Jn. 20.303 | PR |
| 1.15 | | Comm.Jn. 20.367 | PR |
| 1.15 | | Comm.Jn. 20.47 | PR |
| 1.15 | | Comm.Jn. 28.159 | PR |
| 1.15 | | Comm.Jn. 32.193 | PR |
| 1.15 | | Comm.Jn. 32.33 | PR |
| 1.15 | | Comm.Jn. 32.359 | PR |
| 1.15 | | Comm.Jn. 6.19 | R |
| 1.15 | | Comm.Jn. 6.252 | PR |
| 1.15 | | Comm.Jn. 6.35 | R |
| 1.15 | | Comm.Rom. | PR |
| 1.15 | | Comm.Rom. | PR |
| 1.15 | | Comm.Rom. A 1.6.3 | PR |
| 1.15 | | Comm.Rom. A 6.11 | RNF |
| 1.15 | | Comm.Rom. A 7.3 | RNF |
| 1.15 | | Comm.Rom. A 7.5.7 | R |
| 1.15 | | Comm.Rom. A 7.7.3 | R |
| 1.15 | | Comm.Rom. A 7.7.7 | PR |

# Appendix D: Colossians 1.15-20

| Colossians | Early Christian Writer | Early Christian Work | Reference Status |
|---|---|---|---|
| 1.15 | Origen of Alexandria | Comm.Rom. A 8.10 | R |
| 1.15 | | Comm.Rom. B | RNF |
| 1.15 | | Comm.1–145 Matt. 135 | RNF |
| 1.15 | | Comm.1–145 Matt. 33 | PR |
| 1.15 | | Comm.1–145 Matt. 6 | PR |
| 1.15 | | Comm.1–145 Matt. 76 | R |
| 1.15 | | Dial. 2 | PR |
| 1.15 | | Fr.G. 1 | RNF |
| 1.15 | | Fr.Gen. B | PR |
| 1.15 | | Fr.Jn. 186 | PR |
| 1.15 | | Fr.Jn. 92 | PR |
| 1.15 | | Fr.Matt 506 | PR |
| 1.15 | | Fr.Princ. 32 | R |
| 1.15 | | Fr.Princ. 33 | R |
| 1.15 | | Fr.Princ. 36 | PR |
| 1.15 | | Fr.Ps. | R |
| 1.15 | | Fr.Ps. | PR |
| 1.15 | | Fr.Ps.79 | PR |
| 1.15 | | Fr.Ps. 117 | PR |
| 1.15 | | Fr.Ps. 118 | PR |
| 1.15 | | Fr.Ps. 66 | PR |
| 1.15 | | Hom.Ezech. 1.5.1 | PR |
| 1.15 | | Hom.Gen. 1.1 | PR |
| 1.15 | | Hom.Gen. 1.13 | R |
| 1.15 | | Hom.Gen. 16.6 | PR |
| 1.15 | | Hom.Isa. 3.1 | PR |
| 1.15 | | Hom.Jer. 1.8.1 | PR |
| 1.15 | | Hom.Jer. 1.8.5 | PR |
| 1.15 | | Hom.Jer. 15.6 | PR |

| Colossians | Early Christian Writer | Early Christian Work | Reference Status |
| --- | --- | --- | --- |
| 1.15 | Origen of Alexandria | Hom.Luc. 25.7 | PR |
| 1.15 | | Hom.Luc. 8.2 | PR |
| 1.15 | | Hom.Luc. 8.2 | PR |
| 1.15 | | Hom.Num. 11.4.7 | PR |
| 1.15 | | Hom.Num. 3.4 | PR |
| 1.15 | | Hom.Ps. (38) 2.1 | R |
| 1.15 | | Mart. 35 | R |
| 1.15 | | Mart. 9 | PR |
| 1.15 | | Or. 22.4 | PR |
| 1.15 | | Or. 26.4 | PR |
| 1.15 | | Pasch. | PR |
| 1.15 | | Princ. 1.1.8 | R |
| 1.15 | | Princ. 1.2.1 | R |
| 1.15 | | Princ. 1.2.5 | R |
| 1.15 | | Princ. 1.2.6 | R |
| 1.15 | | Princ. 1.2.6 | R |
| 1.15 | | Princ. 1.2.6 | R |
| 1.15 | | Princ. 2.4.3 | R |
| 1.15 | | Princ. 2.6.1 | R |
| 1.15 | | Princ. 2.6.3 | R |
| 1.15 | | Princ. 4.4.10 | PR |
| 1.15* | Pamphilus of Caesarea | Apol. 102 | PR |
| 1.15* | | Apol. 45 | R |
| 1.15* | | Apol. 45 | R |
| 1.15 | Peter of Alexandria | Res. 3.1 | PR |
| 1.15 | Tatian | Orat. 5.2 | PR |
| 1.15 | Tertullian | Herm. 18.5 | PR |
| 1.15 | | Marc. 5.19.3–4 | R |
| 1.15 | | Marc. 5.20.4 | R |

Appendix D: Colossians 1.15–20 — **247**

| Colossians | Early Christian Writer | Early Christian Work | Reference Status |
|---|---|---|---|
| 1.15 | Tertullian | Mart. 5.20.4 | R |
| 1.15 | | Or. 4 | RNF |
| 1.15 | | Prax. 7.1 | PR |
| 1.15 | Theognostus of Alexandria | Hypot.Fr. 2 | PR |
| 1.15 | | Hypot.Fr. 4 | RNF |
| 1.15 | Theophilus of Antioch | Autol. 2.22.1 | PR |
| 1.15 | Victorinus of Pettau | Fabr. 7 | R |
| 1.15–16 | Anonymous | Trim.Prot. | RNF |
| 1.15–16 | Clement of Alexandria | Exc.Theod. 10.5 | PR |
| 1.15–16 | | Protr. 10 | PR |
| 1.15–16 | Valentinian Author cited by Clement of Alexandria | Exc.Theod. 43.3 | R |
| 1.15–16 | | Exc.Theod. 47.2 | R |
| 1.15–16 | Eusebius of Caesarea | Dem.ev. 5.1.7 | R |
| 1.15–16 | | Hist.eccl. 1.2.3 | PR |
| 1.15–16 | | Hist.eccl. 11.19.4 | R |
| 1.15–16* | | Marc. 2.3.4 | R |
| 1.15–16* | | Marc. 2.3.5–6 | R |
| 1.15–16 | Hippolytus of Rome | Pasch. | PR |
| 1.15–16 | Melito of Sardis | Pass. 82 | PR |
| 1.15–16 | Origen of Alexandria | Comm.Matt. 16.8 | R |
| 1.15–16 | | Comm.Cant. Pr | R |
| 1.15–16 | | Hom.Num. 12.2 | R |
| 1.15–16 | | Pasch. 42 | PR |
| 1.15–16 | | Princ. 4.3.15 | R |
| 1.15–16,18 | Clement of Alexandria | Strom. 5.38.7 | R |
| 1.15–17 | Alexander of Alexandria | Depos. | R |
| 1.15–17 | Eusebius of Caesarea | Dem.ev. 5.Pr.34 | R |
| 1.15–17 | | Eccl.theol. 1.20.70–71 | R |

# Appendix D: Colossians 1.15–20

| Colossians | Early Christian Writer | Early Christian Work | Reference Status |
|---|---|---|---|
| 1.15–17 | Eusebius of Caesarea | Eccl.theol. 3.6.5 | R |
| 1.15–17 | | Eccl.theol. 3.8 | RNF |
| 1.15–17* | | Marc. 2.3.4 | R |
| 1.15–17 | | Marc. 2.3.8 | R |
| 1.15–17 | | Praep.ev. 11.19.4 | R |
| 1.15–17 | Lactantius | Inst. 2.8.7 | PR |
| 1.15–17 | Origen of Alexandria | Comm.Matt. 17.2 | R |
| 1.15–18 | | Comm.1–145 Matt. 47 | PR |
| 1.15–20 | | Comm.1–145 Matt. 6 | PR |
| 1.15,18 | | Hom.Jos. 16.2 | PR |
| 1.15,18 | | Hom.Num. 12.2.1 | R |
| 1.15,20 | | Pasch. 10–11 | PR |
| 1.16 | Anonymous | P.Oxy.210 | PR |
| 1.16 | | Trim.Prot. | RNF |
| 1.16 | | Rheg. 44.34–39 | PR |
| 1.16 | | A.Andr. 20 | PR |
| 1.16 | | A.Paul. | RNF |
| 1.16 | | A.Petr.copt. 7 | PR |
| 1.16 | | Barn. 12.7c | PR |
| 1.16 | | Didas.Sil. 22.1 | PR |
| 1.16 | | Ep.Apos. 13 | PR |
| 1.16 | | Evan.Phil. 69 | PR |
| 1.16 | | Evan.Thom. 77 | PR |
| 1.16 | | Evan.Ver. 19.7 | PR |
| 1.16 | | Ptol.Gnos. 1.3.4 | PR |
| 1.16 | | Ptol.Gnos. 1.4.5 | PR |
| 1.16 | Arnobius of Sicca | Disp.Nat. 1.31 | PR |
| 1.16 | Clement of Alexandria | Ecl. 57.1 | PR |
| 1.16 | | Exc.Theod. 19.4 | R |

| Colossians | Early Christian Writer | Early Christian Work | Reference Status |
|---|---|---|---|
| 1.16 | Clement of Alexandria | Strom. 7.82.5 | PR |
| 1.16 | Eusebius of Caesarea | Dem.ev. 5.1.23 | PR |
| 1.16 | | Dem.ev. 5.3.5 | R |
| 1.16 | | Eccl.theol. 1.12 | RNF |
| 1.16 | | Eccl.theol. 1.9.2 | R |
| 1.16 | | Eccl.theol. 2.20.8 | R |
| 1.16 | | Eccl.theol. 3.21.1 | R |
| 1.16 | | Eccl.theol. 3.21.1 | R |
| 1.16 | | Eccl.theol. 3.7.2 | R |
| 1.16 | | Ep.Const. | PR |
| 1.16 | | Ep.Const. | PR |
| 1.16 | | Fr. 2.18 | PR |
| 1.16 | | Fr. 3.1 | RNF |
| 1.16 | | Fr. 4.23 | RNF |
| 1.16 | | Fr.G.I. | R |
| 1.16* | | Hist.eccl. 3.36.9 | PR |
| 1.16 | | Hist.eccl. 7.15.15 | PR |
| 1.16* | | Marc. 2.3.5 | R |
| 1.16* | | Marc. 2.3.6 | R |
| 1.16 | | Praep.ev. 7.15.15 | PR |
| 1.16 | | Comm.Ps. | PR |
| 1.16 | | Comm.Ps. H | RNF |
| 1.16 | Hippolytus of Rome | Antichr. 34 | PR |
| 1.16 | | Comm.Dan. 2.30.6 | PR |
| 1.16 | | Haer. 6.12.1 | PR |
| 1.16 | | Consumm. 39 | PR |
| 1.16 | Ignatius of Antioch | Rom. 5.6 | PR |
| 1.16 | | Smyrn. 6.1 | PR |
| 1.16 | | Trall. 5.5 | PR |

| Colossians | Early Christian Writer | Early Christian Work | Reference Status |
| --- | --- | --- | --- |
| 1.16 | Irenaeus of Lyons | Haer. 1.22.1 | R |
| 1.16* | | Haer. 1.4.5 | PR |
| 1.16 | | Haer. 3.16.6 | R |
| 1.16* | | Haer. 3.7.1 | PR |
| 1.16 | | Haer. 3.8.3 | PR |
| 1.16 | Lactantius | Inst. 4.11.7 | PR |
| 1.16 | Melito of Sardis | Pass. 38 | RNF |
| 1.16 | Methodius of Olympus | Res. 1.1.10 | PR |
| 1.16 | | Res. 1.1.10 | PR |
| 1.16 | | Res. 1.49.1–2 | PR |
| 1.16 | | Res. 1.49.4 | PR |
| 1.16 | | Sang. 7.3 | PR |
| 1.16 | | Symp. 3.6 | PR |
| 1.16 | Novatian | Trin. 1.13 | PR |
| 1.16 | | Trin. 13.2 | R |
| 1.16 | | Trin. 13.7–8 | PR |
| 1.16 | | Trin. 14.16 | PR |
| 1.16 | | Trin. 14.6 | R |
| 1.16 | Origen of Alexandria | Cels. 4.29 | PR |
| 1.16 | | Cels. 6.71 | PR |
| 1.16 | | Comm.Matt. 17.14 | PR |
| 1.16 | | Comm.Matt. 17.21 | PR |
| 1.16 | | Comm.Jn. 1.108 | R |
| 1.16 | | Comm.Jn. 1.108 | R |
| 1.16 | | Comm.Jn. 1.214 | PR |
| 1.16 | | Comm.Jn. 1.216 | PR |
| 1.16 | | Comm.Jn. 1.79 | PR |
| 1.16 | | Comm.Jn. 1.88 | R |
| 1.16 | | Comm.Jn. 10.269 | PR |

## Appendix D: Colossians 1.15–20

| Colossians | Early Christian Writer | Early Christian Work | Reference Status |
|---|---|---|---|
| 1.16 | Origen of Alexandria | Comm.Jn. 13.151 | PR |
| 1.16 | | Comm.Jn. 2.146 | PR |
| 1.16 | | Comm.Rom. A 1.17.2 | R |
| 1.16 | | Comm.1–145 Matt. 62 | RNF |
| 1.16 | | Comm.1–145 Matt. 70 | R |
| 1.16 | | Comm.1–145 Matt. 71 | PR |
| 1.16 | | Fr.Pr. | RNF |
| 1.16 | | Fr.Princ. 32 | PR |
| 1.16 | | Fr.Princ. 36 | PR |
| 1.16 | | Fr.Ps. 12 | RNF |
| 1.16 | | Hom.1 Reg. | RNF |
| 1.16 | | Hom.Exod. 8.2 | PR |
| 1.16 | | Hom.Ezech. 4.1.4 | PR |
| 1.16 | | Hom.Isa. 1.1 | PR |
| 1.16 | | Hom.Jer. 15.6 | PR |
| 1.16 | | Hom.Jer. 15.6 | PR |
| 1.16 | | Hom.Jos. 6.2 | PR |
| 1.16 | | Hom.Lev. 5.1.3 | PR |
| 1.16 | | Hom.Lev. 5.1.3 | PR |
| 1.16 | | Hom.Num. 7.5.5 | PR |
| 1.16 | | Or. 17.2 | PR |
| 1.16 | | Princ. 1.5.1 | R |
| 1.16 | | Princ. 1.5.2 | RNF |
| 1.16 | | Princ. 1.5.3 | R |
| 1.16 | | Princ. 1.5.3 | R |
| 1.16 | | Princ. 1.6.2 | R |
| 1.16 | | Princ. 1.7.2 | R |
| 1.16 | | Princ. 1.7.2 | RNF |
| 1.16 | | Princ. 1.8.4 | PR |

| Colossians | Early Christian Writer | Early Christian Work | Reference Status |
| --- | --- | --- | --- |
| 1.16 | Origen of Alexandria | Princ. 1.8.4 | PR |
| 1.16 | | Princ. 2.11.7 | PR |
| 1.16 | | Princ. 2.6.2 | R |
| 1.16 | | Princ. 2.6.3 | R |
| 1.16 | | Princ. 2.6.3 | R |
| 1.16 | | Princ. 2.9.3 | RNF |
| 1.16 | | Princ. 2.9.4 | R |
| 1.16 | | Princ. 2.9.5 | R |
| 1.16 | | Princ. 4.3.14 | R |
| 1.16 | | Princ. 4.4.4 | R |
| 1.16 | | Princ. A | PR |
| 1.16 | | Res. 2 | RNF |
| 1.16 | | Schol.Cant. | PR |
| 1.16* | Pamphilus of Caesarea | Apol. 82 | PR |
| 1.16 | Peter of Alexandria | Pasch. V.G.Exp | PR |
| 1.16 | Tertullian | Herm. 17.1 | PR |
| 1.16 | | Marc. 1.16.2 | R |
| 1.16 | | Marc. 1.16.4 | PR |
| 1.16 | | Marc. 5.19.4 | R |
| 1.16 | | Marc. 5.19.5 | R |
| 1.16 | | Prax. 14 | PR |
| 1.16 | | Prax. 14 | PR |
| 1.16 | | Prax. 7 | PR |
| 1.16* | | Val. 16.18 | R |
| 1.16–17 | Anonymous | Rheg. 5.37 | RNF |
| 1.16–17 | | Tri.trac.12 | PR |
| 1.16–17 | | Evan.Aeg. | RNF |
| 1.16–17 | | Evan.Ver. 7.33 | RNF |
| 1.16–17 | | M.Quir. 2 | RNF |

Appendix D: Colossians 1.15 – 20 — 253

| Colossians | Early Christian Writer | Early Christian Work | Reference Status |
|---|---|---|---|
| 1.16 – 17 | Aristides of Athens | Apol. 1.1.2 | PR |
| 1.16 – 17 | Eusebius of Caesarea | Eccl.theol. 1.9.2 | R |
| 1.16 – 17 | | Eccl.theol. 3.2 | RNF |
| 1.16 – 17 | | Eccl.theol. 3.3 | RNF |
| 1.16 – 17 | Ignatius of Antioch | Tars. 4.4 | R |
| 1.16 – 17 | Origen of Alexandria | Comm.Jn. 2.104 | R |
| 1.16 – 17 | | Princ. 1.2.9 | PR |
| 1.16 – 17 | | Princ. 2.6.1 | R |
| 1.16 – 17* | Pamphilus of Caesarea | Apol. 45 | R |
| 1.16 – 17 | Victorinus of Pettau | Ad.Just. 9 | PR |
| 1.16 – 18 | Origen of Alexandria | Fr.Jn. 1 | R |
| 1.16 – 18 | | Princ. 1.7.1 | R |
| 1.16 – 18 | | Princ. 4.4.3 | R |
| 1.16,19 | Eusebius of Caesarea | Laud.Const. 12.2 | PR |
| 1.17 | Anonymous | Askew. 10 | PR |
| 1.17 | | Trim.Prot. | RNF |
| 1.17 | | Trim.Prot. | RNF |
| 1.17 | | Tri.trac.1 | RNF |
| 1.17 | | Tri.trac.1 | RNF |
| 1.17 | | Tri.trac.12 | PR |
| 1.17 | | Tri.trac.7 | PR |
| 1.17 | | Evan.Ver. 18.13 | PR |
| 1.17 | | Od.Sol. 16.18 | PR |
| 1.17 | | P.Ber.9794 | RNF |
| 1.17 | Eusebius of Caesarea | Dem.ev. 4.4 | PR |
| 1.17 | | Eccl.theol. 2.2 | RNF |
| 1.17 | | Eccl.theol. 3.7.1 | PR |
| 1.17 | | Hist.Eccl. 7.10.6 | RNF |
| 1.17 | | Laud.Const. 1.6 | PR |

**254** — Appendix D: Colossians 1.15 – 20

| Colossians | Early Christian Writer | Early Christian Work | Reference Status |
|---|---|---|---|
| 1.17 | Eusebius of Caesarea | Ep.Const. 1.2 | RNF |
| 1.17* | Irenaeus of Lyons | Haer. 1.3.4 | R |
| 1.17 | Melito of Sardis | Pass. Fr.1.11 | PR |
| 1.17 | Methodius of Olympus | Symp. 8.11 | RNF |
| 1.17 | Novatian | Spec. 10.4 | PR |
| 1.17 | Origen of Alexandria | Fr.E. | RNF |
| 1.17 | | Fr.Jn. 1 | R |
| 1.17 | | Fr.Ps. 23 | PR |
| 1.17 | | Hom.Jos. 7.6 | PR |
| 1.17 | Peter of Alexandria | Pasch. V.G.Exp. | PR |
| 1.17 | Tertullian | Herm. 4.2 | PR |
| 1.17 | | Herm. 7.5 | PR |
| 1.17 | | Marc. 5.19.4 | R |
| 1.17 | | Virg. 1.2 | RNF |
| 1.17 – 18* | Valentinian Author cited by Clement of Alexandria (parallel to Irenaeus, Haer, 1) | Exc.Theod. 43.2 | PR |
| 1.17 – 19 | Origen of Alexandria | Princ. 3.5.6 | PR |
| 1.18 | Anonymous | Rect.Fide | RNF |
| 1.18 | | Rect.Fide | RNF |
| 1.18 | | Rect.Fide 5 | PF |
| 1.18 | | Orac.Sib. 8.415 | PR |
| 1.18 | | Tri.trac.3 | PR |
| 1.18 | | Tri.trac.3 | PR |
| 1.18 | | A.Thom.A | RNF |
| 1.18 | | Od.Sol. 17.15 – 17 | PR |
| 1.18 | | Ep.Ludg. 2.3 | PR |
| 1.18 | Clement of Alexandria | Ecl. 56.2 | PR |
| 1.15 | | Exc.Theod. 33.2 | PR |
| 1.18 | | Paed. 1.5 | PR |

Appendix D: Colossians 1.15 – 20 — **255**

| Colossians | Early Christian Writer | Early Christian Work | Reference Status |
|---|---|---|---|
| 1.18 | Clement of Alexandria | Paed. 2.8 | PR |
| 1.18 | | Strom. 3.103.3 | PR |
| 1.18 | | Strom. 5.37.5 | PR |
| 1.18 | | Strom. 7.87.3 | RNF |
| 1.18 | Valentinian Author cited by Clement of Alexandria | Exc.Theod. 42.2 | PR |
| 1.18 | Clement of Rome | 1Clem. 24 | RNF |
| 1.18 | Cyprian of Carthage | Test. 2.1 | PR |
| 1.18* | Eusebius of Caesarea | Hist.eccl. 5.2.3 | PR |
| 1.18* | | Marc. 1.2.15 | R |
| 1.18 | | Marc. 2.4.28 | PR |
| 1.18 | | Comm.Ps. | PR |
| 1.18 | Hippolytus of Rome | Ben.Is.Jac. 1 | PR |
| 1.18 | | Ben.Is.Jac. 1 | PR |
| 1.18 | | Ben.Is.Jac. 2 | RNF |
| 1.18 | | Comm.Dan. 4.11.5 | PR |
| 1.18 | | Fr.Reg. | PR |
| 1.18 | | Res. | RNF |
| 1.18 | | Pasch. | RNF |
| 1.18 | Ignatius of Antioch | Smyrn. 1.1 | PR |
| 1.18 | Irenaeus of Lyons | Demonst. 38 | PR |
| 1.18 | | Demonst. 39 | R |
| 1.18 | | Demonst. 39 | PR |
| 1.18 | | Demonst. 40 | PR |
| 1.18 | | Haer. 2.22.4 | R |
| 1.18 | | Haer. 3.15.3 | PR |
| 1.18 | | Haer. 3.16.3 | PR |
| 1.18 | | Haer. 3.16.6 | R |
| 1.18 | | Haer. 3.19.3 | PR |

**256** — Appendix D: Colossians 1.15 – 20

| Colossians | Early Christian Writer | Early Christian Work | Reference Status |
|---|---|---|---|
| 1.18 | Irenaeus of Lyons | Haer. 3.22.4 | PR |
| 1.18 | | Haer. 4.2.4 | PR |
| 1.18 | | Haer. 4.20.2 | PR |
| 1.18 | | Haer. 4.24.1 | PR |
| 1.18 | | Haer. 4.34.4 | PR |
| 1.18 | | Haer. 5.18.2 | PR |
| 1.18 | | Haer. 5.31.2 | PR |
| 1.18* | Lactantius | Inst. 4.19.10 | RNF |
| 1.18 | | Inst. 4.6.2 | PR |
| 1.18 | Methodius of Olympus | Res. 1.1.13 | PR |
| 1.18* | | Res. 1.26.1 | PR |
| 1.18 | | Res. 2.18.8 | PR |
| 1.18* | | Res. 3.22.12 | PR |
| 1.18 | | Res. 3.5.2 | PR |
| 1.18 | | Res. 3.5.4 | PR |
| 1.18 | Origen of Alexandria | Cels. 2.77 | PR |
| 1.18 | | Cels. 6.79 | PR |
| 1.18 | | Comm.Matt. 13.24 | RNF |
| 1.18 | | Comm.Cant. 1.3 | PR |
| 1.18 | | Comm.Cant. 3 | RNF |
| 1.18 | | Comm.Eph. 17 (Fr.) | PR |
| 1.18 | | Comm.Jn. 1.117 | PR |
| 1.18 | | Comm.Jn. 1.121 | PR |
| 1.18 | | Comm.Jn. 1.121 | PR |
| 1.18 | | Comm.Jn. 10.284 | PR |
| 1.18 | | Comm.Ps. I-XXV C 15 | PR |
| 1.18 | | Comm.Rom. A 1.6.3 | PR |
| 1.18 | | Comm.Rom. A 1.6.3 | PR |
| 1.18 | | Comm.1–145 Matt. 113 | RNF |

# Appendix D: Colossians 1.15–20

| Colossians | Early Christian Writer | Early Christian Work | Reference Status |
| --- | --- | --- | --- |
| 1.18 | Origen of Alexandria | Comm.1–145 Matt. 139 | PR |
| 1.18 | | Comm.1–145 Matt. 143 | PR |
| 1.18 | | Comm.1–145 Matt. 55 | RNF |
| 1.18 | | Comm.1–145 Matt. 6 | PR |
| 1.18 | | Comm.1–145 Matt. 73 | PR |
| 1.18 | | Comm.1–145 Matt. 77 | RNF |
| 1.18* | | Fr.1 Cor. A 84 | PR |
| 1.18* | | Fr.1 Cor. A 84 | PR |
| 1.18 | | Fr.E. | RNF |
| 1.18 | | Fr.Eph. 17 | PR |
| 1.18 | | Fr.Jn. 140 | PR |
| 1.18 | | Fr.Jn. 43 | PR |
| 1.18 | | Hom.Gen. 16.6 | R |
| 1.18 | | Hom.Gen. 16.6 | R |
| 1.18 | | Hom.Jer. 15.6 | PR |
| 1.18 | | Hom.Lev. 1.3.1 | PR |
| 1.18 | | Hom.Lev. 7.2 | RNF |
| 1.18 | | Hom.Lev. 7.2.10 | PR |
| 1.18 | | Hom.Num. 11.3.2 | PR |
| 1.18 | | Hom.Num. 14.2.4 | PR |
| 1.18 | | Hom.Num. 14.2.4 | PR |
| 1.18 | | Hom.Num. 3.4 | PR |
| 1.18 | | Princ. 1.3.7 | PR |
| 1.18* | Pamphilus of Caesarea | Apol. 132 | PR |
| 1.18* | | Apol. 143 | PR |
| 1.18* | | Apol. 143 | PR |
| 1.18* | | Apol. 146 | PR |
| 1.18* | | Apol. 45 | PR |
| 1.18 | Peter of Alexandria | Res. 3.1 | PR |

## Appendix D: Colossians 1.15 – 20

| Colossians | Early Christian Writer | Early Christian Work | Reference Status |
|---|---|---|---|
| 1.18 | Peter of Alexandria | Res. 3.1 | PR |
| 1.18 | | Res.(Syriac) 4.2 | PR |
| 1.18 | Tertullian | Virg. 1.2 | RNF |
| 1.19 | Eusebius of Caesarea | Dem.ev. 5.4.10 | PR |
| 1.19 | | Dem.ev. 5.4.6 | PR |
| 1.19 | | Comm.Isa. 81 | PR |
| 1.19 | | Laud.Const. 3.6 | PR |
| 1.19 | | Comm.Ps. | PR |
| 1.19* | Hippolytus of Rome | Haer. 10.10.4 | RNF |
| 1.19* | | Haer. 5.12.5 | PR |
| 1.19* | | Haer. 8.13.2 | PR |
| 1.19 | Origen of Alexandria | Comm.Jn. 20.1 | PR |
| 1.19 | | Comm.Rom. A 3.8.11 | PR |
| 1.19 | | Comm.Rom. A 3.8.7 | PR |
| 1.19 | | Fr.Ps. | RNF |
| 1.19 | Tertullian | Marc. 5.19.5 | R |
| 1.19 – 20 | Anonymous | Rheg. 44.30 – 33 | PR |
| 1.19 – 20 | Origen of Alexandria | Comm.1 – 145 Matt. 37 | PR |
| 1.20 | Anonymous | Rheg. 45.20 – 23 | PR |
| 1.20 | | A.Thom.A | RNF |
| 1.20 | | Evan.Aeg. | RNF |
| 1.20 | Aristides of Athens | Apol. 15.1.1 | PR |
| 1.20 | Eusebius of Caesarea | Fr. | RNF |
| 1.20 | | Comm.Isa.67 | PR |
| 1.20 | | Comm.Ps. | PR |
| 1.20 | Irenaeus of Lyons | Demonst. 34 | PR |
| 1.20 | Origen of Alexandria | Comm.Cant. Pr | PR |
| 1.20 | | Comm.Eph. 12 (fr.) | R |
| 1.20 | | Comm.Jn. 1.60 | R |

# Appendix D: Colossians 1.15 – 20

| Colossians | Early Christian Writer | Early Christian Work | Reference Status |
|---|---|---|---|
| 1.20 | Origen of Alexandria | Comm.Jn. 32.327 | PR |
| 1.20 | | Comm.Rom. A 1.4.4 | PR |
| 1.20 | | Comm.Rom. A 1.9.5 | PR |
| 1.20 | | Comm.Rom. A 10.9.2 | PR |
| 1.20 | | Comm.Rom. A 4.8.8 | PR |
| 1.20 | | Comm.Rom. A 5.10.14 | R |
| 1.20 | | Comm.Rom. A 5.7.6 | R |
| 1.20 | | Comm.1 – 145 Matt. 48 | PR |
| 1.20 | | Fr.E. | RNF |
| 1.20 | | Fr.Eph. 12 | PR |
| 1.20 | | Fr.Jn. 184 | PR |
| 1.20 | | Fr.Jn. 89 | PR |
| 1.20 | | Fr.Lc. 164 | PR |
| 1.20 | | Fr.Matt. 571 | R |
| 1.20 | | Fr.Ps. 70 | PR |
| 1.20 | | Hom.Jos. 3.4 | PR |
| 1.20 | | Hom.Luc. 10.3 | R |
| 1.20 | | Hom.Luc. 13.3 | PR |
| 1.20 | | Hom.Lev. 1.3 | RNF |
| 1.20 | | Hom.Lev. 1.3.2 | R |
| 1.20 | | Hom.Lev. 1.4 | RNF |
| 1.20 | | Hom.Lev. 2.3.3 | R |
| 1.20 | | Hom.Lev. 4.4.3 | R |
| 1.20 | | Hom.Lev. 9.5.4 | R |
| 1.20 | Tertullian | Marc. 5.19.5 | R |

# Bibliography

## B.1 Primary Sources

Aland, Barbara and Kurt Aland, eds. *Novum Testamentum Graece*. 27th ed. Stuttgart: Deutsche Bibelgesellschaft, 2006.
Attridge, Harold W. *Nag Hammadi codex I (the Jung Codex)* Nag Hammadi Studies 22–23. Leiden: Brill, 1985.
*Corpus Christianorum, Series Apocryphorum*. 17 vols. Turnhout: Brepols, 1983–.
*Corpus Christianorum, Series Graeca*. 72 vols. Turnhout: Brepols, 1977–.
*Corpus Christianorum, Series Latina*. 194 vols. Turnhout: Brepols, 1953–.
Horsley, G.H.R. and S. Llewelyn, eds. *New Documents Illustrating Early Christianity*. North Ryde, N.S.W., 1981–.
Migne, Jacques Paul, ed. *Patrologiae cursus completes: Series latina*. 217 vols. Paris, 1844–1864.
Migne, Jacques Paul, ed. *Patrologiae cursus completes: Series graeca*. 162 vols. Paris, 1857–1866.
Musurillo, Herbert. *The Acts of the Christian Martyrs: Introduction, Texts, and Translations*, Oxford Early Christian Studies. Oxford: Clarendon Press, 1972.
Nestle, Eberhard, Kurt Aland, and Barbara Aland, eds. *Novum Testamentum Latine*, 2nd ed. Stuttgart: Deutsche Bibelgesellschaft, 1992.
Pitra, Jean Baptiste, ed. *Analecta sacra (et classica) Spicilegio Solesmensi parata*. 8 vols. Farnborough, UK: Gregg Press, 1966–1967.
Roberts, Alexander, *et al.*, eds. *Ante-Nicene Fathers*, 10 vols. 2nd ed. Peabody, Mass: Hendrickson, 1994.
Robinson, James, ed. *The Coptic Gnostic Library: A complete edition of the Nag Hammadi Codices*, 5 vols. Leiden: Brill, 2000.
Robinson, James M. and Richard Smith, eds. *The Nag Hammadi Library in English*. Leiden: Brill, 1996.
Anonymous, *A Diognète*, edited by Henri Marrou. *Sources chrétiennes* 33. Paris: Cerf, 1952.
Anonymous, *La Chaîne palestinienne sur le Psaume 118, tome I: (Origène, Eusèbe, Didyme, Apollinaire, Athanase, Théodoret)*, edited by Marguerite Harl and Gilles Dorival. *Sources chrétiennes* 189. Paris: Cerf, 1972.
Anonymous, *La Chaîne palestinienne sur le Psaume 118, tome II: Catalogue des fragments: (Origène, Eusèbe, Didyme, Apollinaire, Athanase, Théodoret). Catalogue des fragments, Notes et Index*, edited by Marguerite Harl and Gilles Dorival. *Sources chrétiennes* 190. Paris: Cerf, 1972.
Anonymous, *Ascensio Isaiae. Textus*, edited by P. Bettiolo, *et al.* Turnhout: Brepols, 1995.
Anonymous Apocrypha, *Épître de Barnabé*, edited by Pierre Prigent. *Sources chrétiennes* 172. Paris: Cerf, 1971.
Apostolic Fathers, *The Apostolic Fathers*, translated by Francis X. Glimm. *Fathers of the Church* 1. Washington, D.C.: Catholic University of America Press, 1947.
Apostolic Fathers, *The Apostolic Fathers, Vol I: 1 Clement, II Clement, Ignatius, Polycarp, Didache*, edited by Bart D. Ehrman. Loeb Classical Library 24. Cambridge, Mass: Harvard University Press, 2003.

Apostolic Fathers, *The Apostolic Fathers, Vol II: Epistle of Barnabas, Papias and Quadratus, Epistle to Diognetus, The Shepherd of Hermas,* edited by Bart D. Ehrman. Loeb Classical Library 25. Cambridge, Mass: Harvard University Press, 2003.
Arnobius of Sicca, *Arnobius of Sicca, Vol. 1,* translated by George E. McCracken. *Ancient Christian Writers* 7. Westminster, Md: Newman Press, 1949.
Arnobius of Sicca, *Arnobius of Sicca, Vol. 2.* translated by George E. McCracken. *Ancient Christian Writers* 8. Westminster, Md: Newman Press, 1949.
Arnobius of Sicca, *Adversus nationes,* edited by A. Reifferscheid. *CSEL* 3.1–3. Vienna: Verlag der Österreichischen Akademie der Wissenschaften, 1875.
Athanasius. *Athanasius Werke,* edited by Hans Georg Opitz. 3 vols. Berlin: De Gruyter, 1934–2000.
Athenagoras, *Athenagoras: Embassy for the Christians, The Resurrection of the Dead,* translated by J.H. Crehan. *Ancient Christian Writers* 23. Westminster, Md: Newman Press, 1956.
Athenagoras, *Athenagoras: Legatio and De resurrectione,* edited by W.R. Schoedel. Oxford Early Christian Texts. Oxford: Clarendon Press, 1972.
Chadwick, Henry, ed. *Contra Celsum.* Cambridge: Cambridge University Press, 1953.
Cicero, Marcus Tullius. "De Re Publica; De Legibus," edited by Clinton Walker Keyes. Cambridge, Mass: Harvard University Press, 2000.
Clement of Alexandria, *Extraits de Théodote,* edited by François Louis Sagnard. *Sources chrétiennes* 23. Paris: Cerf, 1948.
Clement of Alexandria, *Christ the Educator,* translated by Simon P. Wood. *Fathers of the Church* 23. Washington, D.C.: Catholic University of America Press, 1954.
Clement of Alexandria, *Clemens Alexandrinus,* edited by O. Stählin, L. Früchtel and U. Treu. 4 vols. in *Die griechischen christlichen Schriftsteller der ersten drei Jahrhunderte.* Leipzig: Heinrich, 1905–1936.
Clement of Alexandria, *The Exhortation to the Greeks, The Rich Man's Salvation, To the Newly Baptized,* translated by G.W. Butterworth. Loeb Classical Library 92. Cambridge, Mass: Harvard University Press, 1919.
Clement of Alexandria, *Le Pédagogue. Livre I,* edited by Marguerite Harl, *et al. Sources chrétiennes* 70. Paris: Cerf, 1960.
Clement of Alexandria, *Le Pédagogue. Livre II,* edited by Marguerite Harl, *et al. Sources chrétiennes* 108. Paris: Cerf, 1965.
Clement of Alexandria, *Le Pédagogue. Livre III,* edited by Marguerite Harl, *et al. Sources chrétiennes* 158. Paris: Cerf, 1970.
Clement of Alexandria, *Protreptique,* edited by Claude Mondésert. *Sources chrétiennes* 2. Paris: Cerf, 1942.
Clement of Alexandria, *Quel riche sera sauvé?,* edited by Otto Stählin, *et al. Sources chrétiennes* 537. Paris: Cerf, 2011.
Clement of Alexandria, *Les Stromates. Stromate I,* edited by Alain Le Boulluec. *Sources chrétiennes* 30. Paris: Cerf, 1951.
Clement of Alexandria, *Les Stromates. Stromate II,* edited by Alain Le Boulluec. *Sources chrétiennes* 38. Paris: Cerf, 1954.
Clement of Alexandria, *Stromateis, Books 1–3,* translated by John Ferguson. *Fathers of the Church* 85. Washington, D.C.: Catholic University of America Press, 1991.
Clement of Alexandria, *Les Stromates. Stromate IV,* edited by Marcel Caster. *Sources chrétiennes* 463. Paris: Cerf, 2001.

Clement of Alexandria, *Les Stromates. Stromate V, tome I*, edited by Marcel Caster. *Sources chrétiennes* 278. Paris: Cerf, 1981.
Clement of Alexandria, *Les Stromates. Stromate V, tome II*, edited by Marcel Caster. *Sources chrétiennes* 279. Paris: Cerf, 1981.
Clement of Alexandria, *Les Stromates. Stromate VI*, edited by Marcel Caster. *Sources chrétiennes* 446. Paris: Cerf, 1999.
Clement of Alexandria, *Les Stromates. Stromate VII*, edited by Alain Le Boulluec. *Sources chrétiennes* 428. Paris: Cerf, 1997.
Clement of Rome, *Épître aux Corinthiens*, edited by Annie Jaubert. *Sources chrétiennes* 167. Paris: Cerf, 1971.
Clement of Rome and Ignatius, *The Epistles of St. Clement of Rome and St. Ignatius of Antioch*, translated by J.A. Kleist. *Ancient Christian Writers* 1. Westminster, Md: Newman Press, 1946.
Colson, F.H., R. Marcus, and G.H. Whitaker, eds. *Philo*. 10 vols. Cambridge, Mass: Harvard University Press, 1929.
Commodianus, *Carmen apologeticum, Instructiones*, edited by B. Dombart. *CSEL* 15. Vienna: Verlag der Österreichischen Akademie der Wissenschaften, 1887.
Cyprian of Carthage, *A Donat et La Vertu de patience*, edited by Jean Molager. *Sources chrétiennes* 291. Paris: Cerf, 1982.
Cyprian of Carthage, *A Démétrien*, edited by J. –C. Fredouille. *Sources chrétiennes* 467. Paris: Cerf, 2003.
Cyprian of Carthage, *De lapsis and De ecclesiae catholicae unitate*, edited by M. Bévenot. Oxford Early Christian Texts. Oxford: Clarendon Press, 1971.
Cyprian of Carthage, *Letters (1–81)*, translated by Rose Bernard Donna, C.S.J. *Fathers of the Church* 51. Washington, D.C.: Catholic University of America Press, 1964.
Cyprian of Carthage, *On the Church: Select Letters*, edited by A. Brent. *Popular Patristics Series* 33. Crestwood, NY: St. Vladimir's Seminary Press, 2006.
Cyprian of Carthage, *On the Church: Select Treatises*, edited by A. Brent. *Popular Patristics Series* 34. Crestwood, NY: St. Vladimir's Seminary Press, 2007.
Cyprian of Carthage, *Opera*, edited by W. Hartel. *CSEL* 2. Vienna: Verlag der Österreichischen Akademie der Wissenschaften, 1868/71.
Cyprian of Carthage, *Saint Cyprian: Treatises*, edited by R.J. Deferrari, et al. *Fathers of the Church* 36. Washington, D.C.: Catholic University of America Press, 1958.
Cyril of Jerusalem, *Catéchèses mystagogiques*, edited by Auguste Piédagnel. *Sources chrétiennes* 126. Paris: Cerf, 1966.
Cyril of Jerusalem, *Cyrilli, hierosolymorum archiepiscopi, Opera*, edited by G.C. Reischl. 2 vols. Monaco: Sumtibus Librariae Lentnerianae, 1848–1860.
Cyril of Jerusalem, *The Works of Saint Cyril of Jerusalem, Volume 1*, translated by Leo P. McCauley, S.J. *Fathers of the Church* 61. Washington, D.C.: Catholic University of America Press, 1969.
Cyril of Jerusalem, *The Works of Saint Cyril of Jerusalem, Volume 2*, translated by Leo P. McCauley, S.J. *Fathers of the Church* 64. Washington, D.C.: Catholic University of America Press, 1969.
Diogenes Laertius. "Lives of Eminent Philosophers," edited by R.D. Hicks. Cambridge, Mass: Harvard University Press, 1925.
Dionysius of Alexandria, *Letters and Treatises*, edited by C.L. Feltoe. London: SPCK, 1918.

Eusebius of Caesarea, *Commentary on Isaiah*, translated by Jonathan J. Armstrong. *Ancient Christian Texts*. Downers Grove, Ill: IVP Academic, 2013.
Eusebius of Caesarea, *Contre Hiéroclès*, translated by Marguerite Forrat. *Sources chrétiennes* 333. Paris: Cerf, 1986.
Eusebius of Caesarea, *Dimonstrazione evangelica*, edited by P. Carrara. Milan: Paoline, 2000.
Eusebius of Caesarea, *Ecclesiastical History, Books 1–5*, translated by Roy J. Deferrari. *Fathers of the Church* 19. Washington, D.C.: Catholic University of America Press, 1953.
Eusebius of Caesarea, *Ecclesiastical History, Books 6–10*, translated by Roy J. Deferrari. *Fathers of the Church* 29. Washington, D.C.: Catholic University of America Press, 1955.
Eusebius of Caesarea, *Histoire ecclésiastique, tome I. Livres I–IV*, translated by Pierre Périchon and Pierre Maraval. *Sources chrétiennes* 31. Paris: Cerf, 1952.
Eusebius of Caesarea, *Histoire ecclésiastique, tome II. Livres V–VII*, translated by Pierre Périchon and Pierre Maraval. *Sources chrétiennes* 41. Paris: Cerf, 1955.
Eusebius of Caesarea, *Histoire ecclésiastique, tome III. Livres VIII–X: et Les martyrs en Palestine*, translated by Pierre Périchon and Pierre Maraval. *Sources chrétiennes* 55. Paris: Cerf, 1958.
Eusebius of Caesarea, *Histoire ecclésiastique, tome IV*, translated by Pierre Périchon and Pierre Maraval. *Sources chrétiennes* 73. Paris: Cerf, 1960.
Eusebius of Caesarea, *History of the Martyrs in Palestine*, edited by William Cureton. London: Williams & Norgate, 1861.
Eusebius of Caesarea, *Eusebius Werke*. 2nd ed. 9 vols. in *Die griechischen christlichen Schriftsteller der ersten drei Jahrhunderte*. Berlin: Akademie-Verlag, 1954–.
Eusebius of Caesarea, *Eusebius Werke*. 7 vols. in *Die griechischen christlichen Schriftsteller der ersten drei Jahrhunderte*. Leipzig: J.C. Hinrichs, 1902–1926.
Eusebius of Caesarea, *The Life of Constantine*, edited by Averil Cameron and Stuart Hall. *Clarendon Ancient History Series*. Oxford: Oxford University Press, 1997.
Eusebius of Caesarea, *The Proof of the Gospel*, edited by W.J. Ferrar. London: SPCK, 1920.
Eusebius of Caesarea, *Questions évangéliques*, translated by Claudio Zamagni. *Sources chrétiennes* 523. Paris: Cerf, 2008.
Grant, Robert, ed. *Irenaeus of Lyons*. London/New York: Routledge, 1997.
Gregg, J.A.F. "Documents: The commentary of Origen upon the epistle to the Ephesians," *Journal of Theological Studies* 3 (1902): 234–244, 398–420, 554–576.
Heine, Ronald E. *The Commentaries of Origen and Jerome on St. Paul's Epistle to the Ephesians*, Oxford Early Christian Studies. Oxford: Oxford University Press, 2002.
Hermas of Rome, *Le Pasteur*, edited by Robert Joly. *Sources chrétiennes* 53. Paris: Cerf, 1958.
Hippolytus of Rome, *Commentaire sur Daniel*, edited by Gustave Bardy. *Sources chrétiennes* 14. Paris: Cerf, 1947.
Hippolytus of Rome, *Hippolytus Werke*, edited by Nathanael G. Bonwetsch, *et al.* 4 vols. in *Die griechischen christlichen Schriftsteller der ersten drei Jahrhunderte*. Leipzig: J.C. Hinrichs, 1897–1929.
Hippolytus of Rome, *Hippolytus: On the Apostolic Tradition*, edited by A. Stewart-Sykes. Crestwood, NY: St. Vladimir's Seminary Press, 2001.
Hippolytus of Rome, *The Refutation of All Heresies*, edited by J.H. Macmahon. Ante-Nicene Fathers Series 6. Edinburgh: T&T Clark, 1868.
Hippolytus of Rome, *La Tradition apostolique: d'après les anciennes versions*, edited by Bernard Botte. *Sources chrétiennes* 11. Paris: Cerf, 1946.

Hippolytus of Rome (pseudo-), *Homélies pascales, tome I: Une homélie inspirée du traité sur la Pâque d'Hippolyte,* edited by Pierre Nautin. *Sources chrétiennes* 27. Paris: Cerf, 1951.
Ignatius of Antioch, *Ignace d'Antioche: Lettres de Martyre de Polycarpe de Smyrne,* edited by P.T. Camelot. *Sources chrétiennes* 10. Paris: Cerf, 1969.
Ignatius of Antioch, *Ignatius of Antioch: A Commentary on the Letters of Ignatius of Antioch,* edited by W. Schoedel. Hermeneia. Philadelphia: Fortress Press, 1990.
Ignatius of Antioch, *Patres apostolici,* edited by F. Diekamp and F.X. Funk, 3rd ed, vol 2. Tübingen: Laupp, 1913.
Irenaeus of Lyon, *Contre les hérésies, livre I. Tome I: Introduction, notes justificatives, tables,* edited by Adelin Rousseau, et al. *Sources chrétiennes* 263. Paris: Cerf, 1979.
Irenaeus of Lyon, *Contre les hérésies, livre II. Tome I: Introduction, notes justificatives, tables,* edited by Adelin Rousseau, et al. *Sources chrétiennes* 293. Paris: Cerf, 1982.
Irenaeus of Lyon, *Contre les hérésies, tome I. Livre III: Introduction, notes justificatives, tables,* edited by Adelin Rousseau, et al. *Sources chrétiennes* 210. Paris: Cerf, 1974.
Irenaeus of Lyon, *Contre les hérésies, livre IV, tomes I et II,* edited by Adelin Rousseau, et al. *Sources chrétiennes* 100. Paris: Cerf, 1965.
Irenaeus of Lyon, *Contre les hérésies, Livre V, tome I: Introduction, notes justificatives, tables,* edited by Adelin Rousseau, et al. *Sources chrétiennes* 152. Paris: Cerf, 1969.
Irenaeus of Lyon, *Contre les hérésies, livre I. Tome II: Texte et traduction,* edited by Adelin Rousseau, et al. *Sources chrétiennes* 264. Paris: Cerf, 1979.
Irenaeus of Lyon, *Contre les hérésies, livre II. Tome II: Texte et traduction,* edited by Adelin Rousseau, et al. *Sources chrétiennes* 294. Paris: Cerf, 1982.
Irenaeus of Lyon, *Contre les hérésies, tome II. Livre III: Edition critique, texte et traduction,* edited by Adelin Rousseau, et al. *Sources chrétiennes* 211. Paris: Cerf, 1974.
Irenaeus of Lyon, *Contre les hérésies, Livre V, tome II: Texte et traduction,* edited by Adelin Rousseau, et al. *Sources chrétiennes* 153. Paris: Cerf, 1969.
Irenaeus of Lyon, *Contre les hérésies, livre III,* edited by Adelin Rousseau, et al. *Sources chrétiennes* 34. Paris: Cerf, 1952.
Irenaeus of Lyon, *Against the Heresies,* edited by D.J. Unger, J.J. Dillon, and M.C. Steenberg. Ancient Christian Writers 55, 64–65. New York: Paulist Press, 1992–.
Irenaeus of Lyon, *Démonstration de la prédication apostolique,* translated by Léon M.Froidevaux. *Sources chrétiennes* 406. Paris: Cerf, 1995.
Irenaeus of Lyon, *Irenaeus' Demonstration of the Apostolic Preaching: A Theological Commentary and Translation,* edited by I.M. MacKenzie. Aldershot: Ashgate, 2004.
Irenaeus of Lyon, *St. Irenaeus: Proof of the Apostolic Preaching,* translated by Joseph P. Smith, S.J. Ancient Christian Writers 16. Westminster, Md: Newman Press, 1953.
Irenaeus of Lyon, *The Writings of Irenaeus,* edited by Alexander Roberts and W.H. Rambaut. 2 vols. Edinburgh: T&T Clark, 1883–1884.
Jenkins, Claude, "Origen on 1 Corinthians" *Journal of Theological Studies* 9 (1908), 231–247, 353–373, 500–514.
Jenkins, Claude, "Origen on 1 Corinthians" *Journal of Theological Studies* 10 (1909), 29–41.
Josephus, *The Jewish War, Volume 1,* translated by H.St.J. Thackeray. Loeb Classical Library 203. Cambridge, Mass: Harvard University Press, 1927.
Justin Martyr, *Justin, Philosopher and Martyr: Apologies,* edited by Denis Minns and Paul Parvis. Oxford Early Christian Texts. Oxford: Oxford University Press, 2009.
Justin Martyr, *Justin: Apologie pour les chrétiens,* edited by C. Munier. *Sources chrétiennes* 507. Paris: Cerf, 2006.

Justin Martyr, *The First Apology, The Second Apology, Dialogue with Trypho, Exhortation to the Greeks, Discourse to the Greeks, The Monarchy of the Rule of God,* translated by Thomas B. Falls. *Fathers of the Church* 6. Washington, D.C.: Catholic University of America Press, 1965.

Justin Martyr (pseudo-), *Ouvrages apologétiques: Exhortation aux Grecs, Discours aux grecs, Sur la monarchie,* translated by Bernard Pouderon. *Sources chrétiennes* 528. Paris: Cerf, 2009.

Lactantius, *Divine Institutes,* translated by Anthony Bowen and Peter Garnsey. *Translated Texts for Historians* 40. Liverpool: Liverpool University Press, 2003.

Lactantius, *De opificio dei, De ira dei, Carmina, Fragmenta,* edited by S. Brandt. *CSEL* 27/1. Vienna: Verlag der Österreichischen Akademie der Wissenschaften, 1893.

Marius Victorinus, *Theological Treatises on the Trinity,* translated by Mary T. Clark. *Fathers of the Church* 69. Washington, D.C.: Catholic University of America Press, 1981.

Marius Victorinus, *Traités théologiques sur la Trinité, tome I,* translated by Pierre Hadot. *Sources chrétiennes* 68. Paris: Cerf, 1960.

Marius Victorinus, *Traités théologiques sur la Trinité, tome II: Commentaire,* translated by Pierre Hadot. *Sources chrétiennes* 69. Paris: Cerf, 1960.

Melito of Sardis, *"On Pascha" and Fragments,* translated by Stewart George Hall. Oxford Early Christian Texts. Oxford: Oxford University Press, 1978.

Melito of Sardis, *Sur la Pâque (et fragments),* translated by Othmar Perler. *Sources chrétiennes* 123. Paris: Cerf, 1966.

Methodius of Olympus, *Le Banquet,* translated by Victor-Henry Debidour. *Sources chrétiennes* 95. Paris: Cerf, 1963.

Methodius of Olympus, *St. Methodius: The Symposium: A Treatise on Chastity,* translated by Herbert Musurillo, S.J. *Ancient Christian Writers* 27. Westminster, Md: Newman Press, 1958.

Methodius of Olympus, *Methodius,* edited by G.N. Bonwetsch. *Die griechischen christlichen Schriftsteller der ersten drei Jahrhunderte.* Leipzig: J.C. Hinrichs, 1917.

Minucius Felix, *The Octavius of Marcus Minucius Felix,* translated by Graeme Clark. *Ancient Christian Writers* 39. Westminster, Md: Newman Press, 1974.

Novatian, *The Trinity, The Spectacles, Jewish Foods, In Praise of Purity, Letters,* translated by Russell J. DeSimone. *Fathers of the Church* 67. Washington, D.C.: Catholic University of America Press, 1974.

Novatian, *de Trinitate Liber: Novatian's Treatise on the Trinity,* edited by W.Y. Fausset. Cambridge: Cambridge University Press, 1909.

Origen, *Commentaire sur l'Évangile selon Matthieu, tome I. Livres X et XI,* edited by Robert Girod. *Sources chrétiennes* 162. Paris: Cerf, 1970.

Origen, *Commentaire sur l'Epître aux Romains. Tome I, livres I–II,* translated by Caroline P. Hammond Bammel and Luc Brésard. *Sources chrétiennes* 532. Paris: Cerf, 2009.

Origen, *Commentaire sur l'Epître aux Romains. Livres III–V,* translated by Caroline P. Hammond Bammel and Luc Brésard. *Sources chrétiennes* 539. Paris: Cerf, 2010.

Origen, *Commentaire sur l'Épître aux Romains, Livres VI–VIII,* translated by Caroline P. Hammond Bammel and Luc Brésard. *Sources chrétiennes* 543. Paris: Cerf, 2011.

Origen, *Commentaire sur l'Epître aux Romains, tome 4: Livres IX–X,* translated by Caroline P. Hammond Bammel and Luc Brésard. *Sources chrétiennes* 555. Paris: Cerf, 2012.

Origen, *Commentary on the Epistle to the Romans, Books 1–5,* translated by Thomas P. Scheck. *Fathers of the Church* 103. Washington, D.C.: Catholic University of America Press, 2001.
Origen, *Commentary on the Epistle to the Romans, Books 6–10,* translated by Thomas P. Scheck. *Fathers of the Church* 104. Washington, D.C.: Catholic University of America Press, 2002.
Origen, *Commentary on the Gospel According to John, Books 1–10,* translated by Ronald E. Heine. *Fathers of the Church* 80. Washington, D.C.: Catholic University of America Press, 1989.
Origen, *Commentary on the Gospel According to John, Books 13–32,* translated by Ronald E. Heine. *Fathers of the Church* 89. Washington, D.C.: Catholic University of America Press, 1993.
Origen, *Contre Celse. Livres I et II: Tome 1–,* translated by Marcel Borret. *Sources chrétiennes* 132. Paris: Cerf, 1967.
Origen, *Contre Celse. Livres III et IV: Tome II,* translated by Marcel Borret. *Sources chrétiennes* 136. Paris: Cerf, 1968.
Origen, *Contre Celse. Livres V et VI: Tome III,* translated by Marcel Borret. *Sources chrétiennes* 147. Paris: Cerf, 1969.
Origen, *Contre Celse, tome IV. Livres VII et VIII,* translated by Marcel Borret. *Sources chrétiennes* 150. Paris: Cerf, 1969.
Origen, *Contre Celse, tome V: Introduction générale, tables et index,* translated by Marcel Borret. *Sources chrétiennes* 227. Paris: Cerf, 1976.
Origen, *Origenes vier Bücher von den Prinzipien,* edited by H. Görgemanns and H. Karpp. Darmstadt: Wissenschaftliche Buchgesellschaft, 1976.
Origen, *Exhortation to Martyrdom,* edited by R.A. Greer. *Classics of Western Spirituality.* New York: Paulist Press, 1979.
Origen, *On First Principles,* edited by G.W. Butterworth and P. Koetschau. Gloucester, Mass: Peter Smith, 1973.
Origen, *Homélies sur le Cantique des cantiques,* edited by Marcel Borret, Luc Brésard, and Henri Crouzel. *Sources chrétiennes* 37. Paris: Cerf, 1954.
Origen, *Origen: Song of Songs: Commentaries and Homilies,* translated by R.P. Lawson. *Ancient Christian Writers* 26. Westminster, Md: Newman Press, 1957.
Origen, *Homilies on Genesis and Exodus,* translated by Ronald E. Heine. *Fathers of the Church* 71. Washington, D.C.: Catholic University of America Press, 1982.
Origen, *Homélies sur la Genèse,* translated by Louis Doutreleau. *Sources chrétiennes* 7. Paris: Cerf, 1943.
Origen, *Origen: Homilies 1–14 on Ezekiel,* translated by Thomas P. Scheck. *Ancient Christian Writers* 62. Westminster, Md: Newman Press, 2010.
Origen, (Jerome), *Homélies sur Ézéchiel,* translated by Marcel Borret. *Sources chrétiennes* 352. Paris: Cerf, 1989.
Origen, *Homilies on Jeremiah and 1 Kings 28,* translated by John Clark Smith. *Fathers of the Church* 97. Washington, D.C.: Catholic University of America Press, 1998.
Origen, *Homélies sur Jérémie (I–XI), tome I,* edited by Pierre Nautin. *Sources chrétiennes* 232. Paris: Cerf, 1976.
Origen, *Homilies on Joshua,* translated by Barbara J. Bruce. *Fathers of the Church* 105. Washington, D.C.: Catholic University of America Press, 2002.

Origen, *Homélies sur Josué,* translated by Annie Jaubert. *Sources chrétiennes* 71. Paris: Cerf, 1960.
Origen, *Homilies on Judges,* translated by Elizabeth Ann Dively Lauro. *Fathers of the Church* 119. Washington, D.C.: Catholic University of America Press, 2009.
Origen, *Homilies on Leviticus, 1–16,* translated by Gary Wayne Barkley. *Fathers of the Church* 83. Washington, D.C.: Catholic University of America Press, 1990.
Origen, *Homilies on Luke,* translated by Joseph T. Lienhard. *Fathers of the Church* 94. Washington, D.C.: Catholic University of America Press, 1996.
Origen, *Homilies on Numbers,* translated by Thomas P. Scheck. *Ancient Christian Texts.* Downers Grove, Ill: IVP Academic, 2009.
Origen, *Homélies sur les Psaumes 36 à 38,* edited by Emanuela Prinzivalli and Henri Crouzel. *Sources chrétiennes* 411. Paris: Cerf, 1995.
Origen, *Homélies sur Samuel,* edited by P. Nautin and M.-T. Nautin. *Sources chrétiennes* 328. Paris: Cerf, 1986.
Origen, *Origenes Werke,* edited by Paul Koetschau, *et al.* 12 vols. in *Die griechischen christlichen Schriftsteller der ersten drei Jahrhunderte.* Leipzig: J.C. Hinrichs, 1899–1955.
Origen, *Trestise on the Passover,* translated by Robert J. Daly, S.J. *Ancient Christian Writers* 54. Westminster, Md: Newman Press, 1992.
Origen, *Sur la Pâque,* translated by Octave Guéraud and Pierre Nautin. *Christianisme antique* 2. Paris: Beauchesne, 1979.
Origen, *Origen: Prayer, Exhortation to Martyrdom,* translated by John Joseph O'Meara. *Ancient Christian Writers* 19. Westminster, Md: Newman Press, 1955.
Origen, *Traité des principes, tome I. Livres I et II: Introduction, texte critique de la version de Rufin, traduction,* edited by Henri Crouzel and Manlio Simonetti. *Sources chrétiennes* 252. Paris: Cerf, 1978.
Origen, *Traité des principes, tome II. Livres I et II: Commentaire et fragments,* edited by Henri Crouzel and Manlio Simonetti. *Sources chrétiennes* 253. Paris: Cerf, 1978.
Origen, *Traité des principes, tome III. Livres III et IV: Introduction, texte critique de la Philocalie et de la version de Rufin, traduction,* edited by Henri Crouzel and Manlio Simonetti. *Sources chrétiennes* 268. Paris: Cerf, 1980.
Origen, *Traité des principes, tome IV. Livres III et IV: Commentaire et fragments,* edited by Henri Crouzel and Manlio Simonetti. *Sources chrétiennes* 269. Paris: Cerf, 1980.
Origen, *Traité des principes, tome V: Compléments et index,* edited by Henri Crouzel and Manlio Simonetti. *Sources chrétiennes* 312. Paris: Cerf, 1984.
Pamphilus of Caesarea, *Apologie pour Origène, suivi de Rufin d'Aquilée, Sur la falsification des livres d'Origène, tome I: Texte critique, traduction et notes,* edited by René Amacker and Éric Junod. *Sources chrétiennes* 464. Paris: Cerf, 2001.
Pamphilus of Caesarea, *Apologie pour Origène, suivi de Rufin, Sur la falsification des livres d'Origène, tome II: Etude, commentaire philologique et index,* edited by René Amacker and Éric Junod. *Sources chrétiennes* 465. Paris: Cerf, 2002.
Pamphilus of Caesarea, *Apology for Origen,* translated by Thomas P. Scheck. *Fathers of the Church* 120. Washington, D.C.: Catholic University of America Press, 2010.
Peel, Malcolm Lee, *The Epistle to Rheginos: A Valentinian Letter on the Resurrection,* New Testament Library. London: SCM, 1969.
Plato, "Phaedrus." edited by Harvey Yunis. Loeb Classical Library. Cambridge, Mass: Harvard University Press, 2011.

Plato, "Protagoras." edited by Nicholas Denyer. Loeb Classical Library. Cambridge, Mass: Harvard University Press, 2008.
Pretty, Robert A., *Adamantius: Dialogue on the True Faith in God*. Gnostica 1. Leuven: Peeters, 1998.
Quintilian, *The Orator's Education, I: Books 1–2*, translated by Donald A. Russell. Loeb Classical Library 124. Cambridge, Mass: Harvard University Press, 2002.
Tatian, *Oratio ad Graecos and fragments,* translated by Molly Whittaker. Oxford Early Christian Texts. Oxford: Oxford University Press, 1982.
Tertullian, *Adversus Marcionem,* edited by E. Evans. 2 vols. in Oxford Early Christian Texts. Oxford: Clarendon Press, 1972.
Tertullian, *Adversus Praxean = Gegen Praxeas,* edited by H.J. Sieben. Freiburg: Herder, 2001.
Tertullian, *Tertullian's Homily on Baptism,* edited by E. Evans. London: SPCK, 1964.
Tertullian, *La Chair du Christ, tome I,* translated by Jean–Pierre Mahé. *Sources chrétiennes* 216. Paris: Cerf, 1975.
Tertullian, *La Chair du Christ, tome II: Commentaire et index,* translated by Jean-Pierre Mahé. *Sources chrétiennes* 217. Paris: Cerf, 1975.
Tertullian, *Tertullian's Treatise against Praxeas,* edited by E. Evans. London: SPCK, 1948.
Tertullian, *Contre Hermogène,* translated by Frédéric Chapot. *Sources chrétiennes* 439. Paris: Cerf, 1999.
Tertullian, *Contre Marcion, tome I. Livre I,* translated by René Braun. *Sources chrétiennes* 365. Paris: Cerf, 1990.
Tertullian, *Contre Marcion, tome II. Livre II* translated by René Braun. *Sources chrétiennes* 368. Paris: Cerf, 1991.
Tertullian, *Contre Marcion, tome III. Livre III,* translated by René Braun. *Sources chrétiennes* 399. Paris: Cerf, 1994.
Tertullian, *Contre Marcion, tome IV. Livre IV* translated by René Braun. *Sources chrétiennes* 456. Paris: Cerf, 2000.
Tertullian, *Contre Marcion, tome V. Livre V,* translated by René Braun. *Sources chrétiennes* 483. Paris: Cerf, 2004.
Tertullian, *De oration liber: Tract on the Prayer,* edited by E. Evans. London: SPCK, 1953.
Tertullian, *Tertullian's Treatise on the Resurrection,* edited by E. Evans. London: SPCK, 1960.
Tertullian, *De spectaculis, De idolatria, Ad nationes, De testimonio animae, Scorpiace, De oration, De baptismo, De ieiunio, De anima, De pudicitia,* edited by A. Reifferscheid and G. Wissowa. *CSEL* 20. Vienna: Verlag der Österreichischen Akademie der Wissenschaften, 1890.
Tertullian, *Apology, De spectaculis,* edited by T.R. Glover. Loeb Classical Library 250. Cambridge, Mass: Harvard University Press, 1960.
Tertullian, *De patientia, De carnis resurrection, Adversus Hermogenem, Adversus Valentinianos, Adversus omnes haereses, Adversus Praxean, Adversus Marcionem,* edited by E. Kroymann. *CSEL* 47. Vienna: Verlag der Österreichischen Akademie der Wissenschaften, 1906.
Tertullian, *De praescriptione haereticorum, De cultu feminarum, Ad uxorem, De exhortation castitatis, De corona, De carne Christi, Adversus Iudaeos,* edited by E. Kroymann. Vienna: Verlag der Österreichischen Akademie der Wissenschaften, 1942.
Tertullian, *Ad martyras, Ad Scapulam, De fuga in persecution, De monogamia, De virginibus velandis, De pallio,* edited by V. Bulhart. Vienna: Verlag der Österreichischen Akademie der Wissenschaften, 1957.

Tertullian, *Tertullian's Treatise on the Incarnation,* edited by E. Evans. London: SPCK, 1956.
Tertullian, *De la patience,* translated by Jean Claude Fedouille. *Sources chrétiennes* 310. Paris: Cerf, 1984.
Tertullian, *La Pénitence,* translated by Charles Munier. *Sources chrétiennes* 316. Paris: Cerf, 1985.
Tertullian, *Les Spectacles,* translated by Marie Turcan. *Sources chrétiennes* 332. Paris: Cerf, 1986.
Tertullian, *Traité de la prescription contre les hérétiques,* edited by François Refoulé. *Sources chrétiennes* 46. Paris: Cerf, 1957.
Tertullian, *La Toilette des femmes: De cultu feminarum,* translated by Marie Turcan. *Sources chrétiennes* 173. Paris: Cerf, 1971.
Tertullian, *Disciplinary, Moral, and Ascetical Works,* translated by Rudolph Arbesmann, O.S.A. *Fathers of the Church* 40. Washington, D.C.: Catholic University of America Press, 1959.
Tertullian; Minucius Felix, *Apologetical Works; Octavius,* translated by Rudolph Arbesmann. *Fathers of the Church* 10. Washington, D.C.: Catholic University of America Press, 1950.
Theophilus of Antioch, *Ad Autolycum,* edited by Robert M. Grant. Oxford Early Christian Texts. Oxford: Clarendon Press, 1970.
Theophilus of Antioch, *Trois livres à Autolycus,* translated by G. Bardy and J. Sender. *Sources chrétiennes* 20. Paris: Cerf, 1948.
Victorinus of Pettau, *Sur l'Apocalypse: suivi de Fragment chronologique et de La construction du monde,* translated by Martine Dulaey. *Sources chrétiennes* 423. Paris: Cerf, 1997.
Victorinus of Pettau, *Opera,* edited by J. Haussleiter. *CSEL* 49. Vienna: Verlag der Österreichischen Akademie der Wissenschaften, 1916.
Vivian, Tim, *St. Peter of Alexandria.* Studies in Antiquity and Christianity. Philadelphia: Fortress Press, 1988.
Whiston, William, transl. *The Works of Josephus: Complete and Unabridged.* Peabody, Mass: Hendrickson, 1987.
Yonge, Charles Duke, tranls. *The Works of Philo: Complete and Unabridged.* Peabody, Mass: Hendrickson, 1993.

## B.2 Reference Works

Arndt, W., ed. *A Greek-English Lexicon of the New Testament and Other Early Christian Literature.* Rev. by F.W. Danker, 3rd ed. Chicago: University of Chicago Press, 2000.
Ashbrook Harvey, Susan and David Hunter, eds. *The Oxford Handbook of Early Christian Studies.* Oxford: Oxford University Press, 2008.
*Biblindex.* Index of Biblical Quotations and Allusions in Early Christian Literature. (*Sources chrétiennes*), http://www.biblindex.mom.fr, 19 August 2013.
Blaise, A. and H. Chirat, eds. *Dictionnaire latin–français des auteurs chrétiens.* Turnhout: Brepols, 1967.
Blass, F., A. Debrunner, and R.W. Funk. *A Greek Grammar of the New Testament and Other Early Christian Literature.* Chicago: University of Chicago Press, 1961.
Boeckh, A., ed. *Corpus inscriptionum graecarum.* 4 vol. Berlin: Deutsche Akademie der Wissenschaften, 1828–1877.
Buchberger, M. *et al,* eds., *Lexikon für Theologie und Kirche,* 3rd ed. Freiburg: Herder, 1993–.

Cabrol, Henri F.L., ed. *Dictionnaire d'archéologie Chrétienne et de liturgie*. 3 vols. Paris: Letouzey et Ané, 1914.
Centre D'Analyse et de Documentation Patristiques, eds. *Biblia Patristica: Index des citations et allusions bibliques dans la littérature patristique,* 7 vol. Paris: Éditions du Centre national de la recherché scientifique, 1975–2000.
*Cetedoc,* Centre de Traitement Electronique des Documents, Library of Christian Latin Texts (Brepols).
Crane, G., ed. *The Perseus Digital Library.* Tufts University, http://perseus.tufts.edu. 19 August 2013.
Dassmann, Ernst, ed. *Das Reallexikon für Antike und Christentum und das F.J. Dölger-Institut in Bonn: mit Registern der Stichwörter a bis Ianus sowie der Autoren Bände 1–16.* Stuttgart: Hiersemann, 1994.
Dekkers, E., ed. *Clavis Patrum Latinorum.* 3rd ed. Turnhout: Brepols, 1995.
Ferguson, Everett, ed. *Encyclopedia of Early Christianity.* 2nd ed. New York: Garland Publishers, 1997.
Geerard, M., ed. *Clavis Patrum Graecorum.* 5 vol. Turnhout: Brepols, 1974–1987.
Geerard, M. and J. Noret, eds. *Clavis Patrum Graecorum, Supplementum.* Turnhout: Brepols, 1998.
Hornblower, S. and A. Spawforth, eds. *The Oxford Classical Dictionary*, 3rd ed. Oxford: Oxford University Press, 1996.
Lampe, G.W.H., ed. *A Patristic Greek Lexicon.* Oxford: Oxford University Press, 1961.
Lewis, C.T. and C. Short, eds. *A Latin Dictionary.* Oxford: Oxford University Press, 1963.
Liddell, H.G. and R. Scott, eds. *A Greek-English Lexicon*, 9th ed. Oxford, Oxford University Press, 1996.
Robinson, James M. and Richard Smith, eds. *The Nag Hammadi Library in English.* Leiden: Brill, 1996.
*Thesaurus linguae Graecae* (TLG) database (University of California, Irving: Packard Humanities Institute), http://www.tlg.uci.edu. 19 August 2013.
*Thesaurus Linguae Latinae.* Leipzig: Teubner, 1900–.

## B.3 Secondary Sources

Aageson, James W. *Paul, the Pastoral Epistles, and the Early Church*, Library of Pauline Studies. Peabody, Mass: Hendrickson, 2008.
Aland, Kurt, Beate Köster, and Michael Welte. *Kurzgefaßte Liste der griechischen Handschriften des Neuen Testament.* 2nd ed. Berlin: Walter de Gruyter, 1994.
Aletti, Jean-Noël. *Colossiens 1,15–20: Genre et exégèse du texte: fonction de la thématique sapientielle,* Analecta biblica 91. Rome: Pontifical Biblical Institute, 1981.
Aletti, Jean-Noël. *Saint Paul, Épître aux Éphésiens,* Etudes bibliques 42. Paris: J. Gabalda, 2001.
Alexander, Loveday. "The Acts of the Apostles as an Apologetic Text." In *Apologetics in the Roman Empire: Pagans, Jews, and Christians*, edited by Mark J. Edwards, Martin Goodman and Simon Price, 15–44. Oxford: Oxford University Press, 1999.
Anatolios, Khaled. *Athanasius.* London: Routledge, 2004.

Anderson, Graham. *Sage, Saint and Sophist: Holy Men and Their Associates in the Early Roman Empire*. London: Routledge, 1994.
Arnold, Clinton E. *Ephesians, Power and Magic: The Concept of Power in Ephesians in Light of Its Historical Setting*, Society for New Testament Monograph Series 63. Cambridge: Cambridge University Press, 1989.
Asher, Jeffrey R. *Polarity and Change in 1 Corinthians 15: A Study of Metaphysics, Rhetoric, and Resurrection*, Hermeneutische Untersuchungen zur Theologie 42. Tübingen: Mohr (Siebeck), 2000.
Ashwin-Siejkowski, Piotr. *Clement of Alexandria: A Project of Christian Perfection*. London: T&T Clark, 2008.
Attridge, Harold W., ed. *Nag Hammadi Codex 1 (the Jung Codex)*, Nag Hammadi Studies 22–23. Leiden: Brill, 1985.
Aulén, Gustaf. *Christus Victor: An Historical Study of the Three Main Types of the Idea of the Atonement*. Translated by A.G. Hebert. London: SPCK, 1931.
Aune, David E. "Romans as a Logos Protreptikos in the Context of Ancient Religious and Philosophical Propaganda." In *Paulus: Missionar und Theologe und das antike Judentum*, edited by M. Hengel and U. Heckel, 91–124. Tübingen: Mohr (Siebeck), 1991.
Bain, Andrew M. "Tertullian: Paul as Teacher of the Gentile Churches." In *Paul and the Second Century*, edited by Michael F. Bird and Joseph R. Dodson, 207–225. London: T&T Clark, 2011.
Bauckham, Richard. "The Ascension of Isaiah: Genre, Unity, and Date." In *The Fate of the Dead: Studies on the Jewish & Christian Apocalypses*, edited by Richard Bauckham, 363–390. Leiden: Brill, 1998.
Bauckham, Richard. *Jesus and the God of Israel: God Crucified and Other Studies on the New Testament's Christology of Divine Identity*. Grand Rapids, Mich: Eerdmans, 2008.
Bauckham, Richard. "The Throne of God and the Worship of Jesus." In *The Jewish Roots of Christological Monotheism: Papers from the St. Andrews Conference on the Historical Origins of the Worship of Jesus*, edited by Carey C. Newman, James R. Davila and Gladys S. Lewis, 43–69. Leiden: Brill, 1999.
Behr, John. *Asceticism and Anthropology in Irenaeus and Clement*, Oxford Early Christian Studies. Oxford: Oxford University Press, 2000.
Behr, John. "Irenaeus on the Word of God." In *Studia Patristica: Papers Presented at the 13th International Conference on Patristic Studies Held in Oxford 1999*, edited by Maurice F. Wiles and Edward Yarnold, 163–167. Leuven: Peeters, 2001.
Behr, John. *The Way to Nicaea*. Crestwood NY: St. Vladimir's Seminary Press, 2001.
Best, Ernest. *A Critical and Exegetical Commentary on Ephesians*, International Critical Commentary. Edinburgh: T&T Clark, 1998.
Bettiolo, Paolo, *et al.* eds. *Ascensio Isaiae. Textus*. Turnhout: Brepols, 1995.
Bird, Michael F. "The Reception of Paul in the *Epistle to Diognetus*." In *Paul and the Second Century*, edited by Michael F. Bird and Joseph R. Dodson, 70–90. London: T&T Clark, 2011.
Blackwell, Ben C. "Paul and Irenaeus." In *Paul and the Second Century*, edited by Michael F. Bird and Joseph R. Dodson, 190–206. London: T&T Clark, 2011.
Bockmuehl, Markus. *A Commentary on the Epistle to the Philippians*, Black's New Testament Commentaries. London: A&C Black, 1997.
Boersma, Hans. *Violence, Hospitality, and the Cross: Reappropriating the Atonement Tradition*. Grand Rapids, Mich: Baker Academic, 2006.

Boismard, M.-É. *L'énigme de la Lettre aux Éphésiens*, Etudes bibliques 39. Paris: J. Gabalda, 1999.
Bouteneff, Peter. *Beginnings: Ancient Christian Readings of the Biblical Creation Narratives.* Grand Rapids, Mich: Baker Academic, 2008.
Boxall, Ian. *Patmos in the Reception History of the Apocalypse.* Oxford: Oxford University Press, 2013.
Brakke, David. *Demons and the Making of the Monk: Spiritual Combat in Early Christianity.* Cambridge, Mass: Harvard University Press, 2006.
Brannon, M. Jeff. "'The Heavenlies' in Ephesians: A Lexical, Exegetical, and Conceptual Analysis." University of Edinburgh, 2010.
Bray, Gerard, ed. *1–2 Corinthians.* Edited by Thomas C. Oden and Christopher H. Hall, Ancient Christian Commentary on Scripture, NT7. Downers Grove, Ill: Intervarsity Press, 1999.
Bright, Pamela. "Origenian Understanding of Martyrdom and Its Biblical Framework." In *Origen of Alexandria: His World and His Legacy*, edited by Charles Kannengiesser and William L. Petersen, 180–199. Notre Dame, Ind: University of Notre Dame Press, 1988.
Brown, Alexandra. *The Cross and Human Transformation: Paul's Apocalyptic Word in 1 Corinthians.* Minneapolis: Fortress Press, 1995.
Brown, Peter. "The Rise and Function of the Holy Man in Late Antiquity." *Journal of Roman Studies* 61 (1971): 80–101.
Brown, Raymond E. *An Introduction to the New Testament*, Anchor Bible Reference Library. New York: Doubleday, 1997.
Bruce, F.F. *The Epistles to the Colossians, to Philemon, and to the Ephesians*, New International Commentary on the New Testament. Grand Rapids, Mich: Eerdmans, 1984.
Bruce, F.F. "St. Paul in Rome, Part 1." *Bulletin of the John Rylands University Library of Manchester* 46, no. 2 (1964): 326–345.
Buell, Denise Kimber. *Making Christians: Clement of Alexandria and the Rhetoric of Legitimacy.* Princeton, NJ: Princeton University Press, 1999.
Burnley, C.F. "Christ as the ARXH of Creation." *Journal of Theological Studies* 27 (1926): 160–177.
Bynum, Caroline Walker. *The Resurrection of the Body in Western Christianity, 200–1336.* New York: Columbia University Press, 1995.
Caird, George B. *Principalities and Powers: A Study in Pauline Theology.* Oxford: Clarendon Press, 1956.
Caragounis, Chrys C. *The Ephesian Mysterion: Meaning and Content*, Coniectanea biblica: New Testament Series 8. Lund: Gleerup, 1977.
Cargal, Timothy B. "Seated in the Heavenlies: Cosmic Mediators in the Mysteries of Mithras and the Letter to the Ephesians." In *Society of Biblical Literature Seminar Papers 1994*, edited by Eugene H. Lovering Jr., 804–821. Atlanta: Scholars Press, 1994.
Carleton Paget, James. "Marcion and the Resurrection: Some Thoughts on a Recent Book." *Journal for the Study of the New Testament* 35, no. 1 (2012): 74–102.
Carr, Wesley. *Angels and Principalities: The Background, Meaning, and Development of the Pauline Phrase Hai Archai Kai Hai Exousiai.* Cambridge: Cambridge University Press, 1981.
Cerfaux, Lucien. *Christ in the Theology of St. Paul.* Translated by Geoffrey Webb and Adrian Walker. New York: Herder & Herder, 1959.

Choat, Malcolm. "Echo and Quotation of the New Testament Papyrus Letters to the End of the 4th Century." In *New Testament Manuscripts: Their Texts and Their World*, edited by Thomas Kraus and Tobias Nicklas, 267–292. Leiden: Brill, 2006.

Christman, Angela Russell. *'What Did Ezekiel See?': Christian Exegesis of Ezekiel's Vision of the Chariot from Irenaeus to Gregory the Great*, The Bible in Ancient Christianity Series 4. Leiden: Brill, 2005.

Clark, Mary T. "Introduction." In *Theological Treatises on the Trinity*, 3–46. Ancient Christian Commentary on Scripture 10. Washington, DC: Catholic University of America Press, 1981.

Cocchini, Francesca. *Il Paolo di Origene: Contributo alla storia della recezione delle Epistole Paoline nel III secolo*, Verba Seniorum 11. Rome: Edizioni Studium, 1992.

Collins, John J. "The Sage in Apocalyptic and Pseudepigraphic Literature." In *The Sage in Israel and the Ancient near East*, edited by John G. Gammie and Leo G. Perdue, 343–354. Winona Lake: Eisenbrauns, 1990.

Conzelmann, Hans. *1 Corinthians*, Hermeneia. Philadelphia: Fortress Press, 1975.

Cribiore, Raffaella. *Gymnastics of the Mind: Greek Education in Hellenistic and Roman Egypt*. Princeton, NJ: Princeton University Press, 2001.

Cribiore, Raffaella. *Writing, Teachers, and Students in Graeco-Roman Egypt*. Atlanta: Scholars Press, 1996.

Crouzel, Henri. *Bibliographie Critique d'Origène*, Instrumenta Patristica 8. Steenbrugis: Abbatia s. Petri, 1971–.

Crouzel, Henri. "La doctrine origénienne du corps ressuscité." *Bulletin de littérature ecclésiastique* 31 (1980): 175–200.

Crouzel, Henri. "Les critiques adressées par Méthode et ses contemporains à la doctrine origénienne du corps ressuscité." *Gregorianum* 53 (1972): 679–695.

Crouzel, Henri. *Origen: The Life and Thought of the First Great Theologian*. Translated by A.S. Worrall. San Francisco: Harper & Row, 1989.

Cullman, Oscar. *Immortalité de l'âme ou Résurrection des Morts?* Neuchatel: Delachaux & Niestlé, 1956.

D'Angelo, Mary Rose "Colossians." In *Searching the Scriptures 2: A Feminist Commentary*, edited by Elisabeth Schüssler Fiorenza, 313–324. New York: Crossroad, 1993.

Daley, Brian. *The Hope of the Early Church: A Handbook of Patristic Eschatology*. 2nd ed. Grand Rapids, Mich: Baker Academic, 2010.

Daniélou, Jean. *A History of Early Christian Doctrine: The Origins of Latin Christianity*. Vol. 3. London: Darton, Longman & Todd, 1977.

Daniélou, Jean. *A History of Early Christian Doctrine: The Theology of Jewish Christianity*. Vol. I. London: Darton, Longman & Todd, 1964.

Dassmann, Ernst. *Der Stachel im Fleisch: Paulus in der frühchristlichen Literatur bis Irenäus*. Münster: Aschendorff, 1979.

Davis, James A. *Wisdom and Spirit: An Investigation of 1 Corinthians 1.18–3.20 against the Background of Jewish Sapiential Traditions in the Greco-Roman Period*. Lanham, Md: University Press of America, 1984.

de Boer, Martinus C. *The Defeat of Death: Apocalyptic Eschatology in 1 Corinthians 15 and Romans 5*, Journal for the Study of the New Testament: Supplement Series 22. Sheffield: JSOT Press, 1988.

de Margerie, Bertrand. *Introduction à L'histoire de l'exégèse*. Vol. 1–4, Initiations. Paris: Cerf, 1980–1990.

Dechow, Jon F. *Dogma and Mysticism in Early Christianity: Epiphanius of Cyprus and the Legacy of Origen*. Leuven: Peeters, 1988.

deLange, Nicholas R.M. *Origen and the Jews: Studies in Jewish-Christian Relations in Third-Century Palestine*, Cambridge Oriental Publications 25. Cambridge: Cambridge University Press, 1976.

Dodd, C.H. "The Mind of Paul: Change and Development." *Bulletin of the John Rylands University Library of Manchester* 18 (1934): 3–44.

Dundenberg, Ismo. *Beyond Gnosticism: Myth, Lifestyle, and Society in the School of Valentinus*. New York: Columbia University Press, 2008.

Dundenberg, Ismo. "The School of Valentinus." In *A Companion to Second Century Christian Heretics*, edited by Antti Marjanen and Petri Luomanen, 64–99. Leiden: Brill, 2005.

Dunn, James D. G. *1 Corinthians*, New Testament Guides. Sheffield: Sheffield Academic Press, 1995.

Dunn, James D. G. *The Epistles to the Colossians and to Philemon: A Commentary on the Greek Text*. Grand Rapids, Mich: Eerdmans, 1996.

Dunn, James D. G. *The Theology of Paul the Apostle*. Edinburgh: T&T Clark, 1998.

Dunne, John Anthony. "The Regal Status of Christ in the Colossian 'Christ-Hymn': A Re-Evaluation of the Influence of Wisdom Traditions." *Trinity Journal* 32NS (2011): 3–18.

Eden, Kathy. *Hermeneutics and the Rhetorical Tradition: Chapters in Ancient Legacy and Its Humanist Reception*. New Haven: Yale University Press, 1997.

Edmonds, Hilarius. "Geistlicher Kriegsdienst: Der Topos der *Militia Spiritualis* in der antiken Philosophie." In *Militia Christi: Die christliche Religion und der Soldatenstand in den ersten drei Jahrhunderten*, edited by Adolf Harnack, 133–162. Darmstadt: Wissenschaftliche Buchgesellschaft, 1963.

Edsall, Benjamin and Jennifer R. Strawbridge "The Songs we Used to Sing? Hymn 'Traditions' and Reception in Pauline Letters," *Journal for the Study of the New Testament* 37.3 (2015), 290–311.

Edwards, Mark J., ed. *Galatians, Ephesians, Philippians*, Ancient Christian Commentary Series NT8. Downers Grove, Ill: Intervarsity Press, 1999.

Edwards, Mark J. "Origen's Two Resurrections." *Journal of Theological Studies* 46, no. 2 (1995): 502–518.

Edwards, Mark J. *Origen against Plato*. Aldershot: Ashgate, 2002.

Edwards, Mark J., Martin Goodman, and Simon Price, eds. *Apologetics in the Roman Empire: Pagans, Christians, and Jews*. Oxford: Oxford University Press, 1999.

Edwards, Mark J., Martin Goodman, Simon Price, and Christopher Rowland. "Introduction: Apologetics in the Roman World." In *Apologetics in the Roman Empire: Pagans, Jews, and Christians*, edited by Mark J. Edwards, Martin Goodman and Simon Price, 1–14. Oxford: Oxford University Press, 1999.

Edwards, Richard A., and Robert A. Wild, eds. The Sentences of Sextus, *Text and Translations*, Early Christian Literature Series 5. Chico, Calif: Scholars Press, 1981.

Ehrman, Bart D. *Lost Christianities: The Battles for Scripture and the Faiths We Never Knew*. Oxford: Oxford University Press, 2003.

Ehrman, Bart D. "The Use and Significance of Patristic Evidence for NT Textual Criticism." In *New Testament Textual Criticism, Exegesis, and Early Church History*, edited by Barbara Aland and Joël Delobel, 118–135. Contributions to Biblical Exegesis & Theology 7. Kampen: Kok Pharos, 1995.

Ellis, E.E. *Prophecy and Heremeneutic in Early Christianity.* Grand Rapids, Mich: Eerdmans, 1978.
Epp, Eldon J. "The New Testament Papyrus Manuscripts in Historical Perspective." In *To Touch the Text: Biblical and Related Studies in Honor of Joseph A. Fitzmyer, SJ*, edited by Maurya P. Horgan and Paul J. Kobelski, 261–288. New York: Crossroad Publishing, 1989.
Erdkamp, Paul, ed. *A Companion to the Roman Army.* Oxford: Blackwell, 2011.
Evans, Ernest. *Tertullian's Treatise against Praxeas.* London: SPCK, 1948.
Fee, Gordon D. *The First Epistle to the Corinthians*, New International Commentary on the New Testament. Grand Rapids, Mich: Eerdmans, 1987.
Ferguson, Everett. *Baptism in the Early Church: History, Theology, and Liturgy in the First Five Centuries.* Grand Rapids, Mich: Eerdmans, 2009.
Ferguson, Everett. "Tertullian." In *Early Christian Thinkers: The Lives and Legacies of Twelve Key Figures*, edited by Paul Foster, 85–99. Downers Grove, Ill: Intervarsity Press, 2011.
Ferguson, John. *Clement of Alexandria.* New York: Twayne Publishers, 1974.
Ferguson, T.C.K. "The Rule of Truth and Irenaean Rhetoric in Book 1 of *Against Heresies*." *Vigiliae christianae* 55 (2001): 356–375.
Fitzmyer, Joseph A. *First Corinthians*, Anchor Bible. New Haven: Yale University Press, 2008.
Florowsky, G. "Eschatology in the Patristic Age: An Introduction." In *Studia Patristica I: Texte und Untersuchungen zur Geschichte der altchristlichen Literatur*, 2:235–250. Berlin: Akademie, 1957.
Fossum, Jarl E. "Colossians 1.15–18a in the Light of Jewish Mysticism and Gnosticism." *New Testament Studies* 35 (1989): 183–201.
Fossum, Jarl E. *The Image of the Invisible God: Essays on the Influence of Jewish Mysticism on Early Christology*, Novum Testamentum et Orbis Antiques 30. Göttingen: Vandenhoeck & Ruprecht, 1995.
Fossum, Jarl E. "Jewish-Christian Christology and Jewish Mysticism." *Vigiliae christianae* 37 (1983): 260–287.
Fossum, Jarl E. *The Name of God and the Angel of the Lord: Samaritan and Jewish Concepts of Intermediation and the Origin of Gnosticism*, Wissenschaftliche Untersuchungen zum Neuen Testament 36. Tübingen: Mohr (Siebeck), 1985.
Foster, Paul. "Polymorphic Christology: Its Origins and Development in Early Christianity." *Journal of Theological Studies* 38, no. 1 (2007): 66–99.
Fraade, Steven D. "The Early Rabbinic Sage." In *The Sage in Israel and the Ancient near East*, edited by John G. Gammie and Leo G. Perdue, 417–436. Winona Lake: Eisenbrauns, 1990.
Froehlich, Karlfried. *Biblical Interpretation in the Early Church*, Sources of Early Christian Thought. Philadelphia: Fortress Press, 1984.
Gaca, Kathy L., and L.L. Welborn. *Early Patristic Readings of Romans.* New York: T&T Clark, 2005.
Gadamer, Hans-Georg. *Truth and Method.* Translated by Joel Weinsheimer and Donald G. Marshall. 2nd ed. London: Continuum, 2004.
Gaffin Jr., R.B. "Some Epistemological Reflections on 1 Corinthians 2.6–16." *Westminster Theological Journal* 57 (1995): 103–124.
Gamble, Harry. *Books and Readers in the Early Church: A History of Early Christian Texts.* New Haven: Yale University Press, 1995.
Gibbs, John G. *Creation and Redemption: A Study in Pauline Theology.* Leiden: Brill, 1971.

Gorday, Peter, ed. *Colossians, 1–2 Thessalonians, 1–2 Timothy, Titus, Philemon*, Ancient Christian Commentary Series NT9. Downers Grove, Ill: Intervarsity Press, 2000.

Gorday, Peter. "Paulus Origenianus: The Economic Interpretation of Paul in Origen and Gregory of Nyssa." In *Paul and the Legacies of Paul*, edited by William S. Babcock, 141–163. Dallas: Southern Methodist University Press, 1990.

Gordley, Matthew E. *Teaching through Song in Antiquity: Didactic Hymnody among Greeks, Romans, Jews, and Christians*, Wissenschaftliche Untersuchungen zum Neues Testament 2.302. Tübingen: Mohr (Siebeck), 2011.

Goulder, Michael. "Ignatius' 'Docetists'." *Vigiliae christianae* 53, no. 1 (1999): 16–30.

Grant, Robert M. *The Greek Apologists of the Second Century*. Philadelphia: Westminster, 1988.

Grant, Robert M. *Irenaeus of Lyons*. London: Routledge, 1997.

Grant, Robert M. *Jesus after the Gospels: The Christ of the Second Century*. London: SCM, 1990.

Grant, Robert M. "The Mystery of Marriage in the Gospel of Philip." *Vigiliae christianae* 15 (1961): 129–140.

Grant, Robert M. *A Short History of the Interpretation of the Bible*. London: SCM Press, 1984.

Greer, Rowan A. "Applying the Framework." In *Early Biblical Interpretation*, edited by James L. Kugel and Rowan A. Greer, 177–199. Philadelphia: The Westminster Press, 1986.

Greer, Rowan A. "A Framework for Interpreting a Christian Bible." In *Early Biblical Interpretation*, edited by James L. Kugel and Rowan A. Greer, 155–176. Philadelphia: The Westminster Press, 1986.

Gregg, Robert C., and Dennis Groh. *Early Arianism: A View of Salvation*. London: SCM Press, 1981.

Gregory, Andrew, and C. M. Tuckett. "Reflections on Method: What Constitutes the Use of the Writings That Later Formed the New Testament in the Apostolic Fathers?" In *The New Testament and the Apostolic Fathers: The Reception of the New Testament in the Apostolic Fathers*, edited by Andrew Gregory and Christopher M. Tuckett, 61–82. Oxford: Oxford University Press, 2005.

Grillmeier, Alois. *Christ in Christian Tradition: From the Apostolic Age to Chalcedon (451)*. Translated by John Bowden. London: Mowbray, 1965.

Haines-Eitzen, Kim. *Guardian of Letters: Literacy, Power and the Transmitters of Early Christian Literature*. Oxford: Oxford University Press, 2000.

Hallström, Gunnar af. *Carnis Resurrectio: The Interpretation of a Credal Formula*, Commentationes Humanarum Litterarum 86. Helsinki: Societas Scientiarum Fennica, 1988.

Harnack, Adolf. *Militia Christi: The Christian Religion and the Military in the First Three Centuries*. Translated by David McInnes Gracie. Philadelphia: Fortress Press, 1981.

Harris, Bruce F. "Biblical Echoes and Reminiscences in Christian Papyri." In *Proceedings of the XIV International Congress of Papyrologists, Oxford 24–31, July, 1974*, edited by International Congress of Papyrologists, 155–160. London: Egypt Exploration Society, 1975.

Harris III, W. Hall. "'The Heavenlies' Reconsidered: Οὐρανός and Ἐπουράνιος in Ephesians." *Bibliotheca sacra* 148 (1991): 72–89.

Harrisville, Roy A. *1 Corinthians*, Augsburg Commentaries on the New Testament. Minneapolis: Augsburg, 1987.

Hauser, Alan J., and Duane F. Watson, eds. *A History of Biblical Interpretation. Vol. 1: The Ancient Period*. Grand Rapids, Mich: Eerdmans, 2003.

Hays, Richard B. *Echoes of Scripture in the Letters of Paul*. New Haven: Yale University Press, 1989.

Hays, Richard B. *First Corinthians*, Interpretation: A Bible Commentary for Teaching and Preaching. Louisville, Ky: John Knox Press, 1997.

Heine, Ronald E. "Cyprian and Novatian." In *The Cambridge History of Early Christian Literature*, edited by Frances M. Young, Lewis Ayers and Andrew Louth, 152–160. Cambridge: Cambridge University Press, 2004.

Helmbold, William, and Edward O'Neil. *Plutarch's Quotations*, Philological Monographs 19. Baltimore, Md: American Philological Association, 1959.

Hengel, Martin. *The Son of God: The Origin of Christology and the History of Jewish-Hellenistic Religion*. London: SCM Press, 1976.

Hengel, Martin. *Studies in the Gospel of Mark*. Translated by John Bowden. Eugene, Ore: Wipf & Stock, 2003.

Hermann, Arnold. *To Think Like God: Pythagoras and Parmenides, the Origins of Philosophy*. Las Vegas: Parmenides Publishing, 2004.

Hill, Charles. *Regnum Caelorum: Patterns of Future Hope in Early Christianity*. Oxford: Clarendon, 1992.

Hoehner, Harold W. *Ephesians: An Exegetical Commentary*. Grand Rapids, Mich: Baker Academic, 2002.

Hoffmann, Daniel. "Ignatius and Early Anti-Docetic Realism in the Eucharist." *Fides et Historia* 30 (1998): 74–88.

Holsinger-Friesen, Thomas. *Irenaeus and Genesis: A Study of Competition in Early Christian Hermeneutics*, Journal of Theological Interpretation Supplement 1. Winona Lake, Ind: Eisenbrauns, 2009.

Hopkins, Keith. "Christian Number and Its Implications." *Journal of Early Christian Studies* 6 (1998): 185–226.

Horsley, R.A. "Pneumatikos Vs. Psychikos: Distinctions of Spiritual Status among the Corinthians." *Harvard Theological Review* 69 (1976): 269–288.

Humphries, Mark. "Material Evidence (1): Archaeology." In *The Oxford Handbook of Early Christian Studies*, edited by Susan Ashbrook Harvey and David G. Hunter, 87–103. Oxford: Oxford University Press, 2008.

Hunt, Emily J. *Christianity in the Second Century: The Case of Tatian*, Routledge Early Christian Monographs. New York: Routledge, 2003.

Hurtado, Larry W. "Christology, NT." In *New Interpreters' Dictionary of the Bible*, edited by Katharine Doob Sakenfeld, 612–622. Nashville, Tenn: Abingdon Press, 2009.

Hurtado, Larry W. *The Earliest Christian Artifacts: Manuscripts and Christian Origins*. Grand Rapids, Mich: Eerdmans, 2006.

Hurtado, Larry W. "Early Christian Manuscripts as Artifacts." In *Jewish and Christian Scripture as Artifact and Canon*, edited by Craig A. Evans and H. Daniel Zacharias, 66–81. London: T&T Clark, 2009.

Isenberg, Wesley W. "Gospel According to Philip." In *Nag Hammadi Codex Ii, 2–7: Together with Xiii, 2\*, Brit. Lib. Or.4926 (1), and P.Oxy.1, 654, 655*, edited by Bentley Layton. Leiden: Brill, 1989.

Ivánka, Endre von. *Plato Christianus: La réception critique cu platonisme chez les Pères de l'Eglise*. Revised ed, Théologiques. Paris: Presses universitaires de France, 1990.

Jaeger, H. "The Patristic Conception of Wisdom in the Light of Biblical and Rabbinical Research." *Studia Patristica* IV, no. 79 (1961): 90–106.
Jensen, Robin M. *Baptismal Imagery in Early Christianity: Ritual, Visual, and Theological Dimensions*. Grand Rapids, Mich: Baker Academic, 2012.
Johnson, L.T., and W.S. Kurz, SJ. *The Future of Catholic Biblical Scholarship: A Constructive Conversation*. Grand Rapids, Mich: Eerdmans, 2002.
Jost, Walter, and Wendy Olmsted. "Introduction." In *A Companion to Rhetoric and Rhetorical Criticism*, edited by Walter Jost and Wendy Olmsted, xv–xvi. Malden, Mass: Blackwell, 2003.
Kannengiesser, Charles. *Athanase d'Alexandrie, Évêque et Écrivain. Une Lecture des Traités contre les Ariens*. Paris: Beauchesne, 1983.
Kannengiesser, Charles. *Handbook of Patristic Exegesis: The Bible in Ancient Christianity, Fathers of the Church* 1–2. Leiden: Brill, 2003.
Karavites, Peter. *Evil, Freedom, and the Road to Perfection in Clement of Alexandria*. Leiden: Brill, 1999.
Karpp, Heinrich. *Probleme altchristlicher Anthropologie: Biblische Anthropologie und philosophische Psychologie bei den Kirchenvätern des dritten Jahrhunderts*, Belträge zur Förderung christlicher Theologie 44. Gütersloh: C.Bertelsmann, 1950.
Käsemann, Ernst. "Epheserbrief." In *Die Religion in Geschichte und Gegenwart: Handwörterbuch für Theologie und Religionswissenschaft*, edited by Hans von Campenhausen, 517–520. Tübingen: Mohr, 1958.
Käsemann, Ernst. "A Primitive Christian Baptismal Liturgy." In *Essays on New Testament Themes*, edited by Ernst Käsemann, 149–168. London: SCM, 1964.
Käsemann, Ernst. "Eine urchristliche Tauflilturgie." In *Exegetische Versuche und Besinnungen*. vol. 1, 34–51. Göttingen: Vandenhoeck & Ruprecht, 1960.
Keck, Leander E. "Is the New Testament a Field of Study? Or, from Outler to Overbeck and Back." *The Second Century* 1 (1981): 19–35.
Keener, Craig S. *1–2 Corinthians*, New Cambridge Bible Commentary Series. Cambridge: Cambridge University Press, 2005.
Kehl, Von N. "Erniedrigung und Erhöhung in Qumran und Kolossä." *Zeitschrift für katholische Theologie* 91 (1969): 364–394.
Kennedy, G. *The Art of Rhetoric in the Roman World, 300 B.C.-A.D. 300*. Princeton, NJ: Princeton University Press, 1972.
Kerferd, George B. "The Sage in Hellenistic Philosophical Literature." In *The Sage in Israel and the Ancient near East*, edited by John G. Gammie and Leo G. Perdue, 321–328. Winona Lake: Eisenbrauns, 1990.
King, Karen L. *What Is Gnosticism?* Cambridge, Mass: Belknap Press of Harvard University Press, 2003.
Kirk, G.S., J.E. Raven, and Malcolm Schofield. *The Presocratic Philosophers: A Critical History with a Selection of Texts*. 2nd ed. Cambridge: Cambridge University Press, 1983.
Kitchen, Martin. *Ephesians*. London: Routledge, 1994.
Knight, Jonathan. *Christian Origins*. London: T&T Clark, 2009.
Knight, Jonathan. *Disciples of the Beloved One: The Christology, Social Setting and Theological Context of the Ascension of Isaiah*, Journal for the Study of the Pseudepigrapha: Supplement Series 18. Sheffield: Sheffield Academic Press, 1996.

Knight, Jonathan. "The Origin and Significance of the Angelomorphic Christology in the *Ascension of Isaiah*." *Journal of Theological Studies (new series)* 63, no. 1 (2012): 66–105.

Knox, Wilfrid L. *St. Paul and the Church of the Gentiles*. Cambridge: Cambridge University Press, 1939.

Koch, Dietrich-Alex. *Die Schrift als Zeuge des Evangeliums: Untersuchungen zur Verwendung und zum Verständnis der Schrift bei Paulus*. Gutenberg: Universität Mainz, 1986.

Kolping, Adolf. *Sacramentum Tertullianeum: Erster Teil*. Regensberg: Münster, 1948.

Kovacs, Judith. "1 Corinthians." In *The Oxford Handbook of the Reception History of the Bible*, edited by Michael Lieb, Emma Mason and Jonathan Roberts, 136–148. Oxford: Oxford University Press, 2011.

Kovacs, Judith, ed. *1 Corinthians: Interpreted by Early Christian Commentators*, Early Christian Commentary Series. Grand Rapids, Mich: Eerdmans, 2005.

Kovacs, Judith. "The Archons, the Spirit, and the Death of Christ: Do We Need the Hypothesis of Gnostic Opponents to Explain 1 Cor. 2.6–16?" In *Apocalyptic and the New Testament: Essays in Honour of J. Louis Martyn*, edited by Joel Marcus and Marion Soards, 217–236. Sheffield: Sheffield Academic Press, 1989.

Kovacs, Judith. "Clement of Alexandria." In *Early Christian Thinkers: The Lives and Legacies of Twelve Key Figures*, edited by Paul Foster, 68–84. Downers Grove, Ill: Intervarsity Press, 2010.

Kovacs, Judith. "Divine Pedagogy and the Gnostic Teacher According to Clement of Alexandria." *Journal of Early Christian Studies* 9 (2001): 3–25.

Kovacs, Judith. "Echoes of Valentinian Exegesis in Clement of Alexandria and Origen: The Interpretation of 1 Corinthians 3.1–3." In *Origeniana Octava: Origen and the Alexandrian Tradition: Papers of the 8th International Origen Congress, Pisa, 27–31 August 2001*, edited by Lorenzo Perrone, 317–329. Leuven: Peeters, 2004.

Kovacs, Judith. "Saint Paul as Apostle of *Apatheia*: Stromateis VII, Chapter 14." In *The Seventh Book of the Stromateis: Proceedings of the Colloquium on Clement of Alexandria (Olomouc, October 21–23, 2010)*, edited by Matyáš Havrda, Vít Hušek, and Jana Plátová, 199–216. Leiden: Brill, 2012.

Kovacs, Judith. "Servant of Christ and Steward of the Mysteries of God." In *In Dominico Eloquio, in Lordly Eloquence: Essays on Patristic Exegesis in Honour of Robert Louis Wilken*, edited by Paul M. Blowers, Angela Russell Christman, David E. Hunter and Robin Darling Young, 147–171. Grand Rapids, Mich: Eerdmans, 2002.

Krentz, Edgar. "Paul, Games, and the Military." In *Paul in the Greco-Roman World: A Handbook*, edited by J. Paul Sampley, 344–383. Harrisburg, Pa: Trinity Press International, 2003.

Kuhn, Heinz-Wolfgang. "The Wisdom Passage in 1 Corinthians 2.6–16 between Qumran and Proto-Gnosticism." In *Sapiential, Liturgical, and Poetical Texts from Qumran: Proceedings of the Third Meeting of the International Organization for Qumran Studies, Oslo 1998*, edited by Daniel K. Falk, Florentino García Martínez and Eileen M. Schuller, 240–253. Leiden: Brill, 2000.

Ladner, Gerhard B. *The Idea of Reform: Its Impact on Christian Thought and Action in the Age of the Fathers*. Cambridge, Mass: Harvard University Press, 1959.

Lähnemann, Johannes. *Der Kolosserbrief: Komposition, Situation und Argumentation*. Gütersloh: Gütersloher Verlagshaus Gerd Mohn, 1971.

Lang, Friedrich. *Die Briefe an die Korinther.* 2nd ed, Texte zum Neuen Testament. Göttingen: Vandenhoeck & Ruprecht, 1994.

Layton, Bentley, ed. *The Gnostic Scriptures: A New Translation with Annotations and Introductions*, Anchor Bible Reference Library. New York: Doubleday, 1995.

Layton, Bentley. *The Gnostic Treatise on Resurrection from Nag Hammadi.* Atlanta: Scholars Press, 1979.

Layton, Bentley. "Vision and Revision: A Gnostic View of Resurrection." In *Colloque International sur les textes de Nag Hammadi*, edited by Bernard Barc, 190–217. Quebec: Les Presses de l'Université Laval, 1981.

Lehtipuu, Outi. "'Flesh and Blood Cannot Inherit the Kingdom of God:' The Transformation of the Flesh in the Early Christian Debates Concerning Resurrection." In *Metamorphoses: Resurrection, Body and Transformative Practices in Early Christianity*, edited by Turid Karlsen Seim and Jorunn Økland, 147–168. Berlin: Walter de Gruyter, 2009.

Lemaire, André. "The Sage in School and Temple." In *The Sage in Israel and the Ancient near East*, edited by John G. Gammie and Leo G. Perdue, 165–181. Winona Lake: Eisenbrauns, 1990.

Lightfoot, Joseph Barber. *Saint Paul's Epistles to the Colossians and to Philemon: A Revised Text with Introductions, Notes, and Dissertations.* 9th ed. London: Macmillan, 1890.

Lilla, Salvatore. *Clement of Alexandria: A Study in Christian Platonism and Gnosticism.* Oxford: Oxford University Press, 1971.

Lincoln, Andrew T. *Ephesians*, Word Biblical Commentary 42. Dallas, TX: Word Books, 1990.

Lincoln, Andrew T. "The Letter to the Colossians." In *The New Interpreter's Bible*, 551–669. Nashville, Tenn: Abingdon Press, 2000.

Lincoln, Andrew T. *Paradise Now and Not Yet: Studies in the Role of the Heavenly Dimension in Paul's Thought with Special Reference to His Eschatology*, Society of New Testament Studies 43. Cambridge: Cambridge University Press, 1981.

Lincoln, Andrew T. "A Re-Examination of "the Heavenlies" in Ephesians." *New Testament Studies* 19 (1973): 468–483.

Lindemann, Andreas. *Der erste Korintherbrief*, Handbuch zum Neuen Testament 9/1. Tübingen: Mohr (Siebeck), 2000.

Lindemann, Andreas. *Paulus, Apostel und Lehrer der Kirche.* Tübingen: Mohr (Siebeck), 1999.

Lindemann, Andreas. *Paulus im ältesten Christentum: D. Bild d. Apostels u. d. Rezeption d. paulin. Theologie in d. frühchristl. Theologie bis Marcion*, Beiträge zur historischen Theologie 58. Tübingen: Mohr, 1979.

Litfin, A. Duane. *St Paul's Theology of Proclamation: 1 Corinthians 1–4 and Greco-Roman Rhetoric*, Society for New Testament Studies Monograph Series. Cambridge: Cambridge University Press, 1994.

Llewelyn, Stephen R. *New Documents Illustrating Early Christianity: A Review of the Greek Inscriptions and Papyri Published in 1982–1983.* Vol. 7. North Ryde, N.S.W.: Ancient History Documentary Research Centre of Macquarie University, 1994.

Lohse, Eduard. *Colossians and Philemon: A Commentary on the Epistles to the Colossians and to Philemon.* Edited by Helmut Koester, Hermenia. Philadelphia: Fortress Press, 1971.

Lona, Horacio E. *Die Eschatologie im Kolosser– und Epheserbrief.* Würzburg: Echter Verlag, 1984.

Longenecker, Richard. *Biblical Exegesis in the Apostolic Period.* 2nd ed. Grand Rapids, Mich: Eerdmans, 1999.

Lorenz, Rudolf. *Arius Judaizans? Untersuchungen zur dogmengeschichtlichen Einordnung des Arius.* Göttingen: Vandenhoeck & Ruprecht, 1979.
Luijendijk, AnneMarie. *Greetings in the Lord: Early Christians and the Oxyrhynchus Papyri*, Harvard Theological Studies 60. Cambridge, Mass: Harvard University Press, 2008.
Lyman, Rebecca. *Christology and Cosmology: Models of Divine Activity in Origen, Eusebius, and Athanasius.* Oxford: Clarendon Press, 1993.
MacDonald, Lee Martin. *The Origin of the Bible: A Guide for the Perplexed.* London: T&T Clark, 2011.
MacMullen, Ramsay. *Soldier and Civilian in the Later Roman Empire*, Harvard Historical Monographs 52. Cambridge, Mass: Harvard University Press, 1963.
MacRae, G.W. "Why the Church Rejected Gnosticism." In *Jewish and Christian Self-Definition*, edited by E.P. Sanders, Albert I. Baumgarten, Alan Mendelson and Ben F. Meyer, 126–133. London: SCM Press, 1980–1982.
Malherbe, Abraham J. *The Cynic Epistles: A Study Edition*, Society for Biblical Study 12. Missoula, Mont: Scholars Press for SBL, 1977.
Martin, Dale B. *The Corinthian Body.* New Haven: Yale University Press, 1995.
Martin, Dale B. *Inventing Superstition: From the Hippocratics to the Christians.* Cambridge, Mass: Harvard University Press, 2004.
Martin, Ralph P. *Carmen Christi: Philippians 2.5–11 in Recent Interpretation and in the Setting of Early Christian Worship.* Cambridge: Cambridge University Press, 1967.
Mazzucco, Clementina. "Il millenarismo cristiano delle Origini (II–III Sec.)." In *Millennium: L'attesa della fine nei primi secoli cristiani. Atti delle III giornate patristiche torinesi*, edited by Renato Uglione, 145–182. Turin: CELID Editrice, 2002.
McGough, Michael E. "An Investigation of ʼEÔYPANIO῀ uin Ephesians." PhD Diss, New Orleans Baptist Theological Seminary, 1987.
McGuckin, John Anthony. "Recent Biblical Hermeneutics in Patristic Perspective: The Tradition of Orthodoxy." *Greek Orthodox Theological Review* 47.1–4 (2002), 295–326.
McKim, Donald K. *Historical Handbook of Major Biblical Interpreters.* Downers Grove, Ill: InterVarsity Press, 1998.
Metzger, Bruce. *Manuscripts of the Greek Bible: An Introduction to Greek Palaeography.* New York: Oxford University Press, 1981.
Minns, Denis. "Irenaeus." In *Early Christian Thinkers: The Lives and Legacies of Twelve Key Figures*, edited by Paul Foster, 36–51. Downers Grove, Ill: Intervarsity Press, 2010.
Mitchell, Margaret M. *Paul and the Rhetoric of Reconciliation: An Exegetical Investigation of the Language of Composition of 1 Corinthians*, Hermeneutische Untersuchungen zur Theologie 28. Tübingen: Mohr (Siebeck), 1991.
Mitchell, Margaret M. *Paul, the Corinthians, and the Birth of Christian Hermeneutics.* Cambridge: Cambridge University Press, 2010.
Mitchell, Margaret M. "Rhetorical Handbooks in Service of Biblical Exegesis: Eustanthius of Antioch Takes Origen Back to School." In *The New Testament and Early Christian Literature in Greco-Roman Context: Studies in Honor of David E. Aune*, edited by John Fotopoulos, 350–367. Leiden: Brill, 2006.
Mohrmann, Christine. "*Sacramentum* dans les plus anciens textes chrétiens." *Harvard Theological Review* 47 (1954): 141–152.
Morgan, Robert. "Jesus Christ, the Wisdom of God (2)." In *Reading Texts, Seeking Wisdom: Scripture and Theology*, edited by David Ford and Graham Stanton, 22–37. London: SCM Press, 2003.

Morgan, Teresa. *Literate Education in the Hellenistic and Roman Worlds*. Cambridge: Cambridge University Press, 1998.

Morgan, Teresa. *Popular Morality in the Early Roman Empire*. Cambridge: Cambridge University Press, 2007.

Moritz, Thorsten. *A Profound Mystery: The Use of the Old Testament in Ephesians*. Leiden: Brill, 1966.

Moss, Candida. *The Other Christs: Imitating Jesus in Ancient Christian Ideologies of Martyrdom*. New York: Oxford University Press, 2010.

Moule, C. F. D. *The Epistles to Colossians and to Philemon*. Cambridge: Cambridge University Press, 1957.

Moule, C. F. D. "St Paul and Dualism: The Pauline Conception of Resurrection." *New Testament Studies* 12, no. 2 (1966): 106–123.

Muddiman, John. *A Commentary on the Epistle to the Ephesians*, Black's New Testament Commentaries. London: Continuum, 2001.

Müller, C. Detlef G. "The Ascension of Isaiah." In *New Testament Apocrypha*, edited by Wilhelm Schneemelcher and R. McL Wilson, 603–620. Cambridge: Clarke, 1991.

Murphy, Roland. "Israel's Wisdom: Dialogue between the Sages." In *Light in a Spotless Mirror: Reflections on Wisdom Traditions in Judaism and Early Christianity*, edited by James H. Charlesworth and Michael A. Daise, 7–25. London: Trinity Press International, 2003.

Murphy-O'Connor, Jerome. "Interpolations in 1 Corinthians." *Catholic Biblical Quarterly* 48 (1986): 81–84.

Murphy-O'Connor, Jerome. "Who Wrote Ephesians?" *The Bible Today* 8 (1965): 1201–1209.

Murray-Jones, C. "Paradise Revisited (2 Cor 12.1–12)." *Harvard Theological Review* 86 (1993): 265–292.

Musurillo, Herbert. *The Acts of the Christian Martyrs: Introduction, Texts, and Translations*, Oxford Early Christian Texts. Oxford: Clarendon Press, 1972.

Myllykoski, Matti. "Wild Beasts and Rabid Dogs: The Riddle of the Heretics in the Letters of Ignatius." In *The Formation of the Early Church*, edited by Jostein Ådna, 341–377. Tübingen: Mohr (Siebeck), 2005.

Naldini, Mario. *Il Cristianesimo in Egitto: Lettere private nei papyri de secoli II–IV. Nuova edizione ampliata e aggiornata*. Fiesole: Nardini Editore, 1998.

Neufeld, Thomas R. *"Put on the Armour of God": The Divine Warrior from Isaiah to Ephesians*. Sheffield: Sheffield Academic Press, 1997.

Nickelsburg, George W.E. *Resurrection, Immortality, and Eternal Life in Intertestamental Judaism and Early Christianity*. 2nd ed, Harvard Theological Studies 56. Cambridge, Mass: Harvard University Press, 2006.

Nielsen, Charles Merritt. "The Epistle to Diognetus: Its Date and Relationship to Marcion." *Anglican Theological Review* 52 (1970): 77–91.

Noormann, Rolf. *Irenäus als Paulusinterpret: Zur Rezeption und Wirkung der paulinischen und deuteropaulinischen Briefe im Werk des Irenäus von Lyon*, Wissenschaftliche Untersuchungen zum Neuen Testament 2.66. Tübingen: Mohr (Siebeck), 1994.

Norden, Eduard. *Agnostos Theos: Untersuchungen zur Formengeschichte religiöser Rede*. Stuttgart: B.G. Teubner, 1971.

Norelli, Enrico, ed. *Ascensio Isaiae: Commentarius*, Corpus Christianorum, Series Apocryphorum 8. Turnhout: Brepols, 1995.

Norris, Richard. "The Apologists." In *The Cambridge History of Early Christian Literature*, edited by Frances M. Young, Lewis Ayers and Andrew Louth, 36–44. Cambridge: Cambridge University Press, 2004.

Norris, Richard. "Irenaeus' Use of Paul in His Polemic against the Gnostics." In *Paul and the Legacies of Paul*, edited by William S. Babcock, 79–98. Dallas: Southern Methodist University Press, 1990.

O'Boyle, Aidan. *Towards a Contemporary Wisdom Christology: Some Catholic Christologies in German, English, and French 1965–1995*. Vatican City: Gregorian Biblical Institute, 2003.

O'Brien, Peter Thomas. *The Letter to the Ephesians*, Pillar New Testament Commentary Series. Grand Rapids, Mich: Eerdmans, 1999.

O'Donovan, Oliver, and Joan Lockwood O'Donovan, eds. *From Irenaeus to Grotius: A Sourcebook in Christian Political Thought*. Grand Rapids, Mich: Eerdmans, 1999.

O'Keefe, John J. "Scriptural Interpretation." In *The Westminster Handbook to Origen*, edited by John Anthony McGuckin, 193–197. Louisville, Ky: Westminster/John Knox, 2004.

Odeberg, H. *The View of the Universe in the Epistle to the Ephesians*. Lund: Gleerup, 1934.

Olson, Mark Jeffrey. *Irenaeus, the Valentinian Gnostics, and the Kingdom of God (A.H. Book V): The Debate About 1 Corinthians 15.50*. Lewiston, NY: Mellen Biblical Press, 1992.

Osborn, Eric Francis. "The Bible and Christian Morality in Clement of Alexandria." In *The Bible in Greek Christian Antiquity*, edited by Paul M. Blowers, 112–130. Notre Dame, Ind: University of Notre Dame Press, 1997.

Osborn, Eric Francis. *Tertullian, First Theologian of the West*. Cambridge: Cambridge University Press, 1997.

Outler, Albert C. "Methods and Aims in the Study of the Development of Catholic Christianity." *The Second Century* 1 (1981): 7–17.

Pagels, Elaine. *The Gnostic Paul: Gnostic Exegesis of the Pauline Letters*. Philadelphia: Trinity Press International, 1992.

Pagels, Elaine. "Ritual in the *Gospel of Philip*." In *The Nag Hammadi Library after Fifty Years, Proceedings of the 1995 Society of Biblical Literature Commemoration*, edited by J.D. Turner and A. McGuire, 280–291. Leiden: Brill, 1997.

Patterson, L. G. "Methodius, Origen, and the Arian Dispute." In *Studia Patristica*, edited by E.A. Livingstone, 912–923. Oxford: Pergamon Press, 1982.

Patterson, L. G. "Who Are the Opponents in Methodius' *De Resurrectione?*" In *Studia Patristics Vol XIX: Historica, Theologica, Gnostica, Biblica et Apocrypha*, edited by E.A. Livingstone, 221–229. Leuven: Peeters, 1989.

Pearson, B.A. *The Pneumatikos-Psychikos Terminology in 1 Corinthians: A Study in the Theology of the Corinthian Opponents of Paul and Its Relation to Gnosticism*, Society of Biblical Studies Dissertation Series 12. Missoula, Mont: Scholars Press, 1973.

Peel, Malcolm Lee. *The Epistle to Rheginos: A Valentinian Letter on the Resurrection*, New Testament Library. London: SCM, 1969.

Peppard, Michael. "'Poetry', 'Hymns' and 'Traditional Material' in New Testament Epistles or How to Do Things with Indentations," *Journal for the Study of the New Testament* 30.3 (2008): 319–342.

Perkins, Pheme. "Gnosticism and the Christian Bible." In *The Canon Debate*, edited by Lee Martin McDonald and James A. Sanders, 355–371. Peabody, Mass: Hendrickson, 2002.

Petersen, William L. "Patristic Biblical Quotations and Method: Four Changes to Lightfoot's Edition of *Second Clement*" In *Patristic and Text-Critical Studies: The Collected Essays of*

*William L. Petersen*, edited by Jan Kraus and Joseph Verheyden, 539–566. Leiden: Brill, 2012.
Playoust, Catherine. "'Written in the Book That I Prophesied Publicly': The Discernment of Apocalyptic Wisdom According to the *Ascension of Isaiah*." In *SBL Annual Meeting*. http://www.sbl-site.org/assets/pdfs/Playoust.pdf, 20 November 2006.
Pope, Martin R. "Studies in Pauline Vocabulary." *The Expository Times* 22 (1911): 552–554.
Porter, Stanley. "The Use of the Old Testament in the New Testament: A Brief Comment on Method and Terminology." In *Early Christian Interpretation of the Scriptures of Israel: Investigations and Proposals*, edited by Craig A. Evans and Jack T. Sanders, 79–97. Sheffield: Sheffield Academic Press, 1997.
Price, Simon. "Latin Christian Apologetics: Minucius Felix, Tertullian, and Cyprian." In *Apologetics in the Roman Empire: Pagans, Jews, and Christians*, edited by Mark J. Edwards, Martin Goodman and Simon Price, 105–130. Oxford: Oxford University Press, 1999.
Rajak, Tessa. "Talking at Trypho: Christian Apologetic as Anti-Judaism in Justin's *Dialogue with Trypho the Jew*." In *Apologetics in the Roman Empire: Pagans, Jews, and Christians*, edited by Mark J. Edwards, Martin Goodman and Simon Price, 59–80. Oxford: Oxford University Press, 1999.
Rankin, David. *From Clement to Origen: The Social and Historical Context of the Church Fathers*. Farnham: Ashgate, 2007.
Rankin, David. *Tertullian and the Church*. Cambridge: Cambridge University Press, 1995.
Reventlow, Henning Graf. *History of Biblical Interpretation*. Translated by Leo G. Perdue. 4 vols, Society for Biblical Study 50, 61–63. Leiden: Brill, 2010.
Rosen-Zvi, Ishay. *Demonic Desires: "Yetzer Hara" and the Problem of Evil in Late Antiquity*. Philadelphia: University of Pennsylvania Press, 2011.
Roukema, Riemer. "Origen's Interpretation of 1 Corinthians 15." In *Gelitten, Gestorben, Auferstanden: Passions- und Ostertraditionen im antiken Christentum*, edited by Tobias Nicklas, Andreas Merkt and Joseph Verheyden, 329–342. Tübingen: Mohr (Siebeck), 2010.
Roukema, Riemer. "Paulus' verhandeling over de opstanding. 1 Korintiërs 15." *Interpretation* 21, no. 2 (2013): 33–35.
Roukema, Riemer, and Saskia Deventer-Metz. *Jesus, Gnosis and Dogma*. London: T&T Clark, 2010.
Rowland, Christopher. *The Open Heaven: A Study of Apocalyptic in Judaism and Early Christianity*. London: SPCK, 1982.
Rowland, Christopher, and Christopher R. A. Morray-Jones. *The Mystery of God: Early Jewish Mysticism and the New Testament*. Leiden: Brill, 2009.
Sanders, Jack T. *The New Testament Christological Hymns: Their Historical Religious Background*. Cambridge: Cambridge University Press, 1971.
Sandnes, Karl Olav. *Belly and Body in the Pauline Epistles*, Society of New Testament Studies Monograph Series. Cambridge: Cambridge University Press, 2002.
Sandnes, Karl Olav. *The Challenge of Homer: School, Pagan Poets, and Early Christianity*, Library of New Testament Studies 400. London: T&T Clark, 2009.
Saxer, Victor. "The Influence of the Bible in Early Christian Martyrology." In *The Bible in Greek Christian Antiquity*, edited by Paul M. Blowers, 342–374. Notre Dame, Ind: University of Notre Dame Press, 1997.

Schencke, H.M. "Das Evangelium nach Philippus." In *Neutestamentliche Apokryphen in deutscher Übersetzung*, edited by Wilhelm Schneemelcher, 148–173. Tübingen: Mohr (Siebeck), 1987.

Schmid, Josef. *Der Epheserbrief des Apostels Paulus: Seine Adresse, Sprache und literarischen Beziehungen*, Biblische Studien (Freiburg) 22. Freiburg: Herder, 1928.

Schmithals, Walter. *Gnosticism in Corinth: An Investigation of the Letters to the Corinthians*. Nashville: Abingdon Press, 1971.

Schnackenburg, Rudolf. *Ephesians: A Commentary*. Edinburgh: T&T Clark, 1991.

Schoedel, William. "Philosophy and Rhetoric in the *Adversus Haereses* of Irenaeus." *Vigiliae christianae* 13 (1959): 22–32.

Schoedel, William. *Ignatius of Antioch: A Commentary on the Letters of Ignatius of Antioch*, Hermeneia. Philadelphia: Fortress Press, 1990.

Scott, Mark S.M. *Journey Back to God: Origen on the Problem of Evil*, American Academy of Religion Academy Series. New York: Oxford University Press, 2012.

Sedley, David. "Philosophical Allegiance in the Greco-Roman World." In *Philosophia Togata: Essays on Philosophy and Roman Society*, edited by Miriam Griffin and Jonathan Barnes, 97–119. Oxford: Clarendon Press, 1989.

Segal, Alan F. *Life after Death: A History of the Afterlife in the Religions of the West*. New York: Doubleday, 2004.

Segel, Alan F. *Paul the Convert*. New Haven: Yale University Press, 1990.

Segel, Alan F. *Two Powers in Heaven: Early Rabbinic Reports About Christianity and Gnosticism*, Studies in Judaism in Late Antiquity 25. Leiden: Brill, 1977.

Seneca, Lucius Annaeus. "Dialogues and Essays." edited by John Davie and Tobias Reinhardt. Oxford: Oxford University Press, 2007.

Setzer, Claudia. "Resurrection of the Body in Early Judaism and Christianity." In *The Human Body in Death and Resurrection*, edited by Tobias Nicklas, Friedrich Vinzenz Reiterer, Joseph Verheyden and Heike Braun, 1–12. Berlin: Walter de Gruyter, 2009.

Setzer, Claudia. *Resurrection of the Body in Early Judaism and Early Christianity: Doctrine, Community, and Self-Definition*. Boston: Brill Academic Publishers, 2004.

Sider, Robert D. "Literary Artifice and the Figure of Paul in the Writings of Tertullian." In *Paul and the Legacies of Paul*, edited by William S. Babcock, 199–220. Dallas, Tex: Southern Methodist University Press, 1990.

Simonetti, Manlio. *Biblical Interpretation in the Early Church: An Historical Introduction to Patristic Exegesis*. Translated by John A. Hughes. Edinburgh: T&T Clark, 1994.

Skeat, Theodore C. "Early Christian Book-Production: Papyri and Manuscripts." In *The West from the Fathers to the Reformation*, edited by G.W.H. Lampe, 54–79. The Cambridge History of the Bible 2. Cambridge: Cambridge University Press, 1969.

Smith, Jonathan Z. "The Prayer of Joseph." In *Religions in Antiquity: Essays in Memory of E.R. Goodenough*, edited by J. Neusner, 253–294. Leiden: Brill, 1970.

Stamps, Dennis L. "The Use of the Old Testament in the New Testament as a Rhetorical Device: A Methodological Proposal." In *Hearing the Old Testament in the New Testament*, edited by Stanley Porter, 9–37. Grand Rapids, Mich: Eerdmans, 2006.

Stead, Christopher J. "Arius in Modern Research." *Journal of Theological Studies (new series)* 45.1 (1994): 24–36.

Stead, Christopher J. "Divine Substance in Tertullian." *Journal of Theological Studies (new series)* 14.1 (1963): 46–66.

Sterling, Gregory E. "Hellenistic Philosophy and the New Testament." In *A Handbook to the Exegesis of the New Testament*, edited by Stanley Porter, 313–358. Leiden: Brill, 1997.

Sterling, Gregory E. *Historiography and Self-Definition: Josephus, Luke-Acts, and Apologetic Historiography*, Novum Testamentum Supplements 64. Leiden: Brill, 1991.

Sterling, Gregory E. "Prepositional Metaphysics in Jewish Wisdom Speculation and Early Christological Hymns." In *Wisdom and Logos: Studies in Jewish Thought in Honor of David Winston*, edited by David T. Runia and Gregory E. Sterling, 217–238. Atlanta, Ga: Scholars Press, 1997.

Streett, Daniel. *They Went out from Us: The Identity of the Opponents in First John*. Berlin: Walter de Gruyter, 2011.

Stroumsa, Guy G. "*Caro Salutis Cardo*: Shaping the Person in Early Christian Thought." *History of Religions* 30, no. 1 (1990): 25–50.

Stroumsa, Guy G. *Hidden Wisdom: Esoteric Traditions and the Roots of Christian Mysticism*, Studies in the History of Religions 70. Leiden: Brill, 2005.

Stuckenbruck, Loren T. "Worship and Monotheism in the *Ascension of Isaiah*." In *The Jewish Roots of Christological Monotheism: Papers from the St. Andrews Conference on the Historical Origins of the Worship of Jesus*, edited by Carey C. Newman, James R. Davila and Gladys S. Lewis, 70–89. Leiden: Brill, 1999.

Stuhlmacher, P. "The Hermeneutical Significance of 1 Cor 2:6–16." In *Tradition and Interpretation in the New Testament: Essays in Honor of E. Earle Ellis*, edited by G.F. Hawthorne and O. Betz, 328–347. Grand Rapids, Mich/Tübingen: Eerdmans/Mohr (Siebeck), 1987.

Sumney, Jerry. "Those Who 'Ignorantly Deny Him': The Opponents of Ignatius of Antioch." *Journal of Early Christian Studies* 1 (1993): 345–365.

Tabbernee, William. "Epigraphy." In *The Oxford Handbook of Early Christian Studies*, edited by Susan Ashbrook Harvey and David G. Hunter, 120–139. Oxford: Oxford University Press, 2008.

Talbert, C.H. "The Myth of the Descending-Ascending Redeemer in Mediterranean Antiquity." *New Testament Studies* 22 (1976): 418–440.

Thistleton, Anthony C. *The First Epistle to the Corinthians: A Commentary on the Greek Text*, New International Greek Testament Commentary. Grand Rapids, Mich: Eerdmans, 2000.

Thomassen, Einar. "Orthodoxy and Heresy in Second–Century Rome." *Harvard Theological Review* 97 (2004): 241–256.

Tibiletti, Giuseppe. *Le lettere private nei papyri greci del III e IV secolo D.C: tra paganesimo e cristianesimo*, Scienze Filologiche E Letteratura 15. Milan: Vita e pensiero, 1979.

Torjesen, Karen Jo. *Hermeneutical Procedure and Theological Structure in Origen's Exegesis*, Patristische Texte und Studien 28. Berlin: De Gruyter, 1985.

Trigg, Joseph W. *Origen*, The Early Church Fathers. New York: Routledge, 1998.

Trigg, Joseph W. *Origen: Bible and Philosophy in the 3rd Century*. Atlanta, Ga: John Knox, 1983.

Tuckett, Christopher M. *Christology and the New Testament: Jesus and His Earliest Followers*. Edinburgh: Westminster John Knox Press, 2001.

Tuckett, Christopher M. "The Corinthians Who Say 'There Is No Resurrection of the Dead' (1 Cor 15,12)." In *The Corinthian Correspondence*, edited by R. Bieringer, 251–261. Leuven: Leuven University Press, 1996.

Urbach, Ephraim E. *The Sages: Their Concepts and Beliefs*. Translated by Israel Abrahams. Jerusalem: The Magnes Press at The Hebrew University, 1975.

van den Hoek, Annewies. *Clement of Alexandria and His Use of Philo in the* Stromateis: *An Early Christian Reshaping of a Jewish Model*. Leiden: Brill, 1988.
van den Hoek, Annewies. "Techniques of Quotation in Clement of Alexandria: A View of Ancient Literary Working Methods." *Vigiliae christianae* 50, no. 3 (1996): 223–243.
van Eijk, A.H.C. "The Gospel of Philip and Clement of Alexandria: Gnostic and Ecclesiastical Theology on the Resurrection and the Eucharist." *Vigiliae christianae* 25 (1971): 94–120.
van Haelst, Joseph. *Catalogue des papyrus littéraires juifs et chrétiens*. Sorbonne: University of Paris, 1976.
van Kooten, Geurt Hendrik. *Cosmic Christology in Paul and the Pauline School: Colossians and Ephesians in the Context of Graeco-Roman Cosmology, with a New Synopsis of the Greek Texts*, Wissenschaftliche Untersuchungen zum Neuen Testament 171. Tübingen: Mohr (Siebeck), 2003.
van Kooten, Geurt Hendrik. *Paul's Anthropology in Context: The Image of God, Assimilation to God, and Tripartite Man in Ancient Judaism, Ancient Philosophy and Early Christianity*, Wissenschaftliche Untersuchungen zum Neuen Testament 232. Tübingen: Mohr (Siebeck), 2008.
van Oort, Johannes. "Biblical Interpretation in the Patristic Era, a 'Handbook of Patristic Exegesis' and Some Other Recent Books and Related Projects." *Vigiliae christianae* 60, no. 1 (2006): 80–103.
van Roon, A. *The Authenticity of Ephesians*. Leiden: Brill, 1975.
van Unnik, W.C. "The Newly Discovered Gnostic Epistle to Rheginos on the Resurrection, I and II." *Journal of Ecclesiastical History* 15, no. 2 (1964): 153–167.
Vermès, Géza. *Christian Beginnings: From Nazareth to Nicaea, AD 30–325*. London: Penguin UK, 2012.
Vermès, Géza. *The Complete Dead Sea Scrolls in English*. Revised ed. London: Penguin Books, 2004.
Vermès, Géza. *An Introduction to the Complete Dead Sea Scrolls*. London: SCM, 1999.
Vinzent, Markus. *Christ's Resurrection in Early Christianity and the Making of the New Testament*. Farnham: Ashgate, 2011.
Walker, W.O. "1 Corinthians 2.6–16: A Non-Pauline Interpolation?" *New Testament Studies* 47 (1992): 75–94.
Welborn, Laurence L. "'Take up the Epistle of the Blessed Paul the Apostle': The Contrasting Fates of Paul's Letters to Corinth in the Patristic Period." In *Reading Communities, Reading Scripture: Essays in Honour of Daniel Patte*, edited by Gary Phillips and Nicole Wilkinson Duran, 345–360. Harrisburg, Pa: Trinity Press International, 2002.
Wengst, Klaus. *Pax Romana and the Peace of Jesus Christ*. Translated by John Bowden. London: SCM, 1987.
Werner, Martin. *The Formation of Christian Dogma: An Historical Study of Its Problem*. Translated by S. G. F. Brandon. London: A & C Black, 1957.
White, Benjamin L. *Remembering Paul: Ancient and Modern Contests over the Image of the Apostle*. Oxford: Oxford University Press, 2014.
Widmann, M. "1 Kor 2,6–16: Ein Einspruch gegen Paulus." *Zeitschrift für die neutestamentliche Wissenschaft und die Kunde der älteren Kirche* 70 (1979): 44–53.
Wiles, Maurice F. *The Divine Apostle: The Interpretation of St. Paul's Epistles in the Early Church*. Cambridge: Cambridge University Press, 1967.
Wilken, Robert L. "Diversity and Unity in Early Christianity." *The Second Century* 1 (1981): 101–110.

Williams, R.R. "The Pauline Catechesis." In *Studies in Ephesians*, edited by F. L. Cross, 89–96. London: Mowbray, 1956.
Williams, Rowan. *Arius: Heresy and Tradition*. 2nd ed. London: SCM Press, 2001.
Wilson, Robert McL. *A Critical and Exegetical Commentary on Colossians and Philemon*. London: T&T Clark International, 2005.
Wilson, Robert McL. *The Gospel of Philip*. London: Mowbray, 1962.
Windisch, H. "Die göttliche Weisheit der Juden und die paulinische Christologie." In *Neutestamentliche Studien für G. Heinrici*, edited by A. Deissman and H. Windisch, 220–234. Leipzig: J.C. Hinrichs, 1914.
Wink, Walter. *Engaging the Powers: Discernment and Resistance in a World of Domination*. Minneapolis: Fortress Press, 1992.
Wink, Walter. *Naming the Powers: The Language of Power in the New Testament*. Philadelphia: Fortress Press, 1984.
Winter, Michael M. *The Atonement*. London: Geoffrey Chapman, 1995.
Witherington, Ben. *Jesus the Sage: The Pilgrimage of Wisdom*. Edinburgh: T&T Clark, 1994.
Wright, N. T. "Jesus' Resurrection and Christian Origins." *Gregorianum* 83, no. 4 (2002): 615–635.
Wright, N. T. "Poetry and Theology in Colossians 1.15–20." *New Testament Studies* 36 (1990): 444–468.
Wuellner, W. "Haggadic Homily Genre in 1 Corinthians 1–3." *Journal of Biblical Literature* 89 (1970): 199–204.
Young, Frances M. *The Art of Performance: Toward a Theology of Holy Scripture*. London: Darton, Longman & Todd, 1990.
Young, Frances M. *Biblical Exegesis and the Formation of Christian Culture*. Cambridge: Cambridge University Press, 1997.
Young, Frances M. "Interpretation of Scripture." In *The Oxford Handbook of Early Christian Studies*, edited by Susan Ashbrook Harvey and David E. Hunter, 845–63. Oxford: Oxford University Press, 2008.
Young, Frances M. "Prelude: Jesus Christ, Foundation of Christianity." In *The Cambridge History of Christianity: Origins to Constantine*, edited by Margaret M. Mitchell and Frances M. Young, 1–34. Cambridge: Cambridge University Press, 2006.
Young, Frances M. "The Rhetorical Schools and Their Influence on Patristic Exegesis." In *The Making of Orthodoxy: Essays in Honour of Henry Chadwick*, edited by Rowan Williams, 182–199. Cambridge: Cambridge University Press, 1989.
Zampaglione, Gerardo. *The Idea of Peace in Antiquity*. Notre Dame, Ind: University of Notre Dame Press, 1973.

# Index of Ancient Sources

This index does not include texts in the Appendices. References to whole texts and ancient authors may be found in the Index of Subjects.

## Hebrew Bible/Old Testament

| Genesis | | | 59 | 78, 90 |
|---|---|---|---|---|
| 1.27 | 140, 143, 165 | | 59.17–21 | 59 |
| 12.7 | 146 | | 64.4 | 35 |
| 32 | 76 | | | |
| | | | *Ezekiel* | |
| *Psalms* | | | 37.1–14 | 101 |
| 49.15 | 101 | | 12.2 | 101 |
| | | | | |
| *Proverbs* | | | *Daniel* | |
| 8.22 | 22, 151–152, 171–173 | | | |
| | | | *Hosea* | |
| *Isaiah* | | | 6.1–3 | 101 |
| 25.8 | 101 | | 13.14 | 101 |
| 26.19 | 101 | | | |

## New Testament

| Matthew | | | 4.13–14 | 40–42 |
|---|---|---|---|---|
| 7.6 | 33 | | 5.28–29 | 119 |
| 13.33 | 38 | | 5.29 | 117 |
| 26.39 | 36 | | 6.53 | 105–106 |
| 22.23 | 101 | | 14.6 | 86 |
| | | | 14.9 | 144 |
| *Mark* | | | | |
| 10.38 | 79–80 | | *Acts* | |
| 12.18 | 101 | | 4.1–2 | 101 |
| | | | 23.6–8 | 101 |
| *Luke* | | | | |
| 12.50 | 79–80 | | *Romans* | |
| 20.27 | 101 | | 6.3–4 | 79 |
| | | | 6.4–11 | 99 |
| *John* | | | 7.14 | 48 |
| 1.1–3 | 162, 166 | | 8.8–15 | 110 |
| 1.1–18 | 22, 138, 162–163, 167 | | 8.14–17 | 11 |
| 1.3 | 154 | | 8.18–25 | 39 |
| 1.10 | 162 | | 8.18 | 40 |
| 1.18 | 144–145, 146–147, 149, 162, 165, 168 | | 8.20 | 59 |
| | | | 8.30–39 | 11, 87 |

| | | | |
|---|---|---|---|
| 8.31 | 87 | 15.50 | 16, 97–98, 99, 102, 104, 105–107, 108–109, 110–119, 120–124, 124–126, 130–131, 176, 179 |
| 13.14 | 86, 103 | | |
| *1 Corinthians* | | | |
| 1.18–24 | 24 | 15.52–53 | 124 |
| 1.18–2.4 | 49–50 | 15.53 | 99, 112–113, 117, 121, 122, 123 |
| 1.19–20 | 35 | | |
| 1.20–24 | 11 | 15.53–54 | 104, 120–121, 124–125, 131 |
| 1.24 | 123 | 15.54 | 103–104 |
| 1.30 | 86, 123 | 15.54–55 | 122 |
| 2.2 | 47, 49, 50 | | |
| 2.4 | 55 | *2 Corinthians* | |
| 2.6–7 | 29–30, 35, 38, 55 | 4.8 | 40 |
| 2.6–8 | 38, 46, 48, 49, 67 | 5.1–5 | 99 |
| 2.6–13 | 47 | 5.1–10 | 106 |
| 2.6–16 | 2, 4, 11, 12, 15, 22, 24–56, 135, 174–175, 179 | 10.3–5 | 62, 64 |
| 2.6 | 31, 32, 35–36, 37, 39, 47, 48, 50, 55 | *Galatians* | |
| | | 3.27 | 83 |
| 2.7 | 24, 28, 29, 33, 48, 52, 55 | | |
| 2.9–10 | 33–34 | *Ephesians* | |
| 2.9 | 15, 26–27, 29, 40, 41, 43, 44, 45, 52 | 1.3 | 60, 62 |
| | | 1.9–10 | 141 |
| 2.10 | 31, 43–44 | 1.20 | 60, 62 |
| 2.11 | 31 | 2.6 | 60, 62, 91 |
| 2.12 | 41 | 2.11–15 | 11 |
| 2.13 | 41, 45 | 3.10 | 60, 62, 91 |
| 2.14 | 33, 40, 43–44, 185 | 4.5 | 80 |
| 2.15 | 31, 33 | 4.14 | 126 |
| 2.16 | 34, 41 | 6.10–17 | 2, 4, 11, 12, 16, 57–96, 174, 175–176, 179 |
| 3.1–3 | 22, 53 | | |
| 4.6 | 41, 53 | 6.11 | 60, 64, 77–88 |
| 11.3 | 161 | 6.12 | 57, 59, 60, 62–68, 69, 72, 74–77, 81, 82, 85, 87, 90 |
| 11.19 | 103 | | |
| 12.4–6 | 31 | 6.13 | 71, 73, 77–88 |
| 13.9 | 31 | 6.14 | 60, 79, 82, 86 |
| 15.1–11 | 97 | 6.14–16 | 82–83, 85 |
| 15.12 | 97–98, 128 | 6.15–16 | 86 |
| 15.22 | 141 | 6.16–17 | 85 |
| 15.28 | 97 | 6.16 | 60, 69–73, 79, 82, 84, 86 |
| 15.42 | 121, 122 | 6.17 | 78, 79, 82 |
| 15.44 | 97, 103, 120 | 6.18 | 81 |
| 15.45 | 141 | 6.17–18 | 71 |
| 15.47–50 | 115 | | |
| 15.50–54 | 110, 113, 117–118, 123 | *Philippians* | |
| 15.50–58 | 2, 4, 11, 12, 16, 22, 97–134, 174, 176–177, 179 | 2.5–11 | 22, 104, 136, 138, 162–163, 167–168 |

| | | | |
|---|---|---|---|
| 2.6–7 | 163–164 | *1 Thessalonians* | |
| 2.6–8 | 11, 165 | 4.13–18 | 99 |
| 2.7 | 104 | 4.15–17 | 126 |
| | | 5.1–10 | 99 |
| *Colossians* | | 5.8 | 59, 78 |
| 1.1 | 136 | 5.8–9 | 62 |
| 1.15–16 | 142–143 | 5.14 | 84 |
| 1.15–18 | 159 | 5.21 | 33 |
| 1.15–20 | 2, 4, 11, 12, 16, 22, 135–173, 174, 176, 177–178, 179 | *1 Timothy* | |
| 1.15 | 13, 125, 135, 139, 140–155, 161, 162, 163–164, 165, 168, 171–173 | 6.16 | 146–147 |
| | | *2 Timothy* | |
| 1.16 | 139, 153, 154, 155–160, 166 | 2.11–12 | 103 |
| 1.16–18 | 159 | 3.16 | 1 |
| 1.18 | 139, 142, 160–161, 166, 169, 184 | 4.7 | 81–82 |
| 1.19 | 143 | *Hebrews* | |
| 2.1 | 136 | 4.12 | 86 |
| 2.2–3 | 38 | 10.1 | 48 |
| 2.8 | 91 | | |
| 2.8–10 | 92 | *2 Peter* | |
| 2.9–15 | 99 | 2.1 | 103 |
| 2.10 | 161 | 3.15 | 1 |
| 2.15 | 59, 91–92 | | |
| 2.18–20 | 136 | *Revelation* | |
| 3.1–4 | 99 | 1.5 | 139, 142, 184 |
| 3.10 | 103 | 1.16 | 85 |
| 3.17 | 136 | 19.16 | 83 |
| 4.13–15 | 136 | 20.4 | 126 |
| | | 20.4–5 | 126 |

## Apocryphal, Pseudepigraphal, and Deuterocanonical Texts

| | | | |
|---|---|---|---|
| *Wisdom* | | 7.14 | 101 |
| 3.7–8 | 101 | | |
| 5.17–18 | 59 | *1 Enoch* | |
| 5.18–22 | 78 | 51.1 | 101 |
| 7.26 | 151 | 91.10–11 | 101 |
| 9.15–16 | 100 | 103.4 | 101 |
| *Sirach* | | *Acta Thomae* | |
| 3.21 | 41 | 1.36 | 38 |
| *2 Maccabees* | | *Apocalypsis Baruch* | |
| 7 | 101 | l.1-li.10 | 118 |

*Apocalypsis Elijah*
1.10 – 11        156 – 157

*Ascensio Isaiae*
7.14        156
7.19        156
7.24        156
7.29        156
7.33        156
8.7 – 10        156
8.11        26
9.24 – 25        156

*Epistula Barnabi*
4.9        74

20.1        74

*Epistula ecclesiarum Lugdunensium et Viennensium*
2        139

*De Recta in deum Fide (Adamantius)*
5        106

*Testamentum Benjamin*
19.8 – 10        101

*Testamentum Levi*
3.8        156 – 157

## Rabbinic Writings

*Sifre Deuteronomy*
45        61

## Philo

*De confusione linguarum*
97        141

*De opificio mundi*
25        140 – 141

*De Somniis*
1.139 – 140        141

2.45        141

*De specialibus legibus*
3.207        141

*De Virtutibus*
1.1 – 4        81

## Josephus

*Antiquitates Judaicae*
18.1.3        101

*Bellum Judaicum*
2.8.14        101

## Nag Hammadi Codices

*Acta Petri*
2        149
39        38

*Didascalia Silvana* 140
94.33 – 95.12        77

96.6 – 15        77

*Evangelium Philippi*
56.15 – 19        107
56.26 – 57.21        100, 105, 120
64.22 – 27        107, 108

| | | | |
|---|---|---|---|
| 66.16–20 | 107 | 44.22 | 103 |
| 67.9–27 | 107, 108 | 47.3 | 103 |
| 73.1–4 | 107 | 49.10–11 | 103 |
| | | 45.14–end | 103–104 |
| *Evangelium Thomas* | | 48.15 | 104 |
| 17 | 38 | 48.27 | 104 |
| | | 49.22 | 104 |

*De hypostasis archontium* 59

*Sentences de Sexte* 24

*Oratio Pauli*
9          38

*Tractatus tripartitus*
12          140

*Ad Rheginum de resurrection*
43.25–26    103

## Ancient Authors and Works

**Alexander of Alexandria**
*Epistula ad Alexandrum Constantinopolianum*
6          136

**Arnobius of Sicca**
*Disputationes adversus nationes*
2.5          85

**Athanasius**
*De Decretis Nicaea*
10.4–6      173
10.13       173
11.4–6      173

*Depositio Arianos*
1.5–6       135
1.9         135
2.37        135
70          171–172

*Orationes contra Arianos*
1.5–6       172
1.9         172
1.63.5      172
2.6–3.1     172
2.37        172
3.5–6       172

**Athenagoras**
*De resurrectione mortuorum*
18          99

**Augustine**
*De doctrina Christiana*
3.10.14–16  114
3.27.38     22

**Cicero**
*De Re publica*
6.24.26     100

**Clement of Alexandria**
*Excerpta Theodoti*
7           140
10          140
19          162
19.4        155
22.6        70
23          102
24.1        70
33          139
43          162
73.1–3      70
85          69

*Paedagogus*
1.6.30.1–2  69

| | | | |
|---|---|---|---|
| 1.12 | 83 | 7.65.1–6 | 80 |
| 1.18 | 58 | 7.84 | 65 |
| 1.37.1 | 38 | 7.86 | 65 |
| 2.8.73.3 | 160 | | |
| 3.86.2 | 44 | **Clement of Rome** | |
| 3.86.2–87.2 | 44–45 | *1 Clement* | |
| 43.2–3 | 108 | 5.5–7 | 51 |
| | | 34 | 38 |
| *Protrepticus* | | 35 | 38 |
| 2.20.4 | 82–83 | 47.1 | 24 |
| 10.23–26 | 140 | | |
| 10.94.4 | 38 | *2 Clement (pseudo?)* | |
| 11.116 | 69, 94 | 9 | 118 |
| 118.4 | 45 | 11 | 38 |
| *Quis dives salvetur* | | *Epistulae de virginitate (pseudo?)* | |
| 23.3 | 38 | 1.9.4 | 38 |
| *Stromata* | | **Commodian** | |
| 1.2.19 | 30 | *Instructiones per litteras uersuum primas adversus paganos* | |
| 1.10.49 | 65 | | |
| 1.50.1–1.53.2 | 33 | 44 | 126 |
| 1.53.3–1.54.3 | 33 | | |
| 1.54.3 | 34 | **Cyprian of Carthage** | |
| 1.55.1–2 | 33 | *Epistulae* | |
| 1.55.1 | 28 | 10.1–2 | 85 |
| 1.55.3 | 33 | 10.2 | 78 |
| 1.55.3–5 | 33 | 28.1–2 | 85 |
| 2.9.45 | 65 | 31.25 | 82 |
| 2.10.46 | 65 | 54.1 | 85 |
| 2.18.81 | 65 | 55.8–9 | 86 |
| 2.20 | 99 | 55.9 | 86 |
| 2.20.109 | 63, 64–65 | 60 | 86 |
| 3.17 | 99 | 73.21.1–2 | 79 |
| 4.7 | 77, 80, 91 | 73.22.2 | 79 |
| 4.65 | 58 | | |
| 5.25.1–26.1 | 43–44 | *Ad Fortunatum de exhortatione martyrii* | |
| 5.25.5 | 33–34 | Pr.4 | 79 |
| 5.40.1–2 | 44 | | |
| 5.80.4–81.1 | 38 | *De bono patientiae* | |
| 5.80.7 | 39 | 12.12 | 62 |
| 6.9 | 65 | | |
| 6.9.74 | 65 | *Ad Quirinum testimonia adversus Judaeos* | |
| 6.68.1–2 | 28 | 2.1 | 139 |
| 7.1.4 | 65 | | |
| 7.3 | 64, 91 | | |
| 7.3.13 | 65 | | |

## Cyril of Jerusalem
*Catecheses illuminandorum*
| | |
|---|---|
| 4.4 | 147, 148 |
| 13.22 – 23 | 161 |
| 17.1 | 45 |

*Catecheses mystagogicae*
| | |
|---|---|
| 3.4 | 69 – 70 |

## Dionysius of Alexandria
*Fragmentum*
| | |
|---|---|
| 204 – 205 | 149 |
| 210 | 149 |

*Ad Sixtus*
| | |
|---|---|
| 3 | 149 |

## Epictetus
*Dissertationes ab Arriano digestae*
| | |
|---|---|
| 1.14.13 – 17 | 84 |
| 1.24.1 – 2 | 74 |
| 2.18.27 | 64 |
| 3.15.1 – 13 | 74 |
| 3.24.95 – 99 | 84 |
| 4.4.11 – 13 | 74 |

## Eusebius of Caesarea
*Demonstratio evangelica*
| | |
|---|---|
| 4.3 – 4 | 150 |
| 4.12 | 99 |
| 4.15 | 148 |
| 5.1 | 150 |
| 5.1.4 – 8 | 152 |
| 5.4.10 | 148 |
| 7.Pr | 155, 162 |
| 7.3.14 | 150 |
| 9.7 | 87 |

*De ecclesiastica theologica*
| | |
|---|---|
| 1.38 | 150 |

*Historia ecclesiastica*
| | |
|---|---|
| 5.2.3 | 139 |
| 5.10.1 | 33 |
| 5.11.1 | 33 |
| 6.4.3 | 79 |
| 6.6.1 | 33 |
| 10.4.58 | 62 |
| 11.19.4 | 162 |

*De laudibus Constantini*
| | |
|---|---|
| 3.6 | 139 |

*De martyribus Palaestinae*
| | |
|---|---|
| 5 | 88 |
| 48 | 38 |

*Praeparatio evangelica*
| | |
|---|---|
| 1.3.5 | 29 |
| 1.3.6 | 30 |
| 5.3.1 | 62 |
| 7.16.4 | 62 |

## Firmilian of Caesarea
*Ad Cyprianum*
| | |
|---|---|
| 9 | 28 |

## Hippolytus of Rome
*De benedictione de Issaci et Jacobi et Moysis*
| | |
|---|---|
| 1 | 92 |

*Fragmentum: Epistula reginam*
| | |
|---|---|
| 1 | 139 |

*Refutatio omnium haeresium*
| | |
|---|---|
| 5.3 | 38 |
| 5.7.14 | 107 |
| 5.19 | 38 |
| 5.21 | 38 |
| 5.22 | 38 |
| 6.19 | 38 |
| 6.29 | 38 |
| 7.14 | 38 |

*Contra haeresin Noeti*
| | |
|---|---|
| 6 | 155 |

*Fragmenta ex libro de paschate*
| | |
|---|---|
| 55.1 | 92 |

*De consummatione mundi (pseudo?)*
| | |
|---|---|
| 44.1 | 38 |

## Heraclitus
*Epistles*
| | |
|---|---|
| 9 | 100 |

## Ignatius
*Epistula ad Ephesios*
| | |
|---|---|
| 13 | 62 |

*Epistula ad Polycarpum*
| | |
|---|---|
| 6.2 | 78 |

## Irenaeus of Lyons
*Demonstratio praedicationis apostolicae*
| | |
|---|---|
| 38–40 | 139 |

*Adversus haereses*
| | |
|---|---|
| 1.Pr.2 | 127 |
| 1.3.1 | 58 |
| 1.5.4 | 62 |
| 1.8.2–3 | 107 |
| 1.8.4 | 28 |
| 1.8.4–5 | 58 |
| 1.9.1 | 28, 32 |
| 1.9.4 | 114, 127 |
| 1.22.1 | 114, 150 |
| 1.26.1 | 70 |
| 2.6.1–2.6.2 | 148 |
| 2.22.4 | 92, 139, 142 |
| 2.28.7 | 31 |
| 2.31.1 | 108, 130 |
| 3.2.1 | 28, 32, 114 |
| 3.2.1–3.3.1 | 107 |
| 3.5.1 | 114 |
| 3.11.1 | 150 |
| 3.15.1 | 103, 127 |
| 3.16.3 | 112, 139, 149 |
| 3.16.6 | 143 |
| 3.19.1 | 112 |
| 3.22.4 | 139 |
| 4.2.4 | 139 |
| 4.20.2 | 139 |
| 4.24.1 | 139 |
| 4.41.4 | 51 |
| 5.1.4 | 99–100, 112 |
| 5.2.2–3.2 | 100 |
| 5.2.2 | 113 |
| 5.2.3 | 58 |
| 5.2.36 | 58 |
| 5.3.1 | 118 |
| 5.6.1 | 31–32, 38 |
| 5.6.2 | 112 |
| 5.9.1–4 | 110 |
| 5.9.1 | 108–109, 111 |
| 5.9.3 | 110 |
| 5.9.4 | 100, 109 |
| 5.10–11 | 110 |
| 5.13.1 | 100, 111 |
| 5.13.2 | 109 |
| 5.13.3–5 | 100 |
| 5.13.3 | 109–110 |
| 5.13.4 | 110 |
| 5.13.5 | 110 |
| 5.14.1–2 | 100 |
| 5.14.1 | 111–112 |
| 5.14.2 | 112–113 |
| 5.14.3 | 113 |
| 5.14.4 | 100, 113 |
| 5.15.1 | 113 |
| 5.31.2 | 139 |
| 5.32.1 | 126 |
| 5.32–36 | 126 |
| 5.36.3 | 142 |

## Jerome
*Epistulae*
| | |
|---|---|
| 57.9 | 26 |

## Justin the Gnostic
*Liber Baruch*
| | |
|---|---|
| 124 | 38 |

## Justin Martyr
*Dialogus cum Tryphone Judaeo*
| | |
|---|---|
| 56 | 147 |
| 60–61 | 147 |
| 75.3 | 153 |
| 80 | 126 |
| 80.5 | 102 |
| 84 | 149 |
| 100 | 149 |
| 125 | 149 |

**Livy** 22.38.2–5  84

**Marius Victorinus**
*Adversus Arium*
1.24F  160
3F  154

*Matryrium Polycarpi*
2.3  38

*Matryrium Fructuosi et sociorum*
3.3  38

*Martyrium Perpetuae et Felicitatis*
10.1–14  74

*Martyrium Apollonii Romani*
92

*Martyrium Pionii*
21.4  101

*Martyrium Polonii*
14.2  101

**Melito of Sardis**
*Homilia in passionem Christi*
82  149

**Methodius of Olympus**
*De resurrectione mortuorum*
1.1.13  139, 141
1.2  119
1.5–6  119
1.12  101
1.12–13  119
2.1.13  139
2.20  119
3.2.1–2  91
3.2.2  77

*Symposium* or *Convivium virginum*
3.6  91
8.12  78

**Novatian**
*De cibis Judaicis*
1.1  80

*Ad Cyprian*
2.5.2  82

*De spectaculis*
2.4  66

*De Trinitate*
3  136
10  99
13.1–2  162
18.1–3  146–147
21.1–6  150
21.9  92

**Origen of Alexandria**
*Contra Celsum*
1.13  28
1.18–19  121
2.24  36
2.25  149
2.31  149
2.77  139
3.20  28, 37, 58
3.34  159
4.29  155, 159
5.1  71
5.14  119–120
5.17  124
5.18–23  122, 124
5.18  126
5.19  122, 123
5.37  149, 150, 151
5.44  91
6.17  149, 151
6.47–48  149
6.47  151
6.63  143
6.63–64  149
6.64  151
6.69  144, 149
6.71  155
7.16  149
7.27  144

| | | | |
|---|---|---|---|
| 7.32 | 122 | 13.429–430 | 121–122 |
| 7.43 | 145, 149 | 19.3 (Heracleon) | 107 |
| 7.46 | 91 | 19.20 | 149, 151 |
| 7.65 | 149 | 20.7 (Heracleon) | 107 |
| 7.70 | 149 | 28.18 | 149, 151 |
| 8.17 | 149 | 32.19 | 77 |
| 8.26 | 149 | 32.29 | 144 |
| 8.34 | 77 | 32.256 | 72 |
| 8.55 | 77 | 32.287 | 72, 77 |
| 8.73 | 82 | | |

*Commentarii in Evangelium Matthaei*

*Commentarii in epistula I ad Corinthios*
| | |
|---|---|
| 15.18–20 | 50–51 |

| | |
|---|---|
| 5.29 | 26 |
| 11.9 | 77 |
| 13.4 | 72 |
| 14.6 | 38 |
| 16.6 | 79, 80 |
| 16.8 | 149, 151 |

*Commentarii in Canticum canticorum*
| | |
|---|---|
| Pr | 149 |
| 1.1 | 149 |
| 1.3 | 139 |
| 1.5 | 38 |
| 2.1 | 149 |
| 2.3 | 87 |
| 3.8 | 71, 72–73, 77 |

*Commentarii in Psalmi*
| | |
|---|---|
| Ps 16.9 | 139 |

*Commentarii in epistula ad Romanos*
| | |
|---|---|
| 1.6.3 | 139 |
| 1.13.3 | 47 |
| 1.13.3–5 | 47 |
| 2.5.3 | 82 |
| 6.12 | 104 |
| 7.4.2–7.4.6 | 40 |
| 7.5.11 | 39 |
| 8.6.5 | 50 |
| 10.3 | 81 |
| 10.15.2 | 81 |
| 10.15.3 | 82 |

*Commentarii in epistula ad Ephesios*
| | |
|---|---|
| 3 | 69, 78, 86 |

*Commentarii in Evangelium Ioannis*
| | |
|---|---|
| 1.18 | 151 |
| 1.88 | 155 |
| 1.108 | 139, 155 |
| 1.117–118 | 139 |
| 1.118 | 149 |
| 1.121 | 139 |
| 1.192 | 149 |
| 1.195 | 149 |
| 2.31 | 153 |
| 6.10 | 71 |
| 6.49 | 143 |
| 6.56 | 80 |
| 10.23 | 162 |
| 10.284 | 155 |
| 10.288 | 38 |
| 13.11–25 (Heracleon) | 107 |
| 13.32–37 | 41 |
| 13.37–39 | 42 |
| 13.38–39 | 42 |
| 13.411 | 28 |

*Fragmenta in Jeremias*
| | |
|---|---|
| 2 | 77 |

*Fragmenta in Evangelium Lucae*
| | |
|---|---|
| fr. 140 | 38 |

*Fragments in Psalmi*
| | |
|---|---|
| 1.5 | 99–100, 123 |

*Homiliae in Exodus*
| | |
|---|---|
| 1.5 | 71 |
| 3.3 | 82 |
| 4.7–9 | 62 |

| | | | |
|---|---|---|---|
| 5.5 | 62, 82 | *Exhortatio ad martyrium* | |
| 11.4 | 81 | 30 | 79 |
| | | 43 | 78 |
| *Homiliae in Ezechiel* | | | |
| 13.1.7–8 | 62 | *De oration* | |
| | | 29.2 | 62 |
| *Homiliae in Genesis* | | | |
| 1.13 | 144, 149, 165 | *De pascha* | |
| 4.6 | 77 | 1.38 | 80 |
| 8.10 | 77 | | |
| | | *De principiis* | |
| *Homiliae in Jeremias* | | Pr.5 | 122–123 |
| 1.8.1 | 149 | 1.1.8 | 144–145 |
| 1.8.5 | 142 | 1.2.1 | 151–152 |
| | | 1.2.6 | 144, 152 |
| *Homiliae in Josue* | | 1.2.9 | 152 |
| 1.5 | 86 | 1.3.7 | 139 |
| 3.1 | 71 | 1.5–7 | 68 |
| 4.1 | 85 | 1.5.1 | 155 |
| 5.2–3 | 71 | 1.5.3 | 155, 157, 158–159 |
| 5.3 | 85 | 1.6.2 | 155, 157 |
| 11.4 | 66–67 | 1.6.4 | 122 |
| 11.11 | 82 | 1.7.1 | 155, 159 |
| 15.1 | 86–87 | 1.8.4 | 155 |
| 18.11 | 82 | 2.1.2 | 151 |
| | | 2.2.2 | 122 |
| *Homiliae in Judices* | | 2.3.2 | 123 |
| 4.11 | 79 | 2.4.3 | 144–145 |
| 5.1 | 1 | 2.6.1 | 136, 155 |
| 5.2–3 | 79 | 2.6.3 | 166 |
| 6.2 | 79 | 2.9.4 | 155, 166 |
| 7.2 | 80 | 2.10.1 | 120, 121 |
| 9.1 | 82, 85 | 2.10.2–3 | 99–100 |
| | | 2.10.2 | 123 |
| *Homiliae in Leviticus* | | 2.10.3 | 120–121 |
| 1.4.6 | 85 | 2.11.2 | 120 |
| 4.6 | 49, 51 | 2.11.2–3 | 126 |
| 7.2 | 155 | 3.2.1–2 | 67 |
| 7.6 | 30 | 3.2.1 | 86 |
| 8.8.1–2 | 71–72 | 3.2.3–4 | 94 |
| 16.7 | 71 | 3.2.4 | 68, 70, 77 |
| | | 3.2.4–6 | 91 |
| *Homiliae in Numeri* | | 3.2.5 | 72, 76–77, 86 |
| 1.5 | 67 | 3.2.6 | 67–68, 76 |
| 3.4 | 139, 149–150 | 3.3.1 | 46, 47 |
| 6.1.2–3 | 49 | 4.2.3 | 41 |
| 25.1.5 | 73 | 4.2.4 | 46, 47–48, 127 |

| | | | |
|---|---|---|---|
| 4.3.12 | 67 | **Tertullian** | |
| 4.3.13 | 53, 174 | *De anima* | |
| 4.30 | 155 | 55.3 | 126 |
| | | 58.8 | 126 |

**Pamphilus**
*Apologia pro Origene*

| | | | |
|---|---|---|---|
| 23 | 28 | *Apologeticus* | |
| 45 | 150, 155 | 48.7 | 116 |
| 81 | 28 | | |
| 102 | 139 | *De baptism* | |
| 128 | 100, 123 | 1.1 | 85 |
| 132 | 139 | 16.1 | 79 |
| 143 | 139 | | |
| 146 | 139 | *De carne Christi* | |
| | | 1.2 | 163 |

**Peter of Alexandria**
*Fragmenta de resurrectione*

| | | | |
|---|---|---|---|
| 4.4 | 99–100 | *De corona* | |
| | | 2 | 85 |

**Plato**
*Timaeus*

*De fuga persecutione*

| | | | |
|---|---|---|---|
| | | 9.1 | 84 |
| 92c | 140 | 9.2 | 83–84 |

**Polybius**

*De idololatria*

| | | | |
|---|---|---|---|
| 22 | 78 | 19 | 85 |

*De jeiunio adversus Psychicos*

**Polycarp**
*Epistula ad Philippenses*

| | | | |
|---|---|---|---|
| | | 17.7–8 | 74–75 |
| 12.1 | 57 | 17.9 | 75 |

*Adversus Marcionem*

**Quintilian**
*Institutio Oratoria*

| | | | |
|---|---|---|---|
| | | 1 | 126 |
| 1.8.1–12 | 7 | 1.2 | 35 |
| 1.8.17 | 29 | 1.28.3 | 85 |
| 10.1.46 | 7 | 3.14 | 51, 85 |
| | | 3.5.4 | 55 |
| | | 3.10.11 | 163 |

**Seneca**
*Dialogue 12: Ad Helviam matrem de consolatione*

| | | | |
|---|---|---|---|
| | | 3.14 | 85 |
| | | 3.25 | 126 |
| | | 4.4.1 | 103 |
| 12.11.6 | 100 | 4.7.1–5 | 163 |
| | | 4.10.16 | 165 |

**Tatian**
*Oratio ad Graecos*

| | | | |
|---|---|---|---|
| | | 4.20 | 57, 75 |
| | | 5.6.1–2 | 35–36 |
| 5.2 | 149 | 5.6.1–7 | 35 |
| | | 5.8.3 | 163 |
| | | 5.10 | 115–116 |
| | | 5.14 | 100, 104, 116 |

| | | | |
|---|---|---|---|
| 5.17 | 58 | *De pudicitia* | |
| 5.18 | 62, 91 | 22.4–10 | 79 |
| 5.19.4 | 154 | | |
| 5.19.4–5 | 155 | *De resurrectione carnis* | |
| 5.20.3–4 | 162, 163–164 | 1.1 | 119 |
| 5.33 | 118 | 2.2 | 118 |
| | | 3.6 | 114 |
| *Ad martyras* | | 19.6 | 127 |
| 1 | 126 | 21.3 | 114, 119 |
| 3 | 51, 78, 85 | 22.8–11 | 114 |
| | | 22.11 | 115 |
| *De Oratione* | | 24.7 | 115 |
| 24.1 | 81 | 26.1 | 38 |
| 29.4 | 81 | 42 | 106 |
| | | 42.1 | 114 |
| *De praescriptione haereticorum* | | 42.3 | 114 |
| 2 | 78 | 48.1 | 114 |
| 20 | 85 | 49 | 99–100 |
| 38–39 | 66 | 49.1–21 | 115 |
| 40 | 66 | 49.1 | 114 |
| | | 49.11 | 100, 116 |
| *Adversus Praxean* | | 50.1–4 | 117–118 |
| 1 | 151 | 50.4 | 114 |
| 5.19.3–5 | 149 | 56.1–57.6 | 118 |
| 7.1 | 149 | 57.1 | 118 |
| 8 | 151, 154 | | |
| 10 | 164 | *Scorpiace* | 51 |
| 14.1–4 | 147 | 4 | 85 |
| 16 | 147 | 6 | 79 |
| 19 | 151, 154 | | |
| 25.621 | 164 | **Theophilus of Antioch** | |
| | | *Ad Autolycum* | |
| | | 2.22.1 | 149 |

# Index of Subjects

Adam  92n138, 111–112, 115–116, 141n21
Adoptionism  70
*Against Heresies* (Irenaeus)  31, 108
*Against Marcion* (Tertullian)  34–35, 115, 132, 163–164
Ambrosiaster 135
anthropology  13, 47–49, 61, 101–102, 113–114, 123–128, 132, 177
*Apocalypse of Elijah*  26, 156n80
apology  3, 10, 16, 27–28, 31, 34, 52, 54–55, 126–129, 131–134, 149, 176
– and formation  129, 131–134, 176–177
Aristotle  29n22
Arius, Arianism  16, 138, 147–148, 150, 155, 157–158, 160n98, 169–173, 176, 178, 180
armour  16, 59–60, 62, 63, 64, 68, 71, 73, 75, 77–88, 89, 92–95, 175
– and baptism  70, 78–80
– and Christ  69–70, 78–80, 86–88, 94–95
– and community  80, 84–85, 94–95
– and prayer  80–82, 93
– Graeco-Roman  59, 69, 77, 83–84, 89, 93–94
– phalanx  84n112
– sword  71n60, 77, 85–86, 89
Arnobius  84n113
Asher, Jeffrey 98
*Ascension of Isaiah*  26, 153, 155–158, 160, 167
asceticism  67n46, 82n98
Athanasius  170–173
– and *homoousios*  171n131, 173
Athenagoras  63n27, 99n12
atonement  91–92, 141n21
– and Aulén  91–92
– Christus Victor  59, 87–88, 91–92
– Attridge, Harold  104
Augustine  22n70, 114
Aulén, Gustav  91–92

Bain, Andrew  154–155
baptism  16, 60, 62–63, 64n34, 69–70, 73, 78–80, 84n113, 87n119, 93, 95, 175–176
battle  16, 60, 62–70, 73, 75, 77–79, 81–84, 87–91, 93–96, 175–176, 178–179
Bauckham, Richard  153
Behr, John  103, 113n88
*Biblia Patristica*  21–22, 182, 185
Bird, Michael  21–22, 182–184
body  47–48, 67–70, 73, 97–107, 109–113, 119–124, 125–126, 128 135n2, 145, 160–161, 163n111, 176–178
Bockmuehl, Markus  163n107, 168n122
Boxall, Ian  15
Brown, Alexandra  107n55
Bultmann, Rudolf  25

Caird, George  59
Cappadocians  171n131
Carleton Paget, James  129n162
catechesis 2, 79n87, 178
catechetical school (Alexandria)  33, 51
Celsus  36–37, 120n120, 123–124, 132, 150–151
– and Origen  36–37, 71, 82, 120, 123–124, 132, 143, 150–151
chiliasm/millenarianism  120, 126n144
Christman, Angela  14n45, 22
Christ (see *Jesus*)
Christology  13, 16, 18, 70, 88, 92, 94–95, 98, 103–104, 111–115, 124–125, 127–128, 132, 137–140, 142n26, 146, 149–152, 155–156, 160–173, 177–179
– begotten  139, 155, 170–173
– Christus Victor (see *atonement*)
– first-born  92n138, 139, 142, 149–155, 160, 165, 167–169, 170, 173
– head of the body  16, 139, 142, 160–161, 169
– image of God  13, 139–149, 151n58, 152, 160–161, 164–168, 171, 173
– novelty of Christ  150–151, 154

- pre-existence 16–17, 139–140, 146–147, 149, 150–152, 154–155, 157–159, 162–163, 166–169, 170–173, 177
- thrones and dominions 139, 153, 155–160, 167, 169
- see also *subordination*
- Chrysostom, John 135, 137
Clement of Alexandria 11, 17, 33–34, 38–39, 43–46, 51, 63–66, 68, 80–83, 108n58, 140–141, 143–144, 146, 148, 160–161
- and *apatheia* 65
- and education 2, 13, 34, 39, 43–46, 65, 83, 108n58, 177, 179
- and faith 43–45, 80, 83, 94, 179
- and opponents 30, 34, 39, 43, 69n53
- spiritual exegesis 39, 44–46
Clement of Rome 1n2, 14n44, 24, 118n115
Colossians 1n2, 16, 57–58, 91–92, 135–138, 153–154, 162–163, 165–166, 167–169, 177–178
- and *Prayer of Joseph* 153–155, 167
*Commentary on John* (Origen) 40–41, 123–124, 153, 185
*Commentary on Romans* (Origen) 39, 50
Conzelmann, Hans 25
1 Corinthians 1n2, 15–16, 24–28, 29, 97–99, 174, 176
- and formation 15, 43–51, 53–56, 95, 173, 174–175, 179–180
- and resurrection 16, 97–134, 176–177
- and the opponents of Paul 97–99
- and wisdom 15, 22, 33, 35, 37, 39–40, 43–51, 52–56, 174–17, 179
2 Corinthians 1n2, 62, 77, 89, 93
cosmology 13, 61–62, 145–146, 157–160, 169, 172, 177
Cribiore, Raffaella 4n9, 7
Cyprian of Carthage 84n113, 86
Cyril of Jerusalem 45n99, 69n55, 147–148, 160–161

Daniélou, Jean 153
demons, devil 60, 64, 66–68, 69–71, 72n64, 84–88, 90n132

dichotomy 40–41, 46n102, 54, 67, 74, 93, 97, 112, 121–122, 124–125, 133, 175, 179
- mortal and immortal 97, 104–105, 122, 133, 176
- perishable and imperishable 97, 104–105, 133, 176
- wisdom of world and of God 15, 24–25, 34–35, 36–37, 40–42, 43–51, 52–53, 174–175
Docetism, Docetists 142n26, 147, 162n104

education 8–9, 10n34, 33–34, 45–46, 47–51, 54–55, 78, 83, 132, 163, 174
- Graeco-Roman education 3–4, 7–9, 28–29, 43n89, 45–46, 51, 131–132
- school exercises 4n9, 7–10
- schools 4n9, 33, 43n89, 51, 76, 178
- teachers 4n9, 8, 28, 34, 43–51, 53–56, 71–72, 85, 87–88, 94–95, 108n58, 128, 174
Edwards, Mark 44, 119n119, 121n126, 162n105
Ehrman, Bart 167–168
Ephesians 1n2, 16, 57–62, 77, 88–92, 94–96, 175, 179
- heavenly places 60–61, 62n25, 90, 91n133
Epictetus 64, 84n113
Epicureans 27n18, 33
epigraphy 10, 87
- and Romans 8 87n119
*Epistle to Diognetus* 21
eschatology 13, 31–32, 38, 40, 45–46, 57, 60n20, 91–92, 101n22, 102, 125–126, 132, 176, 178–180
ethics 28, 93–95, 110–111, 114, 115–116, 125, 133–134, 175–176
eucharist 58, 79, 99–100, 106–107, 109, 112, 177
- and the Valentinians 100, 106–107, 112, 177
Eusebius 11, 17, 29–30, 87–88, 135, 139, 147–149, 152n63

evil 59–61, 67–77, 79–80, 84, 86–88, 91–92, 96, 176, 179
– and baptism 16, 60, 62–63, 64n34, 69–70, 73, 78–80, 87n119, 93, 95, 175
– fiery darts of evil 16, 58–60, 66, 68, 69–73, 78, 81, 93–95, 175
– passions 60, 63–65, 68, 70–73, 75, 78, 80, 89–90, 93, 95
– sin 61n24, 63, 67–68, 72, 89–90,113, 117, 122
– spiritual forces of wickedness 58–60, 61–68, 71–73, 74–77, 78–82, 85–90, 93–95, 175–176
*Excerpts from Theodotus* (Clement) 30, 39n75, 69–70, 102, 135n2
exegesis 13, 15, 28–29, 36, 38–42, 43–44, 52–53, 55, 117–118, 123–125, 127–128, 131–132, 149, 162, 167, 169–174, 176, 182
– and theology 17–18, 100, 114, 116, 124–125, 128, 133–134, 176–178, 180–181
– spiritual exegesis 39, 45–46, 51
*Exhortation* (Clement) 45, 140

faith 16, 30, 34, 43–45, 53–54, 56, 62–63, 65–68, 70–73, 75, 78–81, 83–87, 91–95, 108n58, 110, 131–133, 143, 175–176, 178–180
fasting 74–75, 94
*First Principles* (Origen) 47–49, 144, 156–158
Fitzmyer, Joseph 26, 101n22
flesh (and blood) 16, 66–67, 70, 74–75, 81, 90n131, 93–94, 97–100, 102, 103–107, 108–119, 120–122, 124–126, 133, 176, 179
formation 1–4, 8n28, 12, 15–16, 18, 22, 27, 43–51, 52–56, 94–95, 129, 131–133, 173–176, 178–181
– and persuasion 3–4, 29, 54, 180
– definition 2–4, 15, 53–56, 174–175, 178–181
Fossum, Jarl 145n37, 153

Galatians 1n2, 105n47, 135, 136
Genesis 59n14, 141, 147
genre 11, 18, 56, 59, 94, 131–132, 168

Gnostics, Gnosticism 31–32, 40, 99, 108, 120, 147–148, 179
– and Paul 7n22, 32, 107n55
see also *Valentinians, Valentinus*
Gorday, Peter 6, 9, 40
Gordley, Matthew 137n12, 162
*Gospel of Philip* 105–108, 112, 118n110
Greer, Rowan 98–100, 123n139, 124, 141, 177
Grillmeier, Alois 145–146, 162–163

Harnack, Adolf 67n46, 82n98, 90n132
Hays, Richard 19n53, 20
healing 71–73, 95, 111
– and Origen 71–73
Hebrews 1n2, 93, 105n47
Helmbold, William 20
heresy 52, 55, 78, 93, 102–103, 108, 119–120, 127–128, 130–131
hermeneutics 9, 12, 16–18, 28–29, 37, 41–42, 47–49, 51, 53, 124–128, 132, 169–170, 172–173 , 176–178, 180, 184n12
Hippolytus 17
Holy Spirit (see *Spirit*)
Homer 5n14, 18, 55, 84n112
– and authority 5n14, 15, 18, 55
– and school exercises 7–9
– *Iliad* 8–9
*Homilies on Genesis* (Origen) 165
*Homilies on Leviticus* (Origen) 49–50
Hurtado, Larry 6–7, 146n38, 163
hymns 58, 136–138, 167–168
– 'Christ hymns' 136–138, 167–168, 180
*Hypostasis of the Archons* 59n14

identity 54–55, 73, 101–102, 114–115, 126–128, 130–131, 174–179
– early Christian 3–4, 17, 54, 73, 83, 93, 95–96, 107–108, 114–115, 126–128, 130–131, 174–179, 181, 185
idolatry 66, 140–141
Ignatius 17, 63n27, 78–79, 129
*Iliad* (Homer) 8–9
illness 71–72

image   13, 58–59, 93–94, 138, 140–149, 152–154, 157, 160–169, 173, 175–180, 183
– relation to 'form'   162n104, 165–166
see also *Christology*
Irenaeus   11, 17, 31–32, 92n138, 92n139, 103, 108–116, 118–119, 125–128, 130–131, 135, 141–143, 146–150, 177
– and opponents   31–32, 70n57, 103, 108–110, 127–128, 131n168, 148n47
– and recapitulation, *anakephalaiosis*   2, 13, 92n138, 112–113, 141–143, 177
– and rule of truth   114, 177
Isocrates   7

Jacob   40–42, 76–77
Jerome   26, 78
Jesus   46–47, 59, 70, 76, 85–88, 90–92, 94–95, 111, 114–115, 136, 139, 141, 145, 160, 165–173, 177–178, 180
– and armour   70, 78–80, 86–88, 94
– and baptism   64n34, 69–70
– as mediator 139, 145n37, 158–160, 169
– as phantom   154, 163–164, 169, 178
– as Son of God   139–140, 145–149, 163
– as wisdom   123n136, 140, 151–152, 155, 166
– crucified   24–25, 36, 46–51, 53, 139, 160–161, 169, 179
– divinity of   138, 142–143, 146n38, 147, 149, 151, 154, 157, 160–162, 164, 166–167, 169, 171, 173
– humanity of   99–100, 111–113, 115, 119, 138, 142–143, 146n38, 148, 160–161, 163–164, 166, 169, 173
– passion   36, 79n87, 87–88, 91, 160–161, 177
resurrection 87–88, 101, 103–104, 106, 112–114, 117, 125, 129, 139, 142
see also *Christology*
John, Gospel of   40–42, 106, 111, 144–147, 150, 154–155, 158, 162–163, 165–167
judgement   116–119, 122, 125–126, 133, 176
Justin Martyr   63n27, 102n29, 129–130, 135, 147

Käsemann, Ernst   25
Kingdom of God   97–100, 106–107, 109–118, 120–125, 133, 176, 179
– and flesh and blood   16, 97–100, 106–107, 109–118, 120–121, 124–125, 133, 176, 179
– and judgement   116–118, 122, 125–126, 133, 176
Kovacs, Judith   6, 25–27, 30, 39n72, 44, 69n53, 135n2

Lehtipuu, Outi   127
leprosy   71–72
Leviticus 49–50
Lightfoot, Joseph Barber   137–138, 170
Llewelyn, Stephen   6
Longenecker, Richard   20
Lorenz, Rudolf   171
lust   72–73
Lyman, Rebecca   172

Maccabees 101n25
Marcion   34–36, 66, 103, 108, 115–117, 128–132, 154, 163–165
– and resurrection   115–117, 129–131
– and Tertullian   34–36, 66, 103, 114–116, 129–130, 132, 154–155, 163–165
martyrdom   60, 79–80, 93, 101n25
– and baptism   79–80
– Perpetua and Felicity   74n69
Matthew, Gospel of   33, 38
Menander   7
Methodius   78n79, 119n119, 132, 135, 155n75
Mitchell, Margaret   25, 27–29, 41–42, 48
Morgan, Teresa   7–10, 18
Morray-Jones, Christopher 61n21, 79n87
Moss, Candida   4–5, 19–20, 183

Nag Hammadi   59, 102–107, 182
Neufeld, Thomas   59n16, 90–91
Nicaea, Council of   1n2, 2n3, 149n50, 170, 171n131, 178, 180
*nomina sacra*   10n34
Novatian   17, 66n43, 136n3, 146–147

O'Neil, Edward 20
*On the Pedagogue* (Clement of Alexandria) 44–45, 108n58
Origen 6, 11, 17, 26, 36–37, 39–42, 46–51, 63n27, 66–68, 70–73, 76–77, 78n79, 79–82, 86–88, 92, 94, 108n58, 119–125, 126, 132, 136n3, 139, 142n24, 143–148, 150–152, 155–160, 165–167, 169, 172–173, 177, 179, 185
– and Celsus 36–37, 71, 82, 120, 123–124, 132, 143, 150–151
– misunderstanding of 119n119, 132, 155n75
– opponents of 30, 36–37, 40, 50, 70–71, 119–122, 145–146
– scriptural interpretation 2, 13, 37, 39–42, 46–51, 52–53, 123, 127–128, 177

Pantaenus 33n48
papyrus texts 1n2, 6, 7–10
passions, 60, 63–65, 68, 70–73, 75, 78, 80, 89–90, 93, 95
– and *apatheia* 65
Pastoral Epistles 1n2
Pauline epistles 1, 5n14, 6, 9–10, 12, 27, 37, 57–58, 135, 146n38, 174, 180, 182–185
– authenticity 14–15, 25–27, 57–58, 98, 135–136
– circulation of 5n14, 12
 see also *references*
Paul, the Apostle 1, 24, 28, 29, 31–33, 36–38, 43, 48–51, 54–56, 69, 79, 83–85, 86–88, 91, 102, 109–111, 113, 115, 117–121, 124–125, 127–131, 133, 144, 152, 159, 161, 163–166, 173–174
– and wisdom 1, 18, 28, 37, 49–51, 54–56, 174–175
– as teacher 28, 49–51, 54–56, 85, 128, 174
– authority of 1, 5n14, 15, 18, 28, 54–56, 128, 133, 163–164, 169, 174, 176–178
*pax Romana* 82–83
pedagogy 2, 7–9, 44, 50, 178–179
Peppard, Michael 167
persecution 16, 18, 59–60, 62–63, 68, 78, 83–84, 86–87, 93, 95, 175
2 Peter 1

Pharisees 101
Philemon 1n2
Philippians 1n2, 104n42, 138n14, 162–163, 165, 167–168
Philo 25, 81n90, 101, 140n20, 145n37, 153, 167
philosophy 10, 60n20, 61–62, 101–102
– Graeco-Roman 10, 34n56, 39, 43n89, 45–46, 61–62, 64, 84n113, 99, 131–132
Plato, Platonism 29n22, 30, 33n54, 61, 100–101, 104n44, 140n20, 160
Porter, Stanley 19–20
prayer 16, 70, 78, 80–82, 87n119, 93–95, 175
*Prayer of Joseph* 153–155, 167

Quintilian 7
Qumran 25, 90n131

Rajak, Tessa 133
recapitulation, *anakephalaiosis* 2, 13, 92n138, 112–113, 141–143, 161, 167, 177
reception history 1–2, 4–9, 12, 15, 22–23, 27, 90, 131, 136n5, 137–138, 167–168, 173–174, 177, 180–181, 185
references 1–2, 9–12, 14n44, 15, 18–22, 27n18, 182–185
– definition of 18–22, 182–185
– echoes 18–21, 184
– history of scholarship 19–22
– most frequent, Pauline 2, 4–5, 6–7, 9–10, 11n38, 12–18, 22–23, 99n14, 104n42, 174, 177–178, 180, 185
– texts not cited, Pauline 12n39
resurrection 16, 18, 97–102, 100–107, 108–134, 139, 176–178, 180
– and judgement 116–119, 122–123, 125–126, 133, 176
– and the Eucharist 106–107, 112
– and the Valentinians 102–107, 119
– of the flesh 99–101, 102n29, 106–114, 116–127, 139
Revelation, book of 85, 93
rhetoric 3–4, 28–30, 51, 131–133, 175
– and education 3–4, 28–29, 131–133
– early Christian use of 30–32, 34–36, 51, 52–56, 175

– Graeco-Roman 3–4, 10, 28–30, 131–132, 137n12, 141, 167–168
Romans (epistle) 1n2, 39–40, 86, 87n119, 93, 105n47, 109, 110n71, 135
Rowland, Christopher 61n21, 79n87
rule of truth, faith 114, 177

sacrament, *sacramentum* 84n113, 105–107, 109, 177
Sadducees 101
salvation 2, 35, 39–40, 64, 71n59, 79, 81, 85–88, 91–92, 95, 108, 110–116, 118, 122–123, 125, 127, 133–134, 141–143, 176–177, 179–180
Samaritan woman 40–42
school exercises 4n9, 7–10
Scott, Mark 121n126
Scripture 4, 6, 9, 10n34, 13, 15, 17–20, 22, 37, 38–39, 42, 45–46, 48, 54, 57, 66n41, 98–99, 124, 127–128, 171–173, 177–178, 180–181
Seneca 29n22
Setzer, Claudia 101n22, 102n29, 104–105
sin (see *evil*)
soul 47–49, 61, 63–65, 67–73, 75, 77, 89–90, 99–102, 110, 115–116, 119n119, 121–123, 133
– and Plato 61, 101, 104n44
– and resurrection 98–102, 106, 115–116, 121n126, 122–123
Spirit 44, 53–56, 63, 108–113, 125–126, 150
– and exegesis 27, 37–39, 45–46, 47–48, 51, 55–56
– and wisdom 25, 31–32, 33–34, 37, 39, 41, 44–46, 51, 53
spiritual forces of wickedness 58–60, 61–68, 71–73, 74–77, 78–82, 85–90, 93–95, 175–176
Stead, Christopher 170
Stoics 27n18, 33, 43n89, 64, 65
*Stromata* (Clement) 33–34, 38–39
Stroumsa, Guy 43n89, 100–101
subordination (of Christ) 156, 158–159, 169, 172–173

survey 2, 4–10, 19, 92, 99, 108n58, 174, 182
– methodology 2, 7–10, 12, 17, 23, 174, 180, 184n12
– surveys of Graeco-Roman texts 7–10, 55, 174
– surveys of Christian texts 4–7, 130, 174, 182

Talbert, C. 153
teachers 4n9, 8, 28, 34, 43–51, 53–56, 71–72, 85, 87–88, 94–95, 108n58, 128, 174
– and early Christians 44–46, 49–51, 53–56, 71, 87, 94–95, 174–175
– Graeco-Roman 4n9, 7–9, 45–46
Tertullian 11, 17, 33, 34–36, 51, 62n27, 65–66, 74–75, 77, 81, 83–86, 114–119, 128, 146–147, 151n58, 154–155, 163–166, 173, 177
– and Marcion 34–36, 66, 103, 114–116, 129–130, 132, 154–155, 163–165
– and resurrection 2, 105n48, 114–119, 125, 177
– and *substantia* 13, 115–117, 119, 163–165, 177
Thessalonians (epistles) 1n2, 62, 105n47, 146
Thistleton, Anthony 27, 32
thrones and dominions 139, 153, 155–160, 167, 169
Timothy (epistles) 1n2
Titus (epistle) 1n2
*Treatise on the Resurrection* 103–105, 107

Valentinians, Valentinus 7n21, 14n44, 17, 25, 30, 32, 34, 39, 66, 69–70, 99, 102–107, 108, 110, 114–115, 119, 124–125, 126n144, 130, 131n168, 135n2, 177, 179
– and *Gospel of Philip* 105–108, 112, 118n110
– and *Treatise on the Resurrection* 103–105, 107
van den Hoek, Annewies 21–22, 81n90, 182–184
van Kooten, Geurt Hendrik 62n24, 92

Victorinus, Marius   154n73, 160n98
Vinzent, Markus   129–131
virginity   78n79

Walker, W. O.   25–26
warfare   59–62, 64, 73, 75, 79, 81n97, 83, 87, 90, 92, 95, 175–176, 179
Welborn, Laurence   24
White, Benjamin   40n80, 102
Widmann, M.   25–26
Wiles, Maurice   158
Williams, Rowan   170–171
Wink, Walter   89–91
*Wirkungsgeschichte* (see *reception history*)
wisdom   15–17, 18, 22, 24–37, 38–43, 43–51, 52–56, 62, 65, 68, 71–73, 78, 80, 93–96, 139–140, 145n37, 151–152, 157–158, 173–176, 178–180
– and 1 Corinthians   15, 24–37, 38–43, 43–51, 52–56, 173–176, 179
– and Ephesians   16, 58, 62, 68, 71, 78, 80–82, 93–96, 175–176
– and formation   4, 15–16, 18, 27, 42–51, 52–56, 62, 94–95, 131–133, 173–176, 178–181
– and Paul   1, 18, 28, 37, 49–51, 54–56, 174–175
– and Proverbs   22, 151–152, 155
wounds   68, 71–73, 122
wrestling   16, 58–60, 62, 63, 68, 74–77, 85, 93–94, 175
– and fasting   74–75
– and Perpetua and Felicity   74n69
– and Tertullian   74–75, 77
– Graeco-Roman   59, 74–75
– Jacob and the angel   76–77
Wright, N. T.   101

*yetzer*   61, 67n45, 72n64
Young, Frances   15, 22n70, 178, 182

www.ingramcontent.com/pod-product-compliance
Lightning Source LLC
Chambersburg PA
CBHW070607170426
43200CB00012B/2611